BLOOD
& FIRE

The young evangelists, Cornwall, 1862.
'Strong men, young men, old men weeping like children on account of their sins.'

BLOOD
& FIRE

William and Catherine Booth
and Their Salvation Army

Roy Hattersley

LITTLE, BROWN AND COMPANY

A *Little, Brown* Book

First published in Great Britain in 1999
by Little, Brown and Company

Copyright © 1999 by Roy Hattersley

The moral right of the author has been asserted.

A CIP catalogue record for this book
is available from the British Library.

ISBN: 0 316 85161 2

All photographs courtesy of the
Salvation Army International Heritage Centre

Typeset in Berkeley Book by M Rules
Printed and bound in Great Britain
by Clays Ltd, St Ives plc

Little, Brown and Company (UK)
Brettenham House
Lancaster Place
London WC2E 7EN

Contents

Introduction

On 17 January 1885, *The Times* published a letter from the Reverend J. Hector Courcelles MA which described the horrors of a railway journey between Richmond and Notting Hill. 'In the neighbouring compartments,' Mr Courcelles wrote, 'there were some officers of The Salvation Army.* One of them rose and in violent language, began to address us on the most solemn of subjects.' Worse was to come. 'As the train stopped at Latimer station, there was another train on the up line and into the window of this, our zealous friends shouted, "You will all rot in hell."' The letter ended on a plaintive note. 'Should not the railway companies protect their passengers from this sort of behaviour?'

Had *The Times* of the period not been obsessed with the Salvation Army – describing it in turn as ridiculous, heroic, subversive, heretical, noble and duplicitous – Mr Courcelles' letter would not have been thought important enough for publication. But for all its triviality, the complaint illustrated exactly what respectable opinion hated about William Booth and the great religious movement which he founded.

---

*The trust deed setting up The Salvation Army stipulated that the definite article, with a capital T, was an essential part of the title. Having shown proper respect for that wish, *Blood and Fire* now reverts to common usage.

Much of polite society regarded both the self-styled General and his Army as fanatical, presumptuous, intrusive and vulgar. Those were the characteristics – described by supporters as piety, indomitability, determination and simplicity – which made his extraordinary achievement possible. If William Booth had not been willing to make enemies, he would not have created the only remnant of the hundred-year Wesleyan schism that will survive, independent and self-confident, into the twenty-first century – a new church which, within a dozen years of its inauguration, boasted 3,000 'corps', 10,000 full-time 'officers' and countless adherents in Great Britain alone, and had established outposts in Iceland and New Zealand, Argentina and Germany, the United States of America and South Africa. Unless he had been willing to offend there would have been no campaign for the undeserving poor – the preoccupation of his middle age. Nor would he have helped to change the nation's perception of poverty's causes and cures.

William Booth's success was built on single-minded certainty. At first all that mattered was saving souls – a perfectly rational priority for anyone who believed that we are all born in sin, equally capable of redemption and destined for certain damnation if we fail to grasp the God-given chance of salvation. Even when he became concerned with the material condition of 'Darkest England', he regarded providing help for the 'submerged tenth' (a description he employed a hundred years before it was in common usage) as little more than a way of smoothing their path to heaven. Poverty was the devil's weapon. It drove men to drink and women on to the streets. In an age when even radicals believed that self-help solved all problems, William Booth knew that some men and women were pointed towards eternal damnation by the circumstances in which they were born and lived. Economic determinism – which is what it amounted to – owed more to Marx than to Methodism. But William Booth, who never had time to waste on theories, was not concerned with the philosophical origins of his ideas. They were self-evidently true, so he accepted them.

The poor were his natural congregation and, at least in his early preaching days, the only people to listen to his sermons were the men and women to whom the indolent churches would not reach out. Like John Wesley, his hero and spiritual progenitor, William Booth believed in 'active Christianity' – the moral duty of God's ministers to go out into the highways and byways and make them come in. His style of evangelism was a living reproach to every vicar in whose parish he preached and every minister whose circuit he invaded. He almost certainly never read a word of Milton in his life. But he too had nothing but contempt for the 'blind mouths who scarce themselves know how to hold a Sheep-hook, or have learn'd ought else the least that to the faithful herdsman's art belongs!' The complaint that 'hungry sheep look up and are not fed' might have come straight out of one of his sermons. His wife Catherine was openly offensive about the failures of the traditional churches. Not only were they incapable of making or even keeping converts, they often turned men and women against religion. When she was barely twenty-five – and about to marry William Booth – Catherine published the first of her polemics against religious indolence: 'Not more surely will the sprightly infant born in some pent-up garret (which has for generations been impregnable to the pure air of heaven) pine and die than will the spiritual babe introduced into the death-charged atmosphere of some churches.'

After Catherine Booth died – more than twenty years before her husband was 'promoted to glory' – the General's detractors began to claim that the Salvation Army was her creation, and that without her it would wither and die. They were wrong. But without her it would have been a different movement, as William Booth, without her, would have been a different man. Catherine was not his inspiration, but she added a sense of direction to his sense of purpose. William Booth was lucky in many ways – not least in holding an uninhibited view of religion which matched exactly the robust psychology of the Victorian poor. But his greatest piece of good fortune was meeting and marrying one of the most extraordinary women of the nineteenth century.

Catherine Booth triumphed over every sort of adversity. For years her mother refused to allow her to attend school – afraid that her morals would be undermined by godless girls. So, being an intellectual by nature, she studied the Bible – the one book of which her mother approved – and became such an expert on the text that, in her early twenties, she was able to argue on equal terms with the most eminent biblical scholars of her day. Her greatest triumph concerned the dispute over 'female ministry'. Catherine Booth insisted, with careful reference to the context, that God had intended more for women than the occasional right to preach – itself a scandalous notion. The female ministry would grant women authority over men. Even her husband had initial doubts about her radical view of church governance. But, step by step, he came to accept her heretical view. In thirty-five years of marriage he said little and did less with which she disagreed. Usually the agreement was instinctive and automatic. Sometimes he was convinced by the persuasion of the partnership's stronger member.

Yet, despite her undoubted intellectual superiority and passionate belief that men and women were equal in the sight of God, Catherine managed to fulfil all the conventional obligations of a Victorian wife and mother. She was congenitally ill, yet in just over eleven years she bore eight children – all of whom survived, itself a remarkable feat for the middle of the nineteenth century. At the same time, she was travelling from end to end of Britain with her husband and becoming an evangelist in her own right. Indeed, when they first moved to London her fame amongst the Methodists was far greater than his. Much to his credit, William Booth – contrary to the mores of his age – never stood in his wife's way. She, in turn, always changed from evangelist to wife when her husband needed her special care. There was a time when, although sick herself, she responded to William's hypochondria by sending him away to recover while she ran his Methodist circuit as well as his family.

There was, however, one area of William Booth's life which, despite constant and spirited attempts, Catherine was unable to influence. She failed completely to make him a scholar. It was not for want of trying. Before their marriage she deluged him with messages of encouragement, confidence and even warning. None of them persuaded him that time with books was well spent. Sometimes he replied to her entreaties with the doleful explanation that he had no capacity for study. More often he insisted that scholarship stood between simple believers and uncomplicated belief. At a time when Church of England clergymen read Latin and Greek and the Methodist leadership was built around Doctors of Divinity, William Booth's triumphant ignorance made his assaults on the traditional church seem all the more presumptuous. The fact that Christ had been a carpenter was no reason for a pawnbroker's clerk to imagine that he was entitled to lead a spiritual revival, and to claim that God had chosen him to spread the good news of salvation.

The simplicity of William Booth's faith was his strength. It allowed no room for doubt or delay. It made him God's soldier with no other duty than to march towards the sound of gunfire. But he insisted on drawing his own battle-lines. Before he was thirty he had preached for the Wesleyan Methodists, the Wesleyan Reformers and the Methodist New Connexion – as well as considering the merits of becoming a Congregationalist. And each denomination had, in his judgement, failed to realise his full evangelical potential. The dissatisfaction was more than the result of his justly high opinion of the power his preaching possessed. It was also the product of his rigid, if idiosyncratic, view of discipline. When he imposed it, there could be no relaxation or exception. When it was imposed on him, he insisted that he accepted no other authority than God. It was his reluctance – indeed refusal – to obey the orders of the established denominations, as much as his passion to take the gospel out into the back-streets, which made the creation of the Salvation Army inevitable. William Booth could never have been satisfied with a church which was not made in his own image.

His sins were arrogance and egoism and his excuse for those faults was the certainty with which he believed that God had called him to preach salvation. By temperament he was a travelling preacher – spreading the news of salvation wherever instincts and invitations took him, as did dozens of other Victorian evangelists. There will always be arguments about why he rose from their ranks to become a great international figure. Catherine certainly contributed to his success, but there are rival views about its fundamental cause – personal magnetism, unbridled ambition, simple good fortune or, as he certainly believed, divine intervention. Although it is only possible to marvel at what he achieved, opinions about what made the achievement possible will depend as much on the prejudices and principles of those who judge him as upon the evidence on which the judgement is based. The fundamental cause of his triumph remains his life's enigma. But the nature of the techniques which carried him to glory – like the glory itself – are beyond dispute.

William Booth's technique for encouraging sinners to rally round and remain loyal to his banner was ideal for the type of men and women at whom his campaigns were aimed. He was the greatest publicist of his age and generation. No opportunity to glorify the Salvation Army was ever missed. His children's weddings, his colleagues' imprisonment, even his wife's funeral were all, in turn, exploited to popularise the great work in which he was engaged. He never felt shame, feared ridicule or flinched from danger. Even when, in old age, he became conscious of his patriarchal dignity and toured the world's capitals taking breakfast with kings and tea with presidents, he still insisted on respecting the more embarrassing obligations of his faith. At a time when he was negotiating with half the British Cabinet in the hope of establishing a 'Farm Colony' in Africa, he insisted that Cecil Rhodes kneel down with him to pray in a crowded railway carriage. But he paid a price for the absence of both reticence and inhibition. The public persona that he acquired – bearded old fanatic who called himself a General and wore a frogged tunic with top hat and umbrella – made him ridiculous in the eyes of metropolitan sophisticates. It almost certainly denied him the place in history to which he was entitled as one of the most eminent Victorians. Cardinal Manning's scarlet cassock, General Gordon's fez and Florence Nightingale's wimple were all acceptable to educated opinion. Booth's bogus regimentals were not. So, one of England's great social reformers – as well as one of the world's greatest revivalist preachers – was and is continually underrated.

The idea of using the poor to recruit the poor – reformed sinners who brought the unredeemed to salvation – came to William Booth as the result of hard experience. At first he feared he would not be at home in the rough-and-tumble of a working-class revival. Then he found out that men who would not consider entering chapel were prepared to listen to a rousing sermon if it was delivered from the stage of a derelict music hall or the tap-room of what had once been a public house. He discovered too that, when a repentant sinner testified to the power of the Lord, men and women, as yet unredeemed, listened with an attention which they would not have offered a clergyman who had never sinned. So he recruited reformed drunks, redeemed prostitutes and discharged felons to describe their lurid sins and explain how much they had benefited from acquiring virtue. It turned his services into circuses. But it drew the crowds, and the bigger the congregations, the greater the number of converts. Critics claimed that he relied on carefully induced hysteria to carry his disciples to the banks of the river Jordan, but William Booth cared more about numbers than methods.

The idea of a missionary movement with military pretensions was neither a sudden inspiration nor the result of a carefully planned strategy. It came about haphazardly and almost by chance. The change of name from Christian Mission to Salvation Army was made, without much thought, as the result of a half-joke about 'volunteers' being an inappropriate description for the hard-working members of the Booth family. The military jargon which became a feature of both the Army's rituals and publicity was the casual result of provincial zeal – local branches of the Christian Mission thinking that the promise to 'open fire on the devil' and 'bombard sin' would attract attention. Uniforms were introduced not to improve morale and increase *ésprit de corps* but because they protected the Army's officers from the temptations of fashion and prosperity – not in itself an immense risk from men who lived so near to poverty that instructions had to be issued forbidding them to starve to death. Bands were initially thought to debase the spiritual quality of sacred music, but were accepted when it became clear that they added to the attraction of Sunday services. Flags were never discouraged. They were a spontaneous expression of the devotees' enthusiasm, and were regarded as proper signs of pious commitment. Added together – uniforms, bands, banners and martial affectations – they made the Salvation Army irresistible to the more romantic Victorian poor. William Booth made the penny-plain Christianity of the traditional churches two-penny coloured and, in consequence, brightened some of the gloomiest corners of Darkest England. Men and women joined to experience the gaiety of God.

The Salvation Army offered sacrifice as well as service. The men on the general staff who passed for theologians may have argued about the possibility of 'Holiness' – the achievement of sanctification before death. But whether or not it was possible for William Booth's soldiers to become saints, they had no difficulty in becoming martyrs. From the Army's earliest days, they were in regular physical danger. Often the authorities regarded them as trouble-makers and refused to provide protection. So, throughout the General's lifetime, his followers remained vulnerable to the gangs of thugs who were bribed by brewers and paid by publicans to break up meetings which called for total abstinence from alcohol, and from a special sort of hooligan who took pleasure in assaulting hymn-singing eccentrics who refused to fight back. William Booth invariably turned his assailants into recruiting sergeants. Instead of offering to shield his young recruits from danger, he posted them – men and women alike – to the front line. Volunteers who would not have thought of devoting their lives to a calm and contemplative Christian life signed up for death or glory – believing that one would lead to the other.

Because it was built on hope and survived on often reckless enthusiasm, the Salvation Army can take credit for innumerable little miracles – not sinners proclaiming that the love of God and the power of William Booth's oratory had brought them to redemption, but men and women of a less dramatic inclination inspired by the Army's compassion to do great work on behalf of their fellow men. Despite his contempt for philosophy William Booth actually created his own theory of social responsibility. Like most good Victorian principles it was expressed by analogy. If a London cab horse stumbled and fell, passers-by helped it to its feet without demanding an explanation of its misfortune. Men, William Booth argued, should be treated with no less compassion. He added that if inquiries were made into the reasons for human failure, most often the cause would be revealed as poverty and the vices – particularly drunkenness – that poverty encourages. He was concerned with the cause because he wanted to supply a remedy. But his principal message was the importance of not attempting – before the remedy was applied – to distinguish between the deserving and the undeserving poor.

Until 1890, when he wrote *In Darkest England and the Way Out* – an undoubtedly Utopian description of the better life he thought was possible – William Booth's interest in social policy was far less pronounced than his wife's. Indeed, it was during Catherine's long and fatal illness that, returning home from a south London meeting, he became so outraged by the sight of men sleeping under bridges that he determined to 'do something'. By then Catherine had waged, and at least in part won, her war against child prostitution and (much to her husband's regret) embroiled the Salvation Army in one of the greatest scandals of the century.

Catherine was dying when William Booth began to write *In Darkest England*. Part of his plan for redemption by hard work had already been put into practice. The Salvation Army had run workshops, cheap food stores, women's refuges and workmen's shelters for years. *In Darkest England* demanded that such schemes be extended to cover the whole country, and include new enterprises which ranged from the renovation of worn-out shoes through the production of toys from old tin cans to the distribution of surplus food collected from the wasteful kitchens of Mayfair and Kensington Gore. The schemes provided an easy target for those who had always regarded him as absurd. But he did find thousands of jobs for the unemployed and, over the years, millions of beds for homeless and unemployed workers. Salvation Army vans still distribute tea and sandwiches under the London bridges where the sight of sleeping beggars so offended William Booth a hundred years ago. Most important, he argued for a new view of philanthropy. The Good Samaritan attempted to meet the needs of the poor rather than moralise about how the needs arose.

Yet, for almost half a century, William and Catherine Booth have been virtually forgotten outside the ranks of the Salvation Army. For that the couple's early disciples must take some of the blame. They chose to portray the founding General and his wife as saints. As saints they were, at best, second-rate. As human beings they were remarkable by any standards – heroic, confident, indomitable and full of hope and love for each other and their fellow men. They represented – as much as Brunel or Bright, Paxton, Arnold, Livingstone or Newman – much of what was best in nineteenth-century Britain. They deserve a place in the pantheon of Great Victorians.

1

God's Apprentice

William Booth was born on 10 April 1829 at 12 Notintone Place in Sneinton, now a part of Nottingham too near the city centre to be called a suburb, but then a distant and rarely visited village. It was only famous for 'the high walls of the lunatic asylum from which inmates escaped with a regularity which aroused terror in children living nearby'.[1] Sneinton was also the home of 'Gentleman Morley', the head of the great hosiery company which made Queen Victoria's stockings. His son, Samuel, became a Member of Parliament and a major figure in Victorian Methodism. He would also grow up to defend and support William Booth – whom he never met when they both lived, several social classes apart, in Sneinton.

The baby – Samuel and Mary Booth's third child – was baptised two days after he was born, a precaution which pious parents often took at a time when one child in three lived for barely a month. And the Booths had already lost one son in early infancy. The ceremony was performed at St Stephen's parish church by the Reverend W. H. Wyatt, so blatant an Anglo-Catholic that his parishioners later revolted against his papist inclinations. On the way to the font, the Booths carried their infant along an aisle which was lined with statues of saints and martyrs – each one, in itself, an indication of Roman sympathies. On the day of the christening, the statues were draped in Lenten purple. William Booth – so often, in later life, accused of vulgarising Christianity – received an austere High Church baptism.

Eighty years later, William Booth wrote that he left the Church of England because, in his childhood, he found the services formal and unfriendly.[2] He was not alone in that. The Religious Census of Great Britain – conducted on Sunday, 30 May 1851 – reported that the Church of England had been in decline for years.* More respondents described themselves as Nonconformist than claimed allegiance to the established Church. And, if the census's detailed calculation is to be believed, a majority of *soi-disant* Anglicans (5,573,283 in total) 'neglected religious ordinances . . . of their own free choice' rather than because no Sunday services were held within their locality. England remained a devoutly Christian country. But it seemed to the new industrial working classes that the Church of England responded only to the needs of the old squirarchy. 'For many years [before 1851] it had only infrequently and partially seen itself as a proselytising organisation.' The Methodists did surprisingly little to tend the flocks which the incumbent vicars neglected – even, in some cases, introducing pew rents in their chapels. And pew rents were a barrier – often an intentional one – to regular worship by the poor. William Booth began to learn about the Church's cold detachment in early childhood. His success in building a great international movement was the product of his decision to take religion to the neglected ranks of the disadvantaged and dispossessed.

The Booths of Sneinton were not poor. St Stephen's baptismal records (which describe Samuel Booth as 'gentleman') certainly exaggerated the family's status, but young William was not born into desperate deprivation. The family fortunes fluctuated. Sometimes a new business venture prospered. Sometimes it failed. The curse of William's childhood was uncertainty.

When, in 1797, Samuel Booth of Belper married Sarah Lockitt, he called himself a nailer – though whether he owned a forge or was a craftsman who worked with hammer and anvil is not known. Sarah,

---

* A full analysis of the 'Victorian religious environment' can be found in *The Salvation Army in England*, a Ph.D. thesis written by Dr G. H. Horridge.

who was ten years older than Samuel, died in 1819. In that year her husband was prosperous enough to erect a monument to her memory and, six years later, he could afford to visit Ashby de la Zouch in the hope that its healing waters would cure his rheumatism. But sometime at the beginning of the nineteenth century he invested in land and borrowed to build 'artisan's dwellings' – homes for the new factory workers of the Industrial Revolution. The economic cataclysm which he hoped would make his future nearly destroyed him. The Nottingham enclosures which (by extinguishing common grazing rights) drove the rural poor into towns, flooded the market in land. The glut reduced the value from a pound to a shilling an acre.[3] Samuel Booth was not quite ruined, but he was certainly brought down in the world.

By the time of his first recorded financial disaster, Samuel Booth had married for a second time. His new wife, the former Mary Moss, was born in Somercotes near Alfreton in Derbyshire and was to be described by William as the daughter of a prosperous farmer.[4] Joseph Moss was, at best, a farm labourer, and may well have been an itinerant preacher who settled down to become an odd-job man. His grandson inherited the aquiline profile which, together with his early life as a hawker, encouraged the suggestion that Moss was a Jew – a theory later welcomed by William Booth's most enthusiastic supporters on the principle that all the best prophets are Jewish. Whatever his spiritual origins, Joseph Moss fathered a devoutly Christian daughter who, after the family moved to Ashby de la Zouch, met Samuel Booth in uncertain circumstances. It was 1824 and he, a widower of forty-nine, had just lost his only son. She was thirty-three and, although by the standards of the time was unlikely to receive another offer, refused the proposal which Samuel Booth made within days of their first meeting.

The rejected suitor returned home to Nottingham, more offended than hurt. But in weeks he was back in Ashby where, as Mary Moss later told her son, he 'pressed his proposals to the point where it was impossible to refuse'.[5] They married and she bore him children at regular two-yearly intervals – Ann (1827), William (1829), Emma (1831) and Mary (1833). It is, however, impossible to claim that they, or their only son, lived happily ever after.

William was born in a house which, by the standards of the time, was substantial. And twelve years later – after one financial crisis had driven the Booths out of Sneinton and another one had driven them back – they were certainly not destitute. The 1851 Census revealed that resident at their new address on the corner of Bond Street was 'William Billings, aged 12 years, domestic servant'. Whatever his previous trade, by then Samuel Booth had become an entrepreneur who 'amongst other things bought shop-loads of crockery in Staffordshire and sold them in the markets of the Midlands'.[6] Neither his enterprise nor his energy endeared him to William, who, at least later in life, despised his 'money-making schemes and contrivances'. William Booth described his father as 'a man of considerable force of character, high spirits and a sense of truth and honour combined with a strong desire to get on in the world who knew no greater gain or end than money'[7] who led 'a very unsatisfactory existence'.[8] The tribute to his father's truth and honour was a reference to a single incident. A friend, in desperate need of cash, borrowed against a bond which Samuel Booth recklessly underwrote. When the man defaulted on the repayments and was made bankrupt, Samuel Booth thought it his duty to repay all outstanding debts rather than just redeem the bond. His chivalry provoked the only recorded compliment that his son ever paid him. For William Booth was essentially a mother's boy – an affection, perhaps even a complex, which was to colour his views on women's role in society for the rest of his life. There is no great evidence to suggest that Samuel and Mary Booth were ever in open conflict, but their son always spoke of them as if it were his duty to take sides. And he was for his mother. It must have caused him great pain to concede the coincidence that 'my father's fortunes appear to have commenced waning almost immediately after their union'.[9]

William Booth's only complaint against his mother was that she neglected him in order to guide and comfort his father 'in all his business perplexities. She upheld his spirit in crash upon crash, as one piece of property after another went overboard.'[10] It was William Booth's habit to discount the early help which he received. Indeed he often spoke as if, until he met and married Catherine Mumford, his generous love was never reciprocated. But his true feelings for his mother are best represented in the outpourings of affection which are to be found in both his private correspondence and his public statements between his father's death in 1842 and his own seventy years later: 'I had a good mother. So good she has ever appeared to me that I have often said that all I knew of her life seemed in striking contradiction to the laws of human depravity . . . when my father died, my grief was all but forbidden by the thought that it was not my mother.'[11]

All that is known of Samuel Booth's attitude towards his son is the claim that after committing some minor misdemeanour, the boy had to be saved from a thrashing by a friendly neighbour. We can however be certain that the family lived in constant insecurity. In October 1831 – the month in which Reform Bill rioters passed Notintone Place on their way to burn down Colnwick Hall – the Booths moved to Bleasby, twelve miles north of Nottingham. When their daughter Mary was christened in the local church, her father described himself as 'yeoman'. Small-holder would have been a more appropriate description. The Land Tax assessment for that year listed him as renting ten acres from a John Webster. They were used, according to William Booth, to practise 'fancy farming' – either a derisive way of dismissing an attempt to make a new life or the local colloquialism for specialising in the breeding of rare sheep and cattle. The Booths remained in Bleasby – living in what is now called The Old Farm House – for almost four years. In 1835, when William was six, his father accepted that the agricultural experiment had failed and the family returned to Sneinton.

William Booth 'learned his letters' in the village school at Bleasby – a single vestry room in the parish church where religious instruction was given in the strict language of the Anglican faith. Back at Sneinton, in the house on the corner of Bond Street, Samuel Booth – who had probably become a jobbing builder, working out of what became known as Booth's Yard – regained enough of his old prosperity to send his son to Biddulph's school in Nottingham. Biddulph's had been founded by local Methodists, but Sampson Biddulph and his son, Samuel, had turned it into a commercial enterprise. The Methodist connection was not, however, completely broken: Sampson Biddulph was a Wesleyan Local Preacher and when the new Wesley Chapel was opened in Broad Street in 1837, he was appointed one of the trustees.

The Broad Street Chapel – now a cinema – was a proclamation of Methodist power and strength in Nottingham. The six great pillars of its colonnade dominated the mean streets around it, and its main meeting room was designed to hold two thousand worshippers. The whole

building, together with the land on which it stood, had cost £11,000 –
a fortune by the standards of the time. It was to become the centre of
young William Booth's precocious religious life and the scene of his
conversion. The room in which it took place is still preserved and private behind the cinema's silver screen. Because of its size and
splendour – and thanks to the trustees who paid the generous travelling expenses – the Broad Street Chapel attracted some of the most
famous itinerant preachers of the day. Their oratory held the young
William Booth in thrall. By one of the happy chances which so often
helped him along his way – always identified by him as divine intervention – he was, despite his Anglican upbringing, present in the
Broad Street Chapel during the visits of the great preachers of the
Revivalist movement.

For most of his childhood, William Booth followed the faith of his
father and attended Sunday School at the formal and unfriendly St
Stephen's church. But from time to time Sampson Biddulph as well as
God pointed him in the direction of Broad Street. Not that, in old age,
the General expressed much gratitude for what he learned. 'The school
did very little for me except what I did for myself . . . I never got a helping hand from anybody . . . It seems a pity that somebody did not take
hold of my warm nature and see what could be done with me.'[12] Nor,
according to the recollections of old age, could the Methodists themselves take much credit for the historic moment when he 'decided for
the Salvation of God'. His conversion, he wrote, 'came almost without
the direct instrumentality of any individual'. The insistence that, his
mother's influence notwithstanding, he had found his own way to God
became a constant theme of William Booth's reminiscences. He was in
partnership with the Almighty, who had sent Catherine to be his staff
and comforter. But until she came along, no one intruded into the close
and exclusive relationship.

There were, however, a whole series of incidents in his boyhood for
which William Booth might have felt he owed some gratitude to his
Methodist friends and neighbours. When he was seven a school-fellow
persuaded him to sign the pledge of total abstinence from alcohol – an
event not quite so bizarre as it now sounds since, although teetotalism
had not then become an obligation of Wesleyanism, those who
believed it to be a moral necessity often persuaded uncomprehending
children to swear that they would eschew the demon drink for ever. He

'kept the pledge for seven years, without any encouragement from the family. They took intoxicants in moderation.'[13] Even after the pledge was broken, William – sickly and almost morbidly concerned with his health – only took restorative brandy and recuperative port. But when Catherine Mumford came into his life even that was ended by her unyielding insistence that alcohol's power to restore health was almost as overvalued as its capacity for encouraging sin was underrated.

According to Salvationist folklore, fostered in his time by William Booth himself, a second messenger of God came to him during his tee-total schooldays and beckoned him from the established Church towards nonconformity. A mysterious couple thought that he looked like their long dead son and, in an attempt to integrate him into their family, took him with them to Sunday services at the Broad Street Chapel. Then a cousin, later described as 'a shoemaker who lived a separate and spiritual life', taught him that religion is 'something that comes from outside you'.[14]

Victorian boyhoods were mostly strange by the standards of the late twentieth century. William Booth was particularly moved by the way in which his town responded to the public execution of a labourer who had killed his wife and children. Twelve spectators died in the crush around the scaffold – an event which might have occurred in one of Thomas Hardy's short stories. William's morbid interest in death – and his certainty of divine retribution – was increased by the news that an adulterous Anglican curate, exposed by a parishioner, had committed suicide.[15] William endured a strange upbringing even by the stan-dards of the time. It was made all the more debilitating by his mother never allowing him to forget that the family hovered precariously between solvency and bankruptcy and that she had once known some-thing better. Sarah Osborne, before her marriage best friend to William's sister, Ann, said that there was 'always a mystery about Mrs Booth. She was very proud and reserved and felt her position acutely.'[16] In the summer of 1842, when William Booth was thirteen, at least the insecurity was ended. It was replaced by the certainty of hard times ahead. The mortgages on which his father relied to finance his business were called in and Samuel Booth, builder, was ruined. William was withdrawn from Biddulph's school at once and bound apprentice to Francis Eames, pawnbroker, of Goosegate, Nottingham. Samuel Booth died in September of the same year and Cousin Gregory, the Methodist shoemaker – acting with authority of dubious provenance – led the singing of 'Rock of Ages' around the Anglican death-bed.

It was the habit of William Booth to claim in later life that the devil had tested him by sending him to work amongst the moneylenders. He described the acceptance of his indentures as 'followed by the formation of companionship whose influence was anything but beneficial. I went down morally and the consequences might have been serious if not eternally disadvantageous, but that the hand of God was laid upon me in a very remarkable manner.'[17] That is an example of an old man not so much forgetting as remembering with advantages. In nineteenth-century Nottingham, pawnbroking and piety went hand in hand. If, as the ageing General claimed, his first employer 'although a Unitarian never offered a word to suggest that he believed in anything he could not see',[18] he was not typical of his trade. And it seems unlikely that his fellow apprentices were 'sensuous and some of them even vicious'. The various companies which were in rival business when William Booth was first indentured – Eames, Knight, Dickinson – split off from each other, amalgamated and split off again according to commercial convenience and family alliance. But they all maintained a close connection with the Nonconformist Church. Nathaniel Dickinson, who took over Francis Eames' shop in the Poultry when William's first employer moved to Goosegate, expected his staff to attend Sunday service at the local Baptist Chapel. One of them, John Knight, who later became head of the business, managed both to respect his master's wishes and follow his conscience to the Broad Street Chapel.

When the *Nottingham Citizen* reported the centenary of 'John Knight the pawnbroker, jeweller and antique dealer of 5, The Poultry', it recorded that General Booth (on his way to receive the Honorary Freedom of the City of Nottingham) 'invited Mr Knight to accompany him to the ceremony. Mr Knight was associated with William Booth in his early missionary activities.'[19] So not all his pawnbroking colleagues were godless. Indeed the old General – returning to Nottingham in a more mellow mood – recalled that 'here somewhere at the bottom of the Bluebell Hills, something like fifty-four years ago . . . I knelt down in the Lammas Fields and prayed. My companion was an apprentice to a business in the town and I was also apprentice to another business.' That comrade was almost certainly John Eaton, who 'prospered and became a town councillor'. Indeed, he became Lord Mayor of Sheffield. But he, said William Booth, as proof of his self-reliance, 'had family and friends at his back. I had scarcely a friend in the world . . . Nobody to pat me on the back.'[20] Nathaniel Dickinson was Eaton's uncle, so perhaps young William was right to think that his colleague had begun with a head start. But there was absolutely no reason for him to believe that when he became a pawnbroker he fell amongst thieves.

William Booth and John Eaton knelt down to pray in Lammas Fields on 1 February 1847. The date can be precisely identified because on the same day Fergus O'Connor, the Chartist leader, had been returned as Member of Parliament for Nottingham. William Booth had attended some of O'Connor's meetings and marvelled at his oratory.[21] But the language appealed to him far more than the message which it conveyed. All Europe was on the edge of revolution. William Booth did not show any interest even in reform. The only controversies which concerned him were theological.

William Booth was two years into his apprenticeship when he formally abandoned the Church of England into which he had been born and was 'converted' – not, he would later insist, to Wesleyan Methodism, but to salvation. There was, he said, 'nothing remarkable that led to the conversion',[22] no thunderclap or lightning flash, sudden darkness, mysterious voice or midnight visitation from angels which no one else could see. He simply 'had the advantage of hearing some good preaching and came under the influence of some godly companions'. The good preacher was Isaac Marsden, a revivalist from Doncaster; and the godly companion was Henry Carey, his class leader at the Broad Street Chapel. At first, instruction only convinced him that since 'he was utterly without experience of religion [he was] wholly given up to a life of self indulgence' – an absurd example of sanctimonious self-obsession. His principal preoccupation was earning enough to support his widowed mother who, in an attempt to make ends meet, had opened a 'smallware' (that is to say, haberdashers') shop in a poor district of Nottingham.

In fact, as later described, his 'conversion' was both spectacular and entirely consistent with one of the theories of redemption over which the Wesleyans of the day engaged in constant argument. American revivalists, moving from town to town in New England, had 'rejected the idea that holiness only results from a slow process of change in which a man quietly sets out, with divine assistance, to practise virtue and avoid vice'.[23] They believed in instant and absolute conversion. Indeed, their work demanded that they accepted the immediate availability of God's grace. For the towns they visited always expected (and sometimes even paid by) results. The notion that men and women could be sanctified in life ('The Doctrine of Perfection') had been accepted by John Wesley, and therefore was totally respectable. The dispute was over how sanctification could be *achieved*. One faction regarded it as a spiritual maturity, for which time and gradual development was needed; another thought, with the American revivalists, that sanctity was a gift which God could bestow as soon as a man and woman surrendered to Christ – a view which its advocates insisted was also shared by Wesley, who had endorsed the notion of 'instantaneous deliverance'. Naturally young William Booth held the second view – although he almost certainly knew nothing of the theological argument on which it was based. He was simply in a hurry.

Throughout his long life, William Booth instinctively took up theological positions without even being aware of the scholarship on which they were based. They were almost always consistent with American 'holiness teaching' – the theory that, God having promised redemption, it must be instantly available to every sinner who truly repents and places absolute trust in the Word of the Lord. That is how his own conversion happened. When he wrote that 'although the change that came over me was sudden, it was nevertheless reached by stages',[24] he was explaining that he had to be purified before God's love suddenly descended:

> The entrance to the Heavenly Kingdom was closed against me
> by an evil act of the past which required restitution. In a boyish
> trading affair I had managed to make a profit out of my
> companions while giving them to suppose that what I did was
> all in the way of genuine fellowship. As a result of their
> gratitude, they gave me a silver pencil case. Merely to have
> returned the gift would have been easy, but to confess the
> deception which I had practised upon them was a humiliation
> to which, on some days, I could not bring myself.

William Booth – in old age, little more concerned with theology than he had been as a boy – recalled 'as it were but yesterday, the spot in the corner of the chapel (where God gave him strength), the resolution to end the matter rising up, the rushing forth, the finding of the young fellows I had chiefly wronged, the acknowledgement of my sin, the return of the pencil case'.[25] William Booth had, in the language of redemption, laid his soul on the altar. He was saved.

In his early years as a pawnbroker's apprentice, William grew increasingly certain that the Lord had called him to great work. But, not surprisingly, he was unsure what the work should be. His commitment to itinerant evangelism was certainly encouraged, if not actually created, by the impression made upon him by James Caughey – an American, perhaps the most controversial preacher of his time and a man whose theatricality must have fascinated an impressionable young man. Caughey was tall, dark and cadaverous. To increase the drama of his proceedings, he swept from pulpit to pulpit in a long black cloak. Caughey first visited Nottingham in 1846, and was 'for six weeks the leading figure in stirring spiritual awakening . . . As many as three thousand persons at one time stood, half crushed and stifled, under the spell of the great preacher.'[26]

Between 1841 and 1847 Caughey was almost continuously in England. His preaching technique – particularly the habit of isolating individual members of the congregation and exhorting them to lead the way to conversion – was adapted by the adult William Booth. And although 'English preachers from Leeds, Sheffield and Birmingham all testified that he wrought wonders in their parishes and had the true gift of bringing the indecisive to decision,' the Wesleyan establishment found his histrionics offensive.[27] Notwithstanding the commendation of the provinces, the 1847 Methodist Conference asked Caughey to return to America.

Their antagonism was not surprising. Caughey preached hellfire, if not pure then at least simple. His doctrine of retribution on Earth was both offensive to the emotionally fastidious and heresy to the theologians who insisted that rewards and punishments came in heaven and hell. 'If you resist the Holy Spirit of God, if you grieve Him, He will turn round and grieve you . . . He has plenty of means to do this: through your wife, through your daughter, through one of those boys. Those near and dear to you may help to fill the ranks of the bloated drunkards or the felon's cell. It may be done through your creditors who press you hard or through your debtors who may turn out to be villains, thieves, bankrupts and endorsers of bills which may prove good for nothing.'[28] For reasons we can only guess, 950 members of the congregation saw the light and were saved.

Caughey attributed the Conference's criticism to envy – just as, twenty years later, William Booth was to dismiss demands that he accepted pastoral care of a circuit as no more than jealousy of his success as an itinerant preacher. 'Caughey did not lack ministerial support, but most of his public defenders were incensed local preachers, leaders and trustees and other prominent laymen.'[29] That encouraged young William to believe that Caughey blazed the trail which he should follow. The American had come to England without either invitation or the formal qualifications which the Wesleyans, true to their Anglican origins, thought necessary in a man of God. He had lived off the generosity of the parishes – which was sometimes very substantial. One preacher who visited Salford was paid 100 guineas for his services and his wife received 30 guineas for speaking at women's meetings.[30] Caughey spoke in language which the people understood. His preaching style, 'which manipulated every kind of event from the death of one's wife to the dishonesty of one's friends so as to make one feel more guilty and punished by God Himself',[31] seemed vulgar to elderly Methodists, but not to the young William Booth. The pawnbroker's apprentice had no inclination to consider whether or not his views on earthly punishment contradicted the basic Christian belief in God's ultimate mercy – available right up to the point of death.

Although inspired, William Booth still needed encouragement to begin preaching. It was provided by David Greenbury, a Scarborough evangelist who was struck by the young man's 'earnestness, by the vigour of his personality and by his remarkable appearance'. He was certainly a striking figure – tall, gaunt and with a head, which looked too big for his body, crowned with a mop of unruly hair. Although he was not by any standards handsome, and his shabby, ill-fitting clothes gave him the appearance of a Dickensian clerk, he had a presence which made him impossible to ignore. Contemporaries described him as decisive and stubborn. The young evangelists with whom he preached affectionately called him 'wilful Will' in tribute to his self-confident reluctance to change his mind. But if he was a lion amongst his friends, he was a lamb at home. 'I have heard my mother say that I never caused her a day's anxiety in her entire life.'[32]

Greenbury's encouragement was reinforced by that of William Sansom, the son of a well-to-do lacemaker who, having been brought up in the more prosperous parts of Sneinton, may have known the Booths since his childhood. Sansom's father was, like Sampson Biddulph, a trustee of the Broad Street Chapel, and it was there that the two young men regularly worshipped together. Towards the end of 1846, William Booth fell ill with what he later described as a 'bad attack of fever' – the first recorded example of the constant, though varied, illnesses which punctuated the rest of his life. High temperatures often go with visions and angelic voices. But William Booth survived without divine intervention. During his recuperation, William Sansom visited him with the news that a group of young Methodists from the Broad Street Chapel had begun to preach in the poorer parts of Nottingham, and that joining them would be 'medicine and vocation in one'.

Today, a seventeen-year-old boy who thought it was his duty to call sinners to repentance would be regarded as either intellectually presumptuous or in urgent need of psychological help. In nineteenth-century Nottingham it was regarded as unusual but not extraordinary. Indeed, young William, far from being the only adolescent preacher, was not even the founder of the group that spread the word amongst the slums. By the time he had fully recovered, Will Sansom had clearly set up what he called 'a mission'. William Booth became a member, not its leader. But the great work, to which his life was to be devoted, had begun.

William Booth and Will Sansom became David and Jonathan – 'both closely engaged in business, beginning early and often ending very late', but still finding time to man the mission which had 'set up in a widow's cottage in one of the poorer parts of the town'. At first, in the naïveté of youth, they probably believed that the poor were in the greatest need of redemption, for in the slums, sin is more obvious than in the suburbs. And although there was a good deal of abuse and occasional violence to accept and overcome, the illiterate working class of Victorian England were likely to accept teenage evangelists in a way which could not be expected of more prosperous families. In fact, the poor were the only people with whom the young preachers had any real hope of success. The middle classes, confronted by a group of pre-sumptuous adolescents, would have made short shift of the impertinent suggestion that they needed to be saved. But, as the years passed – and he came to experience real poverty – William Booth began to realise that poverty was the devil's agent and the battle against hunger and despair became an integral part of the war against evil.

At the age of seventeen he was infatuated with the idea of evangel-ism. Forty years on he described the early excitement with an enthusiasm that had not diminished with age:

> As soon as we had got away from business we began visiting
> the sick. At seven o'clock we took a chair into the street which
> one of us mounted . . . I remember one of our converts dying.
> We resolved to improve the situation for the benefit of someone
> else. We arranged with the family and bargained with the
> chaplain of the cemetery to have a turn at the grave after he had
> done. A little group of mourners stood behind us: a few of our
> people who could get a holiday stood around while neighbours
> thronged the doors and windows. We sang, we prayed, we
> exhorted.[33]

That Pump Street funeral was, in General Booth's estimation, 'a proper Salvation Army event'. Indeed, 'almost every branch of subse-quent Salvation Army warfare was unconsciously practised by William Booth during his five years membership of the Nottingham Chapel'.[34] He was, in fact, an evangelist by nature and a populist by instinct who was never prepared to waste time on the contemplation of intentions when they could be put into action. Those were the characteristics which, together with his unshakeable faith, enabled him to build a great world-wide Christian church. And he began to display them all in Nottingham. Indeed, thirty years later he told W. T. Stead – editor of the *Pall Mall Gazette* and William Booth's faithful friend – that, as he moved through his early supervision of the East London Christian Mission to the creation and expansion of the Salvation Army, he con-sciously employed at every stage methods which had proved so successful in the back-streets of Nottingham. 'Go to the people with the message of salvation, instead of expecting them to come to you . . . attract them to within earshot . . . Push the people towards a given end . . . employ the people you have saved to save others.'[35] The tech-nique guaranteed both converts and the creation of bitter enemies.

Despite his claims to have taught himself the preachers' trade in Nottingham, the tactics of the young evangelists were decided by Will Sansom, who was firmly in charge and held William Booth's wilder notions in check. Had Sansom lived, his loyal lieutenant might have stayed in the Midlands and remained a faithful Wesleyan Methodist until he died. But Sansom was a consumptive whose condition deteri-orated so rapidly during the spring of 1848 that he was taken to the Isle of Wight in the hope that he might benefit from the clear air, and then – after three months in which his health got worse not better – was brought home to die. A grieving William Booth was left in undis-puted command of the adolescent crusade.

For two years William preached in the mean streets of Nottingham. If there was anything unusual about his style, nobody remarked upon it. It was not until he had the confidence to set up his pulpit in Nottingham's Red Lion Square that his sermons attracted notice by unashamedly imitating James Caughey's accusatory approach. 'Are you going away from here to the public houses to spend money on drink when your wife needs it for food and your children's shoes?' He hoped to shame repentant sinners into chapel, but did it in a way which deeply offended the more reticent and emotionally fastidious elders of the chapels which he hoped to save. It was the beginning of his life-long conflict with the peaceful complacency of Victorian England. And he was too certain of his cause – or too insensitive – to realise the offence that he caused. He seemed surprised that 'the leading men of the church to which I belonged, believed that I was going too fast and gave me plenty of caution but never a word of encouragement to help me on'.[36]

The willingness to offend in a righteous cause characterises Booth's evangelism from the very start. The Reverend J. E. Page, 'a fellow townsman', recalls that, at the age of eight, he was walking with his mother in the Lammas Fields on the edge of Nottingham when he saw 'a ragged regiment of boys marching two by two down Manvers Street'. They were led by William Booth. Once in the fields they knelt around their leader, who instructed them to pray, 'and this they did one by one'. But that was only the beginning of Booth's work. The converts had to be introduced to formal worship. So over forty of the boys were 'taken to the Wesley Chapel in Broad Street'.[37] The Trustees refused to allow them in the front door. But 'they were admitted through the back door in Beak Lane and, with their leader in front on the right of the high mahogany pulpit', silently took their seats opposite the Page family pew.[38]

As part of William Booth's campaign against Wesleyan detachment from the poor, it was claimed that the young men were required to sit where the pulpit prevented them from offending the eyes of the prosperous parishioners in their reserved pews. The Trustees' behaviour was said to typify the attitude of a church which was increasingly focused on the needs of the well-to-do. The Broad Street Trustees, having become the paradigm of Wesleyan failure, were excoriated so regularly during the early days of the Salvation Army that it was easy to believe that their behaviour had been either exaggerated or even invented to illustrate William Booth's point. The story sounded suspiciously like propaganda. But almost a hundred years after the incident took place, the accuracy of the account was confirmed by M. F. West of Bridgeford, Nottingham. He wrote to the *Nottingham Gazette* in defence of the Trustees' behaviour. Ten years before he was born, his parents had been amongst the distressed – indeed disgusted – regular worshippers. It was, he argued, 'not nice for seat-holders, who had paid for their pews, to find upon their arrival that their places had been occupied by strangers not in a clean condition . . . Some of the pews were nicely upholstered and in order to get rid of the vermin, many of the cushions and hassocks had to be burned.'[39] Although, according to Jesus Christ, the poor are always with us, they were not, in the opinion of Nottingham Wesleyans, to be with them in the Broad Street Chapel.

The West defence, admirable in its filial loyalty, confirmed all Booth's criticisms of nineteenth-century Methodism. A church, built on the principle of universal salvation, could not cry out, 'Suffer the clean little children to come unto me.' And the belief that *every* man and woman could be saved was the rock on which William Booth's faith was built. As an active evangelist he could not afford to believe in Calvin's doctrine of the elect. For if some souls were preordained for heaven, every revivalist meeting would be built on a paradox: conversion would be limited to those who had already been chosen for salvation. But it was more than professional necessity which made him believe in God's absolute and all-embracing mercy; he was called to save souls, and chapels, churches and circuits which did not satisfy his appetite for preaching were, he assumed, morally inadequate. And since his appetite was insatiable he came into conflict with every church in which he worshipped – until he invented his own. Even when he was offered the chance to preach he always thought he had a moral right to take it on his own terms. He had no doubt that his views and God's were indistinguishable.

Certainty that he was called to save did not prevent a cautious pursuit of his vocation when he feared that failure might set him back. The Reverend Samuel Dunn – a Methodist dissident who was later described by one of William's friends as 'helping him more than any other minister'[40] – suggested that he should join the full-time ministry. But William Booth declined, 'on the grounds of youth and health'. The growing hypochondria may have played its part, but there was also a reluctance to accept the intellectual discipline that training for the ministry then required. During his seventeenth year, he began to keep a diary of 'biographical notes'. One of his earliest entries complained that he was 'plagued with theology' and asserted that he 'grew more and more impatient with egotistical introspection'.[41] It was to be a recurring theme of his whole life. William Booth was by nature a soldier, not an intellectual. He wanted to fight the good fight, not study the battle plan. Yet he resented the discipline that every soldier must accept from time to time – a discipline which he was determined to impose on those who followed him. When Samuel Dunn asked him if he wanted to preach, he replied that he was preaching already. And he never forgot or quite forgave the crushing retort which followed – 'On whose authority?'[42] Despite that stern rebuff, Dunn arranged for William Booth to become a properly accredited 'local preacher'. It was the first step along the long road towards what he, even then, believed to be his destiny.

The biographical notes included a statement of his three aims in life – to get on in the world, to work for political change and to 'right himself with God'.[43] The second objective was quickly abandoned. The third he certainly achieved to his own satisfaction. The first was a spur to William Booth's success which his followers – who treated him like a saint, not a man – never considered. Yet there is no doubt that he was ambitious. Walter Jones of Sneinton Hollows recalled that, even in his early teens, he asked, 'Have you no ambition? Because I have. I

intend to do some great thing. I don't intend to belong to the com-
monality.'[44]

There is no doubt that, for all his life, William Booth was driven on –
through every sort of hardship and discouragement – by the love of
God and by a passion to save lost souls. But he also felt an obligation
to get on in the world. That was, in part, because he could only fulfil
his mission as God's messenger if he was a visible 'success', but he was
also a child of the age of self-improvement. The Victorians who
thought that their new society offered a universal chance to rise
believed also in the moral obligation to take advantage of that opportunity. The notion that virtue prospered was accepted by men who
worshipped Mammon far more than they worshipped God. But
William Booth felt the moral obligation to get on long before he
realised that success was part of the Protestant ethic. Some of his contemporaries did their Christian duty by founding great manufacturing
companies, establishing new scientific laws or building the Empire.
William Booth invested in heaven and entered into a partnership with
the Almighty. He dealt not in stocks and shares, but souls.

The nature of the illness which prevented William Booth from heed-
ing the call of God and Samuel Dunn has never been clear, though
there are plenty of possibilities from which to choose. In later life he
suffered from regular headaches, constant indigestion, occasional sore
throats, intermittent rheumatism and chronic hypochondria. Perhaps,
even then, he was over-concerned about his health. For he arranged a
full medical examination with a sympathetic doctor. He was pronounced 'unfit for the strain of a Methodist Minister's life' and, in
consequence, filled with fear that he would be permanently excluded
from the full-time ministry. So the prospective preacher 'implored the
doctor not to give any such opinion to Mr Dunn. He therefore promised to report in favour of the question being delayed by twelve
months.'[45]

Twelve months was too long. Work in the pawnbroker's shop grew
increasingly uncongenial – as indeed would have been the case with
any purely commercial activity. He accepted the long hours but refused
outright to work after midnight on Saturdays, and was discharged.
But much to his understandable delight he was recalled to run the shop
while his employer was on honeymoon in Paris. William Booth clearly
disapproved of both the place and the marriage, for the bride was

fifteen years younger than the groom. Clearly, he had become a trusted and valued employee. But it did nothing to reconcile him to his position. He had become irrevocably alienated from the Nottingham Methodists, who did all that they could to deter his irregular preaching. Where, he asked, were the Wesleyans' 'rich business members who might have given employment to one who was already giving promise of a useful life? . . . No door opened . . . I had to move to London.'[46] He left Nottingham for his new life with only one regret. He was, for the first time in his twenty years, to be separated from his mother.

2

Forward With the Crowd

Although William Booth had completed his apprenticeship and learned his trade to the complete satisfaction of his master, no Nottingham pawnbroker could find him journeyman's work. That in itself was not a matter for great regret. He hated pawnbroking, which he had come to regard as ungodly – a form of usury which particularly exploited the poor. But he was unable to find a job in any other trade. Part of his problem was what would now be called motivation. All he really wanted to do was preach. Out of desperation, he decided to move to London. Unlike other young men setting out for the capital, he was not inspired by hope of fame and fortune. His only concern was earning enough to help support his mother. It was the nadir of a bad year. In the autumn Samuel Dunn – the only patron that William could claim – was formally expelled from the Wesleyan Methodist Connexion. 'Fly sheets' questioning the authority of the Methodist Conference President were circulating everywhere. When Dunn was asked if he was the author, he refused to reply.

The Fly Sheet controversy was only one of the many disputes which convulsed Wesleyan Methodism during the first half of the nineteenth century. John Wesley himself had not intended to split the Church of England, and had died an ordained priest of the established Church.

His tours of England – preaching on village greens and at crossroads – were meant to create a spiritual awakening amongst Anglicans. Each of his offences against his church – from holding open-air services to organising societies for working-class converts – was frowned upon by bishops who would not allow him to preach from their pulpits and vicars who did not welcome the poor into their congregations. Methodism – as a separate denomination – did not come into being until after his death. But once the new church was created, schism followed schism.

Most of the arguments concerned authority – a matter of dispute ever since the death of the founder and the creation of the Conference, which had been created by his followers to exercise the authority which had once been his. Wesley's word had been law. The Conference was certainly the keystone of the circuits and parishes which made up the carefully named Wesleyan Methodist Connexion. But it was not universally accepted as the apex of the structure. The breaking point for all the apostates – the New Connexion, the Primitive Methodists and the Bible Christians – was whether or not one group of Nonconformists had power over another. It was to avoid answering that question that, for years, the title of 'minister' (which sounded like a rank) was abandoned in favour of 'preacher', which was clearly a job. The arguments were augmented by issues of class as one group struggled for respectability and another prided itself on keeping close to the common people. The Salvation Army was the result of the last major schism with the Wesleyan Church, and William Booth was the one apostate to found a separate organisation which remained in permanent independent existence. It was not the result of any settled view about where authority should lie, for during his early years he changed his opinion on that subject according to convenience. But at least he learned about doctrinal differences from an expert. Samuel Dunn's dissent – and consequent support of Booth – had its roots in the most prosaic of events: the decision taken by the Trustees of the Brunswick Chapel in Leeds to install an organ.

Many Leeds Methodists believed that God wanted to hear His praises sung by the human voice unaided by artificial devices. So a meeting of all the itinerant preachers in the District was called and, after due deliberation, a decision was taken to ban the organ. The Trustees, however, appealed to the Conference and the Conference

ruled that the organ could be installed. The cry went up that Dr Jabez
Bunting (President of the Conference) was, by overruling the local
preachers, setting himself up as Pope. A group seceded to form the
Protestant Methodists, but resentment against 'the whole Methodist
Conference being buttoned up in a single pair of breeches' continued
inside the parent church. It grew in strength when Bunting proposed
to create an 'Institution' for the training of Methodist ministers which,
the dissidents assumed, would increase the President's permanent
power. A war of words was declared on 'centralisation and usurped
power', and in 1846 the first of a series of anonymous 'Fly Sheets'
appeared, attacking the autocracy of Dr Bunting and his supporters.
The Conference lost its nerve and demanded that every ordained minister should swear that he was not the author of a 'Fly Sheet'. Six
refused. And in 1849, three of them were expelled. Amongst them was
Samuel Dunn of Nottingham.

Dunn was an independently minded Cornishman, the son of a
Mevagissey sea captain. He spent his early evangelical years in the
West Country before he moved on to the Shetland Islands, following
'nasty gossip and six scurrilous pamphlets against him'.[1] Even then he
was in conflict with the Conference, and between the time he left
Scotland and arrived in Nottingham in 1846 he was publishing a dissident magazine, the *Wesleyan Banner*, and maintaining a remorseless
attack on Bunting. In the single month of November 1847 he preached
on 'The Preparations for a Revival', 'The Time for a Revival' and 'The
Symptoms of a Revival'.[2] Dunn's uncompromising certainty was
immensely appealing to the pious young William Booth, who – recalling with John Wesley that 'to build a new world we first need new
men' – thought of himself as being in the vanguard of the democratic
Wesleyan revolution. He also – almost certainly subconsciously –
absorbed the particular theological message that Dunn's sermons contained. To Methodists the word 'revival' had a special meaning. Those
who spoke of it with passion at least implied that Methodism was in
danger of falling into the Church of England's error and failing to take
the gospel of salvation to the people. It was a message with which temperamentally – and without very much knowledge of how the
Wesleyans worked – Booth was inclined to agree.

The Fly Sheet expulsions were followed by the deepest split in the
Methodists' turbulent history. James Everett, the leader of the expelled

dissidents, formed the Methodist Reform Society and the church from which he had been excluded lost ten thousand members. Not all of them followed him into the new society. They had a wide variety of Wesleyan alternatives from which to choose. The Methodist New Connexion had gone its own way in 1797 when its founder, Alexander Kilham, argued, not altogether consistently, that each local society should have absolute power of discipline over its members and that the trustees of the chapels should have the right to invite whoever they wished to administer the sacraments. In 1810, when the Conference banned open-air 'camp meetings' which were thought to encourage Luddites, sedition and excitement, the Society of Primitive Methodists was formed. Five years later – after the Conference had, with some difficulty, convinced Lord Liverpool's government that Wesleyans were dissenters, not revolutionaries – William O'Bryan denounced the obsession with respectability and was expelled as proof of the Conference's detachment from politics. He formed the Bible Christian Society. The leaders of each new church were accused by the Wesleyan leadership of 'contumacy' – obstinate and wilful resistance to authority. The charge confirmed the apostates' view that they were right, in the name of John Wesley, to challenge the centralisation of power.

William Booth arrived in London almost entirely unaware of the tidal waves of disagreement which were sweeping across Wesleyan Methodism. He had a simple view of chapel. It was the place where ministers preached and the congregation prayed. His innocence was to be shattered within a year of his arrival. So were his hopes of congenial employment.

Like generations of migrants before him, William Booth left for the capital expecting help from earlier pioneers. Ann, the eldest of the surviving Booth children, had married Francis Brown, a London hatter, and her brother assumed that he would be a welcome lodger in their house until he had found a place of his own and a job. His reception was, if anything, too congenial. Francis Brown was a drunkard and his wife, in her brother's euphemism, 'had learned to drink'. Life with the Browns was intolerable but, although he was determined to move, without employment he could not afford to pay for lodgings. Anxious though he was to earn his first wage, he remained steadfastly opposed to returning to pawnbroking, the only trade he knew. His depression was deepened by his powerful dislike of the city he had made his new home. 'The sensation of a newcomer to London from the country is always disagreeable if he comes to work. The immensity of the city must especially strike him as he crosses it from time to time.'[3] The year after he arrived in London, Wordsworth's *The Prelude* (written fifty years earlier) was published. It reflected his mood exactly:

> How often in the overflowing streets
> Have I gone forward with the crowd and said
> Unto myself, the face of everyone
> That passes by me is a mystery.

William Booth was alone in the city and, as he remembered it fifty years later, surrounded by sin, 'manifest poverty . . . the language of drinking crowds . . . people reluctant to bear any witness to the power of God'.[4] His depression was deep enough to be described as misery, but the mood did not last long. Throughout his life, William Booth was subject to sudden changes of emotion and his black pessimism often changed to shining hope. He had intended to put pawnbroking behind him for ever. But when that was the only situation which he could find, he returned to it with great reluctance and became 'shopman' to William Filmer of Kennington. Once he was back with the full status of shopman, with lodgings on the premises, his spirits improved. The earliest letter to survive – undated, but beginning 'arrived safely in London at last' – was, in contrast to the recollection of old age, full of enthusiasm. It was addressed to John Savage, a young Nottingham evangelist: 'Our shop is uncommonly pleasantly situated. No shop in Nottingham has anything equal to it. In front we look on the beautiful common on which there are constantly a number of people playing at cricket, flying kites or some other game and at the back we have a nice garden fountain.'[5]

It was not Booth's way, then or in later life, to enthuse about anything except the love of God and the reception he received at prayer meetings. And his hatred of ball games was so intense that he could barely bring himself to speak about them. But on that day his joy was unconfined. And he seemed as satisfied with the piety of the pawnbroker as he was with the situation of the pawnbroker's shop. 'I think that my Master is an Independent, however we have prayers every evening and we gather round and sing a hymn. My Master then reads a chapter and afterwards prays. This is all to me very agreeable.'[6]

That is not how he recalled his early days in London when the ageing General of the Salvation Army looked back upon his early life and described the shop in Kennington. Nor is it how he remembered Filmer, its proprietor. 'My second Master believed in the divinity of Jesus Christ and in the church of which he was a member, but seemed to be utterly ignorant of either the theory or the practice of experiential godliness. All he seemed to want me for was to help in the sordid selfishness.'[7] By that he meant that he was expected to perform the tasks – taking the pledges and returning the redeemed goods – for which he was paid. Perhaps Booth altered his opinion of Filmer because the optimism of youth was replaced with the cynicism of age. But it is more likely that what really changed was his attitude towards pawnbroking, which he came to see as a dishonourable occupation. The years in the East End of London amongst the slums of the Mile End Road and the stews of Limehouse had introduced him to the hard reality of pawnbroking as it affected the very poor – the sacrifice of the last remaining possessions for the price of a bottle of gin. Even in youth he was unhappy to be part of the trade. In old age he was ashamed that he had even been willing to earn his daily bread by loaning coppers against the security of a workman's tools or his Sunday suit. When he became both an evangelist and a social reformer, he could not deny his past. So he chose to hate it.

The plan, when William Booth came to London, had been to work six days a week and preach on Sundays. Recreation had not figured in his reckoning. But one day a week was not enough to satisfy his religious passion. So late at night, after the shop was closed, he went out on to the streets. Most often he was alone and unsanctioned by the church's authority. Although in mid-Victorian England the public proclamation of religion was more common than it is today, the sight of the gaunt young man sermonising on street corners must have astounded many passers-by. But William Booth never felt the least embarrassment in doing the Lord's work. For all his life he was regularly ridiculed, often abused and occasionally assaulted. He stuck bravely – and perhaps more significantly, without inhibition – to his task.

It may have been because his conduct seemed so perverse that

William Filmer, despite his religious pretensions, did nothing to help and a good deal to hinder his shopman's evangelism. During the day, he was treated 'practically like a white slave'. He found lodging above the shop particularly difficult. 'I had to be home by ten o'clock or the doors were locked against me.' So, out of frustration as much as by a desire to progress, he took refuge in introspection. On 6 November 1849 he made, and wrote down, six rules for life. The resolutions were not set out in any order or priority. 'Strive to live closer to God' came only fifth. First was 'rise early enough for ablutions and five minutes' prayer'. It was immediately followed by the injunction to 'avoid babble' and the commitment to adopt 'a humble and meek deportment'. It seems impossible that he kept his promise to read 'four chapters (minimum) of the Bible each day' or that resolution six – reminding himself of the other five 'every day or twice a week' was necessary.[8]

Perhaps it was his attempts to make himself more worthy in the sight of God that improved his reputation with the local Methodists. For, shortly after he wrote out his list of resolutions, he became an official preacher with the Lambeth Circuit. The immediate result, as confessed in a letter to John Savage, was the awakening of the doubts which followed him through life – the fear that his instinctive aversion to scholarship would reduce his chances of fulfilling his spiritual destiny. 'I am more than ever discouraged. On being acquainted with my congregation, I am surprised at the amount of intellect which I have endeavoured to address. I am waking up as from a dream and discovering that my hopes are vanity and that I literally know nothing.'[9] However, the doubts about the breadth of his knowledge were not strong enough to make him rectify his lack of it with periods of concentrated study. He never felt at home with books. And he knew it. From time to time, he accepted his limitation as a handicap, but he did not allow it to stunt his ambition: 'I preached two sermons yesterday . . . afterwards I had some conversations with one of our local preachers, respecting the subject with regard to which my heart is still burning – I mean full-time work. He advised me, by all means offer myself next month.'[10]

The offer was made and, not surprisingly, rejected. In an age when ministers of every denomination were supposed to have at least pretensions to scholarship, William Booth had knowledge of neither Latin grammar nor Greek syntax and, in the brashness of youth, would happily expand on his view that the careful examination of the scriptures led to interpretation and that interpretation of the literal truth was heresy. He had brought from Nottingham to London a simple view of his destiny: he had a duty to preach salvation. 'How can anybody with spiritual eyesight talk of having no call when there are still multitudes around them who have never heard a word about God, and never intend to, who can never hear without the sort of preacher who can force himself upon them?'[11] Subconsciously he was beginning to develop the philosophy of evangelism which made him, and the Salvation Army, a world-wide force. When he wrote that he would 'force himself upon them', he meant it literally.

William Booth reacted to his rejection as a full-time preacher with anger as well as disappointment. When he was told that 'preachers were not wanted',[12] he seriously considered following in Wesley's steps to the colonies, or becoming a chaplain on one of the convict ships that transported felons to Australia. But he could not, he decided, leave his mother in Britain. So he had soldiered on until the Fly Sheets controversy claimed his patron as a victim. Loyal Methodists had begun to protest about the expulsion of Samuel Dunn and his associates – who had set themselves up as yet another variation of Methodism. They hoped that by calling themselves 'Reformers' they would make plain that, given the opportunity, they would improve their church from within its boundaries rather than split off into another Wesleyan fragment. Their supporters held mass meetings in London and presented great petitions to the Conference. A few chapels had a majority of Reformers as members. Most had a substantial minority. Local ministers grew nervous and began to search out dissidents who might undermine legitimate authority in their circuits.

The Reformers had no great attraction for William Booth. Their arcane arguments irritated him. But Samuel Dunn had been a friend. And since he was fascinated by the *business* of worship, he occasionally visited the Reformers' Walworth Road Chapel in what he claimed was no more than the spirit of pious enquiry. It was, no doubt, difficult for his colleagues on the Lambeth Circuit to imagine him sitting, quiet and contemplative, at the back of the service. So he fell under suspicion. The elders' apprehension seemed confirmed when he decided to resign his commission as lay preacher and instead evangelise independently

on Kennington Common. The decision was personal rather than theological. His resignation letter to John Hall, Lambeth's superintendent
minister, announced that he could 'better serve my generation by
preaching in the streets'. Perhaps the minister could not believe that a
young man, barely old enough to take legal responsibility for his own
debts, could hold such pretentious views of his own abilities. Although
the letter had emphasised Booth's 'wish to continue in ordinary membership of the Connexion', the response was as uncompromising as it
was unreasonable. In old age, William Booth complained that Hall,
'without reply . . . withdrew my ticket of membership'.[13] He had, in
effect, been expelled from the Wesleyan Methodist Church.

His friends suggested that his decision to abandon his lay preacher's
commission was a reaction against the assault on Samuel Dunn and the
Reformers. William Booth himself complained that John Hall 'stated
that my separation from the Wesleyans came about through my rejection as a candidate for the ministry', but added, 'I never was a
candidate. The Reverend Samuel Dunn wanted me to become one in
1848 . . . but it was at my own wish postponed.'[14] Whatever the reasons for his resignation and the expulsion which followed, it had the
predictable effect of driving him towards the Reformers who, until
John Hall returned his membership card, had held no particular attraction for the young preacher. Within weeks of his exclusion, he was
actively working with the Walworth Road Chapel.

It was there that William Booth preached his first Reform sermon.
Edward Rabbits, a wealthy boot- and shoemaker, was in the congregation. 'He was an old-fashioned Methodist who liked to hear "Amens" in
chapel and a "light" in the Reform party.' Rabbits began business, it was
said, on a borrowed half-crown and by 1851 was reputed to be a millionaire. A shrewd, masterful person, he was 'full of energetic interest
in boot-making and religion'.[15] The 1851 Census return records him as
a 'head shoemaker, employing 95 men', and his name appears in the
register of electors for 1849–50 which proved, since universal suffrage
was still twenty years away, that he was a man of property. He was also
a man who was ruled by sudden impulse. One sermon was enough to
convince him that William Booth could awaken the sleeping
Methodists. Helping the young preacher was his way of thanking God
for having made him rich.

Rabbits was a man who liked to control events and he believed, almost at first hearing, that William Booth should throw in his permanent lot with the Reformers. William was not difficult to persuade. He was willing to preach wherever he could command a hearing and, since he was theologically footloose, he regarded the Reformers' headquarters – Binfield House Chapel on the Clapham Road – as good as anywhere else. It was there that Catherine Mumford first heard him. She was so impressed with the force of his oratory that she told Rabbits how moved she had been by the sermon. Rabbits – with motives at which we can only guess – invited them both to tea at his house. The events of the afternoon might well have estranged William Booth from Catherine Mumford for life, but it seems that they, and she, left William Booth absolutely unmoved. When he talked, after her death, about love at first sight, he was describing a later occasion. He did not remember his first meeting with his future wife, constant companion, and unflinching conscience.

Reformers did not waste time on small talk, a discipline with which William Booth would undoubtedly have sympathised. On the day of Catherine and William's first meeting the conversation turned to the evils of drink. William was not, at the time, a total abstainer. The boyhood pledge had lapsed, and although he took the occasional glass of port – thought at the time to be a cure for most known illnesses and therefore indispensable to hypochondriacs – he was regarded by even some devout Methodists as dangerously illiberal on the subject. Some of the company challenged him to defend his views, an idea which he at first stubbornly resisted. But Edward Rabbits, host and elder, either persuaded or bullied William into singing 'The Grogseller's Dream', a song which made up in moral fervour what it lacked in every other sort of merit. The grogseller, in over 210 lines of doggerel, describes with contempt the customers whose lives he has ruined by drink. 'But business is business, so what care I?' he asks before he is chastened, and perhaps redeemed, by an apparition which appears to him in a nightmare:

> And lo! In a corner, dark and dim
> Stood an uncouth form with aspect grim
> From his grizzly head through his snaky hair
> There sprouted of hard rough horns a pair . . .

Forty years later, when his son-in-law was writing the official biography of Catherine (Mumford) Booth, the General was able to repeat the whole poem without error or hesitation.

William Booth made the mistake of admitting to Catherine that he was not a total abstainer and that his mother, the model of sober piety, had given him port as a restorative. In the discussion which followed, Catherine argued the extreme case with an unremitting passion. She attacked not only her future husband but the other middle class Methodists present who, in conforming with the dogma of the time, believed that alcohol was acceptable in moderation.

The only possible explanation for William forgetting the occasion is that he had other things on his mind. Principal amongst them was Rabbits' suggestion, indeed insistence, that he should become a full-time evangelist in what had become the Wesleyan Reform Church. He did not take much persuasion. He still had a widowed mother to think of. But that difficulty was overcome in a conversation which the new recruit to the Reformers' cause recorded verbatim:

> I told him, 'I cannot live on air.'
> 'How much,' he asked, 'do you need to live on?'
> After careful calculation, I told him that I did not see how I could get along on less than twelve shillings a week.
> 'Nonsense,' he said. 'You cannot do with less than twenty.'
> 'All right,' I said. 'Have it your own way if you want. But where is twenty shillings to come from?'
> 'I will supply it,' he said, 'for the first three months at least.'[16]

Rabbits was the first of William Booth's patrons – the first to invest in his evangelism, the first (as it turned out) to want to make him a permanent remittance man, and the first to be abandoned once the ties of dependence seemed too much of a restraint. It was to become a regular pattern of Booth's early life, and there is no reason to believe that he accepted any of the offers of help with anything other than honest enthusiasm and moderate gratitude. Rabbits provided the chance for which he had been looking. He found himself independent lodgings in Camberwell Street with Margaret Wallis, a widow with a fifteen-year-old daughter who, according to the 1851 Census, was a 'drawn bonnet maker'. The rooms were unfurnished, but his five-shilling rent included 'attendance'. His notice to William Filmer expired on his twenty-second birthday, Good Friday, 10 April 1852, and on that day he became a full-time preacher. At last, and for the rest of his life, he was in God's employ.

Overjoyed that he was finally to fulfil his destiny, he rushed across London to tell his sister – and perhaps even her drunkard atheist husband – the glorious news. On his way, he met Edward Rabbits, the architect of his good fortune, and was persuaded to postpone the celebration until he had shared his joy with other Reformers at a tea meeting which was to be held in the Cooper Street school off the City Road. 'On that day,' William wrote, 'I fell head over heels in love with the precious woman who was later to become my wife.'[17] He was also to insist – despite their previous meeting – that it was love at first sight. 'It seemed as if God flashed simultaneously into our hearts that affection which afterwards ripened into what has proved to be an exceptional union of hearts and purpose of life and which none of the vicissitudes with which our lives have been so crowded has been able to efface.'[18]

It was not Catherine's appearance which made William Booth fall so quickly in love. For she was not a physically prepossessing woman. Her dark hair, parted in the middle, fell (tight and severe) down to her ears where it was bound together in 'buns'. She had a small chin, long nose and a pale complexion which, correctly, gave the impression that she was above all else pious. Her clothes were, invariably, the classic black bombazine and white linen of the respectable Victorian spinster, and they added, as Catherine intended, to the aura of sobriety. According to Salvation Army folklore George Bernard Shaw called her the 'least photogenic woman in London'.* She was certainly plain. And she exhibited no obvious wit or vitality. She was both clever and brave. But those major virtues rarely inspire instant attraction – particularly, as was the case with Catherine, when they are combined with a view of the world which was both didactic and censorious. William must have detected 'the pilgrim soul' which W. B. Yeats identified in

---

*Michael Holroyd, Bernard Shaw's biographer, can find no evidence to confirm the story, and regards it as 'out of character' whether or not the description was justified.

Maud Gonne – as well as the moral certainty which he so admired in his mother. In a way, it was the attraction of equals. They were both (by nature) stern, unbending and above all, heroic.

God moved in mysterious ways during the service with which the Cooper Street meeting ended. Catherine was taken ill and William took her home to Russell Street on what he described as 'a little carriage ride' – naturally enough, paid for by Edward Rabbits. With another journey across London in prospect, the Mumfords insisted that their daughter's chivalrous companion stayed the night in Russell Street. So there began with absolute propriety one of the great love affairs of the nineteenth century – born in prayer, continued in sickness and sustained by mutual dependence. It was an almost perfect union. On the great issues of God and Eternity they were in total agreement – though Catherine, without much help and with a good deal of hindrance from her family, had a far more intellectual attitude towards religion than her husband could, or would ever want to, claim.

Catherine Mumford was born in the Derbyshire market town of Ashbourne on 17 January 1829. John Mumford, her father, had been an occasional local preacher, but sometime during Catherine's childhood he had lost his faith. However, Sarah, her mother, had enough religious zeal for them both. When she was old, Catherine wrote, 'the longer I live the more I appreciate my mother's character',[19] but there is no doubt that, even in childhood, she admired as well as loved Sarah Mumford. It could not, however, have been easy to grow up in such a righteous shadow. 'Sarah Mumford rarely allowed her daughter to play with other children in case she caught bad habits. Nor was Catherine allowed to read fiction which her mother regarded as the work of the devil. From time to time she was kept away from school in case she was exposed to some form of impropriety. Sarah was particularly anxious that her daughter should not learn French.' It is not hard to imagine how she reacted to Catherine's several serious illnesses. After the deaths of her three elder boys 'it was a positive joy to her to think that they were in heaven' and she insisted that she 'would not have them back for anything'.[20]

Sometime in 1841 – after the family had moved back to Boston, their Lincolnshire home town – a member of the chapel which Sarah Mumford attended convinced her that the local school could be trusted not to lead her daughter into the ways of wickedness. So Catherine's formal education began when she was twelve. Her main interest was history. Napoleon she heartily disliked because 'he seemed the embodiment of selfish ambition'. Caesar, on the other hand, 'appeared desirous of benefiting the people he conquered'. School days did not last for long. In 1842, Catherine suffered what at the time was called a 'spinal attack'. For months she lay flat on her back, and during the enforced idleness began to study theology. At last she was allowed to read the right sort of fiction. She began with *The Pilgrim's Progress* but 'could not help entertaining a strong antipathy to the Calvinistic tendency in some of its teaching'. West across the Midlands, William Booth, at the same age, had not begun to think about such things. But when he did, his views and Catherine's coincided exactly. Throughout his life he rejected the doctrine of the elect.

At the age of twelve, Catherine Mumford had already begun to develop the strong opinions which came to be her moral trademark. Her 'childhood heart rejoiced greatly in the speculation of Wesley and Butler with regards to the possibility of a future life for animals in which God might make up to them for the suffering and pain inflicted on them in life'. In Catherine theory and practice could never be separated. So she ran down the road in pursuit of a collier whom she had seen hitting his donkey with a hammer and tried to snatch it from his hand. Believing that 'the coloured races of the Earth, Negroes especially . . . were the most oppressed and least capable of defending themselves', she gave up sugar – an example of the self-denial that a hundred years later millions of radicals practised in protest against apartheid in South Africa and fascism in Spain. She also developed a prodigious opposition to 'the practice, now so prevalent amongst superior people, of sending their children to boarding schools before the principles are formed and their characters developed'.[21] Her concern was not the pursuit of privilege. She believed literally in the baptismal promises made on behalf of the person being baptised. It was the duty of parents and godparents to provide a Christian upbringing, not headmasters and chaplains. And after recovery from the spinal attack, her moral commitment grew. She became a young pillar of the Temperance Movement – a cause to which her father had remained devoted despite his estrangement from the Methodist Church.

Some of the claims about Catherine Mumford's prodigious talents are difficult to accept. It is hard to believe that she read the Bible from start to finish eight times before she was twelve years old. And her own account of how she challenged her father's support for the Catholic Emancipation Act would have been more plausible had the Bill not passed into law two years before she was born. Nevertheless, she was an extraordinary child. However faulty her recollection, the insistence that she had always opposed Catholics being given a voice in the government of the country did illustrate the deep suspicion of Rome that she felt throughout her life. The occasional lapse of memory – including exaggeration of her youthful achievements – cannot diminish either the strength of her childhood character or the breadth of her early learning. Catherine Mumford was an intellectual and her interest in ideas was the one part of her life which William Booth was neither able, nor anxious, to share. In most other things, they matched each other exactly. When Catherine Mumford moved to London in 1844, like her future husband, she found it 'cold and worldly'.

The Mumfords settled in Brixton where both mother and daughter became devout and enthusiastic members of the Methodist Church. Then, on 15 June 1846, at the age of sixteen, she experienced the revelation which convinced her, despite earlier doubts, that she was saved. Catherine was reading a Charles Wesley hymn, which she knew well, when the miraculous moment came. 'My God, I am thine. What a comfort Divine. What a blessing to know that my Jesus is mine.' Suddenly she 'felt the assurance of Salvation'. She had read and sung those words 'scores of times', but on that day they carried a special personal message. 'They came home to my innermost soul with a force and illumination they had never before possessed and I no longer hoped that I was saved. I was certain of it.'[22] In those days, her definition of salvation was less complicated than it became after she lost the invincible simplicity of childhood. As her view of redemption became more sophisticated, she was redeemed over and over again.

Even before she was certain of salvation, Catherine had absolutely no doubt about where the path of righteousness led. She had, when an unprepossessing fifteen years old, visited a male cousin in Derby who had become immediately and openly attentive to her. After she returned home he began to write to her almost daily. Catherine ended the correspondence on the biblical precept, 'Be ye not unequally yoked together with unbelievers.'[23] And she was no more lucky in health than in love. In 1846, aged seventeen, she was diagnosed as suffering from consumption. She was sent to Brighton in the hope that the sea air would effect a cure. No doubt because she was lonely, she began to keep a diary. It reveals a preoccupation with death and what might come thereafter which was as unhealthy as it was holy. The first entry set the tone: 'May 12, 1847: While passing through some tunnels I thought, should an accident happen amidst this darkness and hurry me into eternity, shall I find myself in glory?'[24]

There followed a period of self-pity – an unattractive characteristic which disappeared after her marriage. But her despondency about life in this world did not undermine certainty about prospects for the next. 'May 25: I find a want of tender feeling of sympathy but Praise the Lord I have come to him in the house of trial . . . May 27: O how sweet will heaven be to me after the pains and afflictions of life are over.' The devil was a regular visitor to her sick room. 'June 3: Satan is striving to disturb my peace by injecting evil thoughts into my mind. This has ever been the way in which he has harassed me even when engaged in prayer or other sacred duties. O Lord give me true light to discern between temptation and sin.'[25] The distinction was to become central to her future husband's work as an evangelist. Penitents had to be convinced that they might feel temptation but, as long as they resisted it, they remained sanctified. It was one of the contentious propositions of revivalism which would rage in argument for half a century. And Catherine Mumford, as a young girl of eighteen, had begun – without any formal instruction – to agonise about the subject.

Catherine returned home from Brighton in late June – cured but not reconciled to her recovery. 'O it will be sweet to meet my dearest mother again, but still I strive to remember that our meetings are but partings. Perhaps we will soon be separated by the cold pain of death.' However, she was to be spared the ultimate salvation for another forty-three years. Often confined to the house, she used her enforced idleness for study. Her diary entry for 2 January 1848 claims, 'I have read my Bible through twice in the last sixteen months.' Although God, assisted by the fresh air of Brighton, arrested the tuberculosis, Catherine's diary records constant faintness and palpitations during Sunday services. She soldiered on, visiting the Brixton sick as William Booth was visiting the sick in Nottingham and, like him, 'writing down a few daily notes for the coming year'.[26]

William Booth, impatient with theological theory, was always prepared to preach in any chapel which would have him without worrying
about his hosts' particular brand of Methodism. However, Catherine –
believing at that time in a democratic church – was firmly converted to
the Reformers' cause. She moved serenely, and with absolute conviction, from teaching Sunday School for the traditional Wesleyans in
Brixton to leading a class for the Reform Methodists at Binfield House.
So it was that they met at Rabbits' tea party, came together again on the
day that William exchanged pawnbroking for preaching and, on Good
Friday 1852, fell in love. They were formally engaged to be married on
15 May, just over a month later.

To claim that neither William nor Catherine harboured the slightest
doubt would be a romantic fiction. They never doubted their love.
Their commitment to each other was instant and absolute. But
Catherine, who had come into William's life at the very moment that he
became a full-time preacher, worried about coming between him and
his destiny. Four days before their formal betrothal she wrote, 'Do try
to forget me as far as remembrance will injure your usefulness or spoil
your peace. If I have no alternative but to oppose the will of God or
trample on the desolations of my own heart, my choice is made.'[27]
William was appropriately distressed by the thought that Catherine
might be having second thoughts about him – a comforting, if unusual,
moment of human frailty from a man who would normally have
accepted that the wishes of providence were paramount in all decent
people's system of values. So two days before the appointed date, she
wrote to him again. 'You did not fully understand my difficulty . . . My
only reason for wishing to defer the engagement was that you might
not be satisfied that the step was right.'[28] William Booth had the sense
to know that nothing more right had ever been in prospect. The
engagement went ahead as both William and Catherine, despite their
protestations, always knew that it would.
    The letters – which they wrote to each other with inflexible regular-
ity whenever they were apart – no longer needed to offer reassurance
about their mutual devotion. So Catherine embarked upon her life's
work – guiding William Booth. At the beginning of their relationship
she had warned: 'Beware how you indulge that dangerous element of
character, ambition. Misdirected it will be everlasting ruin to yourself

and perhaps to me also.'[29] William, not usually the most humble of men, accepted her strictures with absolute humility. Indeed the constant theme of his letters was the hope that he could become worthy of his future wife. When she urged him to read more and master the theology on which his faith was based, he replied, 'When shall I learn better to require the student habit? When? I fear never.'[30] Catherine was magnificently unsympathetic. 'I am sorry to hear of you talk of *trying* to be a student once more and, if you fail, giving up for ever. Don't say I will *try*, but that I will be one. At least you can study whether you make much out of it or not.'[31] Clearly love was not matched by admiration for William's intellect. But Catherine's determination to lead the way towards a deeper understanding only strengthened the relationship – though it created a partnership which was highly peculiar by Victorian standards.

They shared the same failings and foibles and lived for forty years in something close to complete harmony. The extraordinary quality of their relationship was the way in which characteristics, which might have driven them apart, served only to bind them more closely together. In all nineteenth-century England there could not have been a couple in which both husband and wife held such strong opinions – and felt such an obligation to impose them on other people. And they did not exempt each other from their reforming zeal. But miraculously, on the rare occasions when their views did not coincide, one of them capitulated, so Catherine succeeded in being both a loyal Victorian wife and mother, attendant to her husband's wants and needs, yet at the same time an independent spirit who corrected him when she thought him to be wrong.

William gave as much advice as he received, though it was of a quite different character. He set out, during their often long-distance courtship, what he called the 'rules of the relationship'. They included the insistence that 'ours must and shall be salvation meetings' – meaning that they would be used to inspire greater righteousness. They also had, in William's estimation, a duty to 'enquire closely into our religious experiences and give each other Counsel and Advice as they may be needed'. There was also a mutual obligation to 'avoid desultory conversation and never retire later than after 10'.[32] William Booth's lists of good intentions usually ended in the promise to go early to bed. It was fortunate that they found joy in religion, for they showed little sign of finding it in any of the pleasures which delighted other young couples.

The main subject of their correspondence – copious even when they both lived in London, separated as the demands of both time and propriety required – was William's future. The high hopes of the Reformers' offer, and Rabbits' generosity which made its acceptance possible, were not realised. William was paid enough to preach every day, but his services were rarely demanded more than twice on a Sunday. The problem was the competition which he faced for time in the pulpit. 'They reckon that they are all preachers here,' he wrote to Catherine without pointing out that the presumption which so irritated him was the direct result of the Reformers' belief, which he was supposed to share, that priest and people were one in the sight of God. Catherine, who had once rejoiced in the Reformers' democracy, wondered if she – the fiancée of a full-time preacher and prospective minister – could continue her alliance to a church which so wilfully squandered William's talents. She was, like William, a Wesleyan *in general* without any particular allegiance to any one of its manifestations. However, unlike him, Catherine did take an interest in the theological arguments which enlivened Wesleyan literature. She became particularly interested in the work of Charles Grandison Finney, an American preacher whose evangelism was built on the belief that 'revivals' were not a result of sudden divine intervention, but stimulated by 'a group of people, coming together and praying a church revival into existence'. It was a theory which William was instinctively inclined to accept. At the time of their engagement, Catherine was more interested in Finney as the author of *Lectures on Revivals and Religion*, in particular his thoughts on the 'causes of backsliding' – the drift of converts away from Christianity within a few weeks or months of their redemption. It was a problem which was to cause her and her husband continual frustration. Time after time, during William's years as an itinerant preacher, his new recruits were lost to the church because of the sloth of the resident minister. Finney blamed 'backsliding' on 'having too much worldly business . . . being associated in business with an unconverted partner . . . The influence of worldly companions or marrying one who is worldly . . . the fear of giving offence to worldly friends' and, most important of all, 'the neglect of secret prayer'. Inspired by these notions Catherine began to search for a church which both respected its ministers and retained its members. The Congregationalists came to mind.

The Congregationalists – being the heirs to the Independents who had left the Church of England almost two hundred years before John Wesley was ordained – were not Wesleyans at all. But they were dissenters and literal Nonconformists and, at least at the time of their creation, they believed in the absolute authority of each local church. That, Catherine believed, would provide William with the opportunity to preach to his heart's content. Like all dissidents she believed that the real enemy was the distant establishment, and that the people who knew him would, by the force of his personality, come to support his cause. It was a notion built as much on love as theology. But it stimulated Catherine to argue the case for Congregationalism – a denomination to which she had been attracted by the preaching of the Reverend Dr David Thomas. At the age of twenty-three, Catherine Booth, an essentially serious young woman, could easily be seduced by a sermon. When she was sixty she gladly took responsibility for her future husband's brief conversion:

> William's attention was turned to the Congregational Church.
> I think this was my doing: indeed I know it was, but until he
> came to this dead stop he would never hear of it. I argued that
> once settled in the Congregational pulpit he could impart into
> services and meeting all that was good and hearty and soul saving
> in Methodism . . . With such reasons as these and his soul seeing
> that there was no other way by which he could reach the sphere
> to which his soul believed God had called him, he gave in and
> resolved to seek an open door for the preaching of Jesus Christ
> and to bring lost sinners to God amongst the Congregationalists.[33]

However, there was a problem. The Congregationalists were, or at least had been, inclined towards Calvinism. Most of them had begun to exercise their autonomous rights by asserting only a modified version of that doctrine. But some persisted in the belief that some souls were predestined to be saved, others preordained for damnation. William Booth regarded the idea of an 'elect' as an abomination. In her reminiscences Catherine is gloriously disingenuous about the theological difficulty which they faced:

We knew that the basis of Congregational theology was
Calvinism . . . The idea of anything like the selection of one
individual to enjoy the blessedness of Divine favour for ever
and ever, and the reprobation of another to suffer all the pains
and penalties of damnation, irrespective of choice, conduct or
character on their part seemed to be an outrage.[34]

Nevertheless, Catherine argued, and William agreed, that they
should throw in their lot with the Congregationalists. It was, by normal
standards of behaviour, an act of extraordinary cynicism, and the justification for such open opportunism was barely credible. Most
Congregationalists, Catherine argued, did not believe the basic belief of
their church. The leap was made when Rabbits' stipend ran out and,
true to his independent nature, William Booth declined the offer of a
permanent income in such brusque terms that their friendship was –
despite what by then had become the shoemaker's personal devotion –
briefly ended. It was the life-long pattern of all William Booth's
responses to offers of patronage – the initial grateful acceptance of
essential help, and the rejection of more permanent support out of fear
that it would compromise him. The two distinct stages were usually
followed by an angry parting of benefactor and beneficiary and then,
after years of estrangement, their eventual reconciliation. It happened
time after time. But only in June 1852 was it a prelude to William
Booth joining a church which supported views with which he violently
disagreed.

William Booth and Catherine Mumford began to attend Stockwell
Congregational Church where the Reverend Thomas was the resident
minister. It was not, however, Reverend Thomas who offered William
the chance to become a minister himself. That was provided by
Catherine's encouragement and William's own determination. After
some persuasion he agreed to meet Dr John Campbell, editor and
publisher of *The Banner*, an independent Congregationalist magazine.
It seems that after the meeting was arranged he was suddenly overcome by one of his fits of self-doubt, for he wrote, 'My only fear is that
I have not sufficient ability to be a successful Minister . . . I fear that I
have framed an erroneous estimate of myself, my capacities and
powers and I tremble at the consequences.'[35] William's doubts were
always greatest when it was his intellect, rather than his courage and

convictions, which were to be put to the test. But, no doubt sustained by Catherine, he overcame his fears and asked for help. Dr Campbell did not seem to be over-enthusiastic about the idea of so recent a convert becoming an ordained minister. But he began a process by which William was passed from minister to minister like a package that nobody wants to keep. Campbell arranged a meeting with the Reverend W. Leask of Kensington. Leask suggested that the Reverend W. S. Edwards of the New Chapel, City Road would provide all the necessary information about entry into the Congregational Training Institution at Cotton End. Edwards advised that Dr Massey of the Home Missionary Society might have some useful advice to offer. William's letter of thanks to Dr Campbell – written without a hint of either resentment or irony – describes each meeting, expressed his gratitude that each man had treated him 'kindly' and attempted to tell him all he 'wished to know'.[36]

Unfortunately Dr Massey told him exactly what he did not wish to know. Not unreasonably William was advised to learn something about the faith of which he hoped to become an ordained minister. 'You had better go back to business for about two years, unite yourself with an independent church, sit under an intellectual minister and then, through that church, offer yourself to the society.' It is not clear how William Booth lived through that summer, though it was, no doubt, Catherine's persuasive powers – working through David Thomas – that convinced Dr Campbell to take a more sympathetic view of William's aspirations. But he still had to convince the authorities of Cotton End College that he was a genuine Congregationalist. He had already aspired to ordination in three different churches, seemed to know very little about such complicated issues as 'congregationalism' versus 'connexionalism' (the great debate about local autonomy and central control) and offended serious Congregationalists by the facile explanation of the way in which he had come to terms with residual Calvinism. His justification – supplied by Catherine – was so convenient that the cynics were bound to doubt its sincerity. It was also offensive to pious Congregationalists: 'The doctrine [of preordination] was maintained by the Congregationalists in general . . . but it was not very generally preached, it being only here and there that we heard it mentioned.' Unfortunately preordination was constantly mentioned at Cotton End College.

Dr George Smith, who was put in charge of William's education, suggested that a term's study of theology would be appropriate and expressed the hope that when it was completed, the new student might feel more in harmony with the beliefs on which the college based its teaching. He recommended that William should read Payne's *Divine Society* and Abraham Booth's *Reign of Grace*. Not surprisingly, the new student began with the treatise published by his namesake in 1828. It was written in language which was simultaneously florid and obtuse even by the standard of its time. William Booth claimed that he got no further than page thirty. It seems more likely that he ignored the convoluted introduction and struggled on until he reached the author's classic statement of Calvinism:

> They that are called the elect, in the volume of inspiration, are a
> people distinguished from others, and that all mankind are not
> included under that denomination are truths so evident as
> scarcely to need proof . . . For where all, either persons or
> things, are equally accepted, there is no preference given: there
> is no choice made: there is none left out. But to elect one or
> choose are the same thing – where any are chosen, others must
> be expelled.

It was then, in his own words, that he 'threw the book against the wall'. The minutes of the Home Mission Society for 5 November 1852 give a less dramatic account of his decision to leave Cotton End: 'The application and recommendation of the Reverend W. S. Edwards of Mr Booth as candidate was submitted. It was agreed that he be requested to appear before the examining committee as soon as convenient.' The following month's minutes complete the story: 'The Secretary reported that Mr Booth had withdrawn from being a candidate for admission to Cotton End, disapproving of the manner in which the committee had conducted its examination and the disputed doctrine.'[37] William Booth had not only rejected Calvinism, he had taken exception to being questioned about it.

There is no way in which we can judge how much of his reaction was genuine moral outrage and how much he feared having to study and master the complicated theory of predestination and then produce convincing intellectual reasons for being one of the Congregationalists who rejected the notion of 'the elect'. For the next forty years, he almost always side-stepped theological argument. It was a weakness but not a handicap. The strength of his conviction was that he felt the grace of God and needed no complicated theories to bolster his faith. Contempt for ideas allowed him to pick and choose his principles rather than struggle for some sort of consistency. Forty years later – at the height of his power and fame – he was to set out views on society which were built on economic rather than spiritual determinism. God did not preordain that babies were born to go to hell. But poverty pre-destined them to be wicked. The idea that his religious views on free will were in conflict with his opinions on the causes of evil never entered his head.

So – instinctively confident that Jesus Saves – William Booth ended his brief flirtation with Congregationalism. He had already aspired to ordination in the Wesleyan and the Wesleyan Reform Churches. Both attempts had failed. He was twenty-three and, it seemed, had absolutely no prospects to match either his ambition or his convictions.

3

A Star in the East

Catherine Mumford remained a Congregationalist, no doubt still arguing that Calvinism, which she genuinely abhorred, was not an essential part of that church's doctrine and that the committee to which William had taken such exception 'did not fairly represent the feelings of the Union'.[1] She was not alone in believing that a Congregational minister need not believe in preordination. Dr Ferguson of Ryde – who had heard of William's sudden rejection of formal ordination – wrote to invite the young man to join him as deputy minister and, if all went well, as his successor. Ferguson regarded the abandonment of Cotton End as an added qualification. 'We have,' he asserted, 'a college ministry already,' and went on to ask, 'And what are they doing in reference to saving souls?'[2] The letter exhibited a contempt for scholarship that tempted William Booth to hurry to Kent. But his opposition to Calvinism had grown even stronger. 'I am reading Finney and Watson on election and final perseverance,' he told Catherine, 'and I see more reason than ever to cling to my own views of truth and righteousness.'[3] So he rejected both the 'superior opportunity for mental and moral training' which he preferred to call 'being white-washed at college' and the chance to become a full-time practical preacher without benefit of theological scholarship. The decision to reject the Ryde ministry must have taken a great deal of courage – whether or not it was backed up with the conviction that God would eventually provide.

Providence intervened more quickly than even William Booth could have expected. Within a week of rejecting Cotton End he was invited to become minister at Spalding in Lincolnshire, where the Reformers had wanted more reform than their annual conference would tolerate. Civil war had broken out. Half the Fenland members moved over to the official Wesleyan Connexion. But the rest wanted a dynamic young minister. Although William Booth was regarded as a trouble-maker in London he seemed exactly the right man for Lincolnshire.

In old age, and deceived by the rosy glow of memory, William Booth described his eighteen months in Spalding as amongst the happiest of his life, even though he and Catherine were apart. In fact their separation was not very different from the detached proximity of London. Whether they were divided by half of England or five square miles of the capital, they saw each other rarely but wrote to each other incessantly. Sometimes Catherine started a letter before breakfast and was still adding to it when the time came to catch the day's last post. Somehow, she managed to be simultaneously didactic and affectionate. William had been in Spalding for barely a week when he received a repetition of the familiar message, 'Beware how you indulge that dangerous element of character, ambition.'[4] Seven days later she repeated her concern about another element of his character:

> Do assure me that no lack of effort on your part shall hinder the improvement of those talents God has given you . . . if you really see no prospect of studying then I think you ought not to stay . . . Could you not provide yourself with a small leather bag or a case large enough to hold your Bible and any other books you might require, pens, ink, paper and candle? And could you not rise by six o'clock every morning and convert your bedroom into a study until breakfast time?[5]

The pressure for improvement was remorseless. 'I have been reading Finney's lecture. I have marked it for your perusal when you get your books.'[6] She was equally concerned that he should neither underestimate his own talents nor overrate the importance of material rewards. 'I think you did quite right in saying what you did about salary, it is too little certainly for the amount of labour required . . . But as you are happy . . . I would not advise you to leave because of salary.'[7] Occasionally she warned about the perils of indulgence: 'I don't think too much meat is good for you . . . I wish you would live simpler. I mean abstain from mustard and such like condiments.' But she always returned to the most urgent necessity: 'I would not advise you to leave the circuit on any account if they will give you £60 and there is *the prospect of studying*. But if you really see no possibility of studying, don't stay for any amount of money.'[8]

Far from resenting Catherine's constant advice, and the implied criticism which it contained, William – not by nature a humble man – seems to have welcomed it. Indeed, from time to time he asked for approval and feared that he would only receive condemnation. When he wrote, 'I had to have brandy twice: was really ill: thought much of you,' it seems certain that his thoughts were apprehensive as well as affectionate. The reaction to the additional news that a parishioner had urged him to take port wine makes clear how justified his apprehensions were. Poor William had explained ('he could tell by my voice and his experience that it would do me good') and gone on to ask for her approval. 'My health is of the first importance. What do you say, dear?' What she had to say raised her usual doubts about his strength of character:

I need not say how willing, or anxious, I am that you should have anything and everything which tend to promote your health and happiness. But so thoroughly am I convinced that port wine will do neither that I should not hear of you taking it without unfeigned grief. You must not my love listen to the advice of everyone claiming to be experienced . . . Now my love it is absolutely necessary, in order to save you from being influenced by other people's false notion that you should have settled intelligent conviction on the subject and in order that you may get this, I have been to the trouble of unpacking your box in order to send you a book in which you will find several green marks in pencilling . . . I do hope you will read it, even if you sit up an hour every night until you have done so.[9]

William's letters were rarely so didactic and never so patronising. They had three major themes – the love of God, the misery of separation and the success of his work. Often the discussion of great issues was supplemented by details of his daily life which suggested that, although he was detached from the vanities of the world, he was lonely for Catherine. She was told about problems with socks and shirts, difficulties over diet, washing habits and casual conversations with passing acquaintances. Occasionally the more serious passages reflected the gradual development of the evangelical style on which his later triumphs (and simultaneous unpopularity with the religious establishment) were built. He complained about ministers who 'do not seem to desire that people should be converted under one or two sermons, but that these shall be some time before the truth sinks home'.[10] The experience of Spalding, where a revival had been initiated by local enthusiasts, had convinced him of the virtues of instant conversion without the need to agonise over biblical justification. And his brief time in Lincolnshire confirmed, in his own mind, that he was the man to bring that sort of revival about. William never spared Catherine accounts of his success. 'Last night place crowded, packed – enthusiasm very high – singing good – collections nearly double last year . . .'[11] The list of triumphs seems endless. But there was one success of which she strongly disapproved. Even in those days, charismatic preachers made unintentional conquests, and Catherine was magnificently noble about an infatuation which William reported to her by copying into one of his letters a series of anonymous messages which he had received from an admirer. Certainty that he was true and faithful did not prevent her from offering advice about how his loyalty should be expressed: 'The words on the cards are very pretty, but the sentiments on the one "I'll never forget" is utterly inappropriate. Those of us who sustain a relationship like ours must sincerely *pity* the moral degradation of the being who sent it and loathe such adulterous purposes as, in all charity *must* have prompted it. I do trust that if even for show she can meet you eye to eye again, you will give her unmistakable evidence that you utterly despise such schemes.'[12]

Sometimes she expressed more tender feelings. When William wrote, 'I have brought with me to Spalding a far better likeness than the daguerreotype – namely your image stamped on my soul,'[13]

Catherine replied that she had 'no objection to his profile being considered Jewish [but] rather liked it'. The romantic mood did not last
long. She dismissed suggestions (presumably made by another of his
admirers) that his success might be based on 'elegance of attitude or
gesture . . . I should be sorry for the effects of your preaching to be
attributed to them'. In fact their letters – moral advice going north
and descriptions of triumphs passing them on the way south – bring
irresistibly to mind Macaulay's judgement on Thomas and Jane
Carlyle: 'It was good of God to make them marry each other, thus
making two people unhappy instead of four.' The difference between
the Booths and the Carlyles was that despite behaviour which might
have been intolerable to others, the Booths were happy beyond all
reasonable expectation.

William Booth certainly enjoyed a measure of success in Spalding,
though nothing like as much as he was later to claim. The local papers
of the time put into perspective his achievements on a circuit which
ran halfway across Lincolnshire. On 17 December 1852, the *Stamford
Mercury* reported that, 'The Wesleyan Reformers of Gosberton, having
by a vote of the stewards at the late meeting been deprived of the
entire management of the chapel, have opened a place of meeting near
the Five Bells Inn. The Rev. William Booth of London preached the
opening sermon on Sunday last to a considerable congregation.' A
month later, at Boston, 'The Reverend William Booth, Reform minister
of Spalding, addressed the meeting, detailing the circumstances which
led him to become a Reformer.' The transition from town to country
was complete and the honorary title of Reverend established. There is
no evidence to suggest that the visiting minister explained the reasons
for his brief diversion into Congregationalism.

There were occasional family problems for the couple to face.
Catherine's father teetered on the edge of bankruptcy and William
wrote with regret that he did not know enough about business to offer
any worthwhile advice. A generous spirit in Spalding heard that
William was struggling to help his mother and offered some sort of
contribution, but Catherine warned against making his mother's financial position common knowledge. When she and her mother took
temporary lodgings in Burnham to escape the cholera epidemic which
was sweeping London, her attempts to reassure William about her
safety from infection reflected her often less-than-subtle approach to

life. It also contained a strangely casual confession: 'We have had only one fatal case here and that one of the friends in the village taken and died in 24 hours in the next door house to ours. It made me feel rather nervous when I was seized with violent pain and diarrhoea the other day but I went direct to bed, took a very strong dose of brandy and ginger which made me completely typsy [sic], sent me in a nice perspiration and the next morning I felt better.'[14]

It is impossible to explain why she chose an alcoholic cure, since she had no confidence in the restorative qualities of liquor. It was the only example of backsliding to be recorded in her whole life. During the years that followed, she was to be in constant – often severe and sometimes agonising – pain, yet she refused the palliatives that might provide relief. It is not surprising that William, who already knew her unyielding nature, replied with a mixture of bewilderment, disapproval and anxiety. 'I do trust that our heavenly father will give his blessing to the means you are using so that you may be not only perfectly restored, but enjoy permanent health.' He went on to make a parallel admission which was almost a reproof. 'I finished the bottle of wine last night and am more a teetotaller than ever. I did not think that I profited at all by it. I am drinking camomile tea every morning before breakfast.'[15]

Catherine's lapse and the bland way in which she described it was certainly not the result of the fear of death. It held no terrors for her. Nor had she tried to convince herself, as was the case with some sickly Methodists, that some forms of alcohol were less sinful than others. Whatever her reasons for abandoning one of her dearest principles, the failure of will, nerve or belief was only temporary. Twenty-five years later, when she set out, for the benefit of the young, the five essential ingredients of a happy marriage she numbered total abstinence first amongst them and boasted of the devotion which she and her husband had always felt to that cause.

The other necessary characteristics included attributes which any respectable lady of any denomination would have hoped to share with her husband – identical religious views and common sense. In the case of the Booths, the first of those ideals was easily attained, since each of the partners took up positions over the practice of religion which were identically extreme and held with an unswerving passion. But it was the fourth essential ingredient which set them apart from other couples – and was probably inconsistent with the Married Woman's Property Act as well as the masculine spirit of the age. Catherine expected 'oneness of views and tastes, any idea of lordship or ownership being lost in love'. William Booth had no doubt that both sexes were equal in the sight of God, but at first he did not agree that men and women should have equal rights and responsibilities in the church. He came to accept Catherine's views in the end, just as he came to share her view on sanctity and holiness. But it took time. In maturity she wrote that a young girl should not rush into marriage without being certain that her future husband shared her high standards of belief and behaviour. When, in her youth, William was not quite up to the mark she took the risk because she loved him – and because she intended, as soon as they were married, to educate him in her ways.

Catherine Booth did not, at that time, believe that women could have a fully equal relationship in the home. She assumed (like most clever and strong-willed Victorian women) that in domestic matters she and her husband would show mutual respect while she ruled *sub rosa*. But she had no doubt that the sexes were equal in church, and she had impeccable biblical authority for her belief. St Paul's Epistle to the Galatians was explicit: 'There is neither Jew nor Greek, there is neither bond nor free' and, most significantly, 'there is neither male nor female for ye are all one in Christ Jesus'. That was enough authority for Catherine to insist that to oppose the female ministry was to oppose the will of God. It was a view which would have been regarded as breathtakingly presumptuous had it been advanced by a 24-year-old woman at almost any moment in history before 1950. To hold such views in the mid-1850s was to be accused of scandalous conduct. Yet Catherine actually took issue with ministers of her own church when they failed to accept the same view of God's universal blessing.

Her first assault was mounted against the Reverend David Thomas, the Congregational minister whom she had so admired that she had written to William, rhapsodising about an 'excellent sermon from 49–52 verses of John's gospel'.[16] However, one of his addresses caused Catherine profound offence. It suggested that morally, and perhaps even spiritually, women were inferior to men. Being a woman of confidence as well as of conviction she wrote Thomas a long and carefully argued letter of complaint.* It was the first letter in a lifetime of letter-writing on behalf of the causes she supported and the people she loved, and its grammatical inadequacies only serve to emphasise the strength of the author's conviction. The achievement would have been even greater had she not, at the very last, chosen not to sign her rebuke.

The letter began with the obligatory formal courtesies: '. . . Tho I feel myself but a babe in comparison with you, permit me to call attention to a subject on which my heart has been deeply pained. I had the privilege of hearing you preach on Sunday morning.' Catherine then made the charge direct. 'Your remarks appeared to imply the doctrine of women's intellectual or even moral inferiority to man.' The rhetorical question which followed was almost certainly not intended to be as offensive as it sounds. 'Permit me, Dear Sir, to ask whether you have ever made the subject of woman's equality as a *being* a matter of calm investigation and thought?' She then set out the truth as she saw it and as it came to be accepted a hundred years later:

> No argument, in my judgement, can be drawn from past experience on this point because the past has been wrong in theory and wrong in Practice. Never yet in the history of our world has woman been placed on an intellectual footing with man. Her training from babyhood, even in this highly favoured land, has further been such as to cramp and paralyse rather than to develop and strengthen her energies . . . I cannot believe that you regard woman as morally more remote from God than man or less capable of loving him ardently and serving him faithfully. If such were the case, would not the great and just one have made some difference in his mode of dealing with her. But has he not placed her on precisely the same moral footing and under the same moral government with her companion?[17]

It was a long letter of more than twelve hundred words, and it

---

*The typed copy of the letter in the Salvation Army Heritage Centre dates it 22 April 1855. However, all the evidence (and the early biographies) place it in 1853, before William and Catherine's wedding.

revealed Catherine Mumford's passionate view on the importance of
achieving woman's proper place in the church as a prelude to achieving her proper, though not quite equal, place in society. It contained a
sentence which could have been taken straight out of the leaflets with
which the Church of England General Synod was showered when,
more than a hundred years later, it was considering the ordination of
women priests: 'The thing which, next to the revelation of salvation,
endears Christianity to my heart is what it has done and is destined to
do for my own sex.'

There is no evidence to suggest that Catherine asked William's
advice before she wrote to the Reverend Mr Thomas or that she even
told him about it when the daring deed had been done. If she did, he
was the only one to know that she was the author of her great remon-
strance. The letter was sent and received unsigned. Perhaps she wanted
to protect William from guilt by association with such an impertinent
heresy. Throughout her life, the demands of William's calling and the
fulfilment of his ambition were always her most important concerns.

So, unaware of Catherine's blow for female emancipation, he continued the humdrum work of resident preacher in Spalding. Despite all
the hustle and bustle of a local revival, he wrote to Catherine each day.
But his letters took a new tone. His triumphs in Holbeach, Suttleton
and Pinchbeck no longer satisfied him. One letter reported, 'Mr Poole,
the revivalist, is with us and meditates to go to America. I should
almost like to go with him.' Catherine was brutally dismissive. 'I might
as well spare myself such preparations, if indeed I was mad enough to
attempt such a thing . . . What could you do there? Hundreds now
would give the world if they had it to be home again and hundreds
more are dying of pestilence and climate disease . . . But I presume that
it is only one of your dreams.'[18] William was neither crushed nor
offended. He was convinced that he must dream no more.

Catherine was, throughout her life, openly sceptical about diverting
energies from domestic obligations and towards overseas missions.
But if William was dreaming of America, Catherine had to take some of
the credit or the blame for his fantasies, for she was constantly bringing to his attention both the theology and the preaching methods
explored by Charles Grandison Finney of Warren, Connecticut.
President of a New England college, who usually evangelised in the
vacations, he was the sort of preacher that Catherine believed William

should and could become. William Booth never aspired to the American's erudition, but he certainly adopted – or simply copied – his methods. His theory was Finney's theory. Both men were contemptuous of the notion that evangelists had to wait for God to make the first move, and that ministers must wait for an appropriate sign. Congregations were brought to a high state of emotion by long and passionate prayers followed by an invitation, to those who were already saved, to nominate friends and relations who were on the point, and in need, of salvation. Their isolation of potential converts – sometimes literally in the middle of the chapel as the righteous shrank from them and sometimes metaphorically as they were overcome by the feeling of moral rejection – was described, with unconscious cynicism, as placing them in the 'anxious seat'. From there, assuming that they truly repented, they were invited to approach the communion rail, soon to be renamed 'the penitent form' in conformity with American practice. William Booth adopted the New England methods gradually, but even in those early days in Lincolnshire he was beginning to share the ideas, and copy the technique, of Charles Grandison Finney. The evangelism of high emotion, which was later to characterise the Salvation Army, became William Booth's trademark when he was the resident preacher in Spalding, Lincolnshire.

Despite his success, or perhaps because of it, William Booth had become dissatisfied with life as a Reform preacher. And Catherine, who was missing him badly, and had never been sure of his destiny in the east, began to encourage his dissatisfaction. She had come to a new conclusion. The Methodist New Connexion was the best vehicle for William's talents. It was, she pointed out, 'more widely distributed'[19] and despite the surfeit of amateur preachers in London (which had so inconvenienced him) it generally treated its ministers with a respect which, for some reason, she thought the Reformers rarely showed. As early as May 1853, barely six months after he had taken up the Spalding appointment, William – with staggering presumption – had made at least tentative enquiries about becoming a New Connexion minister. As usual he looked for encouragement and patronage. The vehicle for Providence's wishes and William Booth's ambition was William Cooke, sometime the Connexion President, but in the year of William's renewed interest, Editor and Book Steward.

Dr Cooke was to become a major figure in William's life. He was a gentle man of scholarly disposition, had been President of the Conference at the age of thirty-seven but 'in consideration of his health and literary abilities' was removed from the field of battle after serving in Belfast, Liverpool and Newcastle, and appointed to the more contemplative occupation of librarian and archivist. He remained in that post for twenty-two years, during which time he was President twice more and became notable for his advocacy of Methodist Union – which was in fact reunion of the various sects. He did not enjoy conflict, as William Booth was later to discover. But he sent a firm reply to what he may well have regarded as an impertinent enquiry. 'I think that it is not unlikely that a formal application from you to our President for the year, Rev. J. Hudson of Huddersfield, would result in your reception as a minister in our body.' There was a note of reproof in his judgement that 'the usage of four years' probation would undoubtedly be applied to you just as strongly as it is to those candidates who were chosen from our comrades and are well known to us'.[20]

The Spalding Trustees, unaware that he was already making overtures to another church, but fearful that he would leave the circuit at the end of his eighteen-month contract, offered him new terms. There would, they said, be no objection to him marrying at once, even though it was normally forbidden to young preachers. As well as furnishing him with a house at the expense of the circuit, the Trustees offered to buy him a horse and trap so that he could more easily visit distant parts of the county. William was tempted, but Catherine urged him to 'think of the future, not the present'.[21] In her view the Spalding generosity was not as altruistic as it sounded. She assumed that they at least suspected that he was growing restless, and wanted to buy his loyalty. At the same time – and not entirely consistently – she warned him to eschew ambition and accept the will of God. Fortunately, God's will – at least in Catherine's opinion – coincided with her clear conviction about what was best for her future husband. She often discovered that God supported her judgement.

The Trustees' desire to keep their new, young minister at additional, if not at any, cost was the first example of William Booth's power to impress and to exert an emotional hold over the people who heard him preach. There were always two opinions about the power of his oratory. One was that it was convoluted, florid to the point of vulgarity and littered with complicated images which obscured rather than illuminated his moral and message. The other was that it was irresistible. In Spalding the quality of his sermons and his restless enthusiasm combined to make him the man who, at the age of twenty-four, could revive the divided church.

But his desire was always for 'larger work'. Booth's wish to move on was more than selfish ambition. He felt real affection for the parishioners who loved him. But a minority were less friendly and he was profoundly irritated by what he regarded as the near anarchy of the Reformers' organisation. His solution to his dilemma was ingenious but doomed from the start. He suggested that the Spalding Circuit (which was formally part of the Wesleyan Reform Movement but was in fact entirely independent) affiliate, *en bloc*, to the New Connexion. Catherine was fearful that he would become an itinerant preacher, without any church to call his own and dependent on the charity of chapels which invited him to visit. She argued against his future 'being decided by the quarterly meeting' but remained unswervingly for the Connexion – despite its inferiority, in terms of numbers if not organisation, to the Reformers. While William Booth and the quarterly meeting were still making up their minds, another offer (temptation, Catherine would have called it) was put in his way.

> Yesterday, I received a letter asking me if I would come to the Hinde Street Circuit (London Reformers) salary £100 a year. I have also heard that the Committee in London is about to make me an offer . . . It is certainly enough to make a fellow think and tremble. Here am I in a Circuit numbering 780 members with an increase in the year of nearly 200. I am invited to another with 1,000. And yet I am going to join a church with but 150 members in London and a majority of the circuits with a similar number.[22]

Catherine remained obdurate: 'You are not leaving the Reformers because you fear you could not get another circuit but because you are out of sympathy with its purpose and aims.' Then for a moment she flinched. 'Stay in Spalding and risk all. Rather lose everything than make yourself miserable.' But proper concern for William's happiness could not quite eradicate her conviction about where his future lay. So she insisted: 'The Reform Movement is no home and sphere for you, whereas the principles of the Connexion you live to your very soul.'[23]

Because of his contempt for theoretical discussion, William Booth must have found it difficult to distinguish between the principle on which Wesleyan Methodists, the New Connexion and the Reformers were based. But he was prepared, salvation and predestination aside, to leave theological speculation to his wife who, had he asked her, would not have found it easy to explain why he was a natural member of the New Connexion. On the vexed question of authority, his position was perfectly simple. He wished to govern but would not be governed, and would not even contemplate man-made rules preventing the personal success which was necessary to the triumph of his mission. He had God's work to do and was looking for the church which would provide the best chance of His will being done.

The Spalding Circuit – despite the affection for its new preacher – would not change its allegiance overnight and affiliate to the New Connexion. Nor would it alter the way in which it did its business. William Booth grew increasingly exasperated by his parishioners' casual conduct of their affairs, and 'the ultra-Radicalism which prevailed'. His mind to leave was suddenly made up when the New Connexion – almost certainly after pressure from the ever-forgiving Edward Rabbits, who had begun to support it both spiritually and financially – changed its policy and, in the new recruit's words, 'gave me at my request, a chance to study under a then celebrated theologian'. The teacher in question was Dr William Cooke, the man who had previously warned him that there would be no chance for early ordination. Catherine – who had wanted him to be a scholar far longer than she had hoped that he would join the New Connexion – was delighted by the news. But simple joy did not come to her easily. Concerned that he would not persevere, she wrote, 'I wish you prayed more and talked less about the matter. Try it and be determined to get a clear and settled view as to your course.'[24]

On 14 February 1854 William Booth moved back to London and on the following day took up residence, with half a dozen other students, in Dr Cooke's house at 3, Albany Crescent. From the start he hated the life of study and had no doubt that the fault was in the scholarship, not him. 'I was set to study Latin and Greek and other subjects which I saw at a glance could not help me in the all-important work that lay before me.' Yet he 'visited the British Museum and walked up and down, praying that God would enable [him] to acquire the knowledge to improve the powers of usefulness'.[25] His prayers were answered but not quite in the way that Catherine would have wished. A talent for scholarship was denied him. On the day after his return to London he preached at the Brunswick Street Chapel – itself a tribute to his self-confidence and the high regard in which, despite his excursion to Lincolnshire, he was still held. He went on preaching wherever and whenever he got the chance. And Dr Cooke decided that, although his new student was not a natural scholar, he was a born evangelist.

Dr Cooke's conversion to William Booth's cause was total. The man who, only months earlier, had told William Booth that he must submit himself to the long process of formal admission to the ministry, proposed that the Methodist New Connexion Conference of 1854 should make him the Superintendent of the London Circuit. The General's early biographers claimed that Cooke rallied to William's banner because the student lodger converted the previously godless daughter of the house. Unfortunately for the myth-makers, the lady herself could not confirm the story, and explained that she was 'a little girl at the time'. Again, the likelihood is that the real influence on Cooke was Rabbits, who, with his business secure, devoted more and more time to Methodism. The minutes of the Conference at which the new preacher was appointed record Rabbits as making donations to the Paternal, the Beneficent and the Chapel Funds. He was the sort of man who expected influence and patronage to be the reward of generosity. And he thought of William as his protégé. However, William declined to be nominated on the grounds that he was too young and too inexperienced for the job. His judgement was undoubtedly correct. But that makes it, in the light of William Booth's character, none the less surprising. He emphasised the wisdom of his decision by offering to act as deputy to an older man – a proposition which Dr Cooke would gladly have put to the Conference had it not been for one small problem. The circuit could afford to employ only one minister.

Once again the hand of fate was held by Edward Rabbits who, having preceded William Booth into the New Connexion, had become a Trustee of the new chapel in Pocklington Street which had been built and opened earlier that year. Putting aside all resentment at William's initial rejection of his help, he offered to fund a second

London minister – as long as it was Booth. But the other Trustees at Pocklington Street, to which the Deputy Superintendent was to be attached, added a requirement of their own. The new assistant must live close to the chapel. They added an inducement to their stipulation. Were he to take the job, William Booth, instead of being required to wait for the usual four years, would be allowed to marry after twelve months' service.

So the Trustees, putting aside their preference for rotating ministers, agreed that the Reverend P. T. Gilton should remain Superintendent of the New Connexion London Circuit and that he should acquire a deputy. No doubt William Booth was, at the time, filled with gratitude and joy. But it did not make him look back on his time at Pocklington Street with any great pleasure or much admiration for his old chief. The Reverend Mr Gilton he described as 'still and cold . . . he made up for want of heat and thought in his public utterances by what sounded like a sanctimonious wail!' But Booth found all his superiors wanting. It was his misfortune to make steady progress without the assistance of anyone he was prepared to acknowledge except God. However, he put aside his distaste for Gilton at least long enough to be confirmed in his post as deputy. The New Connexion Conference minutes for 1854 record amongst the 'questions' – a procedural relic of the original Wesleyan democracy – 'What preachers are now received on trial?' The answer was William Booth.

In London, however, the New Connexion did not prosper. But its new Deputy Superintendent became well known as a powerful preacher, and his fame spread with the publication of an article in the *New Connexion Magazine* which repeated his regularly expressed criticism of resident ministers who, having benefited from a local revival, allow the new recruits to 'backslide' into their bad old ways. His article included a barely relevant reference to women's place in the church: 'I believe that it is impossible to estimate the extent of the church's loss where prejudice and custom are allowed to render the outpourings of God's spirit upon his handmaidens, null and void . . . Let the female converts be not only allowed to use their newly awakened faculties but positively encouraged to exercise and improve them.'[26] He was arguing for women preachers, not the female ministry, but Catherine Mumford's influence was beginning to have its effect. And she was beginning to have an effect on his view of the poor. On 19 March 1854 he wrote in his journal, 'I left home at six o'clock for Watney Street. Felt much sympathy for the poor neglected inhabitants of Wapping and its neighbourhood as I walked the filthy streets and beheld the wretchedness and wickedness of its people.'[27] The distaste of his arrival four years earlier had been replaced by compassion and the crucial acceptance that sin and poverty go hand in hand.

The Deputy Superintendent's preaching was universally applauded and his reputation grew at such a speed that Josiah Bates, 'perhaps the most influential member of the New Connexion in London', came to 'regard the appointment of the Rev. W. Booth to this circuit as providential'.[28] Bates' letter to the *New Connexion Magazine* which expressed those sentiments concluded with the hope 'that the next Conference will leave Mr Booth without a fixed circuit so that he may go through the Connexion as an evangelist'. That was certainly what Booth himself wanted, and happily the following year's Conference – meeting in Sheffield on 28 May 1855 – wanted it too. Resolution 16 reads more like a citation than an executive instruction:

That this Conference has pleasure in adverting to the revival services held by the Rev. W. Booth, during the past year, with so much benefit to the Connexion; and the Conference, seeing the manner in which it has pleased God to bless his labours, adopts the recommendation of the Annual Committee, and determines that his time and labours shall, during the next year, be devoted to this field of usefulness, under the direction of the Annual Committee, with a salary of £100, and travelling expenses, to be paid from the Yearly Collection; the Societies paying Yearly Collections for Mr Booth's services, at a rate of £2 per week.

The presidential address was even more complimentary: 'The Ministry of the Rev. Booth has been eminently successful and we trust the results of his evangelistic labours will be more strikingly apparent during the ensuing year.' The minutes also noted that a Mr Rabbits had made donations to several New Connexion churches.

The eminently successful labours had not all been carried out in London. Despite Gilton's distressed opposition and the duty to live in the vicinity of the Pocklington Street Chapel, much of William Booth's usefulness had been enjoyed far from the capital. During the six

months before he was formally authorised to go out into the provincial
highways and byways, he wrote to Catherine – waiting in London
with her parents – from places as far apart as Guernsey and Bristol,
Newcastle, Manchester and Henley, where he addressed 'an imposing
congregation' from which 150 names 'were taken down' as potential
converts. His letters always mixed the sacred and temporal without
even noticing the incongruity. The temporal was often trivial. He
washed his chest with cold water at the beginning of each day, usually
had two eggs and tea both morning and night, and occasionally
became alarmed by the excitement which his sermons created in the
congregation. He 'could not help but reason, Is it right? Is it the best
way?' He came to the conclusion that it was. In Guernsey, 'many went
away unable to get into the chapel. The aisles were crowded and, up to
eleven o'clock, it was almost impossible to get them up to the communion rail, owing to the crush.'[29] William was not, however, satisfied.
He feared that 'many of the more respectable seat holders kept aloof'.
All in all he gave a generally modest account of generally modest success.

Catherine's letters mixed personal emotion and theological advice.
On 13 January 1855 she had responded to the news that his mission to
the north was to continue for another month with what can only be
described as the normal (and therefore uncharacteristic) reaction of a
neglected lover: 'The intelligence of your prolonged absence comes to
my heart most unwelcomely. I have wept myself almost blind.'[30] Two
days later she regretted that she had complained. 'I was mistaken in
what I said on Friday evening. You *do* sympathise with me in this separation more than I first thought you did.'[31] But on 9 April 1855, two
months before the proposed date of their marriage, a sixteen-page
letter created an 'argument between them which rose to such heights as
to threaten their engagement. Miss Mumford was, on this question,
ready to resort to ultimatums and Mr Booth was led by his passionate
love for one woman to justify her claim'.[32] The claim was for sexual
equality within the church – a cause which she had no doubt was
righteous.

> Perhaps you think that I take rather a prejudiced view of it, but
> I have searched the Word of God through and through. I have
> tried to deal honestly with every passage on the subject, not

forgetting to pray for light to perceive and grace to submit to the truth, however humiliating to my nature, but I solemnly assert that the more I think and read on the subject, the more satisfied I become of the truth and scriptural nature of my views.

It seems that William Booth himself had recklessly initiated the discussion on female ministry, for Catherine's letter refers to it as 'that other subject you mention'. He could not have hoped to change her mind. It was Catherine's habit – infuriating to everyone except William – to begin her frequent dissertations on faith and morals with the assertion that she had thought very carefully on the subject. Her tone implied that, since her protagonists had not done the same, she could only hope that they would gradually come to see the truth. There was, she thus made clear, no chance of her own views in any way being altered. Typically, therefore, she asked William, 'See fully with me on it,' and he replied, slightly ambiguously, that he 'felt as deeply on the subject as [she] did'. In fact he did feel that women had a role to play in the promotion of salvation, but it hardly coincided with Catherine's view that 'woman is destined to assume her true position and exert her proper influence by the special exertions and attainments of her own sex'. Her letter was absolutely uncompromising. The reproof with which she had admonished the Reverend David Thomas was repeated to her future husband in a slightly more explicit form. 'Oh, what endears the Christian religion to my heart is what it *has* done and is *destined* to do for my own sex, and what excites my indignation beyond anything else is to hear its sacred precepts dragged forward to hear degrading arguments.' She then delivered what she clearly believed to be the *coup de grâce* – the words of St Paul: 'If indeed there is in "Christ Jesus neither male nor female but, in touching *His Kingdom,* they are one" who shall dare thrust women out of the church's operation or presume to put my candle, which God has lighted, under a bushel?'[33]

Catherine's letter concluded with the same patronising advice which she had given to William on the subject of medicinal alcohol – 'Let me advise you my *love* to get settled views on the subject.' The problem was that William's views were settled already and, at the time, seemed incapable of change either by scriptural authority or by Catherine's polemic. They were progressive by the standards of the time, but not sufficiently progressive for his future wife. On 12 April 1855 he replied in equally portentous language:

> The remarks on *Women's* position. I will read again before I answer. From a first reading I cannot see anything in them that leads me to think for one *moment* of altering my opinion. You *combat* a great deal that I hold as firmly as you do – viz. her *equality*, her *perfect* equality as a whole – as a being. But as to concede that she is men's *equal* or capable of becoming man's equal in intellectual attainment or prowess – I must say that is contradicted by experience in the world and my honest conviction.[34]

The irony of the final assertion probably escaped them both. William, despite his self-doubts, could not believe that her intellect was superior to his, and Catherine was still enough of a Victorian woman not to allow herself to consider such a possibility. She was also a Victorian woman in love, who wanted to find common ground with her future husband, and William, from his position of male superiority, was prepared to make a concession: 'I would not stop a woman preaching on any account. I would not encourage one to begin. You shall preach if you feel moved thereto, feel equal to the task. I would not stop you if you had the power to do so. Altho' I should not like it.' His views on women preachers had been modified by experience. Edward Rabbits, who seemed to appear whenever benign Providence wanted to nudge William in the right direction, had persuaded him to attend a service at which a Miss Buck had preached the sermon. William 'left the chapel saying that he should never again oppose the practice [of women preaching] since Miss Buck had certainly preached more effectively than three-fourths of the men he had ever listened to.'[35] But that was not quite enough to convert him to Catherine's position. He reconciled his admiration for Miss Buck with his general views on the subject of women's rights to preach with the new platitude that they should only be allowed to do so when specifically inspired by God.

William Booth was almost certainly right to describe the difference of opinion as 'the only serious lovers' quarrel we ever had'.[36] It was certainly serious. The argument became so passionate that, even at that last moment, there was real thought of ending the engagement. But

William Booth – out of conviction or love – conceded the essential point. Women could preach – or at least should not invariably be prevented from preaching. The concession – although it turned into mutual agreement over the years – was to have a profound effect on the Salvation Army. 'It became an essential and important doctrine in their creed that in Jesus Christ there was neither male nor female, but that the Gospel combined with nature to place both on a footing of absolute and spiritual equality.'[37]

So, on 17 June 1855, William Booth, Dissenting Minister – who gave his address as Ardwick, Manchester, his latest campaign lodging – was married to Catherine Mumford of Rossel Street, Brixton. The ceremony took place in Stockwell New Chapel in the county of Surrey. Only Catherine's father and William's sister, Emma, were present to witness the wedding. Mrs Mumford almost certainly stayed away to emphasise her disapproval of the match. During their courtship, William had spoken of how the 'high estimation your mother has for you led her, I conceive, to take a prejudiced view of my conduct and make remarks which were unmerited and unjust and calculated to worry my soul'.[38] The absence of old Mrs Booth and William's youngest sister is more difficult to explain. Perhaps the three women, struggling to earn a living in the Nottingham haberdasher's shop, could only afford one fare. And despite his many protestations of affection and anxiety, William had been able to send very little money home in the six years since he set out to London in the hope of providing his mother with the comfort he believed that she deserved. Or it may have been that Sarah Booth would not take part in the form of service that solemnised the marriage. Catherine, who was normally no more emollient, had certainly healed one wound. As if to confirm the young couple's theological inconstancy, the service was conducted by the Reverend David Thomas, the preacher whose views on women in the church had caused the bride such offence and a minister of the Congregational Church which the groom had left because of its inclination to Calvinism.

4

Abundant Labours

In 1855 honeymoons were the prerogative of the prosperous middle classes. So the Booths' week in Ryde on the Isle of Wight was an indication of both their income and their social self-confidence. When it was over, they moved on to Guernsey for the serious business of leading a revival. It was clear, from what Catherine wrote in the autograph album of a friend, that the joys of marriage had not exposed a previously hidden frivolity in her character:

> The woman who would serve her generation according to the
> will of God makes moral and intellectual culture the chief
> business of her life. Doing this, she will rise to the full dignity
> of her nature and find herself possessed of a wondrous capacity
> for turning the duties, joys and sorrows of domestic life to the
> highest advantage, both to herself and to those within the
> sphere of her influence.[1]

After a brief visit to Jersey, where William preached in the New Connexion chapel, they made what seemed the endless sea journey back to England. Catherine was so ill that, when William travelled north to evangelise in Yorkshire, she stayed in London with her parents. Catherine Booth was unwell with such regularity that she can be properly described as susceptible to illness. But she was not, in the normal sense of the term, delicate. In childhood and adolescence she had survived conditions which in nineteenth-century England were almost always fatal, and throughout her life she was to be struck down with disease after disease which would have killed a less hardy and indomitable woman. In fact, she enjoyed robust ill heath. She was certainly obsessed with her own and her husband's physical condition – in turns taking an enthusiastic interest in cures and recovery and displaying a morbid fascination with disease, decay and death. William Booth was the same. In fact husband and wife were immensely *physical* people – though that aspect of their character sometimes dictated that the flesh should be mortified rather than gratified. Throughout their lives they were preoccupied with the body as well as the soul.

The Victorian middle class – particularly those of a particularly religious disposition – were deeply reticent about physical relationships. So when, in the early days of her marriage, Catherine wrote to her mother about the joys of lying next to William and warming her cold feet against his legs[2] she proclaimed the importance which both the Booths attached to bodily love. From the very start, they were separated for weeks at a time. But their willingness to be apart was not the result of a casual or detached affection. It was proof of their devotion to Christ's cause – which included the duty to be fruitful, multiply and replenish the Earth.

The preoccupation with illness and health led Catherine to become a devotee of what, today, would be called alternative medicine. In early middle age she developed an enthusiasm for hydropathy, and under her encouragement, William invariably took the waters as the cure for his many illnesses – most of which were more imaginary than hers. But in the early days of the marriage, Catherine Booth found both physical and emotional relief in homeopathy, the treatment by small doses of drugs which, in a healthy person, would create the condition which they cured in a suffering patient. She was so impressed by the results of the therapy that she recommended it to her mother as a remedy for the internal disorders from which the whole family suffered and by which they were all fascinated: 'If the relaxation comes on again go at once to the homeopathic dispensary . . . I believe in it more than ever.'[3] Catherine Booth and her mother regularly discussed bowels.

The homeopathic remedy certainly worked for her. 'I was sick three times in the public street and about a dozen times during the day . . . I doubt not that under ordinary treatment I should have been in bed. For the attack was very violent.'[4] The improvement was prolonged if not permanent. 'I am very much better than when I wrote last. I have taken homeopathic medicine every three hours or so and am nearly well again and what is wonderful is that my bowels are acting without experiment.'[5] William was so pleased with Catherine's progress that he gave her 'sixteen shillings (16/-) for a book on it [homeopathy] . . . and a *pound* for a case of medicine'.[6] That, in 1855, was a good deal more than a craftsman's weekly wage. The Booths did not live in style or luxury, but at least they lived in comfort.

Thanks to the beneficial effects of homeopathy, Catherine was able to travel north before William's campaign was finished. They met at Selby Junction and completed the journey to Hull together. Unhappily the illness had left her weak and, instead of accompanying her husband on the rest of his tour, she was forced to rest in Caistor with friends William had made during his days as a Wesleyan Reformer. It seems that there was no local bitterness about his apostasy. By late September 1855 she was again fit enough to take to the road. So on they went, first a return visit to Hull and then on to Sheffield. They arrived at what might have been regarded as a propitious moment – the whole country was celebrating the capture of Sebastopol, which by the standards of the Crimean War was a spectacular victory.

Sheffield had been the home of opposition to the Crimean War – not on the grounds of the suffering it caused or the neglect of the British troops who fought in that campaign but for the good commercial reason that it was a waste of money. John Arthur Roebuck, the borough's Member of Parliament, had brought down the Aberdeen administration with his motion for an inquiry into the conduct of the campaign, claiming that it was both misconceived and mismanaged. His electors certainly endorsed his criticism. But that in no way inhibited their celebration of Sebastopol's capture and the news, almost as popular, that Florence Nightingale had recovered from fever and was about to return to Scutari. Catherine, preparing to make the journey from East to South Yorkshire, was not in a similar celebratory mood. 'The bells are ringing and guns firing on account of the news that Sebastopol is taken. But I should think it is a delusion. Anyhow I cannot enter into the spirit of the victory. I picture the gory stain and the desolated homes and the broken hearts attending it and I feel saddened.'[7] It was an unusual excursion into current affairs. Normally they both showed no interest in the world beyond the sound of William's sermons.

William's ability to spread the word of the Lord was all that mattered to Catherine – nothing, not plague or pestilence, war or famine, was as remotely important as saving souls. But in the years before the Booths discovered the relationship between sin and poverty it produced a strange paradox in their behaviour – although they believed absolutely in the need to take the gospel out into the streets, they were detached to the point of pietism from most of what was going on around them. What was surprising about Catherine's attitude towards the capture of Sebastopol and her reference to it was not that she dismissed it as unimportant but that she noticed that it had happened.

William thought that Sheffield 'for smoke rivalled the infernal regions'.[8] But the Booths enjoyed their visit. They stayed with Reverend W. Mills, an ex-President of the Conference, who 'lived ten minutes from the centre of town in a splendid house overlooking the cemetery'. They were, as Catherine's letters show, beginning to take an interest in material things. She told her mother, with girlish glee, 'I have visited one of the most splendid houses I have ever seen.'[9] It belonged to Thomas Firth.

Firth was a steelmaker – not, at least originally, a great industrialist but a craftsman who could add carbon to iron with such precision that the result was the finest steel in Sheffield and (as his son, Mark, therefore rightly assumed) in Britain and the world. At Mark's suggestion, the Firths set up an independent business and became exclusive suppliers of steel to Samuel Colt of America and to Armstrong Whitworth in England. Since the quality of their product made it ideal for the production of gun barrels, they eventually produced a heavier cannon than had ever been cast before – all a triumph to Thomas Firth's skill. Mark Firth went on to become the greatest benefactor in the history of Sheffield – university, park, almshouses – and his father was also famous for his moments of spontaneous generosity. William Booth was a minor beneficiary. 'Yesterday when Mr Firth was bidding him goodbye, he put a £5 note into his hand, apologising at the same time for the smallness of the sum.' Andrew Undershaft had come face to face with Major Barbara.

Old Mrs Booth came over from Nottingham and met her new daughter-in-law for the first time. Catherine had anticipated the meeting 'with some pleasure but much anxiety'. But the apprehension soon turned to admiration. 'She is a very nice *looking* old lady of a very sweet and amiable spirit. William had not at all overestimated her in his description.'[10] In the same letter, Catherine described one of her husband's revivalist meetings in a way which – making allowance for her recently married state – might well have been an overestimation of its success. 'I went to chapel yesterday and saw such scenes as I have never witnessed before. In the afternoon there was a lovefeast – and indeed it was a feast of love.' Catherine was beginning to use the language of the American revivalists and William was beginning to employ their techniques.

> The chapel was packed above and below, so much so that it was with extreme difficulty that the bread and water could be passed about the aisles and the pulpit stairs were full and in all parts of the chapel, persons rose to testify of the power of God in connection with the preaching of my dear William . . . Wm. preached for an hour and ten minutes and everybody was absorbed and riveted. 70 names were taken and many satisfactory cases recorded. The people are becoming increasingly kind and interested in us.[11]

The same could not be said about the press. During the month that he was in Sheffield, the *Sheffield and Rotherham Independent* did not mention William Booth once. There was room for other religious events – the opening of the new Primitive Methodist Chapel in Stanley Street, the meeting of the Auxiliary Bible Society and an ordination at distant Easingwold. But the New Connexion evangelist was ignored. Yet Catherine judged 'the work progresses with mighty power . . . Everybody who knows anything of this society is astonished. Precious souls are being saved by scores. 440 names have been taken and tomorrow is expected to be another mighty day.' And so it was. Amongst the faithful – if not amongst local journalists – William Booth was already an attraction.

In those early years, William Booth only mentioned great events when he thought that God should intervene to rectify man's mistakes.

He expressed his regret that although 'benevolent institutions were rap-idly rising' all over the world, providence allowed the Pope to remain in Rome and Napoleon in Paris.[12] His comments were preceded by the strange enquiry, 'Do you see the papers sometimes?' – an extraordinary question to ask a woman who believed herself to hold advanced views on women's rights and claimed to have held strong opinions on Catholic emancipation since she was seven. It also reveals how little William – separated from Catherine for most of the time before their marriage and much of the time thereafter – knew about his wife. In fact neither of them was interested in politics or, until the slow awakening changed their lives and beliefs, the condition of the English people.

Catherine's attitude towards the world beyond her own hopes and fears was, during her courtship and early months of marriage, less detached than hostile. She was anxious to redeem the unrighteous but not to mix with them before their redemption:

> I am so glad that you feel the importance of *avoiding visiting*.
> Depend upon it dearest, it is an important point and especially
> in your case. I know how impossible it is for *you* to enter into
> *ordinary* social intercourse without having the tone of your
> feelings lowered and your mind in a measure dissipated – and
> my advice is to keep out of company as much as possible.
> Resolutely resist the snare of the enemy.[13]

In a single paragraph, she established both the wickedness of the world and William's difficulty, without her assistance, in resisting it. Catherine's certainty in what she believed remained absolute from the years before her marriage until the day of her death. But her desire to correct and reprove diminished with the years. In the months before the wedding she could hardly have been more didactic about small things. Suddenly adopting the Quaker form of speech, she complained to William, 'Thou spells "till" with one l and encomium with an n instead of an m'[14] – a remarkable reproof from a woman to whom the full stop was virtually unknown and also, in the same letter, gave her opinion on 'sleaves' and 'collers'.

After the wedding, the young bride became increasingly anxious about money. At each of William's moves from church to church, Catherine showed an entirely understandable desire for his salary to reflect the esteem in which he was held by his new employer. But she also exhibited a prickly sort of pride about the way in which they lived. 'Mr Dixon,' wrote William, 'the gentleman with whom I stayed [in Newcastle] made me a present of £2 for my mother, that was very kind was it not, they gave me £3 for my week's services – and every luxury heart could desire to provide for my health and comfort.' Catherine was only moderately impressed. 'It was very kind of the gentleman certainly, but I hope your means by and by will make revelation of your mother's means to strangers unnecessary. I should prefer you to have the means to help her independently of anybody and these thou *oughtest* to have.'[15]

William, whose worldly needs were genuinely modest, glowed in the prospect of rising in the world. 'A gentleman by the name of Bailey who keeps his carriage and pair and who lives in a little paradise two miles out at Longton would very much like us to spend a month to rest at his home next *summer*, but I mean to visit Paris, Switzerland and the Rhine if at all practicable.'[16] Booth's version of the Grand Tour did not take place, but interest in material things confirmed that William's vocation did not require him to take a vow of poverty. In Derbyshire in October 1855, they dined at the local inn – 'First trout, second fowl, third Grouse and mushroom sauce, fourth Plum and Cranberry pie and Bakewell Pudding, rich in the extreme, fifth cheese and sixth wine.' Although Catherine made clear that she would not wish to 'sit down *often* in front of such fare', she felt no need to explain either how William's notoriously weak stomach survived the experience or why the essentially New Connexion meal ended with alcohol. A month earlier, in the same county, she had recorded her relief that 'friends had been exceedingly kind', and that at a meeting of 'office bearers, local preachers and teachers . . . it was carried that . . . a present of £10 independent of the regular salary be presented'. She rejoiced to have received 'little presents from different friends, for the money is most useful, for our expenses recently have been quite up to our income'.[17]

Catherine Booth was human – human enough to rejoice that on winter nights she was not alone. The early hagiographers did her no service by portraying her as a saint, for saints are expected to accept the sacrifices that faith demands. Once canonised in the minds of her biographers, the privations which she willingly endured were discounted as no more than what was expected of her. That enabled them to overlook her faults – some of which undoubtedly contributed to William Booth's unpopularity with colleagues in every brand of Methodism except the one which he created. But he was the real architect of the disapproval which he attracted. However, the couple's least attractive qualities were, like their virtues, complementary. He was sanctimonious and she was generally censorious. Both were intolerant of disagreement (except between themselves) and incapable of considering the possibility that they were wrong. Perhaps understandably, in the early months of marriage Catherine was preoccupied with her wonderful new life – both the glory of her husband's calling and the material pleasures which accompanied it. But her letters home, to parents in increasing financial difficulty, demonstrated a monumental insensitivity. One was from 'the most *comfortable* home I have been in since our wedding. We have a beautiful *warm* room to sit in and a nice bedroom with a four poster bed, quite a luxury . . .'[18] On their Derbyshire tour they passed the house which was occupied by Sir Joseph Paxton, sometime head gardener to the Duke of Devonshire at Chatsworth and architect of the Crystal Palace. Catherine could not resist using Paxton's good fortune to point a moral to her distressed mother: 'Sir Joseph's Paxton's home is between the lodge and the Duke's residence. It is a fine building and quite a gentleman's seat. Yet it is only eighteen years since he came here on the same footing as the man at the keeper's lodge and still a plodding gardener.'[19]

She also had a few words of censure for the Sixth Duke – a bachelor who found consolation for his lonely life in the company of the numerous ladies who lived in what the local residents impertinently called the 'bird cages' which His Grace had built on various parts of the estate. 'The Duke ought to be a happy man if worldly goods can give felicity. But alas, we know they cannot. And, by all accounts, he is one of those to whom they have failed to import it.'[20] The Bachelor Duke was indeed depressed. But the cause was not entirely to his discredit – although it was clearly related to his rank and station. Czar Nicholas was his closest friend. And Russia was at war with England.

It would be wrong to suggest that in youth Catherine Booth found it hard to understand the normal emotions of friendship, but she was certainly incapable of showing sympathy in times of trouble without adding a homily about how the trouble might be avoided in future. When, after months of hints about hard times ahead, Mrs Mumford

wrote with the distressing news that her husband's coach-building
business was on the point of collapse, William sent £2 as a contribution to immediate expenses and ten shillings in stamps with which the
old man could enjoy a distracting day at Crystal Palace. Catherine
offered better long-term advice but less sympathy. She suggested that
her parents take in lodgers and, when she heard that her father was so
depressed that he despaired of the love of God, she added, 'Tell Father
that he must not wait for a change in *circumstances* before he begins to
serve God, but seek first the Kingdom of Heaven.'

The piety increased as the sense of mission grew. 'Pray for us,' she
wrote from Derbyshire, 'our position grows daily more important and
dangerous.'[21] Their conspicuous sense of mission was beginning to
make enemies. Sometimes the young minister's wife seemed to go out
of her way to antagonise potential friends. In Leeds she had blamed
small congregations and poor results on a Mr Stacey, the preacher with
whom William had reluctantly agreed to share his pulpit. But although
the Booths often caused gratuitous offence, part of the antagonism
which they faced was based on jealousy of the young preacher's ability
to hold a congregation in the palm of his hand.

His appeal was based more on style than substance. Certainly there
were members of his congregation who were chastened into repentance
by the threat of hell. But William Booth gave reality to the idea of
damnation by the fervour with which he begged the sinners to be
saved. He rarely shouted. But his rasping voice penetrated the fur-
thest recesses of the chapels in which he preached and the words were
accompanied by illustrative gestures which turned his homely parables
into dramatic monologues. When the ship of life was sunk by the
weight of sin it carried, he sank down in the pulpit. Then he rose,
waving a handkerchief, to represent the one member of the crew who
realised how the vessel could be saved. It was all cheap stuff and would
not have appealed to the parishioners of Great St Mary's, Cambridge or
St Mary Abbots, Kensington. But it was irresistible to the sort of men
and women William Booth hoped to win for Jesus.

On 5 October 1855 William Booth received what, on the face of it,
appeared to be a humiliating rebuff – even though his apologists have
interpreted it as a triumph. Sheffield, a town in which Methodism
prospered, was divided into two districts. William had been invited to
preach in the Northern Circuit. He then received a letter from the

Committee forbidding him to preach in the south of the town[22] – not, whatever his friends may have claimed, because they wanted to spread his unique talents more widely, but because they feared he was getting above himself. Catherine could hardly disguise her resentment that the rewards of her husband's hard work would be enjoyed by the resident minister whose failings he had gone north to rectify. She had to struggle even harder to avoid showing her resentment when, a couple of months later, she heard that Joshua Poole (a local man of barely thirty who was soon to become the author of *The British Revivalist Song Book*) was helping Sheffield converts on their way to heaven. And she did not completely succeed in hiding her feelings: 'Mr Poole has been very successful . . . he went at a very good time. There were scores of wounded who might have been gathered in by *our* people if the Committee could have let us go to the other chapel.' It is almost possible to hear the deep breath which she drew before adding, 'However, it is a good thing somebody has caught them. Poole is a very sincere, earnest good man and we rejoice greatly at his success.'[23]

A month later the same Mr Poole was the subject of a letter, published in the *Wesleyan Times*, which attacked his evangelical technique. Catherine, although not always sympathetic to her friends in distress, invariably defended them against their enemies. And by expressing her support for Poole, she was also asserting the values of her husband's preaching style. Catherine, in her reminiscences, says that Poole's influence had a permanent effect on her husband, who incorporated three Poole precepts into his preaching:

1. Directness of aim. Every word and movement indicating that he was determined to bring the audience, young and old, into harmony with God and that was to be done that night before he parted from them if that were possible.
2. Simplicity of method, the simplest words, the plainest illustrations, the most homely and striking facts being used throughout the discussion.
3. The most direct dependence upon God for the result.[24]

It was all part of the process which increasingly alienated William Booth from the more thoughtful Methodists, who disapproved of the high emotional preaching style which they feared encouraged quick and spectacular, though insincere and brief, conversions. But it was the only style at Booth's disposal. Even his first biographer, Harold Begbie – who excused so much and hid even more – described him as an 'intractable Philistine as regards the entire religion of the intellect',[25] and William responded to the charge of speed and superficiality with a bold, if not very profound, metaphor: 'I know no train that goes fast enough for me.'[26]

The problem, as more thoughtful preachers saw it, was that occasionally he did not arrive at the right destination. One young girl who 'wept sorely and appeared in great distress and to have much rejoiced when she got hope was seen dancing away Thursday and Friday in the Market Hall with half the town looking on'.[27] But William Booth remained an enthusiast for thunder and lightning – and Catherine began to suspect that he was the target for a *Wesleyan Times* campaign against the anxiety seat, the penitent form and instant conversion. A Mr Little of Leeds had led the assault. Catherine – either out of pride or desire to spare her mother pain – wrote home to say that the attacks were not on William. Mrs Mumford, apparently unconvinced, suggested that 'silent endurance is the best expedient for poor persecuted husbands'.

Catherine – partly out of conviction and partly because it was a shrewd defence – agreed that some of Little's comments were 'unquestionably just and *justifiable* when applied to *some* persons using the title of *Revivalist*. I have often been disgusted with the wildness and the extravagance of such and I am the last to tolerate noise without influence or ignorant and profane dealing with sacred subjects . . . *Wm.* does not think that Mr Little knows him or anything about his work at present.' Then she undermined the impression of calm objectivity which she had struggled so hard to create. 'If God gives us such work in Leeds as we had in Sheffield, neither Mr L nor any other "Little man" will be able to disparage us.'[28]

The campaign in West Yorkshire was the success for which Catherine hoped. 'The work here,' she wrote, 'is progressing gloriously though we found the people *frozen* and formal and quite unprepared' – a first impression not unlike that which Mrs Gaskell obtained when she travelled north to write her biography of Charlotte Brontë. However, despite herself, Catherine was becoming increasingly enthusiastic about the 'excitement' which, she wrote, was 'taking over the town.

Sinners are being converted every night!' The good news from Dewsbury was echoed in Hunslet, where 'glorious work was going on. Hundreds of sinners have been converted, many slumbering professions of religion have been quickened and not a few backsliders reclaimed.' The *New Connexion Magazine* (having reported those victories) promised that, in the next issue, the editor would have 'the joy to tell of glorious work in Leeds'. William Booth was becoming a figure in the whole Methodist movement. He was soon to feel both the benefits and disadvantages of his new status.

At the turn of the year, Catherine's spiritual joys were matched by material hardship. In Dewsbury she had been 'prostrate' with a severe attack of inflammation of the lungs – from which, in her own judgement, she eventually recovered thanks to a series of homeopathic remedies. In Leeds she often missed prayer meetings because the heat and the crowd were more than she could stand. In spirit, however, she remained indomitable if not humble, feeling particular regret about her absence from revivalist meetings, because she 'might often render efficient help at the communion rail where a certain amount of intelligence and aptness to speak on divine subjects is often sadly deficient especially in such places as these'.[29] And she worried that, without her calming (and often deflating) influence being constantly to hand, her husband might be lionised to the point at which he lost 'his relish for home and domestic joy'. Despite his God-given calling, Catherine had little faith in William's ability to resist the sin of pride. Without her by his side to remind him that the mighty would be put down from their seats, she feared that 'popularity might turn his head, that social flattery might tempt him from the hard and narrow way'. Catherine should have shared the blame rather than excoriate the sinner. His principal concern was that the lodgings with which he had been provided would meet the needs of his pregnant wife. He threatened that, unless something more in keeping with her condition was found, he would leave Yorkshire without preaching a single sermon.

Perhaps Catherine's concerns about William's character defects were the product of a difficult pregnancy, for fears that William would become prey to the material vices of the world now seem absurd – and they were entirely in conflict with the doctrine on holiness, God's promise to protect from sin all those who truly placed their souls in his

care. Whatever his wife's reasons for her early doubts about his character and conduct, William accepted them with good grace. He even
amended a letter she had written to his mother with a note which
explained that although, in the calm of evening, she had described him
as 'electrifying the congregation', in the heat of the afternoon she had
called him a 'blockhead'. His cheerful acceptance of her constant strictures was, by any standards, proof of his devotion. By the standards of
Victorian England, however, it was indulgent to the point of deviance.

In the autumn of 1855 a letter written to both her parents ended, 'I
enclose a few lines on a personal matter' which only her mother was to
read.[30] It was the confirmation that she was expecting a baby. She was
also expecting help in preparing for its arrival, for Catherine was used
to being looked after. Her needs were set out with an attention to
detail which made her requests sound more like instructions. The letters to her mother simultaneously illustrated her strength of will, her
neat mind and her status as a highly admired as well as much-loved
daughter. From Dewsbury she sent specific instructions about the
clothes she needed for the baby – 'nice thin, long cloth for the four
night gowns . . . nice fine work for 2 of the day gowns and a nice bit
of thread edging for the other. I think scotch combine will do for frills
for the night gown . . . I want the day gowns made very nicely and
trimmed very nicely. I don't want them too long in the waist but just
medium; look at Mrs Brown's. Go and spend the afternoon with her.
Get any nice patterns she may have.'[31] Catherine's exacting demands
might have been excused by the explanation that she was elated at the
discovery that she was soon to become a mother. But the idea that her
thoughts were dominated by maternal delight is undermined by one
undoubted fact. In the early years of her marriage, Catherine Booth did
not like children.

When the Booths arrived at Bakewell during their Derbyshire tour
Catherine had found 'but one draw back' to the accommodation which
had been provided. 'There are five children.'[32] She reconciled herself to
the annoyance with stoic resignation and the sad admission, 'There is
always something'. When they moved on to Leeds, she was relieved to
find that they were 'lodged in a very nice home . . . where there are no
children (quite a recommendation seeing how they are usually
trained)'.[33] She had already developed firm views on child care. 'I hope
that if I have not both sense and grace to train mine so that they shall

not be a nuisance to everybody near them, that God in his mercy will take them to heaven.'[34] The image of the dying infant – about to rise to glory, untainted by vice and redeeming its parents by its spotless example – was a constant source of inspiration to Victorian Methodism. But that was not quite what Catherine Booth meant. During her pregnancy, she actually wrote that, if her children were not well behaved, she hoped that they would die. But, with the intention of avoiding that ultimate necessity, she intended to rear her children as Mrs Gargery reared Pip – by hand. Respect for that precept, combined with her determination not to be parted from William, forced Catherine to accept that she would not enjoy a home of her own. Only a few weeks after the wedding she had 'quite given up the idea of having one'. From the earliest years of the marriage she had been absolutely clear about what the future offered. 'Even if I have a baby, we intend to travel *together* and *carry it with us* and take apartments in every place.'[35] The baby's arrival only hardened her resolve. 'Much as I should like to have a settled home, you know my objections to leaving William and they get stronger as I see the constant need he has of my presence, care and sympathy. Neither is he willing for it himself. He says that nothing shall separate us while there is any possibility of our travelling together.'[36]

The baby was born in Halifax lodgings on 8 March 1856. The proud father wrote to his wife's parents with the joyful news, 'It is with feelings of unutterable gratitude and joy that I have to inform you that, at half past eight last night, my dearest Kate presented me with a healthy beautiful son . . . The baby is a plump, round faced, dark complexioned, black pated little fellow. A real beauty.'[37] The letter provided a clue to the nature of the Booths' strange though strong relationship. It is impossible to imagine Catherine writing in such unashamedly sentimental language, even at a moment of such high emotion. William, by nature, was softer than Catherine. And he moulded himself around her hard will. Her strength was essential to the progress of their great crusade – not simply to drive William on at moments of self-doubt and spiritual agony but, equally important, to convince him that he must press on even when she was too physically weak to follow. The birth of the baby did nothing to make either of the Booths change their mind about service and sacrifice. 'Poor Kate had a dreadful time, but the Lord in His mercy, brought her safely through.'[38] Unfortunately He did not effect so swift a recovery that she was able to travel with her husband to Huddersfield. But he travelled nevertheless as Catherine expected and insisted was his duty. It became a pattern of their partnership.

It took Catherine some time to recover, and even when she was well enough to join William in Macclesfield, her mother accompanied her as nurse as much as companion. It was there that the baby was baptised, during a ceremony in which his father christened thirty children. He was given the name of William Bramwell – partly out of respect for his father, but principally in tribute to an itinerant evangelist who had preached his way across northern England at the turn of the century. It was another reaffirmation of the Booths' theory of evangelism. At his 'lovefeast' in the chapel at West Moon Colliery in 1811, the Reverend William Bramwell had 'commanded all who were determined to forsake their sin and come to Christ to stand up and show themselves . . . Mr Bramwell again and again requested those who remained in distress to stand up till there were none left.'[39] William Booth was to do the same, time after time, for the next fifty years.

William Booth became the hero of the New Connexion Annual Conference. At its sixtieth meeting, held on Monday 12 May 1856 in Chester, he was the only minister to be referred to by name in the presidential address. The language of the praise can only be described as extravagant:

> You will be gratified to learn that the evangelistic labours of
> our beloved brother the Reverend W. Booth will be continued
> through the next year. It is only justice to him to record our
> estimate of his abundant labours, which have resulted not only
> in the quickening of many of our churches and in the
> conversion of many souls but many societies and circuits,
> hearing of the great things which the Lord had done by him,
> have stirred of gifts within them and have realised a revival in
> the fullness of his blessing, thus teaching us that it is not so
> much a specific and extraordinary agency we need as the
> zealous and prayerful use of the means already processed.

The Reverend Henry Watts was doing no more than reflecting the general view of the Conference, but the Committee, which had exercised its authority by refusing permission for William to visit the Southern Sheffield Circuit, insisted on laying down rules to regulate his future activities. Miscellaneous Resolution 57 stipulated that the Committee would decide where and for how long William would perform his duties – a warning that at least part of the Methodist establishment was determined to place William Booth under the firm control of the Annual Conference. But the Booths – infatuated by their own success – were neither subtle nor sophisticated and, in consequence, saw no reason to change their ways. So, unthinking, on they charged towards the inevitable collision.

When, after the triumph of the Chester Conference, they returned to Sheffield to complete their interrupted business by working in the previously forbidden circuit, they immediately found public fault with their hosts. They were particularly angry about the Circuit's inability to prevent the sin of 'backsliding' – the return of recent converts to their sinful ways. It is unlikely that the miscreants took Catherine's strictures with good grace. Even without her complaints and reproofs, the system of travelling preachers seemed designed to make the circuit ministers resent the young itinerant minister and his wife – employed for two or three weeks of emotional evangelism and then moved on to the next town before the permanent results of his mission could be assessed. Catherine's complaints turned resentment into antagonism. William Booth was the favourite of the flock, not the choice of the local shepherds.

In terms of sinners who repented and converts brought to grace, the second visit to Sheffield was such a triumph that, before William left, the Chapel Trustees of the two circuits presented him with a specially commissioned portrait. The practice of presenting visiting preachers with a 'likeness' was common throughout the New Connexion and the presentation to William Booth was endorsed by the presence of the President of the Conference himself, the Reverend H. Watts. But the event 'accentuated the jealousy [with] which a certain section of preachers had begun to regard William's increasing popularity'. Catherine, although too unwell to attend the ceremony, was 'taken aback by the ministerial ill feeling' that it created. Perhaps the offence was caused by the effusive wording of the inscription on the plaque which was attached to the lithograph's frame. It recorded that the gift was made 'in affectionate appreciation of arduous, zealous and successful labours'. The *New Connexion Magazine* reported that 'Mr Booth was received with enthusiastic applause and replied in his usual fervent and effective manner . . . After speaking at some length on the importance of aggressive efforts on the part of the church, Mr Booth sat down amidst protracted applause.' Much to his credit he seized the moment in order to promote his campaign for active Christianity.[40] He certainly enjoyed the recognition of his success, but he always remained single-minded in his determination to do more even if, in his own estimation, he could not do better.

So they moved on, through his home town of Nottingham – where the minister, the Reverend P. J. Wright, received them 'in the coldest possible manner' – to Chester. He travelled alone. Catherine was ill again, so she did not witness the next step in her husband's deteriorating relationship with the elders of his church. She had returned to London and the care of her parents when, on 24 January 1857, the *Chester Chronicle* announced that the Reverend William Booth of London, 'whose labours have been so greatly blessed in various parts of the country', would commence a course of 'SPECIAL RELIGIOUS SERVICES'. In an editorial on the same day, the paper either gave him an extravagant welcome or greeted him with irony so heavy that the compliments seemed genuine. Then the paper sent a reporter to cover one of the services. His account of the proceedings veered wildly from present to past tense and back again. Perhaps what he witnessed had totally unnerved him.

> After the discourse has concluded, the congregation has been called upon to 'come down into the body of the chapel if they wanted salvation'. The preacher then mounts upon a bench and gives out a hymn which is sung to a popular song tune, 'Jim Along Josey', 'Kathy Darling' and 'Charming May' being favourite compositions. As soon as the hymn is finished, the preacher orders everyone to turn round, down on their knees and go to prayer. The congregation having complied with this direction, several men stationed within the rails surrounding the pulpit commence praying, first singly and afterwards in full chorus until the excitement becomes painful in the extreme. The preacher next calls upon 'all who want salvation to come out and kneel down at the rails of the communion table'.

Presently, various persons have gone to the rail where 'leaders' at once fold them in their arms and commence close conversation. After a few minutes the 'penitents' are conducted to the vestry where their names are registered as '*converts*'.[41]

For all its grammatical eccentricity, the *Chester Chronicle's* report provides a classic description of the way in which nineteenth-century revivalist meetings – following the pattern set in New England – were conducted. It also illustrates the reasons why, jealousy aside, William Booth became so unpopular with the Methodist ministry. His 'conversions' were obtained by methods which orthodox churchmen regarded as intellectually absurd, theologically indefensible and – perhaps worst of all in respectable, middle-class Victorian England – deeply embarrassing. The Methodist establishment resented the presumption of the uneducated pawnbroker's clerk who made, or claimed to make, instant conversions. And they were horrified by the translation of religion into the language of the music hall. William Booth was, to them, an upstart vulgarian. His complaint against every church for which he preached was that it neglected the ignorant masses. Their complaint against him was that he promoted the sort of religion that the ignorant masses could understand.

Occasionally even Catherine had doubts about his technique. 'Watch against mere animal excitement in your revival sermons,' she warned. 'Remember Finney's silent and heavenly carriage. He did not shout. There was no necessity. He had a more powerful weapon at his disposal.' Not surprisingly, his replies from Chester were more concerned with the welfare of his new family than the success of his preaching methods. 'So you had to whip him to obtain mastery,' he wrote to his wife, 'and now he is king seeing you are ill.' The king who had been whipped was little Bramwell – in those early days known to his parents as Willy – who was barely a year old.

William's weeks in Chester were a generally unhappy time in the young couple's life. They were separated. Catherine was ill. Their baby was difficult and the local press was doing all it could to denigrate the visiting preacher. William had begun to oscillate between periods of wild elation and long hours of deep depression. In Chester, his spirits sank. 'I have been looking at the dark side of myself. In fact I can find no other side. I seem to be all dark, mentally, physically, spiritually.'[42]

The message home was typical of his occasional lapses into despair. And the *Chester Chronicle*'s attacks were remorseless. He was, the paper made clear, no gentleman. 'On several occasions during the services, Mr Booth has thought fit to adopt conduct of the rudest character . . . The other evening a most exemplary minister of the Gospel in this city was standing in the aisle for a minute, when Mr Booth went up to him and said, "Down on your knees, man; and do not stand there as if you were in the play house."'

As well as being a pioneer of popular evangelism, William Booth was also a progenitor of what modern politicians would call rapid rebuttal. But in Chester he had to wait for seven days before the weekly paper was published again. Then the correspondence column included a letter within a letter. William Booth quoted the Reverend W. Hunter, 'the Minister referred to', who had assured him 'never did you address a word to me individually'. A week later, the *Chronicle* pointed out that the Reverend Mr Hunter had not denied its account of William Booth's bizarre conduct, but merely insisted that the rudeness had not been directed towards him personally. To justify their criticism, the paper gave other examples of how the service had been conducted – including the preacher's improbable 'description of the topography of Hell and . . . a portrayal [sic] of its natural history'.

By then, the travelling preacher had resumed his travels and was on his way to the south. Catherine and their son had joined him to provide support and consolation. The journey to Truro was particularly difficult. The railway line ended in Plymouth and the last part of the journey had to be made by coach – a vehicle so small that there was barely room for Catherine to ride inside with her husband. She was ill again, and 'too ill to take little Willy'.[43] So the baby Bramwell travelled on the box with his nurse – thus illustrating the Booths' view of caring parenthood and the relative affluence of a couple who were always complaining about their poverty. After two hours of exposure to the driving rain, the baby's face was stained blue with dye which had washed out of the nurse's bonnet strings. The child was apparently no worse for his soaking. But Catherine and William (who had himself been ill with a disease which did not respond to homeopathy) decided that Bramwell must be sent to London and kept for a week or two in the care of the Mumfords. It was a desperate decision, taken out of absolute necessity and even then with the greatest regret, for Catherine did not trust her mother to bring up Bramwell in the way his parents thought essential. 'You could not wage war with his self-will so resolutely as to subdue it. And my child would be ruined, for he must be taught implicit and uncompromising obedience.'[44] No child in England endured a harsher upbringing. It did not, however, turn him against his parents. Quite the contrary. But it undermined his confidence to such a degree that, when he achieved some authority within the Salvation Army, the effects of childhood tyranny on his character prompted him to behave with such authoritarian zeal that he almost destroyed the mighty organisation which his mother and father had created. The tyranny began when he could barely walk.

At Truro, mindful of Catherine's strictures and perhaps still debilitated by whatever had afflicted him in Chester, William began to develop doubts about his preaching methods. One evening, 'when the feeling of the meeting was beginning to get warm . . . one dear woman sprang to her feet in ecstasy and began to jump up and down in measured rhythm, keeping in time to the tune we were singing with little shouts of "Glory!" every time she went up. William, fearing that excitement might get beyond bounds . . . gave orders for her to be restrained . . . Physical force was necessary and . . . when it was perceived by the meeting, the atmosphere was destroyed.'[45] Even William Booth had begun to acknowledge that his sort of evangelism could get out of hand – not surprisingly, if he had witnessed a member of his congregation behaving in a way which stimulated mass hysteria. But he was still absolutely unaware of the strength of feeling that was building up against him.

William was too busy preaching, as well as too impatient of authority, to attend the New Connexion's next Annual Conference in June 1857 – even though it was held in his home town. Instead he stayed at his lodgings in Stafford, and it was there that he received from Josiah Bates – Book Room Treasurer of the Conference and an old friend of the Booths – an early and unofficial report of the decision which had been taken about his future. He read the letter with naïve amazement. He had been instructed to become a Circuit Minister in Brighouse in Yorkshire.

The feeling was strong against you – it was yesterday proposed that I should join the Annual Committee in place of Mr Heaps.

But the Doctor [Crofts] opposed it on the grounds that I was
too close to you . . . The principal speakers against you were
Crofts and P. J. Wright. I have no doubt that the decision will
spread widespread dissatisfaction and may have to be
reversed.[46]

William accepted the decision with dignified resentment. His letter
to the Conference in reply to the formal notification of its decision
expressed his surprise that 'no reasons are assigned for this desired
change', and added, 'All I ask, nay claim as my due, is to know what
those important bearings are for which my special labours, acknowledged to be of value, are to be discontinued.'[47] He received no answer.

Catherine, writing to her mother, faced the future with Christian resignation. 'If God wants him to be an evangelist, He will open up his
way.' Next morning she added to the letter – characteristically but not
completely consistently – 'There is to be an attempt this morning at a
compromise, to send him to a circuit and yet let him visit several
places during the year . . . William will not agree to it.' Before the 1857
Conference closed it decided that William Booth be given liberty to
visit three circuits during the year, but not to be absent from his circuit
more than four weeks in succession. Even then the management of his
excursions was to be taken out of his hands. 'Application for his services may be addressed to Mr Booth but no arrangements shall be
entered into without the consent of the circuit.'[48] William himself
wrote to the Mumfords claiming that a faction was forming against him
and accusing Wright and Crofts of plotting his downfall. But he went,
with as much grace as he could muster, to Brighouse to become a circuit minister, and a circuit minister he remained for the next five years.

5

A Fool for God

Catherine found Brighouse entirely uncongenial. There, on 28 July 1857, Ballington, their second son, was born. Bramwell had been christened at a ceremony which he shared with thirty other babies – to prove that preachers' children were no nearer or dearer to God than any other infant. But either because his parents had become proud or because they remained naïve, Ballington was treated differently. In February 1858 the Booths travelled to Sheffield to attend 'a very large meeting' addressed by the great James Caughey himself. After it was over Catherine proudly wrote, 'upwards of twelve hundred people sat down to tea and we were at the same table with Mr Caughey himself and William had some conversation with him'. On the following day, the Booths dined at the house in which the famous evangelist was staying, and 'next morning he called on Mr Wilkins [the Booths' host] and baptised our dear Ballington'. When he left, Catherine 'pressed a fervent kiss on his hand and felt more gratified than if it had been Queen Victoria'.[1]

William took the opportunity to discuss his predicament with his hero who, in his time, had been similarly treated. Caughey uncharacteristically urged caution. It was, he said with more worldliness than was to be expected of a Man of God, better to resign from a position of strength. Wait, he told his young admirer, until after formal ordination allowed him to leave as a Reverend by right rather than courtesy, and in Full Communion with the church he served. He did not have to wait long.

For a year William Booth applied himself to the work of the circuit with a self-effacing devotion, and Catherine began to learn about the life of the northern poor. She described the life of a mill girl with a mixture of horror and disbelief that confirmed her own sheltered childhood.

> They begin as half timers when they are seven or eight years
> and, after a little while, are able to earn eight or nine shillings a
> week. In a family of three or four with perhaps a drunken
> father, it is a great temptation to a mother to let her children go
> to the mill. Indeed, parents seem to lose sight altogether of the
> demoralising and unwomanly influence of the system. I never
> met with such a pound shilling and pence people in my life.
> What pitiable wives and mothers they will make . . . I see no
> help for it but a law prohibiting girls under twenty from
> working in factories before nine o'clock.[2]

That passage reveals all the views about changing society which, typically enough, Catherine developed as soon as she discovered the realities of mill life. The demand for protection by law – unusual though it was at that time – became a constant theme of her work amongst poor women. So did the suspicion that drunken men were at the root of the evil. There was also the common assumption, in no way undermined by her beliefs about equality in the sight of God, that a girl's first duty was to prepare for Christian motherhood. And she took for granted that women managed the family budget, as she did herself. It is unlikely, however, that many other mothers ruled with such uncompromising views on family discipline. 'Willy gets every day more loveable . . . I believe that he will be a thoroughly noble lad if I can preserve him from evil influences. The Lord help me! I have had to whip him thrice lately, severely for disobedience and it has cost me some tears. But it has done some good and I am reaping already the rewards of my self sacrifice.'[3]

William was reaping the rewards of reticence. He did not enjoy being a circuit minister. But he was pleased to record, 'I understand that I have won golden opinions by my deportment during the year – I have not served the Connexion to anything like the extent I have done formerly. But I have kept quiet and for a young man that is very probably best.' Whether or not he really believed in the values of silence, the elders of his church certainly did and they decided to reward him. It was agreed that he should be ordained at the 1858 Annual Conference in Hull. He was admitted into Full Connexion on Monday 24 May 1858.

At the service which preceded the ceremony, 'The Reverend Doctor Crofts put the usual questions to the candidates relating to their religious experience, their call to the ministry and the motives which induced them to engage therein . . . The answers of all the candidates were extremely satisfactory.'[4] The 'charge' setting out the obligations which new ministers must accept was delivered by the Reverend H. Watts, sometime President of the Conference and witness to the Sheffield ceremony at which William was presented with his portrait. He took as his text St Paul's second Epistle to the Corinthians, Chapter IV, Verse 13: 'We also believe and we therefore speak.' His address, which lasted for more than an hour, was too long to be reproduced in a single issue of the *New Connexion Magazine*. It struck a paternal note. 'I am verging on the close, you at the beginning of your ministerial life . . . The brightness of morning gladdens you. Bear with me while I manifest my deep concern for your propriety and all the great work to which you have been called.'

The *Hull News*'s account of the ceremony must rate amongst the greatest missed opportunities of provincial journalism. The issue of 29 May reported, 'First Mr Bishop of Burton related how he became converted. He then claimed that the New Connexion was more in accordance with the enlightened view of the age and also more in accordance with civil and religious liberty . . . than any other branch of the church. He believed in the personality and divinity of the Holy Ghost and the fall and depravity of man.' After several other paragraphs of verbatim reporting the *News* added, almost as an afterthought, 'Three other young men then addressed the congregation following a similar course.' Amongst them (his words now forgotten) was William Booth, the most pyrotechnic preacher of his century.

The now forgotten Mr Bishop was absolutely right to describe the

New Connexion as representing the enlightened view of the age – assuming that he meant the enlightened views on social matters which were held by the progressive minority. For the Connexion, although fundamentalist about the literal truth of every word in the Bible was, nevertheless, positively radical on temporal issues. Resolution 8 of the 1858 Conference reaffirmed 'the necessity of preserving the sanctity of the Sabbath'. But Resolution 9 reminded delegates of their duty 'to raise their voices against all unnecessary wars as contrary to the will of God'. Resolution 10 confirmed that Conference, 'remembering its obligations to the Jewish people . . . would hail their participation in all civil rights belonging to an Englishman . . . and therefore directs a petition to be prepared and signed by the President and forwarded to both Houses of Parliament'. Most surprisingly of all, by the standards of the time, it challenged one of the silliest taboos of the established Church. Resolution 13 asserted that there was 'no valid objection to a man marrying his wife's sister after the death of his wife'. All in all, it was a highly enlightened assembly which welcomed William Booth into full ministry. But if William or Catherine Booth had opinions on any of the contentious subjects which the Conference debated, there is no record of them being expressed.

The formal act of ordination was the laying-on of hands – a ritual in which all ministers present took part. William Booth, still not reconciled to the restraints imposed upon him, had 'no wish to receive the spirit of those who opposed him . . . if the laying-on of their hands involved importation of the character and spirit which they possessed, he would rather dispense with it'.[5] He was not able to avoid the Judas touch. For the physical contact was the act of ordination. But, as always in those early days, he first complained and then submitted. At least he had come to accept that he still had enemies in the Conference – indeed, they were growing in power and increasing in strength.

The Reverend P. J. Wright – the Superintendent Minister of the Nottingham Circuit and an established critic of both William Booth and his methods – was elected to the Conference Standing Committee. Wright, although dismissed by the Booths as motivated by no more than envy, was typical of the Methodists who opposed William's view of ministry. It would have been wise if, instead of questioning his motives, an attempt had been made to understand his principled objection to their views. He had left the Wesleyan Methodists during the Leeds Bethesda Chapel organ controversy – less interested in the merits of organ music than in support of the preachers' right to make decisions for their own circuits. That made him a liberal Methodist in terms of church government. But he 'loved the doctrines, disciplines and ordinances of the body and was religiously conservative'.[6] Wright joined the New Connexion after a colleague advised him that it was a 'respectable denomination whose principles of church government accord with those you seem to hold'.[7] He took the advice and served as an ordained minister for almost thirty years. He represented an austere, though not authoritarian, view of Methodism and was devoted to the principle of ministers as pastors of their circuits. He genuinely disapproved of William Booth's peripatetic (and flamboyant) evangelism, which he thought undermined the essential principle of ministers as leaders of their communities. There was never any chance of a compromise, because the Booths would not believe that he held honest views. It was men like Wright, with a conscientious objection to William Booth's methods, who frustrated the attempts, after his ordination, to get him back on the road.

The year of service in Brighouse had, however, won him some new friends in the Conference. The Reverend Halliwell, who had been completely against William Booth in 1857, suggested a new compromise in 1858. If another twelve months as circuit minister was graciously accepted, the Conference would agree to a roaming commission for the following year. A committee, almost entirely composed of William's friends, was set up to draft the motion. By some oversight they produced a proposition which, although it confirmed the year on the circuit, failed to mention what was to happen thereafter. So the minutes of the Conference recorded that 'although several memorials were presented in favour of the Reverend Booth being again employed as an evangelist, it was deemed inadvisable at present for our beloved brother, in accordance with his own wishes, to be appointed to a circuit'. The Conference either imagined that it could read William Booth's mind, or was misled by the emollient attitude of his friends. He had never expressed the wish which was recorded in the resolution.

Fortunately, although the New Connexion general staff had doubts about William Booth, the troops in the front line of the battle against sin increasingly admired him. So, before the end of the Conference at which he was ordained, Mr Firbanks (a lay delegate from Tyneside) asked if the now fully fledged minister could be sent to the north-east. As always, Catherine was opposed to any agreement to settle down in one place. It was an objection of selfless principle, for the wife and mother inside her longed for a permanent home and stable family life. Of course, in the end she agreed to go and help her husband assume the obligations of a circuit. Gateshead, to which he was posted, had for several years decayed under the supervision of a minister who had lost his faith but not resigned his ministry. There were ninety nominal members on the chapel roll, but less than half that number attended Sunday service. Yet more than five thousand souls waited to be saved in the borough alone and the great city of Newcastle was only the width of the Tyne away. William Booth accepted the Gateshead Circuit in June 1858. By 25 July he was calling sinners to redemption on the Windmill Hills to the south of the town.[8] The event was called a Camp Meeting – though it was more like a picnic than one of the three-day prayerfests of that name which were common in Massachusetts and Connecticut. But that was how he chose to describe his open-air service. He had decided on the sort of evangelist that he wanted to be.

Catherine, who had initially been so opposed to the move north, fell in love with Gateshead almost at first glance. The parishioners were warm and welcoming. Their house had a garden in which Willy could safely play. Told by the leading members of the chapel that her husband had 'the best appointment in the Connexion', Catherine agreed it was 'all she could desire'.[9] And Catherine was pregnant again. Her third child and first daughter, christened Catherine after her mother, was born on 18 September 1858. Giving birth to three healthy children in three and a half years was only one of the achievements of her early marriage. Events in the north-east of England, of a theological rather than personal significance, were to change her life.

Salvationists will call it providential but, however it is described, all that happened to the Booths in their early years now seems like a preparation for the creation of the Salvation Army – not just as a new church which took the gospel of Salvation out on to the streets but, almost equally, as an instrument of care and compassion. At Gateshead Catherine's life-long hatred of drink and drunkenness evolved from an obsession into a campaign. When she saw a woman who was standing, jug in hand, at the door of a slum cottage she confronted the husband who was forcing his reluctant wife to fetch his beer. He promised to change his wicked ways. The assault on the evils of drink had begun. It was in Gateshead too that she found a 'bundle of rags' lying on waste ground and, examining it, found a woman who had just given birth to twins. By today's standards, Catherine Booth's response was less than adequate. She washed the new-born infants in rainwater which she had collected in a broken bowl. All we know of the grateful woman's response is that she told her benefactor that lard was almost as appetising as butter. And there is no record of what happened to her after Mrs Booth's initial ministrations. However the incident ended, Gateshead pushed the poor into the front of her mind. They remained a preoccupation for the rest of her life.

Providence could not have provided William and Catherine Booth with a more spectacular example of Victorian poverty and the personal degradation which it creates. All over Britain hungry children were growing up in festering slums without the benefit of either education or medical care. One child in three died at, or soon after, birth, and a third of those who survived did not live beyond their tenth birthday. But in Gateshead – which had felt but not absorbed the shock of the Industrial Revolution – men and women lived in continual destitution.

A huge influence of Irish – driven out of their homeland by the potato famine and attracted to England by hope of work in the new factories – had helped to double the population in less than fifty years. More than half of the adult men had no regular work. The twin pressures of population and poverty crowded families together like animals. The mid-century census reported that seventy-one persons (members of sixteen separate families) lived in one small house. The result of the overcrowding was three outbreaks of cholera in five years. The Rawlinson Commission into the causes of the second epidemic described living conditions in the poorer parts of the town.

Houses built back to back, usually in squares, drew drinking water from rusty communal stand-pipes at the centre of the yards or at street corners. A whole row of houses – perhaps eight families in all – shared a single earth privy. When they were cleared, the ordure was stored in the yards and then sold as manure. A single sewer, which flowed down the main street, had been badly designed and regularly flooded. So the steep roads which sloped down to the river carried away the refuse of daily living and human effluent. Sheep and cows which grazed on nearby wasteland were slaughtered in the yards, and their hides were tanned on the spot – adding another smell to the stench that always hung in the air. Three years before the Booths arrived a fire helped to cleanse the city by destroying some of the more fetid premises. But the destruction added to the desperation of the poor. The woman Catherine Booth found on the waste ground typified life in mid-century Gateshead. It was there that Catherine learned to love the poor.

William Booth – as always, unreservedly successful as a missionary and evangelist – was greatly loved by his congregation. His power as a preacher and his tireless energy enabled him to transcend his character defects and make friends. William Booth was not an easy man. He had a strong, and often harshly restrictive, opinion on every subject. But his prejudices were the product of conviction and he did not bend his beliefs to suit his own convenience. When he arrived in Gateshead and discovered how the circuit had raised the money to pay for his salary, he had announced at once that there were to be no more bazaars. 'So far as getting money is concerned it has been very successful, having realised £232. But it has been a disappointing godless affair and has exerted an evil influence on our people. There has been a great deal of lotterying which is little better than gambling and the show and display of dress has made us sick at heart.'[10]

Catherine both shared and encouraged his unyielding bigotry – particularly when it applied to what they both regarded as the world's vanities. The severity of their views on children's clothing came as a surprise even to Mrs Mumford, who had underestimated her daughter's dislike of frippery. 'The beautiful frock you bought Willy has never been on him yet as I am altering it to make it less showy so that he may wear it at tea meetings. It would be the most glaring inconsistency if I were to deck out my children as the worldlings do . . . The seed of vanity is too deeply sewn in the young heart for me to dare to cultivate it.'[11]

If the Booths had confined their moral strictures to their family and parishioners – leavening their unyielding righteousness with spontaneous displays of the affection they undoubtedly felt for those around them – William would have become the darling of the Conference as well as the delight of the circuits. But the Booths did not find it easy to express their more gentle emotions. And their moral certainty did not allow a moderation of their opinions, even when those they loved hoped for a moment's respite from the pursuit of virtue. William's high-minded opinions were usually expressed in language which suggested – with a good deal of justification – that William daily thanked God that he was not as other men are. Nothing could have been more offensive to other New Connexion ministers than a constant demonstration by one of their number that he regarded himself as their moral superior.

At the New Connexion Conference of 1859 William Booth was invited to join the group of ministers who were to meet a deputation from the United Kingdom Alliance – a federation of temperance organisations. The one item on the formal agenda was a proposal for a local ballot before a new public house was opened. William, however, insisted on moving a resolution which insisted that no one in any way associated with the production or sale of alcohol should be admitted to membership of the New Connexion. He emphasised what he believed to be the moderation of his proposal by emphasising that he 'did not ask that all members should be teetotal or even that publicans [many of whom were active in Methodism and held offices of considerable importance] should be expelled'. However, his proposal met with 'most vigorous opposition' – including what one of Booth's opponents regarded as an example of how good Wesleyans could combine alcohol and abstinence. A lady publican, their argument ran, was so determined to insulate her daughters from the demon drink, that, during school holidays, she made them stay in nearby lodgings rather than the public house which was their home. William Booth was not impressed. 'I gave the answer that the lady in question only aggravated her offence by inflicting on others the evils which she was unwilling that her own family should encounter. The observation was strongly resented and in the hubbub which ensued my motion was defeated by an overwhelming majority.'[12]

The notion that complete teetotalism was an 'essential part of the virtuous life' was common amongst American revivalist preachers. One of them, Phoebe Palmer, made the formal rejection of strong drink an essential part of the 'doctrine of holiness'[13] – a concept of sanctity in life which, in 1859, she expounded during her English campaign. Her conversion records – kept by all travelling evangelists as testimonials to their success – suggest that her views on abstinence sometimes prejudiced the results of her performance. But she did not flinch from what

she regarded as an article of faith. To Nonconformist total abstainers –
soon to impose their will on the whole Methodist movement – alcohol
was the devil in liquid form. Its rejection was essential to their faith.

It was Phoebe Palmer's gender as much as her ideology which
attracted Catherine Booth, even though the 'lady preacher', in order to
accommodate male prejudices, worked theoretically in junior partnership with her husband. Her meetings usually began with Dr Walter
Palmer reading from the Bible. A local minister – most often the resident of the chapel which they were visiting – would then preach the
formal sermon. Finally Phoebe Palmer brought the service to a climax
by walking to the communion rail 'not to preach according to the
modern acceptances of the term' but to say a few words and invite
those who wished for consecration to come forward. Mrs Palmer then
used what was called 'altar phraseology'[14] – exhortation for sinners to
offer all they had to God in the knowledge that God would, in accepting their offer, sanctify them. The Palmers usually filled the chapels in
which they preached from altar rail to door. Nobody doubted that
Phoebe was the big attraction.

Like the Booths, Phoebe Palmer did not accept that genuine conversion 'resulted only from a slow process of change, in which a man
quietly set out, with divine assistance, to practice the virtues and avoid
the vices, or from the sort of aestheticism which attached moral superiority to abstinence from money and sex . . . It was something that
God gave and gave suddenly.'[15] In *The Way of Holiness* Mrs Palmer
described 'a shorter way' of coming to holiness. The book took for
granted that it was possible to be sanctified without the inconvenience
of first dying and that sanctification might be achieved in a moment. Its
concern was the refinement of those doctrines in a way which met the
needs of professional evangelists who were invited to preach on their
record and were paid on their results. Phoebe Palmer held the view set
out by Adam Clarke nearly ten years before: Christian perfection is a
gift from God bestowed instantly.[16] However, there had to be preparation for the sudden moment. Some Methodists thought it should
include an end to knitting on the Sabbath and the destruction of any
novels which the sinner happened to possess. The Palmer theory combined slow penitence and quick salvation. An inventory of success
was possible when, in a state of fervour, penitents 'laid all on God's
altar', sometimes taking the renunciation of sin so literally that men

handed over pipes and tobacco and women tore feathers (a symbol of vanity) from their hats. Instant redemption allowed supplicants to enjoy the supreme pleasure of experiencing the moment of their own salvation. It also gave them the chance to decide for themselves exactly when it came about and it did not allow the tedious necessity of reading theological texts. It did, however, require the penitent to recognise the moment of second birth. Phoebe Palmer set out how, in the absence of thunder and lightning, it could be identified.

Her contribution to the conversion business was the insistence that there was no reason for redemption to be marked by violent ecstasy. There was a procedure to be followed which, if properly carried out, always produced the desired result. Penitents must first pray. 'Oh Lord I call heaven and earth to witness that I now lay my body, soul and spirit with all their redeemable powers upon Thine altar to be for ever Thine. Tis done. Thou hast promised to receive me. Thou canst not be unfaithful. Thou dost receive me now. From time forth I am Thine, wholly Thine.'[17] God, having been reminded of His duty and His promise, then provided the 'rest of faith' as set out in St Paul's Epistle to the Hebrews, Chapter IV, Verse 3: 'For we which have believed do enter into rest as he said.' Phoebe Palmer's peace did not pass all understanding. On the contrary, if the penitents felt at rest they should, she said, be in no doubt that they had been sanctified.

Phoebe Palmer offered a second essential refinement. Holiness, she said, was achieved when the penitent acquired the *power to resist* temptation, not when the sanctification was so complete that the redeemed sinner was never even tempted. A view of salvation based on 'the rest of faith' and the continued attraction of evil was a strange idea to come from a woman whose evangelism was built around whipping up her audiences into a state of frenzy and urging them to renounce the devil and all his works. But it made the travelling evangelist's work a great deal easier. The Palmer Theory exposed its author to the accusation that she offered the easy route to holiness – 'believe that you have it and you have it', as critics described her do-it-yourself definition – but that was brushed aside as a quibble raised by the hated intellectuals. Phoebe Palmer's formula worked, and that is all that those who supported her demanded. The whole idea was ideally suited to William Booth's theological position. Since her theory relied on feelings rather than thought – and by implication, dismissed scriptural study as a barrier to conversion – it appealed to his essentially anti-intellectual attitude towards theology. It was the perfect vehicle for the conversion of working, and often illiterate, men and women. But as William Booth was to discover, the theory of immediate conversion created instant antagonism.

Phoebe Palmer's progressive theory of sanctification encouraged William Booth's firm if reluctant acceptance of women evangelists. Catherine was simply filled with excitement by the thought that something approaching the female ministry was coming to the north-east. On 16 September 1859 she wrote to her parents, 'The celebrated Mrs Palmer of America, authoress of *The Way of Holiness*, *Entire Consecration* and *Economy of Salvation* is now in Newcastle speaking every night at the Wesley Chapel and getting 30 and 40 of a night up to the communion rail. I intend to hear her when I return.'[18] Ten days later she wrote again, saying that she was determined to visit Newcastle as soon as health and domestic circumstances allowed. A recurrence of what she had downgraded from tubercular spine to 'the back illness' and the obligation to look after her growing and increasingly demanding family made the trip impossible. But by the end of 1859, she had displayed her admiration for Mrs Palmer in a far more dramatic fashion than simply sitting at the back of the congregation. The chance was provided by the Reverend Arthur Augustus Rees, an independent minister from Sunderland who denounced Mrs Palmer and all her works.

The Reverend Mr Rees did not complain about Mrs Palmer's theory of redemption. He objected to her being a woman – or at least, he objected to her being a woman and having the effrontery to preach. He believed, in common with many ministers of his time, that the scriptures explicitly forbade women speaking in chapel, even if they claimed to be doing no more than augmenting a sermon which had been delivered by a man. His initial attack was made from his own pulpit. But his address attracted so much publicity that he repeated his assault at a second meeting – inciting Catherine Booth's contempt for the audience as well as the speaker. 'Would you,' she asked in a letter to her mother, 'believe that a congregation half composed of ladies could sit and hear such self-deprecatory rubbish? They really don't deserve to be taken up cudgels for.'[19] When the Reverend Mr Rees published his address under the title 'Reasons for Not Co-operating in the Alleged Sunderland Revivals', she took up the cudgels nevertheless.

Catherine Booth published her own pamphlet in reply. The letter to her mother which set out her intentions illustrated the strength of her character as well as of her conviction: 'Whatever may be its merits, it is my own and far more original, I believe, than most things that are published for I could get no help from any quarter. William has done nothing beyond copying for me and transposing one or two sentences. I composed more than half of it while he was away.'[20] Much to William's credit – at least by the standard of the time – he made no attempt to persuade his wife not to write or print her polemic. Catherine herself seems slightly surprised by his indulgence. When he read through the draft 'he was very pleased with it and urged me to proceed and not tie myself to space but deal thoroughly with the subject of female ministry [in a way] which would survive this controversy'. In the four years since his marriage, William had, no doubt under Catherine's influence and because of her example, become positively progressive on the subject of women preachers. But, as with so many other complicated questions, he was temperamentally inclined to let others do the hard, intellectual thinking while he relied on his intuition. Although he was undoubtedly on his wife's side, he could not have mounted the argument which she assembled in her counterblast, 'Female Teaching or the Reverend A. A. Rees versus Mrs Palmer, Being a Reply to the Pamphlet by the Above Named Gentleman on the Sunderland Revivals'.

The case for women preachers was set out with a self-confidence that even William Booth could have envied. But her certainty was built on surer foundations than those on which William's arguments usually relied. Her contentions were supported by a careful biblical exegesis which demonstrated so compendious a knowledge of both testaments that it allowed no room for doubt. The arguments were marshalled in a lively style which bore no relationship to the long-winded pomposity of the title:

> Whether the church will allow women to speak in her
> assemblies can only be a question of time: common sense,
> public opinion and the blessed results of female agency will
> force her to give us an honest and important rendering of the
> solitary text on which she grounds her prohibition.
>
> Then, when the true light shines and God's work takes the

place of man's traditions the doctors of divinity who teach that
Paul commands woman to be silent when God's spirit urges her
to speak will be regarded much the same as we should regard
an astronomer who should teach us that the sun is the earth's
satellite.

Having established her position as the Galileo of New Connexion
Methodism, Catherine then developed three distinct but related arguments – more in the style of the biblical scholars who were so despised
by William Booth than in the manner of an uneducated wife of a
provincial minister. First, Catherine dealt with the error of confusing
'nature and custom'. She accepted, for she could do nothing else, that
'the want of mental culture, the treatment of habit, the force of prejudice and the assumptions of the other sex, with their one-sided
interpretations of the Scriptures have hitherto almost excluded
[women] from this sphere'. But that did not mean there was anything
'either unnatural or immodest' in a Christian woman, 'becomingly
attired, appearing on a platform or a pulpit'. She went on more daringly to insist that 'by nature she seems fitted to grace either'. That
conclusion took her radical argument a stage further than the usual
demands for women to make occasional and irregular appearances at
the altar rails and pulpit. Most women preachers – including Phoebe
Palmer, to whose defence Catherine Booth had come – asked only that
they should be allowed to speak on occasions when God granted them
the gift of tongues, a limitation which, had it been imposed on the male
ministry, would have kept many chapels silent for most of the year.
Catherine Booth insisted that all women – properly equipped and genuinely called to service – had the right to preach regularly. As is always
the danger with textual analysis, some of the supporting arguments
seemed arcane and tortuous. Chapter IX of St Paul's Epistle to the
Corinthians insists in Verse 5 that 'every woman that prayeth or proph-
esieth with her head uncovered dishonoreth her[self]'. That, Catherine
concluded with impeccable formal logic, confirmed that female preaching was not excluded *per se*. Had there been a general prohibition,
there would have been no need to prohibit bare heads. However, Verse
34 asserts, more famously, 'Let your women keep quiet in church.'
Catherine resolved the contradiction by what she at least regarded as
'the simple common sense view'. In her judgement, the two passages

referred to distinct and fundamentally different occasions. Women were allowed, indeed should be encouraged, to take a full part in 'devotional and religious services'. They were not, however, entitled to participate in 'political and disciplinary assemblies'. It is not clear how, apart from the exercise of mental agility, Catherine came to that conclusion. Nor does the exclusion of women from the management of chapel and circuit seem, by today's standards, remotely progressive. But at the time the demand for the regular right to preach was the equivalent of scriptural revolution. And Catherine went on to declare theological civil war. For – with equally careful reference to the context – she insisted, as her second contention, that the Bible provides ample authority for full female ministry. That demand was not easy to reconcile with the acceptance that women should be debarred from political and disciplinary debate – a concession which she was happy to withdraw with the passing of the years. But the demand was, in itself, heroically audacious. And the arguments by which it was supported came close to being genuine biblical scholarship.

Deborah, Huldah and Miriam were Old Testament female ministers who had found favour in the sight of God. And there were, she explained, numerous New Testament women who had spread God's word with the Lord's categorical approval. Her star witness was Mary Magdalene – God's choice (as reported in St Matthew's Gospel, Chapter XXVI, Verses 9 and 10) to announce the joyful news of the resurrection. 'Mary was expressly commissioned to reveal the fact to the Apostles; and thus she literally became their teacher on that memorable occasion. Oh the glorious privilege of being able to herald the glad tidings of the Saviour risen!' She went on to wonder why, the case for female ministry being irrefutable, men had rejected it for so long. The answer which she provided to her own question was both a classic statement of woman's moral superiority and an implicit condemnation of male unreliability. Many female liberationists of the twentieth century would endorse it without qualification. Men were ashamed even to consider why a woman had brought the Easter Sunday message: 'One reason might be that the male disciples were missing at the time . . . Woman was there as she has ever been ready to minister to her risen or dying Lord.'[21]

Catherine could have chosen Mary 'the mother of James and John' as the keystone on which her argument rested, for she too had been chosen to reveal the work of God to man. But that Mary had been given no more than a supporting role in the great drama, while Mary Magdalene was selected to occupy centre stage in order to emphasise the importance of a sinner come to repentance. The suggestion that the two women were chosen because no man was available was not conclusive proof that God held both sexes in equal esteem. But Catherine also had the second chapter of the Acts of the Apostles on which to rely. Peter at Pentecost promised that 'your sons and daughters shall prophesy'. But even that was not the strongest point she had to make. What she regarded as conclusive proof of her argument was contained in St Paul's Epistle to the Galatians, Chapter III, Verse 28. It was a text to which, throughout her life, she was to return time after time: 'There is neither Jew nor Greek, there is neither bound nor free, there is neither male nor female, for you are all one in Christ Jesus.'

Inevitably, the Wesleyan establishment spoke out against her. As if to illustrate her point of view (and confirm Catherine's criticism of prejudiced custom) the Reverend James Stacey, editor of the *Wesleyan Times*, asked for a copy of the pamphlet in a letter which he addressed not to Catherine, its female author, but to William, the male head of her household. He disagreed with the views he had still to read. Mrs Booth replied in a soft answer which may have turned away his wrath but ended with an elegant rebuke:

> My dear husband informs me that you have expressed a wish to see one of my pamphlets on Female Teaching . . . I am conscious that I have done nothing like justice to this very important subject but it is my intention shortly to write on it again, in which case I should esteem it a great favour if you would allow me to trouble you for a critical examination of the original with reference to a few controversial places.[22]

The florid assertion of respect with which the letter ended was followed by a postscript. 'Allow me to ask if you have seen *The Promise of the Father* by Mrs Palmer. If not I should have great pleasure in forwarding it for your perusal. It is a large book addressed chiefly to minister and contains much valuable matter on the subject of female agency in the church.'[23] Mr Stacey replied without reference to the 'large book' but with a promise to read the pamphlet at the first opportunity. He then made further criticism of the pamphlet which he had not read, including an offensive reference to one of the authorities whose work Catherine had quoted: 'Dr Clarke's authority weighs very little with me as it has little weight anywhere.' He then wrote, some scholars might think rather belatedly, 'I must read before I criticise.'[24]

However, his letter did contain a brief summary of his general views on the subject and revealed a weakness in his argument. Catherine pounced. Stacey had made the mistake of conceding part of her case – always an error with the Booths, who never took an inch where a yard was available. 'You say, my dear sir, that you do not object to female teaching in the general sense. Then you admit of a *qualification* of the passage, "I suffer not a woman to teach" for taken literally this forbids all sorts of teaching whatsoever. The question to be settled is, what kind of qualification do the principles and general bearing of the New Testament render necessary?'[25]

Stacey's reply – expressing his continued disagreement – still contained no evidence to suggest that he had familiarised himself with Catherine's initial argument, although he repeated his rejection of her conclusions. But he had been forced, whether he realised it or not, to dispute her theology on equal terms. Catherine's letters had been typically punctuated with apologies for writing at such length and 'taking up so much of your time'. But, although unworthy either to contest his scholarship or reasoning, she did not withdraw the smallest part of her original contention or concede any detail of his counter-argument. And she ended with what, if he understood its implications, Mr Stacey could only have regarded as a gross impertinence. After making clear that the pamphlet's references to ignorance and prejudice were not a reference to all teaching in the New Connexion College, she then observed, 'It is not the formal worldly minded professors who experience the urgings of the spirit to open their lips for Jesus, but generally those who are most eminent for piety and unreserved consecration to the service of their Saviour.'

The pamphlet and the correspondence which followed were all part of Catherine Booth's principled concern to establish women's place in the church. But, although her early biographers insist that she was not preparing her own way, there is no doubt that the idea of preaching appealed to her. In Brighouse she had taught a class of thirteen teenage girls and then moved on to 'a senior class of twenty-nine members, many of them elderly'. When, two days before Christmas Day 1857, she had addressed the Band of Hope, she 'got on far better' than she had expected and 'felt quite at home on the platform, far more than I do in the kitchen'.[26] She intended 'one day to become a successful lecturer' – not least in the hope that she could contribute both to domestic expenses and repay some of the help her mother had provided during the year before the Mumford bankruptcy. 'I very much *desire* to earn some money some way . . . When we were in Cornwall I went to hear a very popular female lecturer and felt very *encouraged* to try my hand . . . I only wish I had begun years ago. Had I been fortunate enough to have been brought up among the Primitives, I believe I should have been preaching now.'[27]

According to folklore, 'Nothing is less true than that Catherine Booth took naturally to public ministry. At each successive step, she was drawn forward against her natural opposition.'[28] She was, the mythmakers insisted, urged on by the mysterious voices which, significantly, her husband never claimed to hear. William Booth heard the call to preach as he *recovered* from fever, not while his fever was high. The message was conveyed to Catherine by what she believed to be the 'inward urging of the Holy Ghost', while recuperating from the birth of Emma on 8 January 1860, her fourth child in less than four years. Recalled in old age, it was more than the instruction to preach. It was the demand that she take up the full female ministry.

Catherine undoubtedly welcomed her supernatural visitor. And if, as she later suggested, she was at first too 'timid and bashful' to obey the instruction which she received, her character certainly changed over the years. It was several months before she responded to the call, and even then, according to her own testimony, she needed the Holy Ghost to remind her that she had failed to follow His earlier suggestion.

William Booth planned that Whitsunday 1860 should be marked by a rally on the Windmill Hills, his modified version of a Camp Meeting. But the weather was too stormy for an outside event, so a congregation of more than a thousand was crowded into the Bethesda Chapel. Catherine sat in the front row with four-year-old Bramwell on her knee, while one by one visiting preachers and local dignitaries testified to the goodness of the Lord and their obedience to His will. Suddenly, a voice within Catherine told her to do the same. At first she resisted. Then she recalled the visitation of the previous January and feared that she was defying the will of God. She 'felt that she would rather die than speak. And then the devil said, "Besides you are not prepared. You will look a fool and you have nothing to say."' He over-reached himself for once – it was his words that changed her mind and gave her courage. Catherine decided, 'I have not yet been willing to be a fool for Christ. Now I will be one.' God's will was done.

> Without stopping another moment I rose up from my seat and walked down the aisle. My dear husband was just going to conclude. He thought that something had happened to me and so did the people. We had been there two years and they knew my timid and bashful nature. He stepped down and asked me, 'What is the matter, my dear?' I replied, 'I want to say a word.' He was so taken by surprise that he could only say, 'My dear wife wishes to speak,' and sat down.[29]

According to Catherine's account, William's surprise was increased by her previous outright rejection of every suggestion that she should address the Gateshead congregation – conduct not altogether consistent with her view on the right of women to preach and her stated wish to give regular lectures. But on Whitsunday 1860 she decided that silence was a sin and was able, therefore, to begin her preaching career, on God's explicit instruction: 'I have been living in disobedience and, to that extent, I have brought darkness and leanness into my soul. I have promised the Lord to do so no longer and have come to tell you that, henceforth, I will be obedient to the holy vision.'

Once again Divine Providence – heavily disguised as always when visiting the Booths – intervened to send Catherine's destiny hurtling on. Her career as a New Connexion preacher began almost the moment that she sat down at the end of the first 'testimony'. William, although happier in Gateshead than he had ever been in Brighouse, still believed that he had been humiliated by the church which ordained him. Life in salvation's backwater had become so intolerable that he was near to total collapse. At first he stayed at home and looked after the children while Catherine took on his pastoral duties. Then, at the point of complete breakdown in September 1860, he took up residence in Smedley's hydro in Matlock and there he remained for a full nine weeks. Hydropathic medicine was not a normal treatment for psychological disorders, but Catherine had come to believe that it cured all ills. And she was quite prepared – despite the difficulty of mothering four small children who had inconveniently caught whooping cough – to perform her husband's duties while he was away. In effect she became the New Connexion circuit minister for Gateshead *pro tempore*. And she loved it.

By the turn of the year, she was sufficiently sure of herself to boast to her parents, 'I get plenty of invitations now, more than I can comply with.' At least locally she had become a personality. The newspapers had seen a woman preaching and they reported it with the disapproving incredulity with which they would have described a dog walking on its hind legs. 'In one of them I am represented as having my husband's clothes on! They would require to be considerably shortened would they not?' Her joy – in notoriety as well as achievement – was clearly boundless. But it was a naïve delight that she took in savouring the pleasures of a world from which she remained completely detached. 'Notwithstanding all that I have heard about the papers, I have never had sufficient curiosity to buy one, nor have I ever seen my name in print.'[30] Two months later, the joy was still too great to be disguised: 'I am just in my element in the work. I only regret that I did not commence *years ago*.'[31]

The moment at which her preaching career began might have been chosen by fate. William Booth's relationship with the New Connexion had reached breaking point – principally because he was simply not prepared to accept the restraints which were imposed upon him. He had already enjoyed brief relationships with two other Wesleyan churches and with the Congregationalists. If he chose to leave the New Connexion, all that was available to him was an independent ministry – the dangerous course against which James Caughey had warned him. But although independent, he would no longer be alone. There were two preachers ready to go, hand in hand, out into the wilderness.

6

Not Called but Chosen

If, during the early weeks of 1861, William Booth felt the slightest doubt about his duty to evangelise rather than to perform the humdrum duties of a circuit minister, they had all disappeared by the end of February. For it was then that the Booths entered into the state of 'holiness', the full 'sanctification' to which all pious Methodists aspired. Catherine described the miraculous moment in a letter to her mother which reproduced exactly the language of redemption as it was used by revivalist preachers of both the instantaneous and gradual persuasions. Had the account been copied out of Phoebe Palmer's *The Way of Holiness* it would not have been significantly different:

> I struggled through the day until a little after six, William
> joined me in prayer. We had a blessed session. While he was
> saying, 'Lord we open our hearts to receive Thee,' that word
> was spoken to my soul. Behold I stand at the door. Knock if
> any man hear my voice and open unto Me. I will come in and
> sup with him. I felt that He had long been knocking and oh
> how I longed to receive Him the perfect Saviour! But the
> inveterate habit of unbelief! How good that God should have
> borne so long with me. When we got up from our knees, I lay

on the sofa exhausted with the excitement and effort of the day.[1]

Then, according to Catherine's account, her husband adopted the exact language of instant salvation. William said,

> 'Don't you lay all on the altar?' I replied, 'I believe I do.' Then he said, 'And isn't the altar holy?' I replied in the language of the Holy Ghost. 'The altar is most holy and whoever toucheth it is most holy'. Then he said, 'Are you not holy?' I replied with some emotion and my heart full of faith, 'Oh I think I am.' Immediately the word was given me to confirm my faith, 'Now you are clear through the word which I have spoken to you . . .'

The orgasmic quality of the experience was confirmed by the joyous lassitude which followed. Just as Phoebe Palmer promised, Catherine's 'rapturous joy' turned into 'perfect peace, the sweet rest' which Jesus promised to the heavily laden. 'I have,' she told her mother, 'understood the Apostle's meaning when he says we who believe do enter into rest.'

By their nature, mystical experiences are always open to doubt. And Catherine's account of her instant and spontaneous sanctification is uncomfortably close to what the true believer had been encouraged to expect. She certainly believed that the events which she described happened in the way she set them out. But it is at least possible that, unconsciously, she was following the formula set out by her heroine, Phoebe Palmer. But the origin of the experience hardly matters. Whatever the reason, the Booths believed that they were the instruments of God. And the sanctification of February 1861 helped to confirm the belief that God wanted them to work in partnership. The pronouns used in Frederick Booth-Tucker's biography of Catherine Booth, his mother-in-law – officially sanctioned and published by the Salvation Army two years after her death in 1890 – change after the story reaches 1861. They begin to reflect the idea of a spiritual alliance which characterised the Booths' evangelism for the last thirty years of their married life. After Catherine's 'sanctification' she acquired a new authority. Encouraged by the state of mutual grace, the Booths determined to make one more attempt to follow what they had clearly decided was their common destiny. Their letter to the President of the Conference arguing for a renewal of the roving commission ended by 'offering *themselves* for reappointment to the evangelistic sphere'. The New Connexion could have acquired two preachers for the price of one.

The letter, dated 5 March 1861, began by reminding the President that if he chose to deny William Booth's request he would be arguing with God. 'During the period when I was contemplating joining the New Connexion, the Lord opened my way in a very remarkable manner to the work of an evangelist.' It then set out alternative ways in which the Lord's will (and William Booth's) could be done. The first was clearly William's preference: 'The Conference to employ me in the following or some similar manner; a) To reside in some town centre to our interests and to labour in the churches immediately around it . . . b) To labour under the direction of the President of the Conference . . . c) My salary to be the same as other ministers, to be obtained by the place where I labour giving so much a week for my services . . . d) Every church where I laboured successfully to be requested to make an offering towards a fund to enable me to labour in poor churches . . .' The second possibility, at least in William Booth's mind, was for 'Conference to grant me a location allowing my name to appear in the minutes and recognising me as a regular minister of that body with the privilege of returning to the itinerary when the Providence of God might direct'.[2]

The reply to William Booth did not come until the end of May, and while the Booths were waiting they preached. They went together to Hartlepool where accounts of the services confirm that Catherine registered her first evangelistic triumph:

> On Good Friday March 29th we had public service in the morning, Mrs Booth delivering a most excellent exposition of Pentecost . . . The large congregation listened with the most marked attention – those especially who had come prejudiced against female preaching . . . On Monday evening Mrs Booth preached the concluding sermon of the anniversary services. The sermon produced a most powerful impression and it was evident to all that if Mrs Booth could continue the services, great good would be done. This she kindly consented to do, preaching on the evenings of Tuesday, Wednesday and Friday:

after each service many persons found the blessing of
justification . . . On Sabbath evening April 7th so great was the
numbers flocking to the sanctuary that the chapel was filled to
overflowing . . . Mrs Booth left us on Tuesday April 9th and up
to that date 140 persons had found pardon.[3]

The extraordinary feature of that report was what it omitted. William
Booth was there as well. But he was mentioned only in passing.
Although Catherine was undoubtedly benefiting from sanctification,
the experience had not insulated her from the sin of pride: 'Oh it was
glorious work . . . I hear that they have only taken twenty names since
I left. I hardly expected that Doctor Cooke would put a report in the
Magazine though I knew one had been sent.'[4]

Elated though she was by her success as a preacher Catherine
remained, at least in her own mind, first and foremost her husband's
staff and support. So she prepared for the 1861 Annual Conference in
Liverpool with profound foreboding. She was determined that William
would resume his work as travelling evangelist – perhaps even more
determined than he was himself. But she was the mother of four young
children, the eldest of whom was still not five, and she was married to
a man with no obvious talent except preaching and a tendency to
develop sudden and mysterious illnesses at moments of great pressure.
There was no doubt in her mind that, if William's destiny was denied
him, he would have to resign from the New Connexion ministry. For to
accept that his work must be limited to one circuit was to defy God's
undoubted will. She was certainly not spoiling for a fight. Indeed, she
looked forward to Liverpool with nothing but apprehension. 'My heart
almost fails me in going to Conference and leaving the children
behind.' However, there was no doubt where her duty lay. 'William
would really like me to advise with, in case he is brought into a com-
plexing position.'[5]

The Conference having decided how William Booth should be
employed, only the Conference could change the terms of his employment. As the day of the debate approached Catherine grew increasingly
nervous. 'The time for consideration of our case is now drawing near.
We anticipate some very sharp fighting. Several of the leading preachers are as much opposed as ever but they are prepared to defend it to
the teeth and, as far as one can gather, all the lay members favour the

proposal.'[6] All the old allies had rallied to the cause. 'Mr Rabbits,' Catherine wrote, 'is getting ready for the occasion.' In fact he was doing what today would be described as lobbying, using both his own powers of persuasion and arranging for waverers to meet William Booth himself. Dr Cooke – who had forgiven William his wilful rejection of serious study – was primed to rebut the constitutional argument that to give William Booth a special status would be to found a new branch of the Connexion, an innovation for which the Poll Deed on which the church was founded made no provision.

Unfortunately, Dr Cooke had problems of his own. His re-appointment as editor of the *New Connexion Magazine*, for so long a formality, was being contested. In the debate which preceded a vote on his future, he was accused of 'clinging to office' and the speech in which he defended himself was regarded as 'morbidly sentimental'.[7] Although Conference re-appointed him, his confidence was badly shaken by the demonstration that he no longer enjoyed the wholehearted support of his colleagues. As a result he was not in the best psychological state to defend his protégé during the long and complicated series of debates which the legal advisers to the New Connexion had ruled were necessary to decide William's future. Cooke managed to fight his corner on the opening day. But the effort used up all his reserves of courage.

The Durham Districts' Annual Meeting, held in early 1861, had debated a proposal that William Booth (whose Gateshead circuit was in their area) should be 'set apart' to work as evangelist and, it being carried unanimously, had submitted it as a resolution to the Annual Conference. They had assumed that it would be debated in the usual way and, if carried, the post of peripatetic preacher would be created and offered to their resident minister. But the lawyers had insisted that three resolutions had to be debated. First it was necessary to approve the creation of an 'agency' by which William Booth could be employed – agreeing, either directly or by implication, that the decision was consistent with both the Poll Deed on which the New Connexion was founded and the scriptures which were its fundamental guide. The creation of the agency having been approved, it would then be necessary to appoint William Booth as its travelling evangelist. Thirdly, Conference would have to consider the Durham proposal – not in itself an issue of principle – that the peripatetic evangelist should begin his work in the north-east of England. Had the Durham

Resolution been carried, Conference would, in effect, have adopted the first of the alternatives which William Booth had proposed to the President. It was the scheme which gave him most freedom from the Annual Committee and the President and was, in consequence, the least attractive to delegates who had doubts about gratifying his ambitions. It was not, at least at the time when the letter was written, the only option which William was willing to accept. But as the debate progressed, the Durham Resolution was elevated by both Booths into a question of absolute and unnegotiable principle. It was, they insisted, that or nothing. They knew that God shared their determination for William to make all England his parish. So they had determined to do God's work on their own terms.

> In the afternoon a very long, anxious and spirited debate took place upon a series of resolutions from the Newcastle [Durham] District Meeting . . . The ground taken by some of the brethren was that the agency contemplated would make a fundamental change in the Connexion and that ere such a change could be effected, the circuit should have the proposal submitted to them in due form.[8]

The due form to which the opponents of the scheme referred was a change in the Poll Deed – which they claimed was constitutionally essential to legalise a new branch of the Connexion. Their interpretation of the constitution would have required the change to be proposed at one Conference, endorsed at the next and declared effective six years later. The best they offered William Booth was the prospect of roving evangelism in distant 1869.

The Reverend P. J. Wright – William Booth's old adversary from Nottingham – insisted that the constitution did not allow what amounted to the creation of a missionary institution for the conversion of heathen England. Dr Cooke, obviously nervous about his reception, pointed out that new agencies had been created, without constitutional change, to lead Methodist crusades to India and Ireland and that it would be perverse to ignore the precedent and deny the same blessing to Britain. The Conference decided by a large majority that it was compatible with the Deed Book to 'employ, if found necessary, a special agency for carrying on the work of God amongst us'.[9] It could not, either in conscience or logic, have decided anything else. Only the Booths' most bitter opponents voted with the Reverend Mr Wright. His more moderate critics waited to confound him by deciding that, whether or not a missionary agency was constitutionally possible, William Booth would not become the missionary agent.

It was an indication of Booth's fame in the New Connexion – itself a cause of offence to senior members – that the national Annual Conference should devote three of its sessions to determining his future. Just as Catherine had managed to elevate herself into the highest levels of theological debate, William had succeeded in becoming the centre of the controversy about how the Connexion should evangelise. However, he was not the only subject on the Liverpool agenda, and for two impatient days the Booths fretted while delegates witnessed the ordination of new ministers and the creation of a Methodist College in Sheffield. When what the *New Connexion Magazine* described (without intending offence) as the 'Booth Case' was considered by delegates for a second time, 'the ground being cleared of legal difficulty it was contended that, prior to Mr Booth's appointment as an evangelist being considered, the question should be settled as to the desirability of establishing such an agency',[10] the ever faithful Edward Rabbits spoke eloquently in favour of evangelism in general, though everybody knew that he was arguing the case for one evangelist in particular. The debate,

> while eliciting some diversity of sentiment on the part of
> individual members of Conference was, yet on the whole,
> distinguished by intelligence sobriety and straightforward-
> ness . . . When the debate had reached its climax and had been
> concluded a new and unexpected turn was given to it by a
> proposal which united the parties.

The magazine overestimated the degree of unanimity. The Booth supporters were happy enough, but the Booths themselves were devastated. The compromise resolution read, 'This Conference declares that any circuit, with the consent of the superintendent preacher, is at liberty to make such arrangements with any of our ministers and their circuits as may be found useful for holding revival services among them.'[11] Whether his supporters realised it or not, William Booth was never going to be satisfied with an appointment which amounted to very little more than the occasional excursions which he had been allowed in Gateshead. The wording was almost certainly designed by the Annual Committee in order to confound the pretensions of a presumptuous preacher without humiliating a man whose work was much admired by the rank and file of the New Connexion. The Booths explained their objections to their friends – some of whom had clearly given initial support to the compromise proposal for the understandable reason that they were growing weary of the Booths' continual demands. However, on the evidence of their reactions at the time and their recollections in old age, both William and Catherine believed that the Conference could still be persuaded to elevate William Booth above all others when resolutions, explicitly dealing with his future, were debated.

That was another example of a naïveté that remained with both the Booths for all their lives. For they did not realise why there was so much opposition to the idea of creating a travelling evangelist. To make William Booth special was to diminish the other preachers. Not only was he set apart from the regular circuit ministers. He would be sent into areas where his ministrations were particularly needed – and the necessity could only be the result of the resident's failure. When the *Wesleyan Times* reported the debate, it was clear how much personal resentment the proposal caused. 'Mr John Wittaker felt . . . that by employing such an agency they would be overriding the superintendents of circuits . . . Mr G. L. Robinson thought it would be like an Episcopacy in their church . . . the Reverend A. M'Curdy spoke against . . . any agency of special nature which . . . must shake the confidence of the great majority . . .' The Booths always attributed opposition to jealousy. Often it was the result of reaction against their presumption.

The final act of the drama was the examination of the Durham proposal that William should be appointed full-time evangelist. The Durham delegates made it known that a group of wealthy north-eastern Methodists (led by an anonymous colliery owner) would pay the itinerant's salary and cover the cost of his travel. The Reverend P. J. Wright – as indomitable as he was intransigent in his opposition to William Booth's ambition – insisted that the suggestion was certainly unconstitutional and probably illegal. Then William Booth himself was allowed to read the still unanswered letter which he had written to the Conference President. It did not conclude on a conciliatory note. Indeed its inherent arrogance must have antagonised many of the delegates whose support he desperately needed:

> I should very much deplore any unpleasant discussion at Conference. I could not consent to re-engage in the work by an insignificant majority. I sincerely and strongly desire to spend my time and energies in promoting the highest interests of the Connexion. I wish to labour with the fullest approbation and co-operation of my brethren, neither do I see any righteous reason why this should not be the case.[12]

To William's astonishment and Catherine's fury, Dr Cooke, until then the Booths' most articulate ally, then proposed what delegates were told was a second compromise. In fact it did no more than suggest the particular application of the general role which had already been agreed. It offered Conference the easy way out. So it was agreed that William should resume his duties as a circuit minister but be afforded time to accept invitations to preach in other parts of the country.

What happened next is open to dispute. According to the 'eyewitness' account of a Mr Gibson, who was sitting next to Catherine in the gallery, a general but subdued frisson of resentment ran through William Booth's supporters. Gibson 'saw Mrs Booth and her friends rise up and move towards the steps of the gallery'.[13] The Conference was about to move into private sessions and Gibson was not clear if the Booth supporters were leaving in protest or in anticipation of the call for visitors to withdraw. Whichever version of their exit is correct, folklore demanded something more dramatic. According to both Frederick Booth-Tucker, Catherine's son-in-law, and Kate Booth-Clibborn, her daughter, Mrs Booth rose from her seat in the gallery and, in glorious defiance of both rules and respectability, cried 'Never!' in her loudest voice – which was very loud indeed. The family's version of events (and in consequence the description of the day given in the 'official' biographies) must have been provided or at least confirmed by William Booth himself. Only he could have described how, responding to his wife's call, he stood up, bowed to the President and, waving his hat in the air – either in tribute to his wife or to show his contempt for

squalid compromise – walked out of the Conference followed by astonished cries of 'Order! Order!'

Perhaps the moment of glorious defiance did happen in the way
which, forty years later, Salvation Army leaflets described. If so,
William Booth acted against his usually cautious instincts. Previous res-
ignations had been preceded by at least attempts to find alternative
employment and the letters, which described his dissatisfaction with
the churches which employed him, had rarely failed to balance the
demands of principle against the need to support first his widowed
mother and then his wife and children. Before the Booths left for the
1861 Conference Catherine, fearful that her husband would capitulate
and return to his circuit, had asked, 'Does the security of our bread and
cheese make right what is wrong?' Of course, she came down on the
side of principled starvation, and no doubt she argued the case to
William. But hungry honour did not prevail. The 'walk out', if it ever
happened, was literal on the day but not a symbol of his refusal to
accept the Conference's judgement. If Catherine Booth did cry 'Never!'
to the thought of compromise, her husband ate her words.

Pride and dignity prevented William Booth from capitulating at
once. So, in all probability, did Catherine. They were still agonising
about the future in their Liverpool lodgings when a deputation of delegates – including Dr Crofts – arrived with the request that they make
no immediate or irrevocable decision before the Conference took a
formal vote on the compromise resolution. They also promised, by way
of added inducement, that William could make a final plea to
Conference on his own behalf. After much anxious consultation, the
Booths agreed to wait. And waiting, as Dr Cooke shrewdly calculated,
inevitably led to surrender.

Over the next twenty-four hours, the Booths had two almost equally
unattractive possibilities to consider. William could resign there and
then, knowing that his resignation would not be formally accepted
until the following year's Conference but that he would lose his home
and salary at once, leaving his family to survive on what he might
earn as an independent preacher. The alternative required him to give
prudence precedence over pride. The Cooke delegation described his
second option in the most persuasive language which good Wesleyans
could employ. William, they suggested, had a Christian duty at least to
test the good intentions of the Annual Committee. Their good faith was

symbolised in a formal proposal that William Booth should return to the north-east as Superintendent of Newcastle ('one of the most important in the Connexion'[14]) and that an assistant should be appointed to perform some of the more routine tasks so as to allow time for preaching in other parts of the country. It was in its way a generous offer which, as well as providing the opportunity for roving evangelism, set William apart from other circuit ministers – no doubt to the chagrin of the Reverend Mr Wright. But it was not an arrangement that either of the Booths could accept with anything except reluctance and resentment. They accepted it, nevertheless. Catherine's recrimination makes clear that the break with the New Connexion had not been abandoned – only postponed.

Catherine's reaction to the decision was not a shining example of Christian charity:

> We should have had a majority but for his empty and foolish offer. P. J. Wright only laughed at it and no man of perception could do any other. Mr Cooke lost our cause and I find it very difficult to rid myself of the opinion, and so do others, that he offered up my husband on the altar between the parties in order to procure for himself a reappointment to the Editorship.[15]

The timing of the two debates suggests that she grievously misjudged Dr Cooke. But the Booths did not forgive easily. They were already looking for new friends. In deep despair, Catherine wrote to James Caughey: 'I am sick of the New Connexion from top to bottom. I have lost all faith in its ministry and I see nothing for it but slow consumption.'[16] The members – as distinct from the ministers – of the New Connexion were not sick of William Booth. When his fate was finally decided the people of Gateshead were respectfully informed that his departure from the town 'where he has laboured with great earnestness, zeal and ability for the Spiritual Good of the People' was to be marked by a public testimonial. By a process of logic which does not stand much analysis William Booth believed testimonials to be literally acceptable, as distinct from gifts which had to be refused with thanks. There is no record of how much the Methodists of Gateshead raised. Almost all the Booths' financial affairs, although always proper in virtually every particular, are shrouded in the mystery which both he, and his supporters, thought necessary to his dignity. But the existence of the testimonial – by no means a feature of every New Connexion minister's departure from his circuit – illustrates the high esteem in which he was held.

Catherine was clearly party to the move. William would never have accepted Newcastle without her agreement. But she insisted from the start, 'We will get nothing out of it but trouble and vexation. This I have seen from the beginning and have opposed the coming as far as I could . . . I see very plainly that my husband may spend his life and waste his energies in saving one [circuit] after another for some listless drone to come in and let it down again.'[17] Nothing was right about the Newcastle appointment. The house which had been provided for them was 'filthy in the extreme' and located in what the tribune of the godless poor surprisingly described as 'a wretched neighbourhood'. Within weeks of her arrival she had made up her mind that resignation was, sooner or later, unavoidable. 'Wm. is afraid. He thinks of me and the children and I appreciate his love and care, but I tell him God will provide as long as he goes on the path of duty.' She feared, with good cause as it turned out, that the 'Annual Committee will not even allow the arrangement with the circuit to be carried out and I don't see any honourable alternative for us but to resign'.[18]

In July 1861 the *New Connexion Magazine* virtually advertised William Booth's services as travelling preacher. William's reputation guaranteed that invitations began to arrive in Newcastle within days of the magazine's publication. And his temperament made it equally certain that he would accept them without reference to any authority. The National Committee, with equal consistency, suspected that the Conference's carefully balanced decision was being ignored. So Dr Crofts, the new President of the Conference, wrote to ask that he be sent a copy of 'the arrangements come to with the Newcastle circuit'. Catherine agreed that William should send them as requested but told her mother, 'If they object, I shall urge him to resign . . . The fact is, I am but poorly and almost bewildered with fatigue and anxiety.'[19]

Whether or not William had flouted the Committee's wishes before he received the President's letter, he certainly did so after it arrived in Newcastle. He had assumed that he would be invited to preach all over England. But some circuits – controlled not by members but by

Trustees and ministers – knew that he was in conflict with the Annual Committee and Conference and were, in consequence, reluctant to ask him to speak in their chapels. Perhaps more motivated by insecurity than defiance, William decided to visit London in an attempt to drum up business. He knew that when the inevitable break came, his wife and children would have to live on sermon fees. So he sought advice from whoever was prepared to give it. Mr Hammond, a famous Methodist benefactor, heard his story and advised, 'Cut the denomination and go for Jesus.' He then explained his meaning by suggesting that William get in touch with 'a committee in Glasgow who are only too glad to get the right sort of men and find them a sphere'. But Hammond warned, 'You must not go to them as a Methodist.' George Pearse, a noted itinerant preacher, warned that for the first few months William would 'need a friend or two who would ask the children, have you any bread?' Even William Carter – a famous working-class evangelist who 'held many of the notions of the Plymouth Brethren' – was approached. He received many requests to nominate suitable speakers and offered to set William to work at once.[20] It was not a moment for qualms about consorting with Calvinists.

William Booth did preach once while he was in London – two short addresses given during one service for working men in the Garrick Theatre. But by the end of his visit, he had decided that his future did not lie in the independent ministry. It may be, as his supporters later claimed, that loyalty prevented him from leaving the New Connexion, and that he was eventually driven out by the envious leadership. Conversely it is argued that he accepted the Newcastle circuit because he realised that the demand for independent professional preachers was falling fast, and realised that he did not have the exotic qualities to allow him to succeed in such adverse circumstances.[21] Whatever the reason, he determined to return to Newcastle. Waiting for him when he got home was a letter from the President of the Conference. It accused him of breaking his agreement with his own circuit and demanded an assurance that, in future, he would keep his word. William was about to set off again to fulfil a preaching engagement in Nottingham, but concluded, after much thought, that before he left he must resign as minister-in-charge of the Newcastle circuit.

The letter of resignation began with a tedious and legalistic complaint about the President's failure to refer to alleged neglect of the

Newcastle circuit in earlier letters. The rest was even less conciliatory.
For it was then necessary to explain why, less than two months earlier,
he had accepted the Newcastle commission when he understood the
limitation that it placed upon him. 'I informed the Standing Committee
and afterwards the Conference, both orally and by letter, that I could
not take the responsibility of the Newcastle appointment, but still the
Committee persisted in it.' He had hoped that the Liverpool compromise would allow him another year in the New Connexion 'without
sacrificing conviction'. The President's letters had convinced him that
he had been mistaken. 'Therefore, intensely painful though it be, I
place my resignation in your hands.' There was a heartfelt expression
of regret that his decision would expose people whom he loved 'to loss
and difficulty' and then a final flourish which must have driven Dr
Crofts to fury.

> Trusting in God alone, I offer myself for the evangelistic work,
> in the first instance to our own Connexional churches and,
> when they decline to engage me, to other portions of the
> religious community. I offer myself to co-operate in conducting
> special services or preaching to outlying crowds of our
> populations in theatre, halls or in the open air.[22]

Once again William Booth had chosen to go his own way rather than
accept the discipline of his chosen church. It was an exhibition of
courage as well as of conviction. For, apart from the psalmist's assurance that the righteous are never forsaken, he had no reason to believe
that he could earn a comfortable living outside the New Connexion.
But his sense of destiny was so strong that, after his initial hesitation,
he was not prepared to let anything stand between him and his vocation to convert the world. Certainty about his duty made him reckless,
arrogant and impatient with even the friendliest disagreement – qualities essential to saints and martyrs.

It was left to Catherine, writing her daily letter to her parents, to
describe the trauma they had both felt as the deed was done, 'after a
day's anxiety and fervent prayer'. William announced his decision to
the Nottingham prayer meeting which he attended the day after the
resignation was posted. To Catherine's delight, the resident minister,
'instead of getting up to defend the Connexion, said that while he

deeply regretted the step which Mr Booth had taken, nevertheless could not but honour him for acting on his conviction'.[23]

In the summer of 1861 Catherine, unwell again, travelled down from Newcastle to live with her mother. William and the children followed by sea, the cheapest form of transport. Mary Kirton, the family maid, travelled with them, swearing that she would remain with the Booths with or without pay. It had been a bad year for Bramwell, Ballington, Kate and Emma Booth – at least, if measured against their mother's belief that only close and continual contact with parents can guarantee a proper Christian upbringing. During the early months of the year, when Catherine was enjoying her first preaching triumph in Hartlepool, she assured her mother, 'The children were all pretty well when I heard last . . . William says he does not think they are suffering from my absence, neither do I believe the Lord will allow them to suffer.' Her faith was justified. On her return she was able to report, 'The children are well. Willy gets on nicely with his lessons. They all come on charmingly. Baby gets a real pet – such a mama's girl as none of them have been'[24] – a remarkable attribute in a child who saw so little of her mother. The reunion at the Mumfords did not last long. By the end of August *The Revival*, 'A Weekly Record of Events Connected With the Present Revival of Religion', was reporting a freelance Booth campaign in Cornwall. The children were left once more in London. The Mumfords, either out of concern for their daughter's health or because of a reluctance to continue in the onerous role of surrogate parents, urged Catherine to stay with them until William's future was settled. But she would not even consider the possibility of separation from her husband. The children's moral education was therefore left in the hands of their grandmother – amply augmented by uplifting letters, some of which Mrs Mumford was enjoined to read aloud to Bramwell 'two or three times before he goes to bed at night, so that it may affect his heart the more'. Sometimes the letters contained dire warnings. 'I have never known a naughty child to be happy in my life.' Occasionally they were apologetic: 'I fear you begin to think it is a long time before Papa comes to fetch you.' One at least was prophetic: 'I hope you do not quarrel with Ballington . . .' The quarrel was at least postponed for thirty years.[25]

The Cornwall campaign was the longest separation of the year – so

long that Catherine vowed never to be parted from her children again.
William Booth regarded his instant re-employment as a literal godsend.
It was, in truth, the reward for the record of evangelical success which,
by the age of thirty-two, he had already built up. The Reverend John
Stone – converted during William's 'Chester Revival' and, for a time, his
colleague in Gateshead – had become minister at Hayle and he invited
his old friend to preach in his chapel. The building, the Reverend Mr
Stone warned, was small, the congregation frigid and the prospects of
remuneration at best in doubt. But William had nowhere else to go. So
he accepted. He wrote his own account of the expedition for *The Revival*,
describing himself as 'just having relinquished his connection as preacher
with one of the sections of the Methodist denomination in order to
devote himself more unrestrictedly to the work of itinerant evangelist'.[26]

Cornwall was historically unresponsive to sermons of passion. The
congregations listened attentively and occasionally murmured assent.
But there was rarely the explosion of emotion that an evangelist needs
to stimulate the first conversion that sets the service alight. According
to his own account, William Booth changed all that:

> A strong prejudice prevails here against the custom of inviting
> anxious inquirers to any particular part of the chapel. The
> friends told me that this plan never had succeeded in Cornwall
> but thought it best considering the crowded state of the Chapel
> to try it. Gave a short address and again invited those who were
> decided for Christ to come forward. After waiting a moment or
> two, the solemn silence was broken by the cries of a woman
> who at once left her pew, fell down at the anxious seat and
> became the first fruits of what I hope will be a glorious harvest
> of immortal souls. She was quickly followed by others, when
> such a scene ensued as is beyond description. The cries and
> groans were piercing in the extreme.[27]

William Booth clearly regarded traditional Cornish reticence as the
devil's way of defying the will of God. And he gladly took up the challenge to break down the wall of emotional modesty which stood
between sinners and their conversion. In mid-September there were
'strong men, old men, young men weeping like children, broken-
hearted on account of their sins'.[28] But by the end of the month he was

worrying again about whether the seeds he had sown would be properly cultivated. Hayle had witnessed an 'unquestionably great and genuine revival'.[29] But 'in all great revivals there will ever be some who, unwilling to make the great sacrifice that Christianity receives, obtain false hope and only endure for a season'. When he moved on from Hayle to St Ives – where he arrived at the height of the pilchard season and therefore found most of the population preoccupied – he again noted that 'many live on the church, anxious to do the will of God and yet are perpetually harassed as to whether they are Christians'.[30] His explanation of their trauma was that 'they have never given up the world and forsaken all to follow Christ'. Slowly the idea of a new mass movement was coming into his head – pietists out in the world, a sect which was (in all particulars except its faith) like ordinary men and women and, as well as appealing to the people whom the church ignored, held them fast to the faith by which they lived their daily lives.

Although the intellectual in the partnership, Catherine Booth was, temporarily at least, prepared to live for the present. She rejoiced at the sight of 'great strong men, who cried aloud for mercy, some of them as if the pains of hell actually had hold of them'.[31] Years later, speaking of the Cornwall campaign, she explained (slightly disingenuously) that the

> unusual noise and confusion was somewhat foreign to our notions and practices. William believed very strongly in everything being done decently and in order. Indeed I think that he sometimes mistook the application of this direction . . . How much better to have twenty people smiting their breasts and crying, 'God be merciful to me a sinner' with its necessary consequent commotion than a congregation of equally guilty sinners sitting with still propriety and, in their estimation, needing no repentance.[32]

William Booth's enthusiasm for decency and order was intimately related to his belief in discipline. He wanted his repentant sinners to scream for forgiveness. But he wanted it to happen on the word of command. On the night which followed Catherine Booth's joy at strong men crying he sternly told his congregation, 'When I say "Sing!" we must sing. When I say "Pray!" we must pray. Those willing to co-operate put up their hands.'[33] There was a unanimous vote to follow the preacher's instructions. In consequence the elation, ecstasy and occasional hysteria which promoted repentance were kept firmly under his control. In fact, there were very few devices which William Booth was not prepared to employ or exploit in the pursuit of saved souls. During the Cornwall campaign, a young woman went into a trance and 'held a conversation with her dead father'. It was the first time at which the Booths came face to face with spiritualism – a by-product of the belief in immortality about which they were always sceptical but never totally dismissive. In the south-west William positively welcomed the manifestation and described it as one of the 'signs and wonders' which the gospels promised.

Cornwall proved a hard testing ground and an eloquent teacher. William Booth used his experience to refine his methods. Cornish sin-ners, invited to the communion rail to pray for forgiveness, cried out, 'Cannot we be saved here? Is God not as willing to do it here as there?' There were perfectly respectable theological answers to their ques-tions – all of them concerned with the necessity to make a sign and volunteer complete obedience. But William was not the man to provide them. He had no time for private redemption and the strongest possi-ble professional interest in sinners not only standing up but being counted in public. In Cornwall he expressed his contempt for the closet convert. 'Until he surrenders unconditionally, Christ cannot save him – he will read, weep and pray in secret, but let the Church and the world know that he is a penitent – never!'[34]

Numerically at least, the Booth technique was as successful in St Ives as it had been in Hayle – so successful that the Booths turned down an invitation to join Phoebe Palmer in Liverpool, ready to take her place if it was necessary for her sick husband to return to America. Their admiration did not extend to playing a supporting role in Lancashire when they had a chance to star in Cornwall.

The campaign continued into 1862. His converts were not confined to one class, but amongst them were 'ladies, men of independent means, captains, tradesmen as well as drunkards and swearers . . .'[35] In March the faithful Edward Rabbits, 'being a short distance from the present scene of Rev. Booth's labours . . . determined to pay a visit to St Just'. He gave details of 'the most extraordinary work of God ever witnessed'. William had an unusual capacity to inspire loyalty even in those he treated badly. And, by the early summer, Mrs Booth's labours had won another convert to the feminine cause. *The Revival* began to write of evangelists in the plural, and 'CTS', its special correspondent, was totally won over. 'We confess ourselves to have been disarmed of our criticism and our long cherished antipathy to female preaching somehow melted out of our hearts.'[36] Catherine's sermons could warn that 'flashy dressing leads as many girls to destruction as does drink' without fearing that she would be accused of not living up to her own exacting standards. But when she compared a child brought up without love to a plant brought up without sun, she must sometimes have worried about her continual absence from her own children. There was no doubt that she loved them. But she was not an attentive mother by nature and her husband's vocation, combined with her reluctance to be parted from him, made her conduct difficult to distinguish from negligence. There was a family reunion in St Ives. But even then she did not have an opportunity to pay her children much attention. She was pregnant again – the fifth time in six years. And her condition was complicated by all the old illnesses.

Weighed down both by sickness and by the restrictions imposed by so much child bearing in so little time, Catherine was beginning to feel depressed. 'What I feel most of all is the uselessness of the life I am living . . . I am ready to die at the prospect of another such nine months as in the past.'[37] Inspired by the imminent arrival, when her mother wrote with news of another Mumford financial crisis, she suggested that a baby-linen business might prove profitable. Her second proposal was a return to an old theme. The Mumfords should 'furnish a good house and take in boarders'. She even offered 'to take all the risks and find the capital, if you will go into it and divide the profits'.[38] Perhaps at the time that she suggested it the investment was a practical proposition. But a month later the Booths' own finances came under sudden pressure. William had hoped to earn considerable sums by publishing his sermons in pamphlet form, but unfortunately no one wanted to buy them.

It was not in Catherine's nature to stay despondent for long. When 'the Chairman of the local Methodists declared it contrary to the rules and usage for females to speak in their chapels', she rejoiced that 'no unsympathetic ministerial class of men can whisk us off two or three hundred miles across country. No, that bondage has ended. Never more to be endured . . . We are higher, more useful and more prosperous in every way than we ever were before.'[39] It was just as well that Catherine rejoiced that her husband was no longer bound to the New Connexion. For the bonds were at the point of breaking for ever.

In June 1862, the Annual Conference meeting at Dudley officially accepted William Booth's resignation. The motion was proposed by Dr Crofts, the President, and seconded – no doubt with considerable pleasure – by the Reverend P. J. Wright, who spoke with particular conviction against an amendment that the motion ending William Booth's association should be worded more courteously. In the end, the original proposition was carried by fifty-six votes to fifteen, and the *New Connexion Magazine* reported the parting in a way which was as dismissive as it was offensive. Under the heading 'Various Items of Business Detailed in the Annual Committee's Report', it was recorded that 'the resignation of the Rev. W. Booth and the lamented illnesses of several ministers and preachers were discussed *seriatim*'. The Conference expressed the hope that their departed colleague 'may continue to be useful as a minister of Jesus Christ'.

A few weeks later the Wesleyan Methodists met at Camborne and passed a resolution, proposed by the district meeting of Cornish ministers, that William Booth should be banned from their chapels. The President referred, scathingly, to the 'perambulations of male and female' and added the names of Dr and Mrs Phoebe Palmer to the proscribed list. The Primitive Methodists soon followed suit. Their Conference 'strongly urged all stations and authorities to avoid the employment of revivalists so called'.

Right into old age, William Booth continued to express his astonishment at the behaviour of the Cornish ministers, who had agreed to propose his exclusion and exile at a meeting which took place at the height of his south-western campaign. Their ingratitude was beyond his comprehension and his bewilderment was excusable. Earlier that year, the *Wesleyan Times* had published its appraisal of 'Mr Booth in Cornwall' and concluded that, 'Judged by the practical and personal results, the work here bears every mark of a genuine and thorough revival. It has battled prejudice and subdued opposition. The converts comprised all ages, both sexes and every grade of social condition.'[40] It also reported that when the Booths left St Ives, shops in the town closed down so that their proprietors could take part in his farewell tea.

After he had left, the paper continued, 'We have had many opportunities of noticing the conduct of the converts and their consistent and steadfast adherence to the Gospel of Jesus.' Compliments on the quality of the Booth conversions were rare. The usual complaint was that the repentance that was stimulated by a moment of emotion was invariably brief. But the *Wesleyan Times* judged that he had made permanent recruits to salvation. And the numbers were extraordinary.

> During the eighteen weeks Mr and Mrs Booth conducted their
> services in Redruth and Camborne at least 3,000 souls were
> brought to Jesus . . . At Redruth we hear the Free Church has
> given £1,500 for ground and we are going to build immediately
> the largest chapel in the country . . . Since Mr and Mrs Booth
> commenced their evangelistic work in Cornwall 7,000 souls
> have been awakened and saved.

Neither the quality nor the quantity of converts could reconcile the Wesleyan establishment to either the Booths' methods or character. William offended against the English tradition of gentle conversion. Catherine, lacking all the modesty expected of a minister's wife, preached as though she were a man – and claimed to justify her brazen behaviour by reference to the scriptures. And both of the Booths deported themselves in a way which proclaimed that they were closer to God than those around them. The Booths caused trouble and they caused offence. And their success – far from being regarded as a mitigation of their personal shortcomings – was held against them. William Booth was clearly a potential threat to the cosy complacency of an increasingly respectable Methodism. By driving him out from their churches, they made sure he became their rival as well as their reproach.

7

God's Gypsies

Despite fears that the chapel doors would be closed to them, the Booths decided to continue their Cornwall campaign – partly because they believed that the people, as distinct from the ministers, still wanted them and partly because they had nowhere else to go. Throughout the summer, Catherine – accepting the burdens of wife and mother as well as the obligations of an evangelist – alternated between elation and depression. Penzance lightened her spirits. 'It seems very remarkable that we should come almost straight into a house like this, which is everything we desire and in some ways beyond our dreams.' That was high praise indeed. For, as she had made clear in Newcastle, Catherine was not easily satisfied. The one domestic problem, shortage of help, was increased by the arrival, on 26 August 1862, of their third son, Herbert. 'We were,' she told her mother, 'a week without a servant.'[1]

The Booths' missionary lifestyle made a servant – sometimes assisted by a children's nurse – indispensable to the well-organised existence that Catherine regarded as a Christian obligation. And in mid-nineteenth-century England, where domestic service was the most common occupation, maids were employed by families with very limited resources. But clearly the Booths were never poor. And the week without a maid was far more likely to be the result of Catherine's particular management techniques than the consequence of poverty. Mary Kirton, who had travelled down with William from Newcastle vowing never to be parted from the Booths, left them after barely a year in Cornwall. Letters written after the family had moved on to Wales may illustrate why they had such difficulty in keeping staff. Beating the carpets and blackleading the grates was not enough. There had to be constant signs of redemption. 'The servant whom we engaged a few days ago came out for salvation . . . The girl we had at Cardiff and the one at Newport had also been saved.'[2] No one was completely exempt from the Booths' evangelical attentions. 'A chimney-sweep looked in and asked if we should require his services. Mrs [sic] Booth said that we shall and invited him to come and sit down. He did so with some reluctance, listened while I read and afterwards bowed his head in prayer.'[3]

But a house beyond her dreams was only brief compensation for the ingratitude which greeted her husband's success and her sacrifice. The final weeks of the Cornwall Campaign were frustrating in almost every way apart from the response which they still received from their congregations. The critical resolution which had been passed at the district preachers' meeting had 'materially altered the bearing of the Wesleyans towards the special work', yet 'the people were ripe for it. There was no doubt that a thousand souls might be gathered in.'[4] A meeting at Redruth was so successful that the altar rail had to be extended to accommodate the press of penitents. Yet the Booths still felt like strangers in a foreign land. The invitation to visit Wales – very largely at the instigation of Cornish fishermen who were sailing out of Cardiff – was received and accepted as a merciful release.

Again Catherine vacillated between anxiety and relief. She was worried about the children. Even when she was able to arrange formal instruction, it was unsatisfactory. But early in their marriage they had joined a provident society and Catherine could report, with relief, to her mother that 'the insurance money will be due next month, £14 odd', a considerable sum in those days. By cashing in what should have been kept to meet a sudden emergency, the Booths were to start their Wales campaign with a little capital behind them despite the defeats of Cornwall where, Catherine complained, 'Our expenses have been so heavy and our income smaller.'[5]

At first Cardiff seemed no better than Cornwall. To avoid the embarrassing rebuff which they expected from the local Wesleyans, the first meeting was held in a Baptist chapel, where William 'did not feel at home'. The Cornish fishermen were wrong to think that he would be rejected by the Methodists. The Booths had been in Cardiff for barely a week when they invited Catherine to the chapel for Wednesday evenings. Her reaction was less than gracious. Of course she accepted, but she also said that 'if the Revd Gentleman who talked about the "Male and Female going up and down Cornwall" . . . hears about it, he will think that the "female" is one too many for him'.[6] But in Cardiff Catherine was in an ungracious mood. When she read in the *Wesleyan Times* that P. J. Wright was dead, her reaction was charitable in form rather than in spirit: 'You will have heard of the death of Mr Wright,' she wrote. 'I was very much surprised. Poor fellow I hope he was quite ready. He now sees things in their true light doubtless. I wonder if his views about evangelism are changed?'[7]

Resentment of his Welsh critics, and bitterness at the way they dismissed him as a *parvenu*, made William Booth particularly anxious to preach in respectable premises rather than the rougher venues which some of the fishermen suggested. Since his earliest excursions into evangelism he had never confined himself to chapels. As a youth he had preached from a kitchen chair on the Nottingham back-streets and in the north of England he had organised his version of 'camp meetings' in the fields and on the hills around Gateshead. In Cardiff he would have preferred to preach the Lord's word in the Lord's house. But pride prevented him from building on the offer which the Wesleyans had made to Catherine. And he could not make a habit of preaching on Baptist premises. So he had to consider more secular (and socially less respectable) alternatives. They were helped to adjust their position by two Cardiff grandees who were to remain the Booths' supporters – emotionally and financially – for the next fifty years.

J. E. Billups, a building contractor, became a family friend and, after Mrs Mumford's death, his wife was the recipient of the revealing letters which Catherine felt compelled to write almost every day. When the Booths settled in London, the Billups's daughter became their lodger. The Booths' relationship with John and Richard Cory was far less intimate but the brothers became and remained faithful patrons. The Corys were colliery and shipowners who had developed their father's coastal shipping company into a great enterprise. On Sundays John Cory, the quintessential Victorian self-made millionaire, put aside consideration of business so that he could preach in the local Methodist chapel and superintend a Bible class. When the Booths arrived in Cardiff, he regarded them as part of the Connexion, and even when they moved through churches of their own creation he continued to subsidise their evangelism – first the Christian Mission, then the Salvation Army itself. He actually donated £500 to the 1892 'Self-denial Week' – a special version of sacrifice. The Booths' special brand of religion was essentially the product of Victorian Britain. And it naturally attracted archetypal Victorian figures who behaved in an archetypal Victorian way. The Corys even named one of their ships the *William Booth*, and guaranteed to devote part of its profits to Booth's work. When it sank off the Bermudas shortly after it was launched, the Corys contributed, from their other enterprises, the donations which the ship might have earned. The support of Billups and the Corys gave the Booths confidence to preach on their own terms.

Hindsight provided a theological justification for the decision. 'Undenominated work was just then coming into fashion. The theory was, save the people outside the church and then send them to the churches to be trained and cared for.'[8] Despite what the early biographers claimed, not all the chapels were closed to them. They could, had they wished it, have spent their time in Wales amongst the smaller Bethels and more remote Bethesdas. But they chose to break away. Catherine was absolutely frank about the limitations, as distinct from prohibitions, which convinced them that they should go their own way rather than wait for reconciliation with the Wesleyans. 'There is every prospect of good work, but we are so hedged in with difficulties. We, and the friends who brought us here, want neutral ground but the music hall is an unwieldy, ugly place and the circus is not much better.'[9]

All that would have been lost if they had left Cardiff because there was no venue which they regarded as suitable for their services. Fortunately William Booth agreed to preach in the disused Cardiff circus. Whatever changed his mind, it was changed on the evening of 18 February 1863. That morning Catherine had described it as wholly unsuitable. Next morning she wrote to her mother to say, 'It was decided last night for us to commence in the circus on Sunday. It has been taken for a fortnight at seven pounds a week.'[10] A couple of days later it was grudgingly accepted that 'the circus answers far better than we expected'.[11]

From then on William Booth never refused engagements in the most profane locations. Indeed, he welcomed them. Over the next half-dozen years he came to accept godless surroundings as a positive benefit to the message which he brought to godless men and women. Sinners who would not consider visiting a church or chapel would, he realised, gladly crowd into a circus, a public house or music hall – to scoff if not to pray. Once they were there, it was William Booth's job to win them for redemption.

The Welsh campaign was a success. The 'Revival Intelligence' column in the *Wesleyan Times* reported the Booths' weeks in Wales in the most extravagant language. When they left Cardiff, 'the moral condition of the town had greatly improved and at a season of the year when crime is on the increase, the magistrates had little to do'.[12] And a letter from the Reverend J. Bentley added the considered opinion 'that it would not be possible in this world to know all the good which the labours of Mr and Mrs Booth had brought' to the area. But the paper's editorials, hardly surprisingly, reflected the opinion of the Wesleyan leadership. And for that Catherine could not forgive them. She expressed her disapproval in a rare excursion into irony: 'I have done with the WT [*Wesleyan Times*], it is like most other papers a sycophant. The reviewer says that the Methodist Conference have reasons for their actions with reference to Evangelist. No doubt they had. And it was the place of the WT to drag those reasons into the daylight.'[13]

The *Wesleyan Times*'s attitude towards New Connexion overseas missions made Catherine almost equally angry. It provoked her to express opinions which, had anyone dared to remind her of them twenty years later, she would have found it impossible to defend: 'I have no patience to read a lot of twaddle about New Connexion missions to China and Australia . . . Where is the consistency in spending hundreds of pounds to convert half a dozen Chinamen and leaving thousands of our own population destitute of any means adapted to reach them?'[14] That complaint is impossible to reconcile with the view of the basic belief – which made William Booth so antagonistic to Calvinism – that all men and women are equal in the sight of God and capable of achieving His grace and eventual salvation. But it was, in a sense, the ignoble expression of an idea which, in a less base form, was to motivate the most glorious work in the Booths' lives – their mission to the industrial poor. They might well never have taken up that cause had they not been rejected by the organised Methodists of their day and had they not stubbornly refused to consider the possibility that their opponents' criticisms were justified.

The Booths did not leave Cardiff thinking that their evangelism had leapt forward towards its true destiny. Indeed, they moved on first to Weston-super-Mare and then (at the invitation of the Free Methodists) to Walsall in debilitatingly low spirits. As always in times of emotional stress, William contracted a series of minor illnesses. When his sore throat was compounded by a sprained ankle Catherine took his place in the pulpit for a week, and for a while it seemed that the combination of physical discomfort and spiritual confusion would overcome them. Catherine described the visit to the Midlands as 'a miserable affair' and complained, 'We have not received as much as our travelling expenses and house rent.' Poverty and rejection made her feel 'a good deal perplexed and tempted to mistrust'.[15] Both Booths looked back at Cardiff – regarded as inhospitable when they were there – as a place of unique 'kindness and affection'.

However, despite the many tribulations in the West Midlands, Walsall marked another development, perhaps even turning point, in their evangelism. It was there that William Booth began to develop the technique by which he recruited the dissolute and degenerate men and women whose need for salvation was, if not greatest, most obvious. In his diary* William recorded that 'several noted characters have come over from Birmingham to help us and they went out into the streets singing and exhorting the people. One had been a professional horse racer and gambler. One a prize fighter. Another had been a celebrated thief concerned in some silk

---

*The diary no longer exists. The likelihood is that it was lost when the Salvation Army Victoria Embankment headquarters was bombed during the Second World War. However, it is quoted extensively and, it seems, accurately in Begbie's *Life of William Booth* and Booth-Tucker's *Life of Catherine Booth*.

robberies, jumping on and off trams between stations when going at considerable speeds. It was very gratifying to listen to their earnest pleading and hear them speak of the power of Christ.'[16] The apparent belief that theft and jumping off moving tramcars were sins of equal magnitude should not detract from his discovery that there was a *camaraderie* amongst the wicked that made them listen to advice from one of their own.

It is by no means clear who first had the idea for recruiting reformed sinners to reform and recruit more of their kind. In *How We Began* (his introduction to an early history of the Salvation Army) William Booth naturally took direct credit for the strategy[17] which was meant to overcome Black Country prejudice but became a marketing device of which any high pressure salesman would have been proud:

> The respectable portion of the community were too proud to enter [the chapels] and the lower orders were as positively opposed to anything of that kind as they could possibly be. I went to work to try and make them come . . . Night after night I spoke to large crowds in the market square, processing through the darkest and blackest slums to the chapel into which very few would enter. So far as the door they came, but no further. It was then that I devised a special kind of meeting . . . To attract the people, we invited all the celebrities we knew . . . Men who had been remarkable in wickedness but who, we had reason to believe, were now serving God. We had a morning march, waggons in the hollow of a broken field and meetings all day. We had great crowds of people and souls saved.

It seems unlikely that the respectable portion of the local community reacted with any great enthusiasm to posters which advertised 'Monster Camp Meeting' to be addressed by 'converted pugilists, horse racers and others'. But, at least according to William Booth, the lower orders were entranced to hear such men speaking in a language they understood about subjects which had previously been regarded as only appropriate to the gentry. As always William Booth, the great publicist, invented an irresistible name for the crusading sinners. He called them 'The Hallelujah Band'. The idea of taking religion to the people, rather than issuing a half-hearted invitation for them to make the effort of finding it for themselves, had come to William Booth as a young man in Nottingham. But in Walsall it became a practical reality. And it made him an overnight sensation.

William Booth never thought to question the class system on which Victorian society was based, so while he believed that every man was equal in the sight of God, he had no illusion about them being equal in any other way. In the early days of his independent ministry the conversion of a working man was always noted with as much surprise as delight. And until, five years later, he had been emotionally knocked about by the rough and tumble of London's East End, he always described God's miracles amongst the poor in the language of condescension. In Walsall he ended a market place rally by 'linking arms with a navvy' and 'marching off arm in arm with a great crowd to chapel'. In the meeting which followed many of the sinners who confessed came straight from the 'coalpit and the workshop'.[18] William Booth was beginning to enjoy working amongst 'the worst and poorest classes' in the battle against 'the vast continent of rampant wickedness' which he saw everywhere around him.[19]

When the Booths left Walsall the Hallelujah Band saw them off at the station. And for a month or two the redeemed roughs continued their work of rumbustious redemption, hiring every possible sort of meeting place all over the Midlands and the north of England. But the good work did not last and the band's members soon drifted apart, some to resume their old bad ways. William Booth said that lack of discipline was to blame. When the time came for the idea to be revived – in battalions, not bands, and with hundreds rather than dozens of members – he made sure that the new recruits were subject to proper authority by providing it himself.

There was typhoid fever in Walsall when the Booths left for Matlock, where William was to receive a course of hydrotherapy paid for by an anonymous donor. Once again Catherine was worried about money. So she returned to the idea of supplementing the family income by lecturing on temperance.[20] She had written to her father from Cardiff asking him to send her notes on his speeches, assuming that an 'old stager would have something prepared' and ready for use, but he had failed to reply.[21] Six months later, when they had moved on from Smedley's Matlock hydro to Birmingham, she complained, 'Once more,

I ask father if he can send me a speech on temperance. Wm. wants me to lecture here as I have a good chance of getting introduced and we shall have to do something if things get no brighter with us. Our last collection was £2.13 and the proceeds of the tea will not reach £5.'[22] Until James Cory's ship came in the Booths were forced to live on what they could collect at the end of meetings, and their meetings were designed to attract the men and women who had least to give. By November 1863, Catherine was pawning her jewellery. 'Let Polly have the chain for £2 unless father can get more for it. You see William knows the value of it being accustomed to deal with such things.' For once the years of pawnbroking were acknowledged without shame.

For the next two years the Booths wandered through England preaching where they could but always in the way they wished. Life was hard, and William reacted with violent changes of mood. He was often oppressed by the effect which rejection was having over his wife and children and occasionally elated by the success of a sermon. In Batley there was a 'miserable congregation to begin with . . . but night congregation pretty good'. He had 'a very good week in Pudsey . . . immensely popular with the people'. At first, Catherine was glad to be back in Yorkshire, where they evidently were earning enough to at last maintain a decent standard of living in 'a beautiful house [with] two women servants and a governess'. But by the end of 1863 she had turned against Leeds and 'would rather move every quarter than live like this'. The change of mood had an obvious cause – 'William said last week that he had never seen me look so ill.' The agonising spinal pain had returned, her digestion (as always) made every meal a trial, and she was pregnant yet again.[23] Marion was born during the spring of 1864, just eighteen months after her brother, Herbert.

During their moments of depression the Booths always believed that the next place would be better. They had set off for Yorkshire with high hopes, but the local population was less receptive than they had at first seemed. The Booths were 'unable to get the masses into the chapels' since the northern working classes were 'so awfully prejudicial against all connection with [biblical] texts' that they would not 'come unless under some mighty excitement'.[24] Attendances improved when the services were held, not in regular places of worship, but in the Prince of Wales' Halls. From Cardiff to the West Midlands and on to the West Riding, the message was the same. If the souls of the industrial poor were to be saved, the Lord's disciples would have to excite and entertain before the work of redemption began.

It was not long before the Booths decided they had been invited north under false pretences. The situation in Farsley (then near to, now a suburb of, Leeds) provoked Catherine into un-Christian bitterness against her hosts. 'We find now we get here that the society is split into two parties, associationists and reformers, a *few revivalists* and the great bulk of *anti*-revivalists standing out together from special services. So much for Methodists' truthfulness and sincerity'.[25] So many members of the established congregation had Calvinistic tendencies that William could not persuade any one of them to write reports about the campaign to redeem sinners from outside the ranks of the elect. It was in Farsley that they received news that the good ship *William Booth* had foundered. Catherine – not realising that the Corys would make up the losses – calculated that storms at sea had denied them the prospect of something between £40 and £50 a year. The Booths' only consolation was the 'belief that religion that is pleasing to God consists of doing and *enduring* His will'.[26] It seemed to be His will that the Booths remained not poor but always within sight of poverty. When Catherine wrote to her mother to ask for clothes for Ballington – barely a year after the last discussion of the Mumfords' impending bankruptcy – she ended her letter, 'We are so poor now.' The letter as usual specified her needs in precise detail. But her mother failed to comply with her careful instructions. 'The boots sent for Ballington were not the sort I asked for. They were girls' boots.' For the first time, complaint was turning into self-pity. 'I have been a perfect slave to the needle lately and I don't see what else I can be unless I can afford to put it out, which I cannot afford now.'[27] Putting it out was not a common practice amongst the class which the Booths hoped to convert. There were times when Catherine exhibited ideas above the station to which God had called her.

Occasionally there was a gleam of light. William was invited to preach in Nottingham and Sheffield, where he was reunited with the Hallelujah Band making what was almost its last appearance. The travelling cheerleaders were reinforced by a local version of the same phenomenon which seems to have sprung up almost spontaneously at about the same time. The Hallamshire Battalion – taking their name from the maps of ancient South Yorkshire – all wore 'red shirts. Coats and vests off. Sleeves turned up.'[28] William Booth described their appearance with obvious approval. He had begun to be attracted by uniform.

There is no conclusive evidence that Catherine Booth had begun to persuade her husband that they should return to London, though it is easy to understand why she might have wanted to be close to her mother. In his 1933 biography, St John Ervine refers to a letter (which can no longer be identified) in which she explicitly admits, 'I should like to live in London better than any place I was ever in,' and confesses to having grown weary of 'being God's gypsy'.[29] Whatever her inclination, the idea of moving south was encouraged when she received – independently and in her own right – an invitation from the Southwark Circuit to preach to the Free Church Methodists of Rotherhithe. It was accepted with great and immediate pleasure. William, even before he was converted to the idea of a full women's ministry, never stood in his wife's way and agreed to her mission to London with an enthusiasm which few twentieth-century husbands could have matched. Whether he supported her initiative because he loved her or because he believed that she was called by God to preach is not clear. Whatever the reason, he was – at least for a week or two – prepared, if not happy, to play a supporting role. So Catherine went to London while William stayed in the north to complete a long-standing engagement in Ripon and to keep a paternal eye on his six children – the oldest of whom was still not nine years old.

Catherine Booth's mission was a spectacular success – partly because a woman preacher was a scandalous novelty. The handbills which advertised the sermons (headed 'Come and Hear a Woman Preach') were designed to exploit her special appeal. There were, however, two clouds on Catherine's horizon – Messrs Morgan and Chase, the publishers of *The Revival*, on which William had relied so heavily during his time in Wales and men from whom he would need continual help if he was to make a successful career in independent evangelism. A week before the end of her Rotherhithe crusade, the publishers wrote about Catherine's activities, not to the lady evangelist herself, but to her husband.

We are completely over done with business of various kinds. Nevertheless we hope at least once to hear dear Mrs Booth . . . Let us now say a word on the subject of female preaching. We quite feel that it is to be defended in principle . . . But we are greatly led to question . . . whether it is right for mothers of families to be away from home duties.[30]

Had Messrs Chase and Morgan known the state of the family which Catherine Booth left behind – including a profoundly sick baby girl and two young boys whose disturbed behaviour their mother attributed to the uncertainty of their lives – they might well have been outraged rather than dubious about her conduct. But the Booths, after some initial apprehension, decided that the publishers' doubts would be overcome once they realised how much sanctification Catherine had achieved. So, putting them aside, she preached on and saved enough souls to convince her that she should make the capital her parish. Because she was convinced, William was convinced as well. In an admirable act of self-abnegation, he agreed to settle permanently in London and a house was rented at 31 Shaftesbury Road, Hammersmith. William was too good and too loving a man to think of himself in competition with his wife. That was just as well for his peace of mind. Catherine had become the senior evangelist in the family.

The *Wesleyan Times*, about which Catherine had been so bitter in Wales, described Catherine's preaching style as 'more in the manner of Finney than of many revivalists' – a compliment to rank with the previous comparison between William and James Caughey. 'No empty boisterousness or violent and cursing declamation, but a calm and simple statement of the unreasonableness of sin . . .'[31] The periodical understood that 'the Grange Road Society are anxiously expecting her as soon as she has finished at Rotherhithe'. The professional relationship within the family was illustrated by an announcement in the *Wesleyan Times* of 1 May 1865. The Methodists held a farewell tea to express their gratitude for Catherine Booth's achievement. When the cups were cleared away, William 'delivered the after tea address'.

As summer followed spring, the *Wesleyan Times* reported Catherine Booth sermons in New Town, Kensington and Deptford. One report included a sketch of the preacher which might better be described as an encomium: 'Nearly six and thirty years of age; her appearance rather favouring the supposition that she may not have reached quite so many years. In dress nothing could be neater. A plain black straw bonnet slightly relieved with a pair of dark violet strings, a black loose fitting jacket with loose sleeves, which appeared exceedingly suitable to her while preaching and a black silk dress.' The sketch went on to describe 'a rather prepossessing countenance', a 'calm and precise delivery', a 'quiet manner' and an 'entire absence of unbecoming confidence' – all attributes of a woman with 'no ordinary mind'. Catherine Booth had clearly made a conquest.[32]

Although Catherine had regarded London as home since she was a girl, Bermondsey introduced her to an aspect of metropolitan life that she had not previously experienced. The area was almost entirely inhabited by casual dock labourers and impoverished immigrants – many of them single men living in harsh, if not squalid conditions. It was through the Grange Road Chapel that she met the Midnight Movement, an organisation devoted to the rescue and eventual redemption of prostitutes. It was work to which she became instinctively committed as soon as the hard facts of East End life were revealed to her. Perhaps her admirers were wrong to claim that it was 'her first introduction to the cruelty that women suffer at the hands of men'.[33] But she had certainly never evangelised amongst the brothels and bordellos which were a common feature of the dockland slums. That makes her reaction to the degradation all the more astonishing. She took her message direct to the fallen women. But it was neither sanctimonious nor sententious:

> The Address of Mrs Booth was inimitably pointed, evangelically impressive and delivered in a most earnest and sympathetic manner, drawing tears from many and the closest attention from all. *She identified herself with them* [the prostitutes] *as a fellow sinner, showing that if they supposed her to be better than themselves it was a mistake, since all had sinned against God.*[34]

According to her son-in-law, Frederick Booth-Tucker, 'the paltriness of the efforts put forward to minimise the evil staggered her and the gross inequality with which society meted out its punishment to the weaker sex, allowing the participators in the vice to escape with impunity, incurred her scathing denunciation'.[35] She believed that the Methodists of London's East End, if not of all England, were prepared like the rest of the Establishment to 'wink at such cruel slavery whilst professing to be shocked by the sale of human beings in other lands'.[36] Catherine was developing a talent for righteous indignation.

Had her health allowed it, she would certainly have stayed and worked in London's docklands. And the Methodists of the East End would have been delighted to keep her – after ten weeks in Deptford, her sponsors asked her to extend her stay. But she was pregnant again, and the journey home across the city to Hammersmith (after meetings which often did not finish until midnight) was exhausting. So in November 1866 the Booths rented one of the Cambridge Lodge Villas in Hackney – a respectable, if not spacious, semi-detached house in what she hoped was a quiet suburb. It did not stay quiet for long. Plans were already approved for a new church on the ground immediately opposite. The noise of the building sometimes so disturbed Catherine that she was physically ill.

No doubt, as she prayed and preached, Catherine regretted having so little time for William and the children. But preaching had begun to fill her life as it filled her husband's and it was God's will that, for a time, she should be the family's senior evangelist. There is no knowing how the strange arrangement would have developed had not Messrs Morgan and Chase – either putting aside their objections to women preachers or hoping to strike a blow against one of them – invited William Booth to conduct six weeks of services on behalf of the East London Revival Society, an organisation founded to crusade in London's dockland as missionaries were crusading in Africa. The publishers were 'booking agents' for the Society – a role which involved a good deal more than engaging preachers and arranging for their payment. Selecting preachers gave them control over the sort of sermons which were preached in the Society's missions – both their style and their theological content. Their invitation to William Booth – despite the brief duration of his engagement – was proof that at least some influential Wesleyans approved of him.

William had thought of the Booths' London home as little more than a base from which he could mount expeditions out into the country while his wife worked in the capital. Certainly, William saw London as a good location from which to pursue his career as an independent preacher. But there is no doubt that, in defiance of the general mores of the time, he put the demands of his wife's career ahead of his own. And he was happy, in old age, to make clear what his priority had been. 'My dear wife had always objected to leaving the children for public work and in London we agreed she could find a sphere which would allow her getting home the same evening or, at most, not keep her away very long together.'[37] At first he regarded the Morgan/Chase offer as no more than a London episode in a period of travelling evangelism. His willingness to accept it was all the more praiseworthy in light of the doubts he felt about his ability to identify with the purely working-class mission which Morgan and Chase proposed. 'This, I thought, was not my vocation . . . I had forgotten Nottingham, and the work I did when I was a boy of sixteen, twenty years before.'[38] He had also forgotten – or so he imagined forty-five years later – the more recent triumph in the circus at Cardiff, the Hallelujah Band, the march to the Walsall Chapel arm-in-arm with the sanctified navvy and the camp meetings of the north-east, and he must have forgotten about his wife's (by then) highly developed social conscience. The apparent amnesia is hard to explain. He could not have been insulated from Catherine's increasing concern for the conditions of the poor – a passion which, although it owed no allegiance to any party, was, in the broadest sense of the word, political. She did not choose to keep her strong opinions secret. It was during her early months in London that she launched her assault on His Grace the Duke of Rackrent and the Right Honourable Woman Seducer Fitz-Shameless.

> Is it not too patent for intelligent contradiction that the most detestable thing in the judgement of popular Christianity is not brutality, cruelty or injustice but *poverty* and *vulgarity*. With plenty of money you may pile up your life with iniquities and yet be blamed, if blamed at all, only in the mildest terms, whereas one flagrant act of sin in a poor and illiterate person is enough to stamp him, with a majority of practising Christians, as a creature from whom they would rather keep their distance.[39]

It is impossible to believe that Catherine did not express those sentiments during family meals. For there burned, inside her, something that approximated to the fire of the class war:

> Half the aristocracy of this country mounted on horses worth hundreds of pounds each, which have been bred and trained at a

cost of hundreds of pounds more. And what for? This 'splendid field' are waiting whilst a poor little timid animal is let loose from confinement and permitted to fly in terror from its strange surroundings. Observe the delight of the gentlemen and noble ladies when a whole pack of strong dogs is let loose in pursuit.[40]

William Booth, on his own admission, did not share his wife's early animosity towards '"Mr Moneymaker" [whose] gold sovereigns and crisp notes would look so well in the collection', but concern for the material needs of the poor must have been there, lying submerged beneath his hope of providing them with a better life after death. Catherine awakened the compassion, and Messrs Morgan and Chase provided the opportunity which gave him the chance to dispel his early doubts about where his mission lay. On Sunday 2 July 1865 he preached the first sermon of the East End Revival under the cover of a large marquee on the Old Quaker Burial Ground at Mile End. God's gypsies had found a home at last.

8

When Men Shall Revile You

In his old age William Booth could not make up his mind about the spirit in which he had approached the East London Mission. At one moment he claimed reluctance to take on the job because he feared that he was unsuited 'to deal with people of this class'.[1] But he also claimed, 'At first sight I felt the importance of the place.'[2] The truth is probably less dramatic than either version of his first reactions suggest. He began the work without much confidence in his own ability to appeal to the East End roughs. But gradually he discovered that his Mile End congregations were just as susceptible to his appeal as any other group of potential penitents, and he decided that six weeks was not long enough to complete his mission. 'I found my heart being strongly and strangely drawn out on behalf of a million people living within a mile of the tent – ninety out of a hundred of whom, they told me, never heard the sound of a preacher's voice. Why go further afield for audiences?' It was an absolute reversal of the position which he had taken up when he had refused to become a circuit minister of the New Connexion, and an extraordinary change of heart in a man who had turned his back on three churches because they denied him the right to roam the country in search of lost souls. He had now become entranced by the magnitude of the challenge which faced him:

Mary Booth. 'When my father died, my grief was all but forbidden by the thought that it was not my mother.'

12 Notintone Place, Sneinton, William Booth's birthplace.

The Reverend Dr William Cooke. President of the Methodist Conference, patron and, in Catherine Booth's view, false friend.

Broad Street Chapel, Nottingham. The scene of William Booth's 'conversion'.

The New Connexion minister.
William Booth at Redruth, 1859.

Catherine Booth at the time she
began to preach. 'I only wish I
had begun years ago.'

Never!' The story that William Booth resigned from the Wesleyan New Connexion in response to his wife's cry from the conference balcony is, unfortunately, apocryphal.

3 Gore Road, Hackney. Big enough to be converted from Booth's family home into a training college for female cadets.

The new name was adopted almost by accident. Bramwell Booth refused to accept the casual status of Volunteer. So his father changed the adjective to 'Salvation'.

The Salvation Army excited constant hostility. In Sheffield, during the 1882 Council of War, Lieutenant Emmerson Davidson, leading the procession, was knocked unconscious. Rather than admit victory to the mob, he was held insensible on his horse until the parade was over.

The Salvation Army hoped that 'food and shelter' would lead the way to a better life . . .

. . . possibly in the colonies.

William Booth was slow to accept the importance of band music as an inducement to salvation. The Penzance Band's success helped in his conversion.

Commissioners George Scott Railton and Elijah Cadman: two of William Booth's earliest and most faithful lieutenants.

The moral degradation and spiritual destitution of the teeming
populations of the East of London are subjects with which the
Christians of the metropolis are painfully conversant. Many true
hearted and zealous labourers are toiling in the spirit of the
Master to stop the mighty tide of iniquity and to pour the
glorious light of the Gospel in upon the dense darkness
everywhere abounding – yet seeing these labourers only as a
faint lone star whose light but reveals the surrounding
darkness. A city missionary, living in this neighbourhood, says
that there are hundreds who need to be taught the existence of
God. At a missionary meeting held at Spitalfields Chapel, a few
days ago, it was stated that in a radius of one mile and a quarter
from this Chapel there is a population of two hundred
thousand persons, one hundred and sixty thousand of whom
confessedly never attend any place of worship.[3]

The ratio of four to one in Satan's favour dominated Booth's evangelism like a mystic number that held the secret of salvation.
Sometimes the calculation changed. 'In every direction were multitudes totally ignorant of the Gospel and given up to all kinds of
wickedness – infidels, drunkards, thieves, harlots, gamblers, blasphe-
mers and pleasure seekers without number. Out of a population of
nearly a million souls it was confidently asserted that some eight hundred thousand never cross the threshold of church or chapel.'[4] But the
idea was always the same – in the slums of England the godless always
outnumbered the godly. William Booth concluded that, with the odds
so heavily against him, his war had to be waged with the weapons
which he had employed in Wales and Walsall.

The Morgan and Chase invitation had proved that at least some
influential Wesleyans approved of William Booth, and their plan for
him to preach from a tent offered the prospect of conducting long and
frequent services at any time he chose. But the tent was old and thread-
bare and was torn apart in the autumn wind. So William – with the
Cardiff experience to give him authority – persuaded the Mission to
hire the only room they could find, 'a miserable affair seating but three
hundred and fifty people' which was only available on Sundays
because for the rest of the week it was used, of all things, as a dance
hall. The new meeting place – some local residents called it the New

Royal Assembly Room, others knew it as Professor Orson's Dancing
Academy – was a severe test of William Booth's professed determination to take Christianity to the people. It also taxed his ingenuity as
organiser. For even on a Sunday the building had to be shared with a
professional photographer, 'a Godless man doing a large trade on the
Sabbath. While we were preaching, his customers were passing
through the end of our place to his studio, his wife meanwhile sitting
in the front room, colouring and getting up the pictures.'[5] An added
inconvenience and indignity was the need to move chairs and benches
in and out before and after each session. As a result, the very faithful
went to chapel three times each Sunday – twice in their working
clothes to shift furniture and once in between, dressed in their best, to
pray.

William Booth, who never underestimated the importance of publicity, kept the world aware of his achievements by sending his own
communiqués to the *Wesleyan Times*. 'Hundreds of working men and
numbers of persons who never enter any place of worship have listened night after night to the earnest and soul searching appeals of this
servant of God.'[6] The accounts of general success were illustrated with
examples of particular conversions. 'I am a prodigal, it is twelve years
since I left my mother in Edinburgh. I had not heard the Gospel in seventeen years until I heard you in the Mile-end road last night.'[7] The
evangelist admitted the occasional failure. One backslider told him, 'I
am ashamed to tell you that I have gone back into the world. I have
been led away by friends.'[8]

The problem of 'backsliders' had become a major preoccupation for
the Booths. And it was, in its way, instrumental in the eventual decision
to set up a church of his own. William had wanted to guide his converts into 'neighbouring and sympathetic churches', but never felt
much confidence that the sheep would be kept in the fold. He began
to wonder if the best solution was a pulpit inside a building of his own,
from which he could keep a watchful eye on the new recruits. But there
was no immediate prospect of a permanent mission, so he battled on
with the ambiguous status of a resident preacher operating in the
manner of the itinerant evangelist:

In the morning held services more especially for our workers
and believers in general. Afternoon – public experience

meeting – a precious service. Evening – from five to six in the
Mile-end road a very large gathering. Hundreds appeared to
listen with undivided attention. We then formed a procession
and sang down the Whitechapel-road to our hall . . . from the
adjacent gin palaces the drinkers came forth to hear and see,
some in mockery joined our ranks, some laughed and sneered,
some were angry, the great majority looked on in wonder while
others turned and accompanied us as we went chanting our
song 'There is a Fountain Filled With Blood'.[9]

William Booth's special brand of hubris made him relish the bottles
and the half-bricks which rained down on every open-air meeting.
The devil only struck back when the devil took notice. And the devil
was at home on the Mile End Road. So that was where William Booth –
who had sacrificed so much and caused much trouble in defence of his
right to wander – would stay. 'Oh Kate, as I passed the door of the
flaming gin palaces tonight, I seem to hear a voice suddenly in my ears,
"Where can you find such heathens as these and where is there so great
a need for your labours?" I felt as though I ought, at every cost, to stop
and preach to these East End multitudes.'[10] The problem was how to
keep himself and wife while he laboured.

Paradoxically, Catherine Booth – whose commitment to the poor preceded her husband's and was almost certainly more passionate – began
to spend her time in the more salubrious parts of London; a welcome,
if in some ways uncongenial, extension of her work since she addressed
congregations which could afford to give generously to the collections
which financed both the revivals and the Booths. The *Wesleyan Times*
announced that she was preaching each Sunday and one week night at
the Myddleton Halls in Islington, and because of her success would,
after a break at the end of her engagement, return for a second round of
services and sermons. The advantages of speaking to prosperous
Wesleyans did not corrupt her into mouthing their prejudices. She did
not hesitate to denounce the class divisions in British society:

What sort of taste is it, which, in the presence of the existing
state of things among the poor, spends not fourpence but four
shillings, and double and treble that sum on a single bottle of
wine for the jovial entertainment of a few friends, and from

twenty to forty pounds for a dinner to be swallowed by a dozen
or two of people? I maintain that no splendid furniture, no
well-trained and liveried servants, no costly pictures or display
of finery or jewels, can redeem such a scene, viewed in the light
of the teachings of Christ, from being worthy of being called
'brutal', and all the more brutal because it is delighted in by
persons whose intelligence and knowledge of the awful state of
things in the world around them must make them fully aware
of the good that might be done with the money which they
lavish upon their lusts.[11]

Yet although the antagonism remained, Catherine was at first intim-
idated by the Mr Moneymakers in her congregations. 'It is expected
that a number of very respectable people, so called, would attend the
meeting. To preach to such a class is always supposed to be a more
important and difficult task than to preach to people on a lower scale
of society and consequently possessed of less intelligence and culture.
I believe that I was influenced by such feelings when I was about to
commence.' Catherine recovered her nerve and sense of values, but for
all her advanced views on crime and prostitution her initial concern
was that she lived up to the standards of the upper classes. Not even
Catherine Booth could completely free herself from the mores of
Victorian England.

Life was different outside The Vine on the corner of Cambridge Road
and Whitechapel Road, and in front of The Blind Beggar behind the
Mile End Waste, where William Booth, while preaching in the open air,
was looking for a sponsor to underwrite his efforts when he could no
longer afford to rent the Assembly Rooms. In the autumn of 1865 he
approached, and a month later met, Samuel Morley, son and heir to
John 'Gentleman' Morley of Sneinton and (more important than a native
of William's home village) a major Nonconformist benefactor. Morley –
who became Booth's most regular source of both moral and financial
support – was initially slow to respond. But more immediate help was
at hand thanks to the impression that Catherine had made on the congregation at the Eyre Arms Assembly Rooms, St John's Wood. Two
trustees of the Bewley Fund, a charity set up to encourage spiritual
activities amongst the London poor, had heard and been impressed by
her address. When they discovered that the lady preacher's husband

worked in the East End they went to hear one of his *al fresco* sermons. Convinced that the work should become secure and permanent, they agreed to pay first £12 and then £14 towards the cost of hiring decent premises. There then began William Booth's search for a permanent home for what had, with his decision to extend his six-week stay, become the East London Christian Mission – a title as permanent as it was pious. Property became a minor obsession – a sign that he and his mission were in the East End to stay. He worked his way through a woollen warehouse, a stable (from which he was ejected because loud singing disturbed the athletes in the gymnasium on the other side of the wall), a penny gaff (a low-life music hall which admitted its audience for a minimal price in the hope that they would spend most of their time in a bar), the Eastern Star (a disused public house) and the Effingham Theatre, which he briefly regarded as a 'permanent home'.*

Catherine, who had paid the family's bills for six months, worried about the practical consequences of managing their own mission. For the Bewley Fund was paying rent not wages. 'I remember the emotions it produced in my soul. I sat gazing into the fire and the Devil whispered to me, "This means another new departure – another start in life!"' What she feared was not a settled existence. For that she still longed. But it was a joy which she was prepared to sacrifice for her husband's greater glory. Her doubts concerned family income. 'The question of our support constituted a serious difficulty. Hitherto we had been able to meet our expenses by the collections which we had made from our more respectable audiences. But it was impossible to suppose that we could do so among the poverty-stricken East Enders.'[12] Asked by her husband if she would support the new endeavour, 'she did not answer discouragingly'. After a momentary pause for thought and prayer, she replied, 'We have trusted to the Lord *once* for our support and we can trust him again.'

Before the Booths left for London, they went to hear the Reverend William Haslam preach in the grounds of Dunorlan, the home of Henry Reed, a Yorkshireman who had made a fortune in Australia and

---

*The order in which the premises were obtained is in dispute. W. T. Stead says the Eastern Star was acquired before the Effingham Theatre, George Scott Railton says afterwards. Both were Booth's contemporaries.

returned home a millionaire. The Booths were admirers of Haslam and attended the service as humble members of the congregation. But they could not have been entirely inconspicuous. For Haslam recognised them and introduced them to Reed, who invited William to preach on the following Sunday in his private mission hall. William had already accepted an invitation for that day, but Catherine offered to take his place. Although she was unwilling to accept Reed's exacting instructions about how she should preach and what her text should be, he was so impressed by her performance that he suggested that the Booths accept his permanent patronage – becoming, in effect, his evangelical employees. William Booth was no more willing to be on Reed's payroll than he had been to work for Rabbits ten years earlier. Catherine remained the family's breadwinner.

Fortunately for the family, Catherine's reputation continued to grow. At the end of her series of meetings in the Eyre Arms Assembly Rooms, a deputation of wealthy Methodists offered to build her what they called 'a church bigger than Mr Spurgeon's tabernacle'* – a chapel built in 1861 with the capacity to seat two thousand people. She declined with thanks but without explanation. Perhaps she was inhibited by continual illness and depressed by her eighth and final pregnancy. Or she may have been reluctant to become so obviously the permanent breadwinner of the household.

Lucy Booth was born within two months of the St John's Wood meetings. Catherine was again suffering from the 'continual diarrhoea' – a symptom which probably confirmed her stomach condition as Crohn's disease, the gradual deterioration of the bowel walls. She needed a rest, but as usual decided to combine recuperation with revival. One of her prosperous West End acquaintances suggested that she tour the south coast when wealthy Methodists – of the sort which subscribed liberally to chapel funds and collections – were there for the summer. Catherine's sermons were, as usual, a sensation – at Ramsgate there was no hall big enough to accommodate her congregation, and dozens of believers stood outside the door hoping for a word as she came out.

---

*Charles Haddon Spurgeon (1834–1892), Baptist Minister of the Metropolitan Tabernacle, Elephant & Castle, London. His mild Calvinism antagonised the Booths.

While Catherine Booth was spreading the Gospel and at the same time paying for the groceries, William was thinking of better ways of making the East London Christian Mission a real and permanent church. In November 1868 he believed that at last he had found a citadel. He announced in the *East London Evangelist* – the Christian Mission's official magazine – 'The Conversion of the People's Market Whitechapel into the People's Mission Hall'. The People's Market had been opened for commercial business only ten months earlier by John McAll, a ham and beef dealer who had recently resigned from the committee that William had set up as (the purely theoretical) managers of the Revival Union. McAll had not been able to make the market a commercial success. William Booth believed that he could do better – partly because God would guide customers through his door. He had extended his empire by renting a new Sunday meeting place, but the need for more suitable premises was urgent.

> Ever since the commencement of the mission in the neighbourhood the work has suffered greatly and been persecuted with difficulty for want of suitable premises . . . On the Sabbath we occupy the East London Theatre through the whole of the day and in the morning and afternoon we find it dreary and comfortless in the extreme. Indeed I do not see how we can expect the poor half clad people to attend it in the coming cold weather.[13]

It would be wrong to say that William Booth believed in the gaiety of God, for gaiety implies pleasure and he believed that to be usually sinful. But he did believe that God should be bright enough and light enough to attract attention. He also knew that one of the attractions of God's house was the warmth it provided for families whose members were cold at home. In the evening at the East London Theatre there was 'more gas and the great crowd warms the place', but he wanted more than physical comfort. The chance to turn the People's Market into the People's Hall seemed like a gift of providence.

The announcement in the *East London Evangelist* described the available facilities – tea rooms in addition to the large meeting hall, a shop at the front and a 'soup kitchen admirably filled up with steam engine, coppers etc. all capable of supplying one thousand gallons of soup per

day'. The People's Market's previous attempts to sell cheap soup had
not proved profitable, but they had confirmed that the demand existed.
'Hundreds of poor hungry people frequented the soup kitchen on the
hottest days of last summer while sometimes over one thousand in a
single day were supplied last winter' at a price of two pence per bowl.
William hoped to combine 'a boon to the starving poor' and 'remuneration to the Mission'.

A nine-year lease was available for £3,000. Messrs Habershon &
Price, architects, had confirmed that it was worth the price and tenants
had been identified for both the shop and the soup kitchen. They
would be charged enough to cover the total ground rent of £120 a year.
'The poor people themselves' had raised £300 and might well contribute £200 more. A sale of work was to be held – 'Ladies willing to
co-operate are requested to correspond with Mrs Booth.' The inevitable
appeal included examples of the spectacular blessings enjoyed by the
charitable. One of them might well have been quoted in one of Mr
Caughey's earthly rewards and retribution sermons – a butcher told
William, 'Since my conversion, the Lord has blessed me greatly. I am
feeding eight pigs for Christmas and shall give Him one of them for the
People's Market.' The announcement of the intended purchase contained what by William Booth's standards amounted to an apology:

> Perhaps it will be said that we are always appealing. The other
> day it was to buy a Beer House, then a Unitarian Chapel, then a
> Penny Theatre, now a People's Market. True we did desire these
> places and His people most cheerfully enabled us to serve them
> and Our columns today show that the real work for God and
> Souls and Eternity is being done for them.

The apology was also proof of the speed at which the East London
Christian Mission was expanding. Every time a suitable property
became available, William Booth tried to raise enough money for a
year's rent or purchase of the lease. He felt a proper Victorian respect
for property. Bricks and mortar were a guarantee that the Mission was
in East London to stay. For a couple of months 'amidst much trial and
persecution and notwithstanding the excitement attendant on the
General Election [of 1868], the work of God continued to prosper
through the entire mission'.[14] The election, which William Booth

clearly regarded as an intolerable intrusion into his work, ended with the first of William Ewart Gladstone's great victories. Within a couple of years a New Education Act would provide at least elementary schooling for the children of the slums, and assuming that he read the papers William must have known that a Cabinet with radical ministers – though led by a godly rather than a radical Prime Minister – was about to be formed. But there is no evidence to suggest that he took the slightest interest. Apart from the one dismissive reference none of his letters or papers mentioned the election again. William Booth was only concerned with what William Booth did. It was perhaps the principal reason for his unlikely success.

However, he was beginning – no doubt as a result of the evidence all around him – to see poverty as an intrinsic problem. 'There is every possibility that the approaching Winter will be one of greater destitution in the East of London than the last. Already the workhouses are crowded and cases of death from actual starvation are occurring.'[15] By January 1869 he was echoing Benjamin Disraeli's view that England was two nations, 'all the poverty of the metropolis, together with no small proportion of that from the provinces, seem steadily to be gravitating towards East London, even as the bulk of metropolitan ease and affluence inclines towards the West. London is becoming more and closely divided into two great sections of rich and poor which will ere long prove as wide asunder as the two poles.' He had not completely lost faith in politics, for he grudgingly admitted that 'legislation may do something to counter the mischief' – without suggesting what that legislation might be. But he had no doubt that 'the spread of religious feeling will do more'. Gradually the idea of salvation and social reform marching hand in hand was beginning to dominate his life, even though he had no steady view about remedies for the poverty he had grown to hate. Sometimes he was the Samuel Smiles of Methodism, insisting that 'the true Christian is the real self-helper'; then he argued that unless the conditions for improvement were created – opening new factories and closing old public houses – men would not be able to climb out of poverty and degradation. Forty years later, he denounced socialism in a formal lecture (which inevitably became a pamphlet) not only because he believed it to be godless and materialistic but equally because of its denial of individual economic responsibility. In January 1869 he had just begun to think about how society could become more responsive to the needs of the poor. But he had already decided that 'in bringing the truths of religion before the suffering masses, we are also assisting the great work of social reform'.[16]

That winter the plans to buy the People's Market did not progress in a way which encouraged faith in William Booth's worldly judgement. At first it seemed that a miscalculation of running costs – blamed on Mr Price, the architect – might force the cancellation of the entire project. Henry Reed of Tunbridge Wells was asked to come to the rescue. He refused to help on the grounds that the Mission was only buying a thirty-eight-year lease and he believed, as a matter of principle, in freeholds. But William Booth was determined that the People's Market would become the property of the Mission, and he was not prepared to allow the Revival Union management committee (which had been appointed to act as his agents, not to take independent action) to stand in his way. So he determined to reverse the original decision which he had loyally supported in public but always known to be wrong. A new deal was done. John McAll sold the lease for £750 less than his original price but leased back the shop, house and soup kitchen for £130 a year. Within weeks it was reported that the soup factory was not a commercial proposition and it was moved to new premises in the Whitechapel Road. But at least the Mission had acquired a large and impressive central meeting hall.

After a year of frantic expansion and at least a half-hearted attempt at business, the East London Christian Mission published its first formal balance sheet. Amongst the Mission's sponsors – their names proudly printed on the official letterhead – were Samuel Morley, by then a Member of Parliament; Morgan and Chase, the founding fathers; George Pearce, 'a member of the stock exchange' and, more significant in terms of his power and influence, son of the man who had made Middlesbrough what Mr Gladstone called 'an infant giant and an infant gentleman'. The list was completed by two captains (one naval and one military) and three ministers of religion.

The annual report which accompanied the accounts was even more impressive than the list of patrons and sponsors. It listed thirteen 'preaching stations in which the Mission held one hundred and forty services (indoor and out) every week'. Some of them were no more than street corners. The list included new 'stations' in Stepney and Bethnal Green. Others were the assorted premises – the Oriental

Theatre in Poplar High Street, the New East London Theatre in Whitechapel as well as the Eastern Alhambra in Limehouse and a 'large shop' in Hackney Road – which William Booth had acquired after the long series of appeals for which he had come close to apologising. Between them the actual meeting rooms could accommodate a total congregation of '8,000 persons, every seat free'. William Booth calculated that 14,000 people attended mission services each week and participated in the extraordinary variety of activities which the report listed with such obvious pride. They included (as well as Bible classes and mothers' meetings) tract societies (which examined contemporary theological work) and a whole range of social activities that encouraged those limited pleasures which William Booth regarded as respectable. Evening classes were held 'in reading, writing and arithmetic'. 'Relief of the Destitute and Sick Poor' was provided by 'the distribution of bread, meat, small amounts of money and soup kitchens'. A reading room – full of biblical and morally uplifting materials – was soon to be built. A 'penny bank' had proved too ambitious an undertaking for the first years, but the idea would be resurrected as soon as the time and circumstances were opportune. In 1868 the principles on which the Salvation Army was to be built – the encouragement of virtue through the provision of shelter, food and clothing – were already established in William Booth's mind. All he lacked was a permanent cadre of full-time enthusiasts – his sovereign remedy against backsliding – and money.

Perhaps the Mission was the victim of its own success. For as well as reporting the vast expansion in its work, William Booth had to record what he described as constant 'petty victimisation'. The details of the persecution made his description of the assaults sound like a brave understatement:

> If we opened the windows, mud and stones and occasional
> fireworks were thrown through. Consequently we had to sit
> and endure the stifling heat until it was impossible for delicate
> people to remain in the place. Sometimes trails of gunpowder
> were laid, the dress of one devoted sister was thus actually set
> on fire during the service.[17]

Perhaps more disturbing, 'the open-air gatherings were harassed by the police and the landlords and frequenters of adjacent public houses'. The partnership between publicans and police officers was, over the years, to put William Booth and his followers in constant danger. When the roughs and publicans' hired louts attacked the preachers, the police sometimes looked on with amused detachment. Occasionally they took the part of the assailants against their victims. But they rarely came to the defence of the persecuted evangelists until an outcry in the House of Commons forced reluctant Justices of the Peace to do their duty.

The violence escalated week by week.

> From Whitechapel, for the last three Sundays, a band of brethren has gone out to labour on the Ratcliffe Highway. The neighbourhood is beyond comparison the foulest sink of moral corruption in the metropolis . . . Much opposition has been encountered: at first the persecutors contented themselves with ridiculing and mutilating the tracts which they were given, tearing them into shreds and throwing them over the speaker. The next Sunday, they threw the brother down three separate times: the Sunday following, potatoes, cabbage and other refuse was thrown at them. While Brother Rose was speaking, about one hundred Irish fell upon him . . . one young man, very well dressed, seized him by the throat, another struck him a heavy blow to the cheek.[18]

The police 'compelled the preachers to desist, dragging them away and threatening to lock them up unless they went away. In obedience to the police, the brethren departed . . .' In Three Colts Lane 'so soon as Brother Rose and Fisher had commenced the open-air service, a policeman came up and ordered them away . . . Brother Rose said that it would be an honour to be locked up for the Master.' The distinction which he sought was granted: he was arrested and charged with obstruction. When the case came to court, the magistrates judged that the evangelists had 'shown too much zeal'.[19] They were bound over for six months on their own recognizances not to repeat the offence. 'Notwithstanding the bitter persecution . . . the brethren continued their meetings.'[20]

The pattern of violent opposition which was to stalk the Booths for thirty years was gradually being established. It was the product of several factors – brewers' fears that the teetotal evangelists would reduce their trade; popular resentment at the uninvited intrusion into private lives; police impatience with behaviour which provoked violence in others. As William Booth's campaigns gained momentum and became more successful, the reasons to hate him and his work multiplied. The only possible response was the soft answer and the turned cheek. 'A young man came along and interrupted us . . . one of our brethren remonstrated with him . . . at which he threatened to knock the Brother down.' William made an offer to arrange a prize fight – on the understanding that it was preceded by prayers. 'Then a drunken man came up and, with curses, threatened to break up the meeting.' William Booth 'took hold of him and, drawing him to the centre of the meeting, said "Let us pray" and, falling on his knees, called on God to have mercy on the poor drunkard.' The effects, at least according to William Booth, were spectacular. 'When I arose, instead of the small congregation with which we had commenced, there was a large concourse of people.'[21]

The opposition was, in its way, a tribute to William Booth's success. At the end of the 1860s he was everywhere in the East End of London, and it was impossible to pass a public house without being urged to accept one of his pamphlets. His preachers were on every street corner and the sound of his hymns disturbed Sunday morning rest from Limehouse to Whitechapel. He would have been less than human not to rejoice at the success with which he did the Lord's work and the distress he caused to the devil's local representatives. In the heady atmosphere of conquest, he did not even pause to consider the risks of expanding more quickly than his resources allowed. Even if he had realised the dangers, he would still have rejected the idea of proceeding with caution.

On New Year's Eve 1868, William Booth was preparing for the Watch Night Service when he received a telegram from Henry Reed. It invited him to travel down to Dunorlan on the last train. That William accepted the invitation, at such a time and on such a night, illustrates his continued susceptibility to men of power and wealth – a weakness which grew with the years. So, abandoning the Mission's New Year observances, he travelled down to Tunbridge Wells. Reed welcomed him with a reiteration of his concern about the Mission's financial future. He wanted to provide it with a permanent headquarters – rented, not leased. But his help was contingent on no further use being made of any of the theatres in which Sunday services were held. In Reed's view, by paying rent for them on the Sabbath, the Mission was helping to finance their godless weekdays.

Reed had taken the option on a piece of land near to the site where William had held his tented services. He could buy it for £3–4,000, and would gladly spend up to £7,000 more building a hall which would accommodate a 2,000-strong congregation – as long as William Booth would agree to fill it. But it was clear that, although he would be called Superintendent, William would not superintend in any practical sense. Reed was explicit that, unless the new mission was run in the way he chose, he would reclaim the deeds. And one of the requirements was that his resident minister would preach there and nowhere else.

Perhaps William was already growing restive. Or perhaps the idea of being formally tied to the East End unnerved him. But once again he rejected salaried employment on the grounds that it would be a sin to turn his back on the work to which God had called him – wherever it might be. William Booth, although years away from commanding an army of his own, was already a general in spirit, and he was not about to become anybody's mercenary chaplain. He had bigger and better ideas of his own. His New Year message to the Mission asked, 'What are you going to do in 1869?', and then answered his own question: 'The great test of character is *doing*. God, the Church and the world all estimate men not according to their sayings, feelings or desiring, but according to their doings.'[22] William Booth was fulfilling his destiny as John Wesley's heir. 'Eschewing sin' was not enough. One convert had to make another. Godly men and women struggled to create a heaven on earth. 'Doing' was everything.

During 1869 the doings in East London were already set in the pattern which was to characterise William Booth's endeavours for the rest of his life. New recruits were sent straight into the front line. Conversions were recorded at The Blind Beggar – not a public house which maintained its reputation for sanctity. Nine hundred paupers were given breakfast in early April and five hundred more took tea on Good Friday. William Booth described venial transgressions in the language of mortal sin. Two young men from Sclater Street who 'had formerly spent their Sabbaths gambling in a coffee house . . . were pulled out of the fire'.

Although on 20 April Samuel Morley wrote from the House of Commons with 'pleasure in sending my cheque', there was a moment in May when William Booth almost despaired – all confidence 'spent in the conflict with ignorance and vice and woe'.[23] But a month later his spirits were uplifted by a new initiative – Christian Female Pioneers. 'A few sisters, anxious to work for Jesus, formed themselves into a Christian Pioneer Band and meet together on the Friday evening from seven to eight. They have already established a cottage prayer meeting in one of the darkest streets in Bethnal Green . . . They will specially work amongst the children.'[24] Ten years later the Female Pioneers' natural successors were called 'Hallelujah Lasses'. A hundred years on, their lineal descendants were going from public house to public house on Saturday nights selling copies of *The War Cry*. William Booth's ideas of the development of active Christianity barely changed in half a century; they were just adapted and applied with increasing success.

The wisdom of rejecting Henry Reed's suggestion that he should limit his activities to East London must have seemed to be confirmed in August when he visited Edinburgh, where 'the question of amalgamation of the two missions, to be worked under one superintendence, was urged [upon the London Mission] by the Edinburgh Friends'.[25] Not surprisingly, 'after much deliberation and prayer', William Booth 'agreed to the proposed amalgamation and . . . consented to remain in Edinburgh a week longer than intended in order to make all the necessary arrangements for working the mission on the plans and principles acted upon in the East of London'. It went without saying that 'the two missions would be worked under one superintendence'. There was no question about who the superintendent should be. The hopes encouraged in Scotland were to some extent compensation for the pain caused in England by the 'several slanderous letters and articles . . . of the most scurrilous kind [which] have been written and freely circulated'. William Booth was proud to announce, 'We have not replied, neither have our hearts fainted. We have fallen back on Matthew, Chapter V.'[26] For the rest of his life, William believed the absolute truth of Verse 12: 'Blessed are ye when men shall revile you and persecute you and say all manner of evil against you, falsely for my sake.' Abuse and assault became the symbols of success. But, as William Booth's fame grew, his attitude towards the slanders changed. Instead of allowing them to pass without contradiction, he refuted the libels at once. Instant rebuttal – the technique of modern politics – was invented by William Booth.

The decision to amalgamate with (or colonise) Edinburgh was announced in September. The following month, Mrs Booth was in Brighton at the request of the chapels where she had scored such a success two years earlier. She had a second triumph and, before she left, plans were laid to open a Mission Hall at the turn of the year. Suspicions that William Booth was beginning to develop wider ambitions than those which the East End Mission could gratify were confirmed by the October editorial in the *East London Evangelist*. It was entitled 'The Conversion of the World'. It recommended nothing more ambitious than that 'each converted person endeavour to bring one soul to God in the course of one year'. But it was an indication of how his mind was moving. Like John Wesley, he was coming to believe that the world was his parish.

9

Suffer Little Children

When, in November 1865, William and Catherine Booth moved into 1 Cambridge Lodge Villas, Hackney, the change of address was the result of one of Catherine's rare admissions of weakness. She was pregnant for the seventh time in barely nine years and, because she meant to go on evangelising until a month before the birth, she found the journey to and from Hammersmith more than she could bear. Evangeline, born on Christmas Day, was therefore the first of the Booth children to enter the world in permanent accommodation. Catherine had good reason to be cautious. Marion, born eighteen months earlier in Leeds, had immediately developed 'convulsive fits'.[1] But Catherine was preaching again five weeks after the invalid baby's birth – and continued to do so even when Marion contracted the smallpox which 'permanently weakened her health'. The care with which Catherine approached Evangeline's arrival was wholly untypical of her general attitude towards her children's health and welfare – the one cavalier aspect of her whole character. She certainly worried about them, but not enough to provide constant attention. And she regularly reminded them – very often in letters from distant places – that no mother had ever loved her children as she loved hers. The protestations of affection guaranteed stability of a sort. The letters were enough to convince the children that they had the most loving mother in the world, and made them feel wanted.

The move to Hackney at least provided the Booth children with a settled home just at the time when the scars of their strange life began to show. Their conduct confirmed that they were, by modern standards, 'disturbed'. William Booth, when he was actually with his family, encouraged long walks. 'It makes a great difference when they are done in, all of them. They're not half the trouble.'[2] Bramwell was the most difficult to persuade to do his spiritual duty. In Cardiff in 1863, the seven-year-old boy had outraged his parents by declining the offer of redemption. Six months later, in Walsall, he agreed to approach the penitent form and ask for forgiveness. The condition of holiness which he thus acquired did not provide the protection from temptation which Phoebe Palmer had promised. William Booth – again separated from his family – wrote to Catherine with the good news that he had acquired two white mice from the Sheffield Hallelujah Band. They were to be a present to Ballington. The attached message to Bramwell – known in the family as Willy during those formative years – was more severe. 'Tell Willy that if he does not obey Miss Macbean [the latest governess] and set his brothers and sisters a good example . . . he must be prepared not only to lose his dog but to live in the attic while I am at home, for I will not see him.'[3] However, the rewards of obedience included 'a party on Friday evening and . . . a great many more nuts'.

Bramwell was hyperactive. From Leeds his mother was able to report that he was 'getting on nicely with his lessons' under the supervision of Mr Hurst, a Free Church Minister who taught him twice each week. Latin was included in the syllabus, despite William's contempt for the study of dead languages. Mr Hurst found his pupil 'sharp as a needle but lacking application'. Both parents endorsed that judgement. His father said that 'he hops about like a pea in a frying pan and is as mischievous as a monkey'. His mother, less poetic, described him as 'very active with a restless disposition'. She did not think 'that he ever sat five minutes at a time on anybody's knee'.

The idea that their children lived under continual strain – moving from town to town, left in the care of unknown governesses and forced to accept an entirely adult view of religion – never troubled either Catherine or William Booth. When he was only eight, Bramwell shared both his parents' anxiety about their future and the resentment they felt against the Wesleyan establishment – knowing that the hero father, who could hold the crowds spellbound, 'was cold-shouldered, his preaching not wanted'.[4] Bramwell had every right to be disturbed.

Catherine accepted that, during the years of William's wanderings, Bramwell was not being properly educated. 'Nobody takes any pains with him when they know that he is only going for a few weeks. The last school, we thought, was a first-rate one, but the master took nearly all his books away and put him to babyish spelling which he learned years ago.'[5] But the difficulties continued. Tutors came and went. One was 'a Roman Catholic, something of a traveller . . . but he had been broken down by drink'. Bramwell thought that the brilliance of this 'remarkable man' contributed to his failure as a scholar. It made him dissatisfied with more pedestrian teachers, and, in consequence, contributed to his inattention. But another 'brilliant and attractive' man came along and convinced his pupil 'how fine it was really to know things'.[6]

The situation became so serious that Catherine briefly abandoned her fears of corruption through contact with ungodly boys and sent Bramwell to the City of London School. The experiment, which only lasted from January to April 1868, ended in catastrophe. Other boys, less godly than Bramwell, mocked his piety. One day he was tied to a tree while his heathen classmates charged at him like wild animals and demanded that he renounce his faith. Although crushed and bleeding, Bramwell remained true to his beliefs. A few days later Bramwell developed pleurisy. His mother regarded it as a direct result of his martyrdom.

Ballington was even worse behaved than Bramwell. In Walsall he 'became dreadfully unstable' and had to be kept out of the nursery because he 'knocked the little ones down without mercy'.[7] But Emma was a paragon of virtue. She 'lived in the memory' of one governess, 'intensely upright, scorning deceit and withal so very affectionate'.[8] Seeing a boy beating a donkey, she snatched the stick from his hand and beat him about the head and shoulders and asked him, 'How do you like it?' – a more violent replication of her mother's encounter with the pony's tormentor twenty years before. At the age of ten she was reluctant to speak at a tea meeting for orphan paupers, not because of diffidence or nerves but because, having been impatient with a servant earlier in the day, she did not feel in the necessary state of grace. Emma

was rarely subject to the criticisms with which her siblings were deluged. But she was not completely exempt from the barrage of moral
instruction and spiritual advice which was launched almost every day
against her less saintly brothers and sisters. Catherine's letters always
asserted how much her children were loved and missed. But the
protestations of affection were usually followed by terrible warnings
about the consequences of sin. The nineteenth-century biographers –
writing in William Booth's long shadow and with the admitted intention of confirming his greatness – attributed the constant illness of his
children to their parents' regular and fearless visits to slums in which
contagious diseases raged. A century later an alternative explanation is
at least possible. All the children were subject to pressure which their
infant minds could not accommodate. Even judged against the behaviour of the most pious Victorian Nonconformists, the Booths' treatment
of their children was bizarre. Long after Catherine was dead, it was
described by Jane Short, one of the two lodgers who were taken into
the house in Hackney to help meet the household bills.

Jane Short and Mary Billups – the daughter of the contractor who
had befriended William Booth during his Welsh campaign – moved in
with the Booths during 1867, the year in which Lucy (the eighth and
last of Catherine's children) was born. Miss Billups (who did not fit into
the strange household and was accused of holding herself aloof) made
it clear that she did not want to become 'one of the family'. She was not
used to life as it was lived by the Booths – constant prayer, absolute discipline and rice pudding every day. Even the amusements, in which the
children were allowed to indulge in moderation, underlined the
family's peculiarities. Competitive games were forbidden and cricket
and football denounced as frivolities which distracted grown men from
serious pursuits. Outside they played 'fox and geese', which involved
William Booth – always the fox – chasing and catching his children.
The favourite indoor pastime – apart from having his head rubbed –
required William Booth to lie on the floor. His children then tried to
pick him up while he imitated a rag doll which had lost most of its
stuffing.[9] The garden had become a menagerie but the only inhabitants
in which William was really interested were the industrious silkworms.
For years he believed that fiction only aroused temptation and he constantly warned his children against Charles Dickens. However, some
time during the late 1860s he read and enjoyed *Jane Eyre*, *Les*

Misérables and the collected works of James Fenimore Cooper. His interests expanded from Red Indians to the French Revolution, and he became a great defender of Danton and Robespierre.[10] Religion was never far from his mind. One day, during a picnic, he picked up the kettle (which mercifully had not yet been put on the fire) and splashed everyone around him with the water which was to be boiled for tea. As he splashed he cried, 'I will sprinkle you with water and you will be cleansed from your sins!' He then demanded a general assurance that his wife, children and lodgers all accepted the promise of Ezekiel. Nobody present thought that he was joking.

The second lodger, Jane Short, was of a less aloof disposition. In old age she talked with a cheerful lack of discretion about life with the Booths in the 1860s. She had met Catherine in 1866 at a service in Margate, became first a regular member of her East London congregation and then a regular visitor to Cambridge Lodge Villas. Her admiration for Catherine did not prevent her from describing the Booths' peculiarities. The man who became patriarch as well as General of the Salvation Army refused, as an indication of domestic humility, to sit at the head of his own table, carve the family joint or pour the tea. The joint was available for carving only during William Booth's early married life. As he approached middle age his diet became increasingly peculiar. 'For the greater part of the last forty years of his life, he did not eat butcher's meat nor did he care for poultry . . . the dish he fancied most was vegetable soup.'[11] The tedium was occasionally relieved with toast and baked apples. Even when he had a young family to feed, his idea of a feast was currants in the daily rice pudding, a feature of high days and holidays. Believing that cleanliness was at least related to godliness, he insisted that every member took a cold bath on six days a week and a hot one on Sundays.

It was Jane Short who, recalling her first Christmas with the family, described William Booth's discovery of why the tap room was such an attraction. The Dickensian Christmas was not, by then, part of the English tradition, but Prince Albert had brought the Christmas tree to England and presents had become a feature of Boxing Day. The young Booths had to wait for their gifts until their father returned from preaching in Whitechapel. When he got home, instead of satisfying their impatience, he sat morose and silent. Then he began to pace the room. They knew better than to interrupt his meditations and waited patiently for him to address them. 'I'll never have a Christmas Day like this again. The poor having nothing but their public houses. Nothing!' The following year the Booth family gave away one hundred and fifty Christmas puddings – most of them cooked in the copper boiler in their own kitchen. By the end of the century the Salvation Army was distributing 30,000 puddings each Christmas in London alone.[12] No doubt the recipients did not worry much about the motives. But William Booth's purpose was clear. He wanted to provide a cheerful alternative to the public house. He had decided that the way to a man's soul was through his stomach.

The description of William Booth's character was a noble attempt to match candour and loyalty. 'The General was a *force*. He dominated everything . . . You knew the difference in the house directly he opened the door. You felt his presence. Of course he was odd. He often used to say, "Sister Jane, the Booths are an odd lot" . . . I've known him suddenly kneel down in the middle of breakfast and give thanks to God because a letter he had opened contained money for the Mission'.[13] Reading Jane Short's account of those early days, it seems astonishing that any of the Booth children achieved even comparative normality. They were certainly strange. But they were not as strange as their upbringing entitled them to be.

Miss Short was almost unique in speaking frankly about Catherine Booth's undoubted character defects. Perhaps she wanted to diminish the 'Mother of the Army' in the hope of further exalting its General, whom she clearly worshipped. Whatever the reason, she was alone in describing Catherine as a burden, a 'great invalid whose suffering at times made her irritable and exacting'. The adjective by which Mrs Booth's condition was qualified carries overtones of hypochondria. But it was the cures which were bogus, not the illness, and she bore her undoubtedly genuine suffering with a fortitude which guaranteed that she rarely allowed her pain to cloud her senses or diminish the commitment to the cause. No doubt Miss Short was right to praise William's kindness. 'Never once did he say a harsh word, never once did he try rallying her with rough encouragement.' He was sometimes 'cross and irritable' and often 'too stern with the children'. But he was always gentle with his wife.

He was so stern with the children that he would 'often whip them when another would have tried gentler methods, particularly Bramwell

who came into more whipping than any of his brothers'. Poor
Bramwell was the first of all the young Booths to show any inclination
to break away from the thrall in which William and Catherine thought
their sons and daughters should be held. As soon as he realised that
there was a world outside his family he wanted to be a doctor. He was
forbidden even to think about such a thing, and was pressed in the
Booth mould until he resembled the shape of his father and was
thought fit to follow in the great man's footsteps. His inheritance was
the Salvation Army and a ruined life.

Bramwell was certainly prepared for the task with great care. His
sister Kate built a penitent form in the nursery at which their dolls were
required to kneel each day. And he was left in no doubt that the Booths
regarded redemption as involving a good deal more than constant religious observance. All the children were taught and came to understand
the need to live a Christian life. Jane Short's father – 'an old-fashioned
man who smoked a church warden pipe' – drank gin and water, a regular working-class cordial in Victorian England. On a visit to the old
man, Ballington (aged seven) took a sip from the glass and then ran
home shouting, 'I've broken the pledge.' He was first beaten and then
forgiven. William Booth usually reacted to the children's confessions by
offering them the chance of praying convincingly or being whipped.
Poor Ballington was always anxious to improve but invariably found
improvement difficult. He tried desperately to live as his parents would
wish and spent hours at what he called 'the observation point' at the
end of the school garden. 'I sit and pray and talk with God and point
out my faults and ask Him to forgive me.' His mother, no doubt hoping
to offer welcome advice, replied, 'Choose the boys to be your companions who most fear God, love God and pray together when you can
and help each other.' Even the messages about mundane family matters
were written in a tone which was simultaneously didactic and censorious. Catherine told Ballington, 'I am willing for you to have raw eggs
for lunch but not for tea' – though whether she was applying the
restraint for moral or dietary reasons was not made clear. Ballington
was as much distressed by the envelope as by the message it contained. 'Mind,' he pleaded, 'that you don't put Ballington on the letter
again because all the boys will see it and call me by that name.'

The letters from Catherine to her children and their often fraught
replies tell their own sad tale. Bramwell, when only thirteen, was

moved to write to his mother with a confession of evangelical failure: 'I have tried to use my influence over A, but it does not seem that I have done him any good, at least as far as I can judge. The elder brother came home this afternoon and made a great change in them which is not the least for the better. They both, especially the younger, dislike prayer.' Kate, at the same age, was sent to visit a friend who, having been attracted to evangelical Christianity, was reluctant to break the news to her High Church parents. Catherine advised her daughter, 'Be much in prayer and wisdom to do the Lord's errand there . . . You must explain to her that confession is the only way to keep her blessing. Tell her never to mind if he cannot help crying. I wish more people cried about their sins and cried after their survival.' Emma, aged eleven, was given special uplifting advice. 'You see where your mistake is. Now take hold of the help of the Lord to remedy it. When you are crying to the Lord to give you back your blessing, believe that He does it just then and afterwards. If Satan says, "No, you have not got it" and tempts you to feel naughty, say, "Oh yes I have."'

Occasionally Catherine's other children won their mother's approval. But even then the congratulations were laced with stern injunctions. None of the children could ever have felt that their parents were satisfied with their behaviour. A letter from Catherine to Bramwell announced that she was 'better pleased' with his last effort since it showed 'more trouble and care', and also contained comments on the sporting life as he enjoyed it with his brother:

> I told you my opinion about Christian boys joining in games
> and I thought you would give them up at once . . . Now it is
> bad enough to have to live with unconverted boys without
> playing with them; this is unnecessary and you see what comes
> of it. Why should the accident have happened to you, instead
> of some other boys? Because you had no business there! It will
> not surprise me if Ballington's eye is injured for life . . . What a
> pity to have to reflect, if it should be so, that I got this at
> hockey, joining with the world. I hope he is keeping his eye
> constantly wet bandaged . . . You and Ballington can play ball
> together. Never mind if there is not so much fun. There will be
> a good conscience and that will more than make up for it.[14]

Not satisfied with condemning hockey as the devil's pastime and warning that those who played it risked God's instant retribution, Catherine Booth concluded with a warning against 'light and foolish talk' and a complaint that he had not written to his sister Emma for some time. It ended with what must have been the most dispiriting passage in the whole litany of complaints: 'Is the spelling in your last letter your own or did Ballington help you? You should play games at spelling as you go along. Spell, spell, *spell!*'

By the time that the older children were in their early teens, Catherine was more or less a permanent invalid – a permanent invalid who travelled and preached, but a permanent invalid nevertheless. And after the birth of Lucy in 1867 – from which William said she never quite recovered – Catherine's own physical condition began to have a morbid effect on her mind. Her moods still changed dramatically and without perceptible cause. But the gloom, when it came, was deeper: 'I know I ought not, of all saints and sinners either, to be depressed . . . but I cannot help it . . . The doctor says, "Never mind. Regard it as the result of your affliction." But this does not satisfy me . . . I cannot fight nor run. I can only endure – oh that I could always say with patience.'[15] Inevitably her mood affected her children. After a summer visit to Henry Reed in Kent, Bramwell wrote a letter to his mother which, for a thirteen-year-old boy, was as disturbing as it was extraordinary. 'Friday, July 16 1869, Good class. Great blessings. Very happy . . . May the Lord keep ever the work. Heart not well at all.' By the time he got back to London his mother had left to preach in the provinces. He wrote her an apology for his whole existence: 'I do feel very low in spirits tonight. I am quite disappointed with myself. I feel quite despairing with regards to future health. It seems as if my Heavenly Father did not think it best for me to be strong and well but it is a great trial to me to think that I shall be a burden to those close to me.'[16]

Bramwell's depression was, although encouraged by the strange atmosphere in which he lived, almost certainly genetic. Both his parents suffered periods of black despair, his mother's fuelled by a genuine chronic illness and his father's increasingly by hypochondria. The maternal genes were probably the stronger. For old Mrs Mumford was similarly afflicted. The Mumford syndrome would, these days, be considered just another illness to be treated (and almost certainly cured) by drugs which corrected the chemical imbalance that was its cause. But in the middle of the nineteenth century melancholy was thought to be a disease of the spirit and the soul. Despair, a denial of God's power and love, was heresy. For an evangelist, periodic gloom was the ultimate blasphemy. And Catherine became increasingly depressed by her depression. Life for her children – moved from town to town, left for long periods in the care of barely known nurses, subject to oppressive discipline when their parents returned, obliged to behave with piety far beyond their years and obliged to live in the shadow of their mother's periodic depressions – must have been truly terrible.

Some times must have been worse than others. In the summer of 1867, Mrs Mumford was diagnosed as suffering from cancer. For a few weeks she moved in with the Booths. Then they rented a house which was near enough to Cambridge Lodge Villas for her daughter to be in constant attendance. As the pain increased, Catherine administered the morphine. Mrs Mumford went to her Maker so sure of redemption that she was able to 'cast a look of mingled love and triumph and pass away into the presence of the Redeemer' in the serene certainty of eternal life. Her progress was accompanied by the singing of her family, assembled at her bedside. If she heard, and understood the words, she was not left in any doubt about her prognosis: 'We are waiting by the river / We are waiting by the shore / Only waiting for the angels / Who will come and bear us o'er.'

The children were brought to the bedside for the final moments, not in itself an unusual arrangement at a time when death was accepted as a normal event. But Bramwell 'was thrown into a highly nervous condition of grief' which his father only partly remedied when he 'explained the Christian hope of reunion'. William Booth still had his own ordeal to face. An autopsy was performed on Mrs Mumford, not to determine the cause of death but to see if medical science could learn anything about the treatment of her fatal disease. It was a strange decision for Catherine to take. For she was normally so opposed to modern medicine that she regarded vaccination as a dangerous superstition. Even more bizarre was her insistence that William be present when the autopsy was performed. It was all part of her strange preoccupation with things of the flesh – a characteristic which her husband shared. However he felt about the experience, he met his wife's wishes and watched the dissection of his mother-in-law.

It seems unlikely that he found the experience intolerably traumatic. The body was, after all, no more than the home of the soul and after death became an empty shell. In any event, he was clearly a man of profound insensitivity. No other assessment of his character can account for his reaction to his children's distress at the death of the family dog. It had been shot on his orders after it snapped at a servant who scolded it for leaping at bed linen which she was hanging out to dry. The dog was shot in haste and William Booth regretted his decision when he realised what he should have already known. The children were heartbroken. He decided, in an attempt to ease their pain, to retrieve the carcass and have the pelt made into a rug. When they reacted with hysteria rather than thanks, he was bewildered by their lack of gratitude.

Acting on the information provided by the grieving family, the registrar entered 'widow' on the death certificate. Catherine's father was alive and well, but dead to the church and therefore to his daughter. God was the head of the Booths' only family. The whole family was expected to fulfil their obligations to the only authority William Booth acknowledged. As soon as they could mouth the necessary words, the children began to imitate their parents' evangelism – preaching to their dolls and converting the animals in the garden. Long before they could have been expected to understand the true meaning of religion they were introduced into the reality of revivalism. Emma, always described as 'shy and retiring', conducted children's services in the front room of the family's Hackney home when she was thirteen, and at seventeen was preaching to adult congregations. Her mother rejoiced (with some surprise) when, in conformity with the family tradition, she stepped forward to save the day at St Leonard's by shouting down the roughs who were disrupting the meeting.

Young Catherine – Kate to her father until she acquired the absurd sobriquet *La Maréchale* – preached at prayer meetings when she was still a child, often being brought on like the precocious daughter of fading music hall artistes to win the sympathy of noisy hecklers. Indeed, she saved the Army from so many catastrophes that her father often called her 'Blücher', in tribute to the number of occasions when she had rescued the day with the reinforcement of religious passion. When she was only thirteen she routed the drunks who had shouted down brother Bramwell outside The Cat & Mutton in Hackney.

There is no doubt that Kate was the star performer of the family, and that Bramwell, although older and clearly being prepared to inherit his father's kingdom, accepted hers as the more lively talent. Indeed it was Bramwell who encouraged his sister to preach and reconciled his mother to Kate's precocious evangelism. During one of Mrs Booth's southern tours, Bramwell was sent out to address the open-air meetings which acted as advertisements for his mother's evening rally. When Mrs Booth heard that he had persuaded his sister to add a sermon of her own, she was initially dubious as to the propriety of one so young exposing herself to the hooligans who hung around the fringes of the congregation. Bramwell told her, 'You will have to settle this question with God, for Kate is surely called and inspired by Him for this particular work as you are yourself.' God and Mrs Booth came to an arrangement and, for some time, Bramwell shepherded and chaperoned his sister as she moved from meeting to meeting. The activity was, in itself, a strange way for a sixteen-year-old girl to pass her time. The way in which she approached it was more extraordinary still. Bramwell wrote, with something approaching awe, of her addressing 'a crowd assembled at the theatre then used by us on Sabbaths. It was composed of many of the lowest and roughest in town.' When the teenage girl announced that her text for the evening was 'Death of the Righteous' the whole auditorium – families in the stalls and circle as well as the roughs by the exits – collapsed in derisive laughter. Kate advanced from the table at the back of the stage and, from immediately behind the footlights, began to sing, 'The rocks and the mountains will all flee away and you will need a hiding-place one day.' In the silence which followed, she announced her text in full, 'Let me die the death of the righteous and let my last end be like His.'

Kate had begun to put Bramwell in the shade and tempt her father to commit the sin of pride. 'William writes that he is utterly amazed at Kate,' Mrs Booth told Miss Billups. 'He had no idea she could preach as she does. He says she is a born leader and will, if she keeps right, see thousands saved . . . Dear friend, join me in praying that she may be kept humble and simple.' But Kate was beginning to show signs of worldly ambition. She even wanted a proper education. Naturally her mother would not hear of it:

I have not changed about the school. I still think that a great

deal of teaching would be useful to you and I would like you to
have it, but I fear the associations will lead you to strive after
too much and to imbibe a worldly spirit and aim . . . You talk
my darling girl about Herbert becoming a mighty man in God's
Israel. Mightier youths than he have fallen. Besides, where did
he get the principles you have such faith in? Under his mother's
thumb and eye, not in a school for little boys preparing for
college and where deception and lying and infidelity are the
order of the day.[17]

For the Booth children, the 1860s was a disturbed decade. Even
when it seemed that at last they had a settled home, Catherine insisted
that they moved on. Cambridge Lodge Villas was no longer tolerable to
her – largely because of the constant noise from the building site on the
other side of the road. She had set her heart on Belgrave House in Gore
Road, a quiet backwater off Victoria Park Road in Hackney. It was a
substantial, detached, three-storey property opposite the park – not
quite the house that a Forsyte would have found acceptable but certainly, with its garden, railings and bow windows, far above Mr Pooter's
aspirations. William feared that the rent and upkeep were beyond the
family's means. But, as usual, Catherine's will prevailed. They moved in
just before Christmas 1869.

10

Singing All the Time

William Booth was a man of unrestrained ambition. His principal aspirations were for the great cause which he had been called to serve but, like so many men of destiny, he did not believe that it could prosper without him. His success and the success of his mission could not, at least in his own mind, be separated. The possible extension of his empire to Edinburgh and Brighton – with prospects of further expansion in Croydon – had confirmed, in his mind, that the Lord had not intended him to limit his work to the East End of London. And his discovery that the poor liked their religion twopenny-coloured rather than penny-plain convinced him that God's work was best done from appropriately spectacular premises.

He therefore regarded the development of a People's Mission Hall as a moral duty. He discharged his obligation by negotiating a new and immensely complicated deal with John McAll. The financial details – McAll's acceptance of a reduced price and the lease-back of part of the property – were not regarded as information which the rank and file supporters of the East London Christian Mission needed to know.

The decision to move the soup kitchen from the Mission Hall to Whitechapel Road was announced in February 1870. According to the official explanation, the Whitechapel site had been chosen because there was 'an abundance of room' where it was hoped to provide, in addition to the soup kitchen, 'various kinds of cheap refreshment and a reading room'. The notice ended with what was, in fact, a statement of William Booth's basic evangelising philosophy: 'We intend the People's Soup Kitchen to be a half-way house to the People's Mission Hall and this satisfying of the outer man with bread that perishes, we hope will lead on to the satisfying of the inner man with the bread that comes from heaven.'[1] The People's Hall was to become the symbol of his success in the capital, but his real aim was expansion throughout the United Kingdom.

William Booth had become so certain of the wider prospect that the East London Christian Mission had become the Christian Mission – without any territorially limiting adjective preceding its name.* Once the Mission had a title which encompassed the whole world, the name of the magazine was changed to match the new expectation. The *East London Evangelist* became the *Christian Mission Magazine*. Such were the aspirations of the new Mission and its celebrated resident minister that the great Charles Grandison Finney wrote an original article for the March issue. It denounced the desire to conform with fashion as an attitude 'at war with the spirit of the gospels'. Men and women who were slaves to the mood of the moment were described as 'ungodly sinners'. It is hard to believe that the people of East London, to whom William Booth preached most days, needed to be warned against dressing *à la mode* or aping the fleeting fancies of the Prince of Wales, but William Booth took up the subject with enthusiasm. The April issue of the magazine set out all the possible objections to Finney's call for the rejection of worldly ways and then knocked each one down with clubbing blows. Objection 7 suggested, 'No matter how we dress if our hearts are right?' That suggestion was met with the stern if slightly incomprehensible rebuke, 'Then your heart may be right when your conduct is wrong.' More severe still was his refutation of Objection 3, 'You carry religion too far away from the multitude. It is better not to

---

*In his Ph.D. thesis *The Salvation Army in England*, Dr G. H. Horridge dates the four changes in name in four years from membership cards and reports thus: August 1865 – Christian Revival Association; January 1866 – East London Christian Revival Union; September 1867 – East London Christian Mission; September 1869 – Christian Mission.

set up an artificial distinction between church and world.' The splutter of indignation spattered the page: 'The direct reverse of this is true. The nearer you bring the church to the world the more you annihilate the reasons that ought to stand out in the view of the world for their changing sides and coming over to the Church.' William Booth had never been completely able to suppress his quietist instincts – the desire to feel that he had been chosen and, at the same time, to insist that no one was excluded. He wanted to lead an exclusive sect which was deeply integrated into society, to be *in* the world, but not of it.

Throughout the year the *Christian Mission Magazine* offered its readers unremittingly uplifting advice. In October, it published no less than fifty-four objections to tobacco. As well as warning, with remarkable prescience, about the damaging effect on throat and lungs, the denunciation claimed that nicotine addiction had 'done much to fill poor-houses and lunatic asylums'. The industry which profited from the devil's weed was 'one main upholder of slavery in the United States of America'. The article concluded, 'To young and old we say, TOUCH NOT TOBACCO. A CURSE IS ON IT.'[2]

At the same time, the Soup Kitchen and the Poor Man's Dining Hall in Whitechapel was 'working admirably'. On a single day two thousand men and women had 'received soup and other food. And this, it must be remembered, is with the place still unfurnished.' However, the work was, or was said to be, progressing at great speed. 'Our soup hall will accommodate one hundred and fifty, the coffee and reading room one hundred. We can bake for two hundred and fifty people and boil for as many more. We want large soup pans going which will make, under the system we practise, four thousand one hundred and sixty quarts daily.' The precision of the calculation was matched by the optimism of the management. 'The whole affair, when in operation, will be *self-supporting*. For every guinea we receive, we send one hundred tickets to various clergymen and dissenting ministers, bible readers, missionaries and Bible women to be distributed among the starving poor – [they] entitle the bearer to one quart of meat soup and a slice of bread . . .'[3] It was morally as well as financially essential for both enterprises to balance their books. Unrestrained charity, William Booth believed, only damaged the recipient. Every item of help had to be paid for in cash or in kind.

On 10 April 1870, when the People's Hall was officially opened,

William – still struggling to overcome the unknown illness which had inspired a March editorial on the duty to battle on against adversity – was too unwell to preach the Sunday evening sermon.[4] Catherine took his place. But fortunately, four days later, he was sufficiently recovered to attend the emergency committee meeting which he had called immediately the opening ceremonies were completed. He had disturbing news to report. The Christian Mission faced a financial crisis.

The report revealed that the Mission's budget had been exceeded by several hundred pounds. The cost of the building alterations alone had risen to £1,411 and the removal of the soup plant was estimated at £95 – an item for which no one had budgeted. The whole operation had been conducted without the slightest attempt at financial control. Although it had been agreed that all the sub-contracting should be allocated by open tender, the work had not gone to the lowest bidder. Booth paid what bills he could from his own small savings – an obligation of pride and propriety – but clearly the debts were not his. That, however, was not the view of the architect, who wrote to say that he would hold Booth personally responsible for the outstanding amount. He had signed a contract with the Mission's General Superintendent, as William Booth had come to be described, not with its committee and unless his bill was paid he would sue the individual, not the institution.

There was no way in which the Booths could hope to clear the debt. They lived comfortably enough on gifts, lodgers' rent, royalties, pamphlets and lecture fees. But what little savings they had been able to make had been used to pay off the early People's Hall bills. Determined not to make another appeal – and publicly admit the existence of the crisis – William had written to Henry Reed in Tunbridge Wells with a plea for help. It must have been a hard letter to write. Reed's reply could only have added humiliation to embarrassment. It made the emergency committee meeting unavoidable.

> I have boasted that you have adopted the principle of no debt, not one penny. I do not wonder now that you were ill . . . [knowing] the dishonour you are bringing on the cause of Christ . . . if all you have in the world was sold, I question if you could pay 20/- in the pound . . . I should put my house into the hands of a respectable house agent for sale, taking the

first reasonable offer . . . hundreds of clerks have to live on
£100 a year, thousands of respectable artisans on 30 shillings a
week. Thousands are in Glory who have made greater sacrifices
than living upon £100 a year for the Master's sake.[5]

Reed's reaction represented Methodism at its harshest. He was not
simply saying that it is a sin to borrow beyond your power to repay.
There was, in his condemnation, an echo of Caughey's – 'if you resist
the Holy Spirit of God, if you grieve Him, He will turn round and
grieve you' . Failure was proof of wickedness to be redeemed, just as
Reed's own success was proof of virtue rewarded. Perhaps poor William
agreed with him. For he did not, as might have been expected with a
man of spirit, break off all relations there and then. Indeed, their
friendship was barely affected by the rebuff. Chastened, William Booth
considered other ways of paying off the debts.

Driven back on his own resources and with a sick family to support,
he hit on the ingenious solution of running the soup plant himself, as a
commercial operation which would, in time, make enough profit to
clear his debts. It was an honest enough arrangement. But it was not a
deal which the committee would have made had they operated purely
on commercial considerations and it was the sort of cosy arrangement
which gets voluntary associations a bad name. For if the soup kitchen
could be run at a profit, the Mission should have been the beneficiary.
However, the minutes of their May meeting record a unanimous decision to sell the equipment to the Superintendent and allow him to pay
for the purchase as and when his circumstances allowed. It also agreed
to relieve him of the burden of paying the premiums on his life insurance policy – essential if his family was to retain protection against his
death. The decisions weighed heavily on his conscience for the next
forty years. Neither of the arrangements was the sort of deal of which
auditors approve, and – even allowing for admiration and generosity –
it made plain that the committee was the instrument of Booth's will, not
the executive authority which determined and supervised his duties.
But at least its faith in his probity was justified. The equipment in the
soup kitchen was valued at £140. Every penny was repaid within the
period which the committee judged a bank would regard as reasonable.
In old age he also returned to the Salvation Army the accumulated cost
of the insurance which the Christian Mission had bought on his behalf.

Technically the Mission was out of debt. It was now the creditor of its resident minister. However, it was still based on dangerously inadequate foundations. But William Booth did not believe that shortage of funds need prevent a multitude of activities. By the spring of 1870 it was able to boast that it had built a very substantial organisation. The opening of the People's Hall was celebrated with the publication of what, these days, would appropriately be called a 'mission statement'. It began with a reaffirmation of increasing warfare against the 'appalling temporal and spiritual destitution . . . squalid poverty . . . hideous and most dreadful crime which afflicted society'. William Booth had already developed a taste for slightly spurious statistics, never quite realising that exact figures, where precise calculations were impossible, undermine rather than confirm credibility: 'In the Walworth Road, only half a mile in length, 18,600 persons may be seen entering the public houses on the Sabbath.' The failure of existing churches to reach such people – indeed their reluctance even to stretch out in their direction – was made plain by the promise to concentrate efforts and energies on 'outlying crowds which are not reached by other instrumentalities'. But it was the activities listed under the heading 'means employed' which proclaimed the scope of both the achievement and the aspiration. As well as 'PREACHING in the OPEN AIR and in THEATRES, VISITING from HOUSE to HOUSE, BIBLE CARRIAGE for the sale of BIBLES, TRACTS and SOUL SAVING LITERATURE and MOTHERS MEETINGS', there were a number of other listed activities which might have been rendered unto Caesar rather than to God. They included, 'RAGGED SCHOOLS, A PENNY BANK and RELIEF of the DESTITUTE by distribution of bread, meat and small sums of MONEY'.[6]

There is no evidence to suggest that all the activities were being carried on with the same degree of success. Some of them – the penny bank and the ragged schools – were not being carried out at all. But the wording of the statement was sufficiently ambiguous to provide a defence against the accusation of outright deception. The list of 'preaching stations' – from Hyndford Close in Edinburgh to Windsor Street, Brighton – read as if they were all established and in active use. Since it also included St Leonard's Music Hall in Shoreditch, which the Mission had yet to purchase, it was at best inaccurate and at worst dishonest. William Booth's flair for publicity often got out of hand.

Although he claimed to be a pillar of formal rectitude when he described his work – both its size and its scope – he always erred on the side of hope rather than truth.

The occasional exaggeration of his achievement must have helped William Booth accommodate the vicissitudes of both his private and public life without losing nerve or hope. His faith was beyond destruction but his health was not. Catherine, who was genuinely ill, complained about her condition, but struggled on even when in great pain. William complained less but capitulated more. It was a fortunate, perhaps even providential, combination of rival attitudes. For Catherine's fame as a preacher was enhanced time after time by the way in which she performed when acting as a substitute for her sick husband – often when she was the more sick of the two.

From June to August 1870 William was back at the Matlock hydro taking the remedial waters once again. During his absence Bramwell and Miss Billups contracted rheumatic fever (a rather more serious condition than William's indisposition), which it was left to God and the local doctor to cure. At about the same time Emma caught her hand in a door and reacted to the injury with hysterical depression. Catherine's technique for overcoming strain and fatigue was to do more for the Mission every time she was obliged to do more for her family and vice versa. But there is no doubt that she felt the weight of her extra burden. The June 1870 edition of the *Christian Mission Magazine* was dominated by her views on 'The Uses of Trial'. Her message was that 'the blood of martyrs has ever been the seed of the Church'. Catherine clearly believed that she was making a substantial contribution to her own martyrdom as she heroically fulfilled the duties of mother and preacher, not by balancing one against the other but by increasing her zealous commitment to both church and children. 'Mrs Booth, having had to visit Hastings in order to obtain change and the advantages of the sea air for an invalid daughter, availed herself of the opportunity to hold a few Sabbath services in the Music Hall.'[7] No doubt the cost of seaside recuperation was in part met by whoever sponsored the Hastings meeting – a second advantage of combining convalescence and campaigning. But questions still arose about how William was able to pay for so many, often prolonged, courses of treatment in one hydro or another. It was the sort of question that critics asked increasingly often as his fame grew, but they rarely received conclusive answers. The secrecy that surrounded the Booths' finances was more the result of William's stubborn pride than the need to hide disreputable dealings. But the doubts did damage. James Bradlaugh – who in this as in so much else spoke for the radicals of intellectual England – was near obsessed by the subject. His dying words were 'We must see Booth's accounts'.

William Booth was back at work in the late summer of 1870 and determined to secure a regular income by extending the operation of the soup kitchens – ideally on the model of the successful business which was operating in parallel with the Cheap Provision Store in Whitechapel. By 1872 he owned, controlled or at least enjoyed some income from five 'Food for the Millions' shops –in Limehouse, Brick Lane, Shoreditch and two in Whitechapel.[8] He certainly did not exploit the poor – indeed, his retail business enabled hundreds of families to buy food which, without the shops, would have been beyond their means – but, without the knowledge of his followers, his excursion into the provision trade made a small contribution towards the cost of his own groceries. It also provided paid employment for Bramwell who, at the age of sixteen, was made general manager of the whole enterprise. Bramwell was not suited to the task of managing the individual depot superintendents – all of whom were older and far more commercially experienced – and the needs of the pauper customers could only be met by selling the merchandise at prices which produced virtually no profit. So Bramwell was constantly attempting to make an economic success out of a project that had little commercial justification. The 'Food for the Millions' experiment was not a success. And in a couple of years it was all over. But for a time – together with the soup kitchens – it contributed to the solution of the Booths' financial problems. And it helped to focus William's mind on the extent of poverty in London.

At the same time they agonised about their own, always inadequate, finances. Before the beginning of her Hastings campaign, Catherine Booth wrote to the sponsors insisting that the costs be covered by collections at the meetings and services.[9] But the local organisers feared that, if the handbills which advertised the meeting warned that money would be solicited from congregations and audiences, the impression of an entirely *spiritual* gathering would be lost. In consequence potential converts, who were reluctant to pay a price for their salvation, would be deterred from attending. But Mrs Booth would not be moved. 'I cannot help feeling that I have, to some extent, compromised my position by allowing my services to rely on the support of a few private individuals.' The Booths – despite their rejection of full-time employment by Rabbits and Reeds – often relied on patronage. But it was a mark of their strange integrity that, although they accepted the gifts and sponsorships of wealthy benefactors, they were never prepared to give anything except their preaching skills in return. They were answerable only to God. Over the next five years they worked assiduously to ensure that no one else could make demands upon them.

On 15 November 1870* – when, according to their nineteenth-century biographers, the 'time of trial' was at its most severe and the Booths' vicissitudes almost beyond endurance – William Booth held the Inaugural Conference of the Christian Mission. It was five years before a Foundation Deed was deposited in the Chancery Court, but the preamble to that document made explicit that 'the form of government' envisaged at that first, formal meeting was meant to meet the needs of an organisation which spread the word of the Lord far beyond the East End of London. It made equally clear that the Christian Mission belonged to William Booth, not William Booth belonged to the Mission: 'A number of people were formed into a community or society by the said William Booth.'[10] He had founded his first benevolent autocracy. It was one in which – thanks to his wife – men and women enjoyed an equal status under God and the secretary.

The constitution which the Inaugural Conference approved could not have been clearer on the subject of female preachers and ministers. Section XII reflected Catherine Booth's views on the subject in every detail:

As it is manifest from the scriptures of the Old and especially the New Testament that God has sanctioned the labours of

---

*In Roger Green's *Catherine Booth* the date of the annual conference is given as 15–17 June 1870. A Quarterly Meeting of the Christian Mission was held at Brighton on 1 July 1870, and it was reported in the *Christian Mission Magazine* for 1 July 1870. There is no record of any June meeting.

Godly women in his Church; Godly women, possessing the necessary gifts and qualifications shall be employed as preachers, itinerant and otherwise, and as class leaders and as such shall have appointments given to them on the preacher's plan: they shall be eligible for any office and to speak and vote at all official meetings.

A revised edition of Catherine's original 1862 pamphlet on female ministry was published to provide a biblical justification for the Conference's position – even though the constitution moved a giant step forward from her original view that the Bible gave women authority to preach but not to take part in church government. As if to prove how far events had moved on, the new pamphlet was published by Morgan and Chase, the partnership which, only two years before, had invited William Booth to London *despite* his wife's bad habit of usurping the male prerogative by preaching. When the pamphlet had first been published their magazine, *The Revival*, had argued that both nature and the scriptures forbade the innovation and had gone on to complain that 'her caustic tone' did nothing to attract them to her arguments. Eight years after the denunciation, they published its third edition.

Every leap forward was matched with a lurch back. A month after the Inaugural Conference, the Brighton Mission – part of what William Booth increasingly saw as his empire – dissociated itself from its London partner. The pattern of its defection was to become a regular feature of secession. The preacher sent by the Booths to the Sussex coast had won the patronage of a Mr Wilson – a wealthy local who, with Booth's approval, had been appointed Mission Treasurer. When he agreed to keep the books in balance with constant injections of his own money, there seemed no point in maintaining allegiance to East London. Catherine Booth, whom 'God had enabled at great personal sacrifice and labour' to establish the Mission, took the desertion very hard. There was, she insisted, no justifiable cause for the Brighton brethren *'very unwisely* and *very ungraciously'* to go their own way. 'When,' she asked, 'will people of God learn wisdom? Satan's grand plan to frustrate God's benevolent designs in the salvation of men is first to separate Christians and then to weaken and to scatter them and to destroy their work.'[11] The enthusiasm for Christian unity had not been a feature of her husband's early years in the three denominations which he first served and then abandoned. It had, however, become a key element in the management in the Christian Mission's outposts.

At least in terms of numbers, the loss of Brighton was soon to be redeemed. Catherine Booth established a new branch in Hastings and stations were opened soon afterwards in Bethnal Green and Carshalton. In August, the Mission obtained temporary use of the Apollo Music Hall in Shoreditch – 'a singing and drinking den of the lowest character'. The theatre was empty and available to let on a lease too short to attract a commercial tenant, so the owner offered it rent-free to the Christian Mission. The Booths, as always, did not hesitate to accept what amounted to grace and favour from what they must have regarded as a morally reprehensible force. The arrangement was, they hoped, only temporary. The Shoreditch brethren were told that they 'must either obtain permanent possession or must build a hall'. William Booth recommended ownership rather than rent.[12] The Christian Mission was building to last.

William Booth was gradually developing the strategy for establishing a permanent church of his own based on the moral needs (and ready availability) of the neglected poor. He had discovered, and meant to exploit, a gap in the evangelists' market. When, in April 1871, he visited a band of gypsies in Whitechapel – largely to offer his protection against the antagonism of the local residents – he could write with absolute conviction that he was grateful for 'being given the privilege to listen to some of the rougher, more unpolished gems, but to men who were nonetheless God sent, heaven taught messengers of truth'.[13] The middle classes were either contented in their Christianity or were convinced that religion had little to offer them. The poor were ready for redemption in their thousands. William Booth was so confident of his ability to redeem them that he thought it right to offer advice on the subject to other evangelists. *How to Reach the Masses With the Gospel: A Sketch of the Origin, History and Present Position of the Christian Mission* was advertised as 'Containing a description of the means and instrumentalities employed in the East of London and elsewhere, together with some of the results which have followed in the remarkable conversion of numbers of common people, including infidels, thieves, drunkards etc. With engravings in paper 6d: cloth 1/-.'[14] It set out the principles on which William Booth's evangelism was built – beginning with the evenings in Nottingham when he preached on a kitchen chair to half a dozen paupers:

> We believe that God has given us a mission to the throngs in the great thoroughfare roaming about on the Sabbath day and all other days, thoroughly unconcerned about death, judgement and eternity . . . our experience tells us that although their aversion to Chapels and Churches is as strong as can well be conceived, they will nevertheless eagerly listen to any speaker who will, with ordinary ability, in a loving and earnest manner set before them the truths of the Bible in the open air.

William Booth was not a man to concern himself with literary style. Nor did he set out his theory with ruthless logic – having insisted that the masses could hardly wait for the offer of salvation, he went on to insist how to react 'if the speaking fails to draw a crowd or, as is sometimes the case, fails to keep it when it is gathered'. Very often the failure was, he said, attributable to the harassment which was often experienced and always anticipated in the poorer areas. 'This kind of work ensures opposition and persecution, it raises the hatred of men and devils.' The alternative to facing evil head on in the streets he dismissed with contempt. 'If you will stop quietly in your church or chapel or meeting place, you may talk of religion forever and, beyond a little passing ridicule, the ungodly will let you alone.' But 'only proclaim the truth at the gates of the city or in the crowded market place and they will gnash upon you with their teeth and hate you as they hated Him who went about all the cities and villages of Palestine.' Comparisons with Christ were a constant feature of William Booth's writing and preaching. Booth had discovered, either by chance or design, what was to become the irresistible technique of both the Christian Mission and the Salvation Army which succeeded it. He promised persecution and made it a symbol of righteousness. There was nothing which he could offer his members except blood, sweat, toil, tears and redemption.

In *How to Reach the Masses* he drove home his message of salvation by sacrifice with examples of how evangelists had been treated in East London and must expect to be treated in every town in England. 'In Shoreditch, a man warned of hell's fire, threatened to knock a young

preacher down.' Catholics in Croydon threw a saucepan, 'But our
Heavenly Father guided it so that it fell outside the circle.' When the
evangelists were daubed with whitewash, 'the grace of God kept them
from resenting this treatment in any other way than by falling on their
knees and praying for the conversion of their persecutors'. Whatever
happened – pushed, tripped, 'pelted with . . . flour, mud, stones and
cabbage stalks' – William Booth 'felt like singing all the time'.[15] It was
clear enough why the campaigners were directed towards the largely
illiterate poor – a more sophisticated audience would have found such
behaviour near to ridiculous. William Booth, the super-salesman of
emotional Christianity, had identified a growing demand for his product in the slums.

The stories from the early years of the Christian Mission passed into
the Salvation Army's folklore. The most famous was the 'Battle of
Sanger's Circus'. The circus, William Booth explained, 'fixed themselves up near to our usual stand' – a double offence since the Booths
(although not all their supporters) disapproved of performing animals
and the cruelty which it involved. The Mission members started to
sing hymns, but 'notwithstanding . . . they just commenced their
evening performance'. Circus employees pelted the evangelists with
'clods of earth and tufts of grass'. They then 'brought out their brass
band which made a most hideous noise' in competition with the
Mission's performance of 'I Am a Pilgrim, Bound for Glory'. Finding
the evangelists 'brass band proof . . . the next scheme was to send out
a large bass and side drum', which were deployed in front of the
speaker 'whilst behind him stood a man who clashed in his ears a pair
of cymbals'. The preacher continued preaching. 'They then brought
out a large elephant and two dromedaries which they led up and
down among the people . . . The roughs shouted, women and children shrieked and every moment we expected some dreadful accident
to occur . . . The persecution lasted just an hour and a half but God
was with us.'[16] The evangelists continued to evangelise and ended the
day triumphant.

When William Booth paused to consider why he attracted such
antagonism, he always attributed the animosity either to the influence
of the devil (which needed no further explanation) or to the brewers
who feared that he would put them out of business. Often the reasons
that his followers attracted violence were more complicated than he

realised. The willingness of Mission members to accept insult and assault without fighting back encouraged instinctive bullies to see how far the disciples of passive resistance could be provoked without them descending to retaliation in kind. Booth's followers were eccentrics, and in Victorian England eccentricity often provided an excuse for persecution. Above all, they were obtrusive. They marched, they sang, they approached complete strangers in the street, and they thrust themselves, as well as their opinions, on everyone they met. It was the secret of their success and of their unpopularity. The more successful they grew, the more unpopular they became.

The unpopularity – the excitement of risking life and limb in the name of Jesus – inevitably attracted recruits from the wilder shores of religion. The earliest volunteer was John Eason, 'once in a position of affluence with a comfortable home and excellent prospects'. However, he had 'met with a reverse of fortune which had stripped him of everything'. Eason had become minister at the Hackney Mission, and when the Booths took it over they gladly accepted him as a valued member of their organisation. He was influential in the local community and willing to work for next to nothing. So they were prepared to overlook his unusual theological views. Not only was he a Second Adventist who anticipated the imminent arrival of the Son of God, he had also identified the signs which would be sent by heaven to signify that the Second Coming was at hand. The Revelation of St John the Divine (Chapter XIII, Verse 18) predicted that the Great Beast would arrive before the reappearance of the Messiah and that the man, whose human form it occupied, would be recognised by his association with the number 666. Eason had, by manipulation of that mystic symbol, come to the firm conclusion that Napoleon III, Emperor of France, was the Great Beast. The Booths disagreed, but it did not prevent them from making him a valued lieutenant. Undoubtedly he was more eccentric than many of the Mission's members. But he was not alone in his eccentricity. The idea that William Booth and his followers were 'peculiar' seemed, to some nineteenth-century minds, to justify the assaults upon them.

The Booths' ready acceptance of Eason made their doubts about George Scott Railton all the more incomprehensible. Certainly Railton was 'the radical of radicals' who 'would have burned a field of wheat rather than tolerate the chance of the existence of a single tare'.[17] But he was right to argue when his brother warned him not to join the Christian Mission that 'Mr Booth and I are so much one that I cannot separate myself from his work'. He based that judgement on the evidence of *How to Reach the Masses*. For he was a passionate opponent of what he called 'ecclesiasticism' – the rigid hierarchy, the complicated liturgy and the arcane ritual of the established Church and those branches of Methodism which had not quite managed to break away from the bad old habits of the Church of England. His opposition to flummery and formality was expressed in pungent terms, and his advice on how to deal with ecclesiasticism was uncompromising: 'Fix it as your pole star and then sail with all your might in the opposite direction.'[18]

George Scott Railton was born into Methodism. His father, Launcelot Railton, had intended to become a teacher but was suddenly called to the Wesleyan ministry and was posted to the West Indies where he became part minister, part administrator of the Nonconformist community already established in Antigua. It was there that he met and married Margaret Swift, herself a Methodist missionary. Their first son, Launcelot like his father, was born in 1843. Six years later – incapacitated by illness and converted to total abstinence – the Railtons returned to Scotland. Their second son was born in the Wesleyan Manse in Arbroath in 1849. Little George was brought up with exactly the sort of care and attention which Catherine was later to lavish on Bramwell. And he responded in much the same way to his treatment. 'My dear mother made upon me the unalterable impression in favour of the old-fashioned whipping system . . . when worthy of whipping I would be sent upstairs and then before punishment she always prayed with me and talked with me as to the will of God.'[19]

Despite enjoying the advantages of a strict Scottish Nonconformist childhood, George Scott Railton did not truly find God until, at the age of ten, he was struck down by what he believed to be influenza. It was no more than a bad cold, but a flu epidemic was sweeping Scotland and George – in childhood though not in later life – showed William Booth's tendency to overstate the seriousness of his ailments. He decided, 'If I lose consciousness and die as I am now – determined to have nothing to do with God – I am lost for ever.' Then he heard his pious mother discussing salvation with a friend. 'The joy of God made me for the moment completely free from the head ache and pain which had burdened me all day. I marched round the little room, singing and praising the Lord . . . Hearing my mother at the front door, I rushed to tell her the good news that I was born again.'[20] Railton was a religious prodigy and, like John Eason and so many more of William Booth's followers, slightly mad.

Railton was sent to a school for Methodist ministers' sons at Woodhouse Grove in the West Riding of Yorkshire, where he was commended for being one of the very few 'really praying boys' in the whole institution. However, he did not follow his brother Launcelot into the ministry. Instead, at the age of fifteen, he joined a firm of Anglo-Spanish merchants in London. A year later both his parents – who had taken semi-retirement on the Isle of Man – died in the cholera epidemic which swept the north-west of England. Almost alone in the world, he turned to southern Methodism for comfort. He found that in London, Wesleyans had begun to call their chapels 'churches' and were using the Book of Common Prayer. Railton determined to halt the drift back to the established Church, single handed if necessary. So he turned to independent evangelism and appointed himself assistant to a preacher who worked amongst the Spanish sailors on the London docks. As if to complete the parallel with his future chief, he denounced commerce as the devil's work and publicly confessed that often he had been obliged to speak less than the complete truth about the goods which he bought and sold. To prove his point, he refused to write what he regarded as a fraudulent contract. Dismissal, which he must have known would follow, left him free to become a full-time evangelist.

All that Railton had in the world was £20, his share of the proceeds from the sale of his father's library. He used it to buy a steamship ticket to Morocco, where he bore silent witness with a home-made banner with the strange device 'Repentance, Faith, Holiness'.* His money ran out within weeks. When the British Consul heard of the destitute Englishman who thought that 'if it is God's will to take me where I desire to go, He will provide the means',[21] he was less concerned with the dubious theology than with the embarrassment which resulted

---

*Bramwell Booth and (quoting him) St John Ervine say that the banner was borne through Morocco. Booth-Tucker says that he carried it in England.

from a subject of Her Britannic Majesty wandering penniless through the souks of North Africa. A letter was sent to Launcelot Railton saying that his unbalanced brother was probably in physical danger and, what was worse, making an exhibition of himself. Arrangements would be made for him to work his passage back to England as a ship's steward.

We will never know why Railton, if he was so sure that God had called him to be a missionary, was prepared for an official of the temporal power to pack him off home to England. Nor is it easy to imagine how a man of his aesthetic temperament and teetotal convictions could serve food and drink to the first-class passengers. However, he managed somehow to reconcile the conflicts and prevent the ignominious end to the Moroccan adventure from dampening his religious ardour. As soon as he landed at London Docks he set off on the long walk to Cornwall, where he believed he could find employment in the tin mines. Work was more scarce than he had hoped it would be and he spent more time preaching than mining. Again he had to be rescued from starvation. An uncle found him a job in Stockton-on-Tees. A year later, having come to terms with Mammon, he was promoted and moved to Middlesbrough where he preached, as William Booth had preached before him, whenever he could encourage anyone to listen to him. His regular Sunday engagement was in a butcher's shop which was scrubbed out every weekend in preparation for the service. The chopping block was used as a pulpit. There was talk of him becoming a candidate for the Wesleyan ministry.

He was still working in Middlesbrough when, in the autumn of 1872, William Booth was again 'set aside by affliction' and again 'wandering about from home . . . seeking health'.[22] As always his wanderings took him to Matlock where Mr Smedley, the proprietor of the hydro, had become a friend of his regular visitor. There he met the Reverend Lancelot Railton, who was also taking the waters. The minister told William Booth about his dangerously impetuous young brother who was determined to devote his life to evangelism – though it seems unlikely that he also admitted his antagonism to young George joining the Christian Mission. His opposition was an attempt to prevent a liaison designed in heaven. After George Railton read *How to Reach the Masses*, he was William Booth's man for life. As soon as he was able to leave his job in Middlesbrough he made his way south and, without any preparation or warning, called on the Booths. The Booths were dubious about his suitability to work for the Mission and only agreed to employ him for a brief trial. They invited him to lodge with them in Gore Road. He lived there – half son and half brother – for the next eleven years.

The Reverend Launcelot Railton remained implacably opposed to his brother joining the Mission, but there was no stopping George. He wrote home describing his duties in a way which was clearly intended to comfort and reassure his brother. 'I may compare the post to that of a second preacher in an old-fashioned Methodist Circuit reaching from Hastings to Edinburgh. Besides the editing of a magazine . . . Mr Booth cannot require of me too many duties for I wish to do whatever he will let me do.' William Booth took a week or two to make up his mind if Railton was really his man. When he decided to make the appointment, he at least convinced his new lieutenant that they shared a passion to work together. 'He too says that when I left them [briefly and only to make arrangements for his move to London] he and Mrs Booth felt that they lost one who had suddenly become a pleasure and a power to them.'[23] Perhaps he overstated his new chief's enthusiasm. Booth-Tucker, writing with the insight of a son-in-law, devoted two pages of Catherine Booth's biography to an account of Railton's impetuous lack of judgement. He concluded that the success of the man who became Mission Secretary was the result of William Booth's 'iron hand in a velvet glove', restraining Railton's reckless nature. He was to become Augereau to William Booth's Napoleon. Time after time he charged without waiting for orders. But very often it was his charge that saved the day.

Whatever his temperamental shortcomings, George Railton provided the Christian Mission with an intellectual dimension which it had previously lacked. Many of his ideas, like his life, were bizarre. But he did not lack imagination. Catherine, although held back both by the restraints imposed on her sex and the early limitation of attempts to break out from those restraints, had produced a historic pamphlet on women's ministry. Railton produced pamphlets on everything. Their titles – from 'Heathen England' to 'Captain Ted' – made them sound far less serious than they were. And he stood shoulder to shoulder with Mrs Booth in the cause of female emancipation, first in the Christian Mission and then in the Salvation Army. His own biographer actually awards him the primary place in the move towards sexual equality:

'Railton was the leading protagonist, perhaps the decisive influence, in causing William Booth to give women equal place in the Salvation Army command.'[24] Bramwell Booth gets very close to endorsing that judgement. Railton certainly favoured entrusting women with 'the responsibilities and authorities which had previously been given only to men'.[25] Inevitably Catherine began to treat him like a son and, even when William turned against him, her love endured. Both were right, in the early years of Railton's association, to regard him as indispensable to their success. Without him, the Salvation Army might still have evolved from the Christian Mission, but it would not have swept the world in ten years.

11

Well Instructed Saints

George Railton's admiration for William Booth was perilously close to idolatry. But it was based on a devout belief in the aims and methods of the movement which his hero led. In January 1873 he described his first impression of the organisation itself. The spirit of the Christian Mission was even better than reading *How to Reach the Masses* had led him to expect:

> Instead of finding a mere community enjoying a common vitality or suffering a common lassitude, I saw constant evidence of real individual life, a life which will propagate itself irrespective of any association with which it may stand connected . . . Though nearly everyone seems capable of leading all seem glad to be led . . . I expected to see a company of powerful but irrepressible volunteers, whereas I found myself in the presence of a battalion of trained male and female soldiers quite as remarkable for their steadiness as for their readiness.
>
> The East of London has long worn the aspect of a heavy thunder cloud hanging over the future of the country. Now I

think I have seen a bow in the cloud. The charity of London may pour ceaselessly into the 'East End' and yet be lost in the ocean of drink and vice. But when the working classes on the spot become the workers together with God we have reached the goal of a 'native agency' and hope to find a solid resting place.[1]

The two paragraphs showed how completely Railton understood and supported William Booth's philosophy of evangelism – the importance of taking the gospel to the people who wanted it the least but needed it most, and the necessity for the gospel to be spread amongst the poor, not by well-meaning outsiders but by the poor themselves. That required William Booth to appeal in the language of the people whose souls he hoped to save. He was, by necessity, a religious populist who adopted whatever methods were needed to rally recruits to his cause. His technique was never to appeal to the head, and his appeal to the heart was often embarrassingly emotional. Railton approached the whole business of revivalism in a more intellectual way. In some ways he was too cerebral for his own good and the good of the missions which he served. He was inclined to follow an idea wherever it led – sometimes with disastrous consequences.

By 1873 Railton was firmly established as the Christian Mission's ideologist, but he was also an activist who argued for militant Christianity and asked the long-established churches, 'Where is the holy war? Where is the terrible energy displayed in the attacks upon sin? Where is there a hard, unbending advance to exterminate wrong?' He concluded with a rhetorical question, 'Is not Christianity today a sentimental attempt to please all men and to give no offence to any?' and, by way of an answer, set out a very different philosophy of evangelism: 'The Christian Mission is war, war to the knife.'[2] That sort of language went down wonderfully well in the slum parishes whose inhabitants liked a fight and felt totally neglected by both the Anglican vicar in the big house at the edge of the cemetery and the Wesleyan minister who found their vulgarity distasteful. Despite his fundamentalist theological views, Railton represented what in the mid-nineteenth century was the 'New Christianity'.

The Church of England had failed to come to terms – indeed in some ways refused even to acknowledge – the Industrial Revolution. Its organisation was still built around the rural parishes. Country parsons – remote from towns – ran their godly race in deserted villages while nearby incumbents of urban livings wrestled to save thousands of souls from the new temptations of factory life. Often the task, being too great for them to accomplish, was not even attempted. All thought of going out and making converts was abandoned. Instead the Church retreated into its traditional territory and, reinforced by tithes and pew rents, became more and more the preserve of the country gentry and old middle classes with the clergy alienated from the new industrial poor. It was the failure in the Anglican Communion to recognise the changes in society – as much as disputes over doctrine – that had brought about the Wesleyan revolution and the demands for 'active Christianity'. And it was, at least in part, because William Booth feared that Methodists had fallen for the same respectable temptation that he created a church of his own. He succeeded in that unlikely enterprise because, at a time when more conventional preachers waited to hear polite requests for redemption, he chose to take religion to the people. Railton came to personify the view that sinners must be taken by storm. He was, in the early days of the great enterprise, William Booth's ideal lieutenant.

Respectable citizens were scandalised by William Booth's willingness to expose his emotions in public. But their disreputable neighbours did not feel that William Booth was patronising them. Railton's language was as wild and sometimes wilder, than his chief's. But he was able to combine fighting metaphors with a broader and more sophisticated view of the world than that which William Booth possessed. He arrived at the Christian Mission at the providential moment.

After a year under Railton's direction, the *Christian Mission Magazine* – doubled in size and substantially increased in circulation – began to show interest in subjects which, before his arrival, had not so much been ignored as not even noticed. 'People are beginning to wonder if Spain will ever be governed again, and if so by whom. As we read of Carlists and Republicans and the Intranisegente, we begin to think that national wretchedness is, in that sad country, about to reach its climax'. But despite his Spanish associations, Railton was not interested in Spain for Spain's sake. He had a moral to draw. 'The condition of Spain just now is, after all, very similar to that in which most Christians are now satisfied to live.' The condition to which Railton referred was 'endless anarchy'[3] – his description of the democratic reform which he feared would replace the autocracy of a Christian monarchy.

Politics of a sort began to appear in the magazine: 'The Chief Minister of the British Government has once more moved, and the House of Commons consented, to lay aside the business of the country in honour of Derby Day.'[4] From time to time the editorials argued a case which was more concerned with economics than with faith and morals:

> The question of the relationship of labour and capital seems at last to be coming to that decisive struggle which has been foreseen in our country . . . The working classes, accustomed for centuries to take whatever was offered them and be thankful, or at any rate only complain in whispers to one another, are almost universally beginning to talk about their rights and treat with other classes as equals.[5]

Unfortunately, having set out the terms of the coming conflict, Railton – whose inimitable style was clear in every line – felt unable to come down firmly on either side of the argument. Perhaps by implication he had sympathy for labour. But in his explicit conclusion, which should have been the climax, he collapsed in bathos. The best he could do was support virtue and endorse justice: 'All this cannot last for ever. There must come, and there must come very quickly, a time when men will look the question of right and wrong fairly in the face . . .'

The *Christian Mission Magazine* also began to develop a house-style which was built around military metaphor. Report of 'the opening of a new battery of artillery on Southsea Common, Portsmouth' was followed by news that 'the regiment presented itself in most correct style' in Hastings and Rye. At the same time the Mission began to promote its activities in a way which was neither spiritual nor martial but unashamedly commercial. A notice was composed in the style of an insurance advertisement. It was headed 'Christian Passenger Assurance Company – President, King of Kings' and promised 'protection against accidents of all kinds – spiritual and temporal'. The scheme was guaranteed by a unique form of 'paid up capital – the love of God in Christ Jesus our Lord'. Railton's imaginative publicity undoubtedly increased the Mission's appeal amongst the classes from which it hoped to recruit members and make converts. But the one intellectual in William Booth's high command increased the alienation of those respectable, if dormant, Christians who regarded selling God like an insurance policy as both blasphemous and lacking refinement. The sales technique was a huge success. The Christian Mission had discovered a patent method of making both new recruits and new enemies.

It was no more than coincidence that, almost exactly at the time when the Mission was engaged on the second stage of its domestic expansion, it also took its first tentative steps to becoming an international organisation. New stations were being opened almost every month and old ones were being rebuilt. The Whitechapel People's Hall, where work had been held up by the discovery that the glass roof was beyond repair, was at last fulfilling its promise to accommodate congregations of two thousand and more – under two brand-new domes. A beerhouse and brewery in Stoke Newington had become a Mission Hall, a brand-new 'station' was to be built in Hackney, and a railway arch in Bethnal Green (right opposite a gin palace known as The Salmon & Ball) was to be bricked in and used as a meeting place and school rooms. The expansion was William Booth's response to the demand for his ministrations accelerating at a rate which he regarded as confirmation of his calling. Not once, during the whole history of the Mission and the Army, did he feel the need to slow down the rate of expansion – although he often worried that the income by which his work was supported did not grow as fast as his congregation. However, he greeted the news that a self-styled branch of his Mission had been established in America with irritation rather than enthusiasm. An American station would be beyond his control and might, by its general conduct, bring the work of the parent Mission into disrepute. At first he was completely unmoved by the heroic tale of what the unauthorised missionary described as 'Unfurling the Flag of the Christian Mission in America'. Brother James Jermy, at one time a member of the Bethnal Green Branch of the Mission, who had originally emigrated to Canada, wrote to tell William Booth of the spiritual odyssey which had taken him south across the 39th Parallel and encouraged him to plant the mission flag in Cleveland, Ohio:

My happiest times in Canada were with the coloured

people . . . When I was preaching, power came down . . . They
shouted and jumped and danced . . . But brother, I cannot live
on a good meeting now and then . . . I must see souls saved. So
I prayed about it and said to my wife, 'I must go to the States.'
When I got here, I found thousands going the way of death.
Some parts of this city look like Whitechapel. Here human
nature is the same, with drunkardness and every other sin.[6]

Jermy explained how, on his third Sunday in America, he 'went to a
little hall' in which he 'found a young man in the pulpit'. After the service he introduced himself to James Fackler, the preacher, and told him
of the work being done by the East London Mission. According to
Brother Jermy's account, Fackler responded with the excited admission,
'This is what I have been waiting for.' And the young American was as
good as his word. He abandoned the little hall and, together with
Jermy, founded a replica Christian Mission.

William Booth – being once again immobilised by illness – had time
to reply to Jermy at length. His letter did not mention that fighting
poverty was an absolute Christian obligation, but it did comment on
the subject of church government – including the merits of a 'small
executive' on the model of the one which advised him in London. The
advantages of keeping the controlling committee in its place were
described with admirable frankness. 'I am free to adopt such measures
as seem to me calculated to sustain the advance of the mission.'[7] The
letter concluded with a postscript which revealed William Booth's naïve
view of America and perhaps the world. 'Mrs Pengelly is somewhere in
Canada . . . I feel sure that she will find you out if she can . . . She had
good temporal prospects but weeps that there is no mission.'[8]

For a while the American Mission prospered without much direct
help from London except agreement that Railton's articles could be
published in the *Mission Harvester*, the magazine of the Cleveland
'headquarters branch'. If William Booth wished to be rid of the certain
distraction and possible embarrassment of the American connection,
providence was again on his side. Within months of the Cleveland
Mission's formal opening, Jermy had to return to England and the
American enterprise – not being grown from native seed – withered
away. When the Mission had become the Army, and crossed the
Atlantic for a second time to set up a station in Philadelphia, the

pioneers were careful to respect the lessons which had been learned during the not altogether unwelcome Cleveland failure. They confirmed the rules laid down by William Booth and George Railton and relied on local enthusiasm. As a result, it prospered.

The overseas – indeed, what became the imperial – development of the Christian Mission had a false start and proceeded slowly. But in Britain William Booth led what was swiftly growing into a national organisation. A cadre of full-time preachers was being built up – most of them, in the manner of Eason and Railton, men whose eccentricity prevented them from feeling at home in the longer established churches. Typical of them was Elijah Cadman, a Rugby chimney-sweep whose regular entertainment, until he found God, was drinking and fighting. In those days 'all sweeps were drinking people. At every comfortable and kindly house, the sweep and his boys were given beer. Six-year-old Elijah was often drunk.'[9] The habit persisted well after his sixth birthday. But all that was put behind him when he experienced a moment of sudden revelation.

In Cadman's case – and true to his history, character and role within the Christian Mission – the cause of instant conversion was dramatic even by the standards of Victorian redemption. Watching a public hanging at Warwick, he feared that he was witnessing the fate which awaited him. He reacted in a way which in the modern West Midlands would have resulted in his detention and confinement in a place of safety. On the night of the hanging, the people of Lutterworth were disturbed by a 'tremendous clamour . . . It was Cadman ringing the town-crier's bell before each inn' and announcing that 60,000 men and women died of drink each year. A series of mystical experiences followed, including a vision of Christ and a voice from God which instructed him to marry forthwith. He obliged with a parlour maid from Rugby School.

Mr and Mrs Elijah Cadman – having achieved prosperity as well as respectability – joined a Hallelujah Band, one of the groups of evangelising working men which William Booth had first met during his early tour of the West Midlands. Elijah then discovered from his brother-in-law that men whose status and education were no greater than his were preaching the gospel in London. So, 'wearing a well-cut suit and tall silk hat' to confirm that he was a successful tradesman 'owning a thriving shop besides the chimney-sweep business',[10] he went to

London and presented himself at the Whitechapel Hall. He was allowed
to meet William Booth, who was by then called Superintendent as well
as minister. But his offer of service was treated with even more caution
than had been displayed when George Scott Railton knocked on the
Mission's door. A number of tests were devised to determine his suitability. One was participation in a revivalist meeting at Wellingborough.
He passed by leading the audience in vigorous singing and sitting
astride the rail that ran round the platform in order to illustrate that
'wobblers' had only themselves to blame if they were injured when they
fell. He was sent to subdue Hackney – a particularly violent part of
William Booth's kingdom – and succeeded with the help of another
handrail, which he somehow used to illustrate that the wages of sin is
death. Throughout his term of trial, and during his early months of probation, Cadman's mental stability was not questioned. The Mission
were right, if reckless, to take his character on trust. He became a key –
and wholly responsible – member of the high command.

In its early days – despite the respectability of the wealthy men who
backed its work and, occasionally, underwrote its activities – the
Christian Mission had to rely on the ranks of working-class eccentrics
to provide its leadership. It occupied a position which was simultaneously theologically extreme and socially unacceptable, and could
hardly expect to recruit its officer class from the sort of men who were
ordained in the Church of England. So it came to rely on peculiar
men like James Dowdle – 'the saved railway guard' who, after he had
joined the Mission, became famous for stopping a young girl in the
street, insisting that they knelt down on the pavement and 'praying the
flower out of her hair'. Dowdle had played a bass violin in one of the
church orchestras which were common during the early part of the
century. But he went to the bad and began to play in a music hall band.
A converted actor persuaded him to abandon his wicked ways and he
became 'The Hallelujah Fiddler'. After being employed on the rebuilding of a Christian Mission Hall he offered his services as a full-time
evangelist. Together with his wife, he began to work for the Mission
managing the Shoreditch Food Depot, 'selling to the poorest of the
poor, penny worth's of bread'. Mrs Dowdle acted, when necessary, as
chucker-out. She described her technique of ejection in simple language: 'I stick my knuckles into their necks and out they go.'[11]

It was not surprising that a Mission officered by such men attracted more and more disapproval from the Christian establishment. They were ideal for the task which William Booth set them, but the result of their rough enthusiasm was the polarisation of public opinion. As working-class sinners filled his meetings in increasing numbers the respectably virtuous began to fear as well as loathe him. And the pattern of recruitment perpetrated itself. Dowdle, on duty in the city in Bradford, met and recruited James Lawley, a bearded youth of barely eighteen who initially became famous for the extravagant way in which he gesticulated – to attract attention – with his umbrella. He also perfected the trick of tearing his prayer book apart as he preached, to illustrate the way in which the devil destroyed the godly who are not on guard. He then scattered the pieces over the congregation to illustrate the rain falling on both the just and the unjust.

William Booth's appeal to his officers was more than the attraction of a vibrant personality. He certainly exuded vigour and the excitement of constant struggle for greater achievements. But he also possessed characteristics which were irresistible to men and women whose religious beliefs were the product of emotion rather than reason. He made no compromises with what he regarded as evil – even if his obduracy made him influential enemies. He was absolutely certain of both the God he served and his own vocation to serve him, even at times when his destiny was being frustrated. And he was absolutely tireless in his work of conversion and redemption – always willing to make the sacrifices which he expected of others. Because of his indomitable faith in his eventual triumph he was, despite the occasional setback, immensely successful – itself an immense attraction to instinctive revivalists who want to see the Lord make progress here on earth.

So the work of expansion went on. As well as the converted breweries and beerhouses in London, new branches of the Mission were created from Portsmouth to Fife. 'Stations' and 'branches' – the first steps to full mission status – were established in Southsea, Hastings, Tunbridge Wells and Northumberland.[12] It seemed that, with the Booths in charge, nothing could hold back the Mission's work. That was certainly William Booth's own view. And he grew increasingly impatient with the restraints which were occasionally imposed on his authority. He determined to remove the impediments to his successful leadership by rewriting the Mission's constitution.

Eighteen seventy-five started badly for the family, with the death of

William's mother on 13 January. The death certificate described her as the widow of a farmer – one of the few occupations which Samuel Booth had not performed. The coroner had been told that Catherine's mother was a widow, when her husband was still alive. So both parents were sent to heaven on false papers. It was all part of a pattern of posthumous promotion into the middle classes which elevated Samuel Booth from jobbing builder to crockery factor to farmer, a strange deceit for a man of God to practise, and evidence of William's growing concern for his position in society. The paradox – identification with the poor matched against a will and desire for respect which the poor could not command – made him increasingly dissatisfied with the *al fresco* constitution which did not provide the professional status which he thought was his by right.

Within weeks of her mother's death, Catherine was herself so ill that William was worried that his wife might well not see the summer. 'She would writhe in agony on the bed and floor and then, white and cold as marble, fall into a swoon from which it appeared that nothing could restore her.'[13] The doctors diagnosed *angina pectoris*. Fortunately William was at home more than usual. He was preparing a new constitution for the Christian Mission. It was drafted in the form of a Deed Poll which was approved by the Mission's 1875 Annual Conference and registered as the Foundation Deed in the Court of Chancery.

The Christian Mission's Deed replicated the form of document by which John Wesley had incorporated his dissenting church. It began with a brief history of the Mission's origins, followed by eleven articles of doctrine – none of them exceptional or unusual – and five paragraphs which set out 'the Rights Etc. of William Booth'. They began with the uncompromising declaration that 'the said William Booth is and shall continue to be for the term of his natural life, the General Superintendent of the Christian Mission unless he shall resign or unless he shall be, by disease or some other cause, disqualified for [*sic*] discharging his duties'. At the Annual Conference – a body which, like the Methodist Conference itself, was dominated by full-time preachers – no objection was raised to the clause which gave the Superintendent plenipotentiary powers for life:

> The said William Booth while holding the office of General
> Superintendent shall possess the power of confirming or setting

aside all or any of the decisions and resolutions of any
Conference and of the Official Society or other Meeting held
throughout the said Christian Mission which may in his
estimation be contrary to the laws and usage of the said
Christian Mission or prejudicial to the object for which the said
Christian Mission was established.[14]

The account of the Conference which appeared in the *Christian Mission Magazine* did not report William Booth's assumption of autocratic powers. The message sent to the members concentrated on other aspects of the Deed. The Mission had, for some time, been concerned that the buildings which it owned might one day be used for undesirable purposes – or, in the case of the many converted beer halls, revert to the degradation from which William Booth had rescued them. It was happy to announce: 'We have at length completed and enrolled in Chancery a deed which will, we think, render the use of any of our halls for other than purely evangelistic purposes utterly impossible.'[15] No mention was made of William Booth's assumption of the powers previously held by the Conference.

As soon as the Conference was over Catherine, who had been too ill to attend, was reunited with her husband. Both of them agreed that orthodox medicine having failed, the time had come for a course of hydrotherapy. But Mrs Booth was too ill to travel to Matlock. So she took the cure from Richard Metcalf in Paddington Green. Then, leaving the management of the Mission to George Railton and nineteen-year-old Bramwell – who, although being prepared for the succession, was (because of his upbringing) young for his years. William took his wife for what he hoped would be her convalescence at Hardness, near Canterbury. He was immediately the victim of an incapacitating accident.

For the second time in his life, William Booth set out for a ride in a carriage to which the horse had not been properly harnessed. In Darlington ten years before, Catherine had watched as her husband was pulled to near disaster. In Kent, they were riding side by side when the bridle came loose. William leapt out in the hope of refastening it, but the horse bolted and he was dragged along the ground for several hundred yards. His left leg was so badly damaged that, for a time, he feared that he would never walk again. But, as was so often the case with his illnesses and incapacities, he overstated the seriousness of his condition. However, both William and Catherine were out of action for most of the second half of 1875. In their absence, the Christian Mission lost one of its most important stations. Portsmouth – the scene of Catherine's first evangelistic triumph – had become a hot-bed of secession.

Rotation between circuits had always been the Wesleyan way of preventing their ministers from sinking into the complacent comfort of familiar surroundings, and the Conference of 1875 had decided, in traditional Methodist fashion, that it was time for the Portsmouth minister to move on. He had refused, and the congregation had backed his rebellion. When it became clear that the decision to leave must stand, the minister declared unilateral independence. The Foundation Deed, approved at the same Conference, preserved the Mission's ownership and control of the property, but the claim was only legally established after weeks of expensive litigation. The experience confirmed the growing opinion (encouraged by George Railton) that, since democracy was an inappropriate system by which to run the Mission, the constitutional reforms of 1875 had not gone far enough. Bramwell Booth – being prepared for the succession by working under his father's oppressive supervision – encouraged the general disapproval of democracy:

> Sometimes the local meetings would last for three or four hours
> and would then be adjourned without anything being settled.
> The worst feature was that the chief power slid gradually into
> the hands of those who were least fitted for it. The most
> spiritual and most earnest members would remain silent while
> a few interminable talkers would have it all their own way.[16]

Bramwell was reporting on the situation in one mission station, but he was also describing what was generally believed to be the position in most of the missions.

Success as well as failure encouraged the move towards increasing William Booth's absolute authority. After a brief decline in membership during 1874 – probably the result of Catherine's several illnesses keeping her out of the front line – new missions had been set up and plans had been made to mount a sustained campaign in the north of England. The Christian Mission had become a national institution. It owned and ran twenty-nine separate missions and employed thirty full-time ministers. In a single year its membership had risen from 980 to 2,455. Four local societies had more than 200 members and Stockton, the largest, had 320.[17] And the numbers grew month by month. The credit went to William Booth and his patent recruitment technique. 'As soon as a man or woman was saved, the Mission asked that person to stand before the crowd and relate their experience of conversion. Other denominations insisted that evangelists required education and special training. But the Christian Mission was nothing more than its converts.'[18] William Booth's contempt for Latin and Greek – and perhaps his difficulty with book learning – kept the Christian Mission close to the soil from which it grew. Nobody doubted that serious decisions had to be taken about how the growth was to be controlled. William Booth was certain that new regulations were necessary to confirm his control over what had become a national organisation.

The 1876 Annual Conference met in the People's Hall in Whitechapel on 5 June, and William Booth – almost certainly on the instigation of George Scott Railton – used the occasion to impose his will on the increasingly unruly army as, in the previous year, he had taken complete control of the general staff. The General Superintendent dominated each day of the Conference, and the direction in which he determined to move the delegates was made clear by a passage in a 7,000-word lecture – 'How to Manage a Mission Station' – which he delivered as part of the official proceedings. Section (7) was headed 'Govern It' in the published version, and began with the insistence that the evangelist was *servant* not *master*. Then it advised:

> Sit upon the box and hold the reins, grasp them lovingly but firmly. It is never safe to let the high-spirited horse feel that you are driving with a slack rein. If they do, they will take liberties with your vehicle . . . it is safest and best for society in all its grades and relations to feel that there is a real authority which must be respected and a real law and authority which must be obeyed.[19]

One entirely autocratic resolution was carried without dissent. It was

agreed that 'no circuit plans are to be printed and no committee meetings are to be held in any station except in such instances and in such
manners as the Conference may decide'. But the shift of authority away
from the individual missions towards the General Superintendent – the
centralisation which many Methodists believed was the sin of the
established Church – was not the only radical move made at the 1876
Conference. It was agreed also that women could take sole charge of
missions.

Bramwell Booth believed that his mother 'had never quite contem-
plated placing women in positions which would involve their authority
over men. That would be going further than anything ever recorded in
the early church.' He thought that the credit for the reform should go
to George Railton, 'who was always ready for new departures'.[20] But
Bramwell did Catherine less than justice. The 1870 Inaugural
Conference of the Christian Mission had accepted that women were eligible for any position in the organisation. And it is inconceivable that
William would have accepted either that step forward or its repetition
in 1877 had Catherine made the slightest reservation about putting
women on an equal footing with men. Almost everything that William
Booth – and through him, the Christian Mission itself – did, reflected
her views. She was undoubtedly the author of the 1876 Conference
resolution on fund-raising: 'Bazaars, fancy sales, spelling bees and
entertainments to be opposed in the spirit of the Mission and are therefore unadvisable and inadmissible.'[21] That prohibition was happily
accepted, but William Booth's attempt to turn the Mission into a temperance organisation failed. He had hoped that total abstinence would
be made a condition of membership. The most he could persuade his
followers to accept was a motion 'strongly urging upon evangelists
and office bearers of the Mission the duty of persuading all members
and converts to abstain from intoxicating drink'.[22] The failure of the
Conference to follow his lead on the subject confirmed that, although
he had gone a long way towards establishing his autocratic authority,
he had not gone far enough. More constitutional reforms were essential.

Railton, enjoying the advantage of being one of the few members of
the Mission who took theology seriously, had been turning his
thoughts to 'holiness' – a notion which William Booth had considered,
though not very deeply, many times during the previous twenty years.

Railton had thought about its meanings and implications with the same passionate intensity that characterised all that he did. And he drafted a statement which, in almost every detail, reflected the conclusion of 'The Brighton Holiness Conference' – a conclave held the previous year with the admirable, if slightly *outré*, object of convincing Nonconformists that sanctity in life was possible:

> We believe that after conversion there remain in the heart of a believer inclinations of evil or roots of bitterness, which, unless overpowered by divine grace, produce actual sin but that these evil tendencies can be entirely taken away by the Spirit of God . . . And we believe that the persons thus entirely sanctified may, by the power of God, be kept unblamable and unreproachable before him.[23]

The impetus behind the acceptance of 'holiness doctrine' clearly came from Railton. But William Booth raised no serious objection to the Mission formally taking up a theological position which some of its members might find unacceptable. By agreeing to such a text he was risking the populist appeal on which he relied, but William rarely bothered to concentrate on even the consequences of theological dispute. Railton drafted the 'holiness' statement because the idea appealed to him. William Booth gave his instinctive support because it was associated in his mind with Phoebe Palmer and evangelists whom he admired – and because he felt no urge to consider the mysteries of sanctification.

The preamble to the Articles of Faith, which were published that year, were more typical of William Booth in both tone and content: 'The object and work of this Mission is to seek the conversion of the neglected people who are living without God and without hope.'[24] But the Articles of Faith which followed included the conviction that it is the privilege of all believers to be 'wholly sanctified' and that 'their whole spirit and soul and body' may 'be preserved blameless unto the coming of our Lord Jesus Christ (I Thessalonians, 5 v. 23)'. Much was subsequently made – by the sort of scholar whom William Booth so despised – of the total absence of the word 'Holiness' from the foundation articles. But it appears in the preamble (with the necessary capital 'H') and the notion of complete sanctification was mentioned time after time in the main text. In fact, 1876 was the one 'Holiness moment' in the life of both the Mission and the Army which it became. From then on the idea was in steady decline – denied a central place in doctrine because its metaphysical complications were not to William Booth's taste and only what he regarded as important survived.

William Booth's theology was built on instinct, not intellect. So, without much thought, he took the most extreme view about the love of God, and when challenged on the subject of 'instant sanctity' replied, without needing to ponder, that redemption was available to all who repent. But the notion of complete redemption – and the obsession with the constant examination and textual verification of the idea – was generally the preserve of groups who chose, being sanctified themselves, to hide away from possible contamination by the wickedness of the world. His psychological problem – throughout his life and particularly in the mid-1870s – was that, far from insulating himself from the infection of sin, he spent far too much of his time confronting it face to face. His morals were never under threat but his composure constantly was. Anxiety always produced the symptoms of ill health.

On 29 July, six weeks after the 1876 Conference delegates had returned home, Catherine Booth wrote to Bramwell – still barely twenty – with the news that his father was 'working as hard as he did before Conference and I am daily expecting a breakdown'.[25] Catherine, although sympathetic, had no doubt where the blame for her husband's condition should be laid. 'It is useless talking. He says he cannot help it. He will not be persuaded to get a man of ability into the office.'[26] As always with the Booths, one illness led to another. In October, William Booth told Henry Reed, 'My dear wife broke down completely in nursing me and she has been very ill since.' Catherine and William again went to Kent to convalesce. But recovery was slower than either of them had hoped. Bramwell, who had himself been unwell, was called down from Scotland – where he had been following the usual Booth custom of combining recuperation and revivalism – to take command of Mission headquarters. He was prepared for his ordeal by a five-page letter from his father. It offered advice which would have been more appropriate ten years earlier:

On one thing alone I insist upon. Be something – be master of

one branch of labour. Now, as to the present I think that you should lay down and act upon some plans that would
    1. improve your mind
    2. increase your intelligence
    3. improve your gifts
    4. add to your education.[27]

William Booth went on to urge upon his son disciplines which he never accepted himself. It was typical of his intellectual inconsistency. His sudden enthusiasm for learning was not the result of age bringing wisdom. The advice he gave his son was the whim of the moment. 'To be able to read a *Latin sentence* or your *Greek Testament* is I think desirable, although not necessary. All this may be done by a moderate and, to you, an easy amount of reading. To hold your own with preachers and *public* you must have information and skill in controversial theology. There need be no excuses here. *You have a mind for it.*' The speculation about whether or not a period at college was either necessary or desirable – coloured by the fear that too many theological 'institutions are Calvinistic, cold-blooded and, while improving the mind [are likely] to damage the heart' – confirmed that he still had no fixed ideas on the importance of education. The plea to his son to 'pray a great deal about everything' and the repetition of his belief that revivals must be stimulated from earth not heaven represented William Booth's more consistent philosophy. His letter ended with a combined nod in the direction of 'holiness doctrine' and a simple statement of how to make and keep sanctified Christians. 'I have been reading Tynerman's *Wesley* in my illness and have, by comparing his experience with my own, I think, derived some *important lessons*. One is that, under God, Wesley made Methodism not by converting sinners but by making well instructed saints.'[28] Bramwell was notoriously susceptible to his father's will and wishes, and no doubt he found that the letter, didactic though it was, provided great encouragement. The improvement to his morale could not have come at a better time.

For while his father was 'recovering his old strength' and telling friends 'I must be careful of myself . . . I have been doing too much', Bramwell was required to resolve the problems which had arisen at the Mission headquarters during the summer. Two of the women evangelists – Sisters Stride and Pullet – wished to resign in order to marry, not

in itself a sin but in the eyes of the Booths a sign of deep disloyalty. Two
other staff matters were outstanding. One was the retirement of Brother
Tetley, which the Mission refused to accept until he abandoned a claim
for back wages to which, in his employer's view, he was not entitled.
The third problem was rather more serious. The Poplar Mission Station
had been so offended by its resident minister's uncompromising view
of Christian duty that it had demanded that he should be removed.
The resident minister was George Scott Railton.

Bramwell Booth, not yet twenty-one and not completely recovered
from his own debilitating illness, was faced with the most difficult
decisions of his life. Nothing in his upbringing had encouraged him to
believe that his father welcomed him taking independent action. So,
not surprisingly, he wrote and asked for advice. The reply was less than
saintly in tone or content. 'Let me, for mercy's sake, have a day's rest. I
won't serve you and Railton so when you go away . . . Every day you
have bothered me . . . Do the best you can. *Please* do, let me alone.'[29]
The only possible excuse for Booth's behaviour was that he had just
been diagnosed as, in addition to his other ailments, suffering from gas-
tric fever. Bramwell rose to the occasion. Brother Tetley retired with
a small *ex gratia* payment. Sisters Stride and Pullet resigned with
honour. Poplar was reconciled to Railton.

It is impossible to imagine how long the Booths' convalescence
might have gone on had they not received terrible news from London.
Early in November Mary, the family maid, was diagnosed as suffering
from smallpox. Lucy, the youngest of the Booth children, caught it
two days later. Mary was moved – at her own request, Catherine was
anxious to make clear – to the local isolation hospital. But Lucy
remained at home in a house which was effectively quarantined.
Catherine and William hurried back to be near to their sick daughter
while Railton (who was still living with the Booths) believed himself so
safe in the hands of the Lord that he insisted on visiting the maid
during her dying days. He immediately developed the distinctive
symptoms of rash but refused to accept that he needed medical treatment.

I got into a beautiful perspiration which continued all the way
home and all today while I am getting on with the Report. Why
should not the thing be got right by work just as well as by

baths which only serve to promote the same end when a person cannot exert themselves enough to attain it . . .[30]

William Booth's comment on the way in which Railton had contracted his illness was made all the more curious by his own long record of hypochondria: 'I have never shrunk from danger and have never scarcely taken a complaint. Cannot we all trust and not be afraid? I would not run heedlessly into danger. I think that Railton did wrong.'[31] Then, having condemned Railton for misguided heroics, he changed his diagnosis and charged him with feigning illness – even though the smallpox patient had insisted on continuing to work at home. Booth saw Railton's potentially mortal illness entirely in personal terms – first of all his feelings, then his convenience. Indeed it was because Railton was needed by the Mission that he concluded that God would not incapacitate or kill him. 'It came over me in the Holiness meeting last night like an avalanche and crushed me to the ground . . . I felt that I could not give him up . . . could not do without him.'[32] Railton had certainly contracted smallpox, but he persisted in claiming that, since his face was 'smooth though red spotted' he was fit for work, although infectious. He went into voluntary quarantine and spent his time writing.

The result was *Heathen England* – a book which, because of its title, is often thought of as the precursor of *In Darkest England*, the monumental work on poverty which was published, under William Booth's name, fourteen years later. *Heathen England* revealed that Booth and Railton had quite different views about who should be the object of their labours. By 1876, William Booth was for the poor. Railton wanted to convert families 'whose houses are thoroughly respectable in position, construction and appearance as any man could wish'. However, Railton was worried about the temptations of prosperity – which he associated with culture as well as physical comfort. It was his suspicion of pleasure and prosperity which led him recklessly to attack Matthew Arnold.

Matthew Arnold and Professor Thomas Huxley – the most vocal of Charles Darwin's many disciples – had been engaged in a long public agreement about the best way of combating the vice which both aesthete and atheist agreed lay just below the cheerful surface of Derby Day. Railton intervened in the dispute with an attack not on the scientist but on the moral philosopher:

Even supposing that culture was a great success in the cause of individuals, it is manifestly impracticable for the mass. How many Bethnal Green Museums, how many National Galleries, how many conversations and lectures would be necessary to 'culture' the people of East London? But is there no possibility of making that rough great fellow over the way a gentleman? Thank God! There is. The culture of God can make that man to sit down at the table of the King of Kings.[33]

Railton's absolute failure to understand Arnold's dream of 'sweetness and light' – the dissemination of culture throughout society – was the product of a nature which attracted him to authority, discipline and order. *Heathen England* – basically a description of the Christian Mission's onward march – was positively Nietzschean in its insistence that success depends upon the 'direction of one controlling will'. But he then revealed that, for all his interest in ideas, his enthusiasm for the Christian Mission blinded him to its true nature. The Mission, and the Salvation Army which followed, were the high water mark of Methodist enterprise in Britain. The Mission was and the Salvation Army remains part of the Wesleyan heritage. But Railton really believed that the organisation was above such narrow consideration. 'We are a corps of volunteers for Christ, organised as perfectly as we have been able to accomplish, seeking no church status, avoiding as we would the plague any denomination in order perpetually to reach more and more of those who live outside every church boundary.' The pretensions of the Mission were infinite.

The idea of a Salvation Army was clearly already in Railton's mind. Indeed, in all but name and uniform, the Salvation Army was already in being. Railton had become convinced that God's will would only be done if William Booth assumed complete and absolute control of the Christian Mission.

12

Into Battle

The date on which the historic meeting took place has never been precisely determined, but the message which George Scott Railton and Bramwell Booth carried to the General Superintendent of the Christian Mission is not in doubt. Railton was the spokesman for the two-man delegation which offered advice that William Booth was happy to accept. 'We did not give ourselves to form a little church to be an appendix of Methodism. We gave ourselves to you to be guided by you.'[1] Booth, the contemporary biographers claimed, was, like Caesar on the Lupercal, reluctant to adopt full autocratic powers. He had already tightened his grip on the organisation and did not, according to his loyal chroniclers, believe that he needed to do more. But Booth-Tucker (the son-in-law who in all things represented the view of the early leadership) illustrates by his language the impatience, indeed the disdain, with which Booth's immediate lieutenants viewed 'the democratic system into which . . . the Christian Mission had fast been drifting'. It was not difficult to convince the General Superintendent of the need for a 'purely military constitution'.[2]

The drift towards democracy was largely in Railton's imagination. Booth had already limited the authority of both the Christian Mission's Committee and Conference by proposing, without the slightest consultation, changes to the constitution which increased his personal power. Railton used those changes as a reason for taking the process a stage further. Formally emasculating the Conference and abolishing the Committee was no more than formalising what was, in practice, already the reality of its purely theoretical power. Even before the constitution was changed, nothing about the central direction of the Mission – with the single exception of the rejection of his call for total abstinence – had been decided without William Booth's approval since at least 1875. But Railton wanted – and Booth was less reluctant to accept than he pretended – the formal acceptance of the General Superintendent's supreme authority. In many ways that intention was in conflict with the democratic traditions of the Methodism which William Booth had adopted. But the changes had reduced the risk of the local revolts which had caused so much difficulty in every other branch of the Wesleyan Church and were threatening to slow down, if not stop altogether, the onward march of the Christian Mission. William Booth's response to the revolt in Brighton, the revolution in Portsmouth and the secession in Leicester (which, he feared, might encourage a trend in evangelical separatism) was the conspicuous assumption of absolute power.

The Booths had always had their doubts about the Leicester mission which, they feared, was too dependent on the grace and favour of a local philanthropist named Walker. But they had accepted the assurances of the 'rich merchant' that he was satisfied for William to take complete command – 'to govern and manage' in what Walker described as 'whatever way you think best'. But some of the congregation objected to what the Mission called 'straight hitting' – the uncompromising denunciation of sins which might be common amongst prosperous Christians. At first Walker stood by his promise and the Mission. But then he was persuaded by Brother Lamb, his senior evangelist, to spend his money on a chapel of his own. It was a common pattern of behaviour amongst rich Methodists – indeed William Booth had been offered employment by both Edward Rabbits and Henry Reed. The relationship between democracy and defection was set out in Railton's biography of his chief. The words are Booth's, the sentiments Railton's:

The work began to spread and show wonderful promise and

then when everything was looking like progress a new trouble arose . . . Some of the evangelists whom I had engaged to assist me rose up and wanted to convert our mission into a regular church with a Committee of Management and that sort of thing. They wanted to settle down in quietness. I wanted to go forward at all costs. I was not to be defeated or turned back from the object on which my heart was set . . . I called them together and addressing them said . . . 'I want to make an Army. Those among you who are willing to help me to realise my purpose can stay with me. Those who are not must separate from me.'[3]

Railton did not divulge where and when (if at all) William Booth actually spoke those words. But the reference to 'an Army' suggests that they were the reflections upon, rather than the sudden emotions caused by, the schisms of 1876. Railton's own gloss on the explanation is a reflection on both the state of the Mission and on Victorian society. Rich patrons were an unnecessary risk. 'It had been found that congregations of workmen gathered in the provincial towns would give collections large enough to defray the local expenses.'[4] So the Mission could manage without sponsors – the men who came to conferences and committees and when William Booth's will prevailed rather than theirs, broke away and founded independent missions of their own.

No doubt it was Booth himself who decided to proceed with caution, for caution was not Railton's style. On a Tuesday and Wednesday, 23 and 24 January 1877, all the full-time evangelists, thirty-six in all, met at the Christian Mission headquarters in the Whitechapel Road. They were to be prepared for the changes which William Booth was to propose to the Conference and, by becoming committed to them in private, prevented from opposing them later in public. Railton was there because he was Poplar Minister as well as Mission Secretary. Bramwell Booth had, in effect, been promoted over Railton's head and was now, in fact if not in form, both second-in-command and heir apparent. For the Christian Mission had become more than an autocracy. It was a hereditary monarchy. William Booth asking for his colleagues' agreement to change was little more than a courtesy.

Much emphasis was placed on the defection at Leicester and Abraham Lamb's desertion. His aggressive resignation letter was read out as evidence of the moral deterioration which follows apostasy. Its more truculent passages were greeted with gratifying exclamations of horror. The way to avoid the repetition of such deplorable conduct was, the evangelists were told, to concentrate all power in the hands of William Booth himself – though there was no explanation of why that should be so. None of them, they were forcefully reminded, had supposed when first they joined the Mission that they had been appointed to govern it. On the contrary, 'they had been given to believe that they were to carry out the orders of the General Superintendent'.[5]

Not all of the ministers were in favour of other, and more draconian, constitutional changes – not least because, during the previous year, they had lost members as a result of the Mission's enthusiasm for dramatic conversions, emotional sermons and the pursuit of Holiness. They blamed Railton for the emphasis on excitement which turned into frenzy and they rightly suspected that he was also the inspiration of the constitutional 'reforms'. But William Booth, whom they revered, had put his name to the proposals and for him they were prepared to accept meetings being held in public houses and women being given dominion over men. So they agreed and Booth assured them that the new discipline would stifle dissent. In June, the Annual Conference would discuss (and no doubt agree) a new constitution.

As the year passed, William Booth began to interpret both history and his own youthful relationship with the New Connexion in a way which gave his enthusiasm for autocracy the spurious justification of consistency. He had come to believe that he was John Wesley's heir and that the Mission was what Wesleyan Methodists would have been had it not been corrupted – by which he meant 'gone soft' – after the founder's death. The theological bequest was the belief in 'instantaneous sanctification'. But part of the inheritance was the understanding that evangelism only prospered under strong leadership. By a remarkable rewriting of his personal history, he went on to explain that his several conflicts with other branches of the Nonconformist Church had always been the result of the inevitably inefficient, and usually corrupt, committee system.

Wesley had certainly been an uncompromising autocrat. But after his death, the Conference which he had created to take his place faced challenge after challenge. The founder's aura of omnipotence could not be re-created. And the Methodist membership was changing. Wesley was a gentleman and a scholar in a society which was built on, and respected, class differences. His followers instinctively accepted his authority.[6] As the century progressed and the ties to the Church of England loosened, the difference between leaders and led narrowed. For the Wesleyans a measure of democracy became inevitable. The Christian Mission was able to move in the other direction because it maintained its essential working-class constituency. And its officers were men and women who had risen from the ranks – a class of person famous for its belief in discipline. And they were, at least according to Bramwell Booth, entirely uncorrupted by personal ambition. The ever charitable Bramwell judged that, throughout his lifetime, every officer was ready to die for the cause. But after the death of William Booth they wanted to die with the rank of Commissioner. Before his death, they did not care what they were called as long as they were allowed to serve. His problems, from Reed to Walker, usually involved rich and independent men who regarded themselves as his social superiors.

The thirty-six evangelists assembled again on 11 June for the Annual Conference which had been charged with the duty of formalising the decision which had effectively been taken in January. Its deliberations were summarised on forty-eight pages of the *Christian Mission Magazine* in July. After expressing what he claimed to be the widespread disap- pointment which had followed previous conferences, 'so large a proportion of the time being consumed in discussion of comparatively trivial matters', William Booth set out to justify his proposals to avoid 'leaving essential principles and practices to be mangled about and decided by mere majorities'. He then described his plans for stifling democracy in a way of which any politician would have been proud. Answering his own question 'Why emasculate the Conference?', he avoided giving an answer by explaining that he proposed to replace the legislative assembly with a Council of War – which was represented as a superior form of democracy. In modern constitutional jargon, the Conference-turned-Council of War was purely advisory. The com- mander-in-chief, by 'resolving upon a programme of action', removed all necessity for an executive committee to take decisions between Councils of War or at any other time. Clearly there was no need, in the circumstances, for a cumbersome executive to take decisions between conferences. That was the role of the commander-in-chief. Suddenly, the logic of the Presidential Address seemed impeccable: 'We thereby give up the Conference Committee. It seems almost useless to go into the reasons fully, but I may point out one or two. It seemed impossible to get a truly *representative* committee. Some of the oldest and most experienced brethren go to the country, perhaps three hundred miles away.'

In any event, reality about where power really lay made the change imperative: 'If you are in any trouble, you don't want to go to the Committee, you want to come to me and say, "I want to see you alone".'

Having established his control of the whole Mission – spiritual and administrative, local and national – Booth went on to resolve the one outstanding doctrinal dispute in his own favour. The previous year he had failed to make total abstinence a mandatory obligation of membership. When he returned to the subject at the 1877 Conference he committed the Christian Mission to absolute rejection of alcohol by explaining that the time had not yet come to make a commitment. 'Let us wait until we can arrive at something with unanimity. Until we have made up our minds to some definite plans it will be useless to talk. But, in the meantime, *let us make all our people abstainers*.'

William Booth committed the Mission to the most austere, indeed extreme view of abstinence. That was only the beginning of his demands for self-denial. Having established the necessity to behave in a sober fashion, he moved on to the need for sobriety in dress. The Earl of Shaftesbury had told him of the rapid increase in the number of women serving prison sentences, and reported an explanation of that deplorable trend which had been suggested by a London prison chaplain. 'He attributed it to three causes, drink, trashy literature and flashy dress, and said that anyone would be surprised to see the tawdry feathers and flounces and flowers' which the prisoners wore then they were arrested – 'to gain which they had, no doubt, been tempted to commit crime'.

His belief that 'nothing can be more influential in this important question than the example of evangelists' wives' was slightly diminished as a tribute to virtuous women by a grudging aside. 'Our young men will, I suppose, have wives' – a strange complaint from a man who knew how much he had benefited from his marriage. He went on to express what could only be interpreted as doubts about the wisdom of his young men's choice and their ability to overcome temptation: 'I say to you, if you meet with young women wearing showy dress, don't look at them. And if you are now engaged to somebody you met by moonlight long ago before you came to the Christian Mission, make a bargain before they marry that they dress neatly and scripturally.'

The enthusiasm for modest dress was genuine. But – almost as an aside – William Booth offered another reason for dressing 'as becometh Godliness'. He wanted his evangelists 'to be more readily recognised by our most godly and reliable people. When I go to a society, I always feel that I want to see who are its backbone.' He had no 'definite plan to propose' and the battle over uniforms was still to come. But the idea of tunics and badges was clearly in his mind.

For the second year in succession, Catherine Booth missed the Conference. In 1877, she was at Tredegville in Cardiff, the home of the Billups, where she was again resting and convalescing. Her letter to the assembled delegates arrived too late to be read out at one of the sessions, but it was nevertheless published in the *Christian Mission Magazine*'s account of the proceedings. The Booths were already treated differently from other evangelists. 'The hand of the Lord is still upon me and I bow to His will and trust whatever his purpose concerning me I may be better fit to fulfil it in consequence of this affliction.' Mrs Booth's continual illness, during the crucial years of retrenchment and reform, is often quoted by her husband's hagiographers as proof that she was not – as some of William's detractors suggest – the driving force behind the conversion of the Mission into a form that made it fit to be an army. But to prove that Mrs Booth was not the only true begetter is not to prove that Mr Booth was. He played a major part. But the Salvation Army came about because of William Booth's vision, Catherine Booth's determination, George Railton's impatience, Bramwell Booth's industry and the undoubted fact that, either by design or good fortune, its spirit and organisation fitted exactly the needs of the time.

It was, however, the force of William Booth's character – as well as the strength of his convictions – which held together a naturally fissiparous organisation. In 1877, he had the task of uniting his Mission behind a common view of 'Holiness'. He resolved the disagreements not with a compromise but by a balancing act. 'Sin,' he said, 'must not only be held in bondage but completely destroyed.' But sometimes virtue had to be approached in stages: 'It may be that the pride, envy, anger, malice, lust and all or whatsoever other evils ruled him with a

rod of iron before may be there. Bruised and broken and faint they may
be but they still exist, but the Master has taken them from the throne
of the soul and given the saint power over them. He is no longer under
sin but under grace.'

That, according to his 'Holiness Address' at the 1877 Conference,
was only the first step towards sanctification. 'There is another state,
and that is WITHOUT sin . . . The God of peace sanctifies wholly and
the whole body, soul and spirit is preserved blameless.' Booth knew
that perhaps half his audience – and rather more of his potential audience in the country – did not believe a word of what he told them.
Indeed, some of his most pious and committed supporters heartily disapproved of the concept of Holiness – which they regarded as
theologically disreputable – and the Holiness Meetings that went with
it, which they feared often became exhibitions of hysterical excess
rather than inducing grace and encouraging penitence. So William
Booth nodded in the direction of the sceptics: 'Now I am free to confess that about this state, there may be difficulties and perplexities. I
simply insist that it is described in the Bible and that the descriptions
in the Bible have been verified by thousands of saints.'

That view, even when supported with references to Ezekiel and St
Paul's Epistle to the Thessalonians, might not have been enough to
unite the Conference behind him. So a second explanation – almost a
disclaimer of what he had already said – was necessary:

We don't say that it is possible to be without imperfections,
both physical and mental. We still suffer, as the consequence of
the faith, from disease and are liable to mistake and errors,
although I am not going to limit in this respect the power of the
Holy Ghost to guide into truth and keep us from error.

So the conference was offered – by a combination of contradictions
and gibberish – whichever definition of Holiness individual partici-
pants wanted to accept. It was not an heroic way to solve the dilemma.
Indeed, it was a stratagem which was less appropriate to Messengers of
God than Members of Parliament. But it sent the evangelists home
satisfied and content that the new autocracy would not drive them all
into seeking full and instantaneous sanctification. Many of them must
have taken it for granted that the new discipline would make very

little difference to their daily lives. The nature of their commitments – to the Mission and to its leader – made them susceptible to discipline, and the commander-in-chief had always expected his subordinates to accept orders without argument or question. Elijah Cadman – bellicose by nature and a prize-fighter in his time – was once assaulted during an open-air meeting but, in the great tradition of passive resistance, got up when the assailants had finished with him and resumed his sermon. So they knocked him down again. Cadman picked himself up for a second time. He was about to continue his address when Bramwell Booth arrived and told him, 'Get into the Hall, Cadman.'[7] Despite his natural inclinations, Cadman agreed. Ministers of the Mission obeyed the orders of their superiors. So they accepted the Superintendent's injunction on their attitude towards Holiness – whatever it meant.

It must have taken an effort of will on Bramwell's part for him to exercise such authority. For at the time he was going through a crisis of confidence from which he never fully recovered. Twenty years later, he was to compensate for his insecurity by subjecting his brothers and sisters to such fierce discipline that three of them left the Army. And when his time came to take full command he found that without his father's strength and wisdom behind him, he was unable to discharge a General's duties. But in 1877, he was simply uncertain of both his abilities and the esteem in which he was held by God and man.

On Monday 14 May 1877, he wrote in his journal, 'Much agitated in mind as to the future. I seem to lack the force, ability and application which is positively necessary to work which I am attempting. A secular employment would certainly be much easier than this.' By December his spirits had improved. 'For months since a line was written in this book . . . I have passed through more conflict than I could have thought possible on the matter of preaching and public work generally, but I feel more settled lately.'[8] Bramwell attributed his recovery to his mother's support and encouragement. In November 1877 she told him, 'Don't be discouraged at difficulties. Those who lead in the fight must be prepared to see their comrades fall.'[9] There is no mention of support in troubled times from his father. Indeed, a letter from mother to son, sent in the following year in response to Bramwell's suggestion that he should volunteer for demotion, suggests that William Booth was part of the trauma's cause. 'No: the General will not *have you*. You are a man yourself and as much worth for spiritual work as himself. Don't think that you are going to be anybody's second.'[10] At that time 'General' was used as an indication of authority and power, not military rank. It all confirmed how hard it was to be William Booth's son.

The instinct for good order – which was so highly developed in William Booth – was shared by even the most unlikely evangelists. Even George Railton – regarded by the Booths as pathologically reckless and irresponsible – hoped to emulate an almost unknown soldier, John Nicholson, a general at thirty-five who died saving India for what the Secretary of the Mission believed to be the Christian Empire.[11] He was immensely impressed by the reforms of the British Army which were initiated by Edward Cardwell, the Secretary of State for War in Gladstone's first administration. Cardwell had, Railton believed, created citizen soldiers. The military influences within the Christian Mission were strong, strange, diverse and irresistible.

Both Cadman and Railton expressed their fervour in martial images. Railton's articles discussed the need for 'Reinforcements' and the use of 'Torpedoes'. He constantly challenged his readers with the question, 'Shall it Be Peace or War?' Cadman called his Bible his sword[12] and described himself as a captain in the King's Army. When he led a campaign in Whitby during November 1877, the posters with which he advertised his arrival were headed 'War! War! 200 Men and Women wanted at once to join the Hallelujah Army'. He described himself as 'Captain', a title which, when he first assumed it, was thought by his followers to owe more to the patois of dockers and navvies than to the Army List. But his account of the campaign left no doubt that he saw his evangelism as a battle against evil.[13] It was headed 'Latest War News' and reported that, 'The troops had a review at 7 p.m., marching through the streets in good order.' There was 'hard fighting throughout the day . . . Sinners were cut to the heart but would not yield . . . On Monday the victory was won and the devil defeated . . . by The Hallelujah Army.'

Whitby was under siege for six months. The poster which advertised the July big push was an absurd caricature of a military communiqué: 'WE ARE RUSHING INTO WAR. The battle has begun: thousands killed and wounded, a few have been saved from death. It is a field of blood already but what will it be?' The poster promised reinforcements – 'THE MIDDLESBRO' ARTILLERY is to arrive at 9.30 a.m.

with their big guns.' It then became a chapel notice again: 'A public
ham sandwich tea will be provided in the Congress Hall at 3 o'clock.
Tickets 9d each,' to be followed by a 'HALLELUJAH LOVE FEAST in
the hall'. The notice then returned to its original warlike theme: 'HOS-
PITAL FOR THE WOUNDED and all who want to be healed from sin.'

That advertisement – military metaphors aside – illustrated a characteristic which was common amongst William Booth's followers and
was both a strength and a weakness. Few of them possessed the slightest capacity for understanding how ridiculous they could sound. The
absurdity of much of their publicity attracted support in the slums, but
it increased the contempt in which they were held in the respectable
suburbs. They should not have been surprised when their expansion
into a national institution was initially greeted with derisive incredulity
as well as bitter opposition.

Whitby became the Christian Mission's Bunker's Hill, the battle in
which the citizen army discovered that it knew how to fight. Mrs
Dowdle, wife of the Mission's minister in Bradford, addressed the
January Rally in St Hilda's Hall. She set out the Mission philosophy in
uncompromising language which proclaimed that the Christian
Mission 'did not want the respectable members of religious society
amongst them – it was the outsiders they were seeking to bring to
God'.[14] It seems that they attracted exactly the sort of congregation
which they were after – at least at the tea meeting. 'It took the captain
and his lieutenants to prevent some of their guests from taking their
teas and then walking off with not only lots of cake but the tea plates
in their capacious pockets . . . At the evening meeting Cadman
implored those who had possession of plates to bring them back to
him.'[15]

The *Christian Mission Magazine* reported the 'latest war news' as the
'Arrival of Mr Booth, General of the Hallelujah Army' – language not
altogether consistent with the later claim that the title had first been
used not to denote military rank but in comparison with the chief
officer of a religious order. From Whitby onwards the military
metaphors grew increasingly popular. In Bradford, Lawley was 'advancing every battery in full play against the enemy'. One Sunday morning
in March 1878 he 'mustered full force at City Road and opened fire'.
The martial images did not increase the aggression with which the
evangelists advanced their cause. Their tactics were already so bellicose

that no further increase in belligerence was possible. But it did antagonise members of other Christian denominations who, as well as
resenting being treated as the enemy, thought of the wild talk of shot
and shell as either building conversions around hysteria, rather than
reason, or simply unspeakably vulgar. Vulgarity was one of the
Mission's most deadly weapons. In the summer of 1877 it organised a
'Great Exhibition of Trophies; given up for Christ's sake', which
included 'Feathers, Flowers, Jet Ornaments, Lockets, Brooches, Pipes
and Tobacco Pouches'. The whole announcement was another metaphor. The trophies were on display 'over the mantelpiece in the homes
of some of our evangelists and others'.[16]

When William Booth took advantage of his new authority to draw
up 'Orders and Regulations of Membership, To Govern the Conduct of
Officers', he guaranteed that the publicans and brewers, who had previously regarded him as an irritant, began to see him as a threat who
must be destroyed before he destroyed them:

> No one shall be allowed to hold any office in the Mission who
> is not a total abstainer from intoxicating liquors, tobacco and
> snuff – except in cases of absolute sickness. No person shall be
> received or continue as a member who shall keep a public
> house or brewery or be engaged in the demoralising traffic or
> sale of intoxicating drinks or shall frequent any public house or
> dram shop except on business.

That was a direct challenge to an industry which made and broke
politicians. The publicans and brewers responded with a literal violence that matched Captain Cadman's bellicose images. During its East
London days, the Christian Mission preachers were often harassed by
louts and occasionally assaulted by hooligans – some of whom were
given half a guinea by the local landlords for their trouble. But after it
became a national movement – thriving and expanding most quickly
amongst the drinking classes – the attacks became general and regular.
The evangelists' constant complaint was that neither the police nor the
magistrates would protect them, and there were dark suspicions that
sometimes the forces of law and order were in the pay of the licensed
trade.

Sarah Sayers, in court as the plaintiff where a man was charged with assaulting her, insisted in her evidence that she was not a preacher but a citizen who 'exhorted sinners to flee from the wrath to come'. That, and the 'continual blessings which she gave the court' provoked – according to the *Salisbury Times* – continual laughter.[17] Sarah Sayers' assailant was convicted, but her treatment illustrated both the ridicule which Mission members attracted and the sort of behaviour which attracted it. And the way in which they gloried in the abuse and assault increased the amused contempt in which they were held. The soldiers for Christ capitalised on their treatment. Men and women joined the Mission to prove that they were the stuff of which martyrs are made.

With the rules and regulations in place, the Superintendent, Commander-in-Chief and General decided – with the encouragement of his son Bramwell and George Railton – to consolidate his position by calling a Council of War. Once again he prepared for the formal event with a 'consultation' with the full-time evangelists. He prepared for their deliberations with a 'night of prayer' which two hundred and fifty people attended. It lasted from the end of a Holiness Meeting at ten o'clock on the evening of 16 January 1878 until eight o'clock the following morning. It provided a perfect example of the induced hysteria about which the more fastidious Methodists complained:

> From the very first, Jehovah was passing by, searching,
> softening and subduing every heart. The power of the Holy
> Ghost fell on Robinson and prostrated him. He nearly fainted
> twice. The brother of Blandys entered into full liberty and then
> he shouted, wept, clapped his hands, danced amid a scene of
> the most glorious and heavenly enthusiasm. Others meanwhile
> were lying prostrate on the floor, some of them groaning aloud
> for perfect deliverance.[18]

Thus fortified, they came together to prepare for the Council of War. 'A little band of unlearned and ignorant men met in the great metropolis, determined by the Grace of God to shake the whole country out of the sleep of sin.'[19] Between 3 and 8 August there were six days of hard discussion. They ended with the evangelists satisfied with what William Booth had proposed and confident that they could persuade the lay delegates to accept it too. So the Council of War – the Conference by another name and denied even the appearance of power – came together to endorse the 'Deed of Amendment' and the 'Deed of Constitution' which were necessary to give legal force to the previous year's decisions. Thus, 'he who was so much against the restraints imposed by religious elders in societies to which he had once belonged, now imposed restraints on people under him'.[20] The authority which the Deed conferred was absolute – 'The said William Booth shall continue to be, for the term of his natural life, the General Superintendent of the Christian Mission unless he shall resign such office' – and he was endowed with every power that he could possibly need, from the appointment of his successor to the right to acquire the legal ownership of Mission property. He was also given the right to 'expend on behalf of the Christian Mission all money contributed to the general purposes of the Christian Mission'. The statement of doctrine did no more than refer to the Deed of the previous year. The theological decision of 1878 was the exaltation of William Booth above all others. It was the year of power, not of principles.

General Superintendent Booth hoped that the Deed Poll, by regularising his authority, would 'destroy the influences of those slanderers who, taking advantage of the fact that the supreme governing power of the Mission lies in the hands of the General Superintendent, have pretended that he could apply the property of the Mission to his own use'. The result was quite the opposite of that for which he hoped – as a more worldly man than Booth would have realised. Railton traced the origins of the slander to a man identified as 'Old Scotty . . . a wretched individual whose natural home was the public house'. Scotty attended most of the Mission's Mile End open-air meetings and, standing near to the preacher, constantly interrupted prayers and addresses with a demand to know what would happen to the proceeds of the collection. But even if that was how the calumny began, it was taken up by more serious, and better respected, critics of Booth and the Mission.

The suggestion that the Booths were milking the Mission was clearly absurd. In many ways William was the model of propriety. Throughout the 1870s, Richard Crossley, a Manchester businessman, constantly offered blank cheques for either the Mission funds or the Booths' private use. They were regularly refused until, at the depth of Catherine's terminal illness, he was allowed to donate to the Salvation Army – largely to compensate for the loss of income from collections after Mrs Booth's meetings. For most of his life as a full-time evangelist, William drew a salary which was too small to pay the family household bills and the deficit had to be met by the (often not very large) income from the sale of pamphlets and published sermons. Yet, although the Booths never lived lavishly, their living standards improved. They were never without a servant. Sometimes they had two. And each of their frequent illnesses was followed by a period of convalescence at a spa or by the sea. It seems almost certain that he was offered small gifts in cash or kind and that he accepted them. William Booth was an honest man. He was also, by nature, incapable of understanding why his critics accused him of double standards – even though, while he was comfortable in Gore Road, his officers were so badly paid that he had to issue a 'General Order Against Starvation'. It warned his evangelists not to endure such privation that they 'put at risk the strength and life of the officers which are of unspeakable value'.[21] Even then he could not forbear to add a note which destroyed all thought that he was concerned for his officers' welfare. A death from starvation would, he feared, 'bring great discredit to the army'. The good grace with which his officers accepted the disparities are an indication of their devotion. Evangelists in the field were rarely given help in times of sickness. Yet the constantly sick Booth family were regularly sent for long periods of recovery and convalescence. The double standards caused much comment outside the Mission and the Army, but there was no revolt amongst the officers themselves.

The Order was issued in December 1878. By then the Mission was the Army and there was no doubt why William Booth was called General – a title which, at first, he had not welcomed. According to Jane Short – who first lodged with the Booths in 1867 – 'in the family circle he was called the General during the early days of the Christian Mission rather as a tribute to his commanding and autocratic temper' than in imitation of a military rank.[22] He led the forces during Cadman's Whitby campaign initially as the Christian Mission's General Superintendent. Then, in the midst of battle, the title 'Superintendent' was consciously abandoned. When the Christian Mission became the Salvation Army, it was natural for him to assume a rank suitable to the commander-in-chief.

According to Bramwell Booth – who was witness to the event – the Mission's change of name came about almost by accident. William Booth, working (as was his early morning habit) in his bedroom, strode about in carpet slippers and long yellow dressing-gown as he dictated his orders of the day. Railton, who sat at a table by the window, was drafting a statement to be issued that afternoon. Its peroration drew a parallel between the Mission and the Volunteer Movement – effectively territorials – which was coming into being as part of the Cardwell Army Reforms which he so admired. He was so pleased with the idea that he interrupted William Booth's dictation with a reading from his draft. 'We are a volunteer army.' Bramwell was outraged. 'Volunteer!' he cried. 'I am not a volunteer. I'm a regular or nothing!' William Booth stood silent for a moment. Then he strode across to Railton, leaned over his shoulder, took the pen from his hand, 'crossed out the word "Volunteer" and wrote in its place the word "Salvation"'.[23]

Booth-Tucker heard the story from his mother-in-law, who was presumably about the house at the time. He wrote, in Catherine Booth's biography, that Railton was helping William Booth prepare his Christmas message. The date is certainly wrong and so, therefore, is his description of the article which the two men were writing. They were working on the September 1878 edition of the *Christian Mission Magazine*. His account does, however, reveal the caution with which the new name was adopted. 'By the early summer of that year, the whole new vocabulary was in use . . . Official recognition of the title only took place by degrees. At first the notepaper used for correspondence bore the heading *The Christian Mission* or the Salvation Army. A few months later, the order was reversed.'[24] The appeal of the name (which had made George Railton leap in the air with excitement when he first heard it) was irresistible. And the idea of an army had been in the members' minds since Whitby. By October advertisements were announcing the 'opening of the Great Salvation Factory in Coventry' and promising that 'William Booth, the General of The Salvation Army, will enter the town at the head of the 35th (Coventry) Corps'. Mission members were described as 'troops' and the Coventry order of battle announced 'forces will encamp on Pool Meadow'. The name 'The Salvation Army' was not entered as an amendment to the 1878 Poll Deed until 24 June 1880, and only confirmed in the Court of Chancery on 20 April 1906. But neither formality was of any consequence. From the autumn of 1878 onward *General* Booth was the commander-in-chief of *The Salvation Army*.

There were three Booths at its head, and Bramwell was playing an increasingly important part in the triumvirate. Catherine Booth – in national terms still a more famous evangelist than her husband – continued to preach but, where the organisation of the Army was concerned, chose an advisory rather than an executive role. Despite the decision – which she had inspired – that women could be given authority over men, she was never made an officer of the Army. Although she advised the high command in private and defended its decisions in public, she was never given formal rank. She had received God's commission and that was all the warrant that she needed. The title 'Army Mother' which she acquired during her declining years summed up her position exactly. She had immense influence but little power, immense respect but no formal responsibilities. It was, she had no doubt, her duty to help her husband in all his endeavours. So it was Catherine Booth who, despite initial doubts, announced in November 1878 that the Salvation Army was going into uniform.[25] It would be 'the same old friend, neither altered in dress or person, bringing the same message'.[26]

William Booth had already told his soldiers that it was important that they should be able instantly to recognise each other. And he knew that uniforms, by extending the feeling of community, would give an immense boost to morale. But the selection of a suitable livery posed a problem. The Army had to be visible without being vain or glorious, smart but not extravagant in dress or ostentatious in badges of rank and insignia. Anything remotely flamboyant would create a barrier between the soldiers and the civilians they had enlisted to serve.

George Railton shared the commitment to austerity which had at first made Catherine Booth doubt the wisdom of introducing uniforms of any sort. But it had led him to the opposite conclusion. As early as 1875 he had begun to agonise about the propriety, as well as the practical advantages, of Christian Mission ministers and members sharing common dress. To clear his mind, he had written a memorandum to Catherine who, as if she did not have enough children of her own, increasingly took a maternal interest in Railton's constant moral dilemmas.

I puzzle to know what line to take . . . it seems to me that the strongest line of argument is that this desire to dress up is a lust and to insist that if anyone follows a lust which is so universally manifest amongst the unconverted, they are evidently going with the multitude to do evil . . . I cannot see that Christ ever *definitely* touches the question – a remarkable reticence . . . Is there any other proper way to deal with dress but to bring everyone to a uniform system, just as we brought people to total abstinence?[27]

The merit which Railton saw in uniform depended on the idea being applied in the literal sense of that word – identical dress which bound the organisation together and, in its simplicity, united them with the poor sinners they hoped to save. He suggested clothes 'so rough, coarse and plain that no one would wish to wear it for the sake of its appearance or texture'. His proposal, for all ranks, was 'a short unbraided jacket of common serge with brass Ss on it'. Once the idea was adopted – if not accepted in every mission – he became the first staff officer to wear the red jersey. Indeed he became so enthusiastic about the anonymity of cap and tunic that 'for years he possessed no outer garments that were not uniform'.[28]

Catherine Booth – despite her contempt for the vanities of the world – was less austere in her approach. Indeed her son-in-law and biographer thought it necessary to explain why 'in the question of uniform, Mrs Booth took a particular interest'.[29] She had always believed that modesty alone was not enough. Fashion, in even its most unostentatious form, was an evil which, 'within the borders of the mission, had crept in despite the most strenuous efforts to guard against it . . . Left to their own discretion, some of the wives of the evangelists had dressed in a manner which to some degree resembled the fashions of the world. Others in their anxiety to avoid this evil (and naturally destitute of taste) had adopted costumes which were unsuitable and even ridiculous.'[30] The outcome of Catherine's deliberations was the 'Hallelujah Bonnet', chosen (in consultation with her daughter Kate) from so many examples of different designs and colours that they filled a room. Catherine stipulated that the bonnet should be worn far enough back on the forehead to expose the beginnings of the hairline and tied securely under the chin with a ribbon.

Whatever its merits as a hat, the Hallelujah Bonnet became the symbol of all that was best in the Salvation Army – unpretentious, practical, durable and not noticeably out of place in either the most pious Holiness Meeting or the roughest public house. Mrs Booth was far too practical to invest it with any spiritual qualities. When the Sisters went to spread the word in hot climates, the bonnet was replaced by a shawl or veil. For she did not wish it to be 'unalterable as in the case of monks and nuns'. Despite Railton's sudden suggestion that it might be exchanged for a three-cornered hat which could be worn (with minor adaptations) by either sex, the bonnet remained in use for almost a hundred years.

The turbulence of 1878 proved an effective recruiting sergeant – though it was perhaps the new uniform and new name, rather than William Booth's assumption of absolute power, that called men and women to the colours. Whatever the reason, during the year in which the Christian Mission became the Salvation Army, it prospered as never before. At the time of the 1877 Conference there were twenty-nine Christian Mission stations. At the end of 1878 there were eighty-one Army 'units'. The number of full-time ministers (evangelists in the summer of 1877, officers by 1878) rose from 31 to 127 – more than a hundred of them recruited from the ranks of recent converts. In less than a year, the number of weekly services (in and outdoor) almost doubled, and the average total Sunday night congregation increased from 11,675 to 27,280. The Salvation Army was on the march.

13

The Voice
of the Rabble

The change of name from Christian Mission to the Salvation Army was the result of a moment's whimsy – a rare event in the life of William Booth. But it symbolised the popular appeal of 'God's Irregulars', and the assumption of the martial name, combined with the adoption of military ranks and uniforms, appealed to the jingoistic Victorian working classes.

The flag, which became the symbol of the Army's militancy, was a tricolour – red to represent the blood of Christ, yellow for the baptism of the Holy Spirit and blue to symbolise the condition of true holiness which was available to those who trusted the Lord. To the men and women who lined the streets as the parades passed by – and even more to those who followed the colours – it was an oriflamme that proclaimed the Salvation Army's eternal war against evil. 'Blood and Fire', the motto, which surrounded the cross in the centre of the battle honours, was an even more dramatic demonstration of the heroic image that the Salvation Army chose to assume. The Army was sanctified by the blood of Christ and inspired by the fire of the Holy Spirit. 'Blood and Fire' sounded like, and was, a call to arms. The response was more recruits to the colours than the high command could reasonably accommodate.

The Salvation Army was expanding at so great a speed that it risked being destroyed by its own momentum. It did not possess the bureaucracy necessary to sustain a large organisation, and the men who had been given executive authority had no executive or administrative experience. It was chronically short of funds – living from day to day on the sacrifice of its employees and the generosity of its congregation. Apparently unaware of the dangers by which he was beset, and the antagonism which he attracted, General Booth chose to assume the new military persona which required him to behave in a way which compounded the offence caused by the emotional appeal of his evangelism and the uncouth nature of his preachers. The Salvation Army – in musical comedy uniforms and claiming ranks to which they were neither suited nor entitled – completed the pastiche by playing martial music which disrupted the quiet Sundays of the streets in which they proselytised. It would have been bad enough if their behaviour had been no more than profane. But it was also risible. The Old Testament prophet at the head of the battalion took to wearing the frogged coat of a real general – often with a top hat and umbrella. And dressed as if to proclaim his eccentric respectability, he behaved with a scandalous disregard for the mores of the time. Women – some of them recent sinners – were expected to expose themselves to dangers and degradations about which more delicate ladies chose not even to think.

Most scandalous of all were the Hallelujah Lasses – girls barely out of their teens who supported the trained evangelists with cries of joy and hymns which they sang to their own accompaniment on banjos, concertinas and tambourines. After the hymns came adaptations of music hall songs. Railton, despite his emotionally fastidious reputation, wrote new sacred words to go with old profane music. 'Dixie' became 'Oh Every Land is Filled With Sin'.[1] In Torquay a potential benefactor withdrew his support when he heard Salvationists sing 'Elijah was a jolly old man / And was carried up to heaven in a fiery van.'

Some of the Hallelujah Lasses achieved a moment's fame. In the Rhondda Valley Kate Shepherd – who would tell her audiences, 'We know you are miserable' and somehow elicit the response, 'We know we are miserable' – received six offers of marriage during her first six weeks of preaching. Two of them were from ordained ministers. 'Happy Eliza', a recruit who was sent to liven up a flagging Nottingham campaign, marched through the town with streamers flying from her hair and jacket and singing the Salvationist version of 'Marching Through Georgia':

> Shout aloud Salvation, boys, we'll have another song
> Sing it out with a spirit that will move the world along
> Sing it as our fathers sang it many millions strong
> As they went marching to glory . . .

Glory, according to Salvationists, was what followed the death of redeemed sinners. When she moved to Marylebone – and was driven round the streets playing her 'Salvation Violin' – music hall songs were written about her and Happy Eliza dolls appeared in the shops.

Despite the Booths' efforts being focused on the needs (and susceptibilities) of the huddled masses, they both remained, at least for the success of their Army, in part, dependent on donations from wealthy patrons. By the end of the 1870s Catherine – far more in demand than her husband in polite society – was preaching regularly in the West End. And she was feeling guilty about it. At least she was for part of the time. Her attitude was an uneasy combination of disapproval and awe. She said and she meant, 'Oh friends, give up the sentimental hypocrisy of singing, "Reserve the perishing / Care for the dying" in a drawing room, to the accompaniment of a piano, without dreaming of going outside to do it,'[2] but a few weeks later, she proclaimed the pleasure to be found in the company of the middle and upper classes: 'The audience was very select, we never having published a bill, only advertised in *The Christian* and the daily papers.'[3] She later wrote to tell Bramwell that foreign royalty were expected: 'Princess – and Prince to be present. I am to tell them of the effect of our work on drunkards etc.'[4] There seems to have been no question of Their Highnesses being told to repent their sins – only how evil can be driven out of commoners. In a letter to Mrs Billups, Catherine was overcome with girlish delight by the discovery that 'both Kate and I are beset with invitations to drawing room meetings'.[5]

William Booth was less ambivalent about doing business with the rich. He had less hope of bringing them to the penitent form than of sending them to heaven by the power of good work. The good work he had in mind was investing in the Salvation Army. Samuel Morley hit on the idea of arranging a confrontation between William Booth and some of his more vociferous critics. Morley, 'with tears in his eyes', told Catherine that her husband had 'carried them every one and by the end, they agreed with his every word'. William Booth, in a letter to his son, Herbert, gave most of the credit for their conversion to Catherine and predicted, 'They will help us but I am not sure to what extent.' He listed those attending with careful respect for rank and position – 'The Honourable Cowper Temper MP, the Honourable Captain Moreton'. He ended with rejoicing that 'the papers are working for us all over the country and are mostly favourable'.[6] They were not favourable for long.

One or two rich benefactors were caught in Morley's net. John Melrose, an Edinburgh tea blender, helped to meet the cost of Scottish campaigns and T. A. Denny, a bacon merchant with a house overlooking Hyde Park, made a tour of the Army's London stations with his brother, Edward. The two men were so impressed with what they saw that they became regular donors and close friends to both the Booths. Much to William Booth's delight, they complained that he was 'inclined to take the money without taking the advice' – clear proof that his beliefs were not for sale.

There were other converts and conquests. But the newspapers, which Booth had judged to be on his side when he met Samuel Morley's wealthy associates, proved to be fickle friends. One journalist did, however, remain faithful to him from the foundation of the Salvation Army until the end of his life – more loyal than in some ways William Booth deserved. W. T. Stead was the editor of the *Northern Echo* and therefore a witness to the Newcastle Council of War which assembled in May 1879. His report makes clear why his support endured even when Booth turned on him. His article began with a comparison between the Council of War and the enthronement of the Bishop of Durham which had taken place during the previous week:

> The Salvation Army services on the fringes of the Council were
> conducted by men and women who were destitute of any
> pretensions to culture. In place of the organ, on which Dr
> Adams discoursed sweet music in the Cathedral, the Tyneside
> congregations had to content themselves with the Hallelujah
> fiddle. Rough and shock-headed processionists followed,
> banners emblazoned with the representation of the sun at

noonday and bearing the rude mystic inscription Blood and
Fire whilst Hallelujah Lasses walked backwards precentor
fashion.

It was the 'disorderly gathering of the Hallelujah Lasses' which capti-
vated Stead and made him a Booth supporter for ever.

> Ridicule as we may the doggerel hymns, the incoherent prayers,
> the wild harangues, the violent gesticulations and all the rude
> sensation of a country fair imported into public worship, the
> fact remains that the Salvation Army has saved for the time
> being, numbers of the very lowest of the community from vice
> and crime. The testimony of the police and of the magistrates in
> Gateshead is conclusive as to the gentleness of their work.[7]

The Hallelujah fiddle, a feature of the procession which Stead so
admired, was – like so many of the Army's most popular innovations –
incorporated into the Salvationists' services by chance and despite
William Booth's strong initial reluctance. Will Fry, a Salisbury builder,
joined the Salvation Army during the summer of 1879 and, together
with his three sons, attended William Booth's open-air rally in that
town. All three men had played in the orchestra which augmented the
hymn-singing in the local Methodist Chapel – a common feature of
services in every denomination during the nineteenth century as
immortalised by Thomas Hardy's *The Woodlanders*. The General initially
thought that artificial music profaned the sacred atmosphere of his
services. Then he realised that it could become an immense attraction
to the sort of people he hoped to recruit. It did not take long for music
to become an essential part of every Salvation Army meeting and for
William Booth to decide that its incorporation into the military rituals
was one of his best ideas. He probably never said that all the best
tunes should not be left to the devil. But that certainly represented his
view.
     The Booths were populists by nature and never even thought that
they were debasing their beliefs by making them intelligible to the
working classes. However, with the explosion in the size and scope of
the Salvation Army, they did agree that it was necessary to educate
prospective officers. Railton was against formal training, which he

believed would dilute the purity of their preachers' evangelism and come between God and the Army's officers. But Catherine Booth was adamant, and a training home was set up. In order to spread the Salvation Army's appeal it was first situated in Manchester. It did not prosper. It was, therefore, moved to London, where it succeeded within the limited terms that the Booths set out. They had not quite overcome their suspicion of scholarship:

> We abjure all learning for its own sake. Moreover we believe that a great deal of it is calculated rather to unfit than aid its recipients for actual warfare . . . We say teach the builder how to build houses, the shoemaker how to make shoes, the soul winner HOW TO WIN SOULS – Every cadet is seen privately, talked to and prayed with and counselled according to his or her individual necessities.[8]

Individual 'counselling' was not to become fashionable for another fifty years. So in that one particular, William Booth was a progressive far ahead of his time. But his syllabus could not be described as innovative. He was preparing the converts from the slums of Britain to go out and make more recruits amongst the people they knew best. 'We try to train the *head* so as to put our affairs a little in advance in intelligence and information of the people to whom they minister. To this end we teach the three Rs and the rudiments of history, geography and composition . . .'[9]

The decision to set up a training home was further evidence that the Salvation Army had begun to see itself as a national organisation. In December 1879 the *Christian Mission Magazine* was abandoned and the first edition of *The War Cry* was published – another indication of the Army's growing pretensions. But, although Bramwell had refused to be called a volunteer, the organisation was, in many ways, still run by amateurs. Indeed, it was part of their appeal. It did not, however, equip them to run a weekly popular newspaper.

Self-help being a matter of principle as well as a financial necessity, Railton planned for the Salvation Army to produce the paper itself. He bought a second-hand printing machine and 'after various attempts to print condemned the engine as being utterly useless and the machine's only value as old iron'.[10] Railton, called sub-editor out of respect for the

General but in charge of every element of the paper's production, judged (without the benefit of any knowledge on the subject) that the machine could be made to work if the power was increased and various 'details' of its gears adjusted. The changes were made and it 'did two and tore up three and then two more and stopped'. He persevered, for perseverance was part of the Salvation Army's creed. Eventually 17,000 copies were printed and sent, through a London pea-soup fog, to the five great railway terminals. A year after the first edition came reluctantly off the press, the circulation of *The War Cry* had increased to 110,000.

Although William Booth was not a man who ever felt satisfied, he must have regarded the turn of the year from 1879 to 1880 as the time when God's choice of evangelist was vindicated. The Salvation Army in Britain was established as a permanent organisation – glorying in the number of its new recruits and proclaiming that its unpopularity with the godless confirmed its closeness to the Mercy Seat. In the early months of the new decade William Booth – certain that as long as he fulfilled his destiny, God would provide – led the most rapidly expanding, as well as the most controversial, evangelical organisation in Britain. And it seemed that, like John Wesley before him, he was about to have the whole world as his parish. For the Army was about to build a second – and this time successful – bridge-head in America.

The efforts of James Jermy to found a branch of the Christian Mission in Cleveland, Ohio, had ended in dispiriting defeat when he returned to Britain and the 'converting work' which was 'going on gloriously' collapsed without him. But in April 1878, three soldiers from the Coventry Corps – Amos Shirley, his wife Anne and their daughter Eliza – had set sail for America to start a new life which, they took for granted, included founding a branch of the Salvation Army. Shirley found a job as foreman in Adams & Company's silk factory in Philadelphia. While Amos was at work, his daughter (who had been an officer of the Army in Bishop Auckland) and his wife evangelised so successfully that they became known (and were described in the local newspapers) as 'The Two Hallelujah Females'. Such was their success, and their determination, that they soon acquired permanent premises in Philadelphia, 'The Old Chair Factory at the corner of 6th and Oxford Street . . . consisting of a room 40 by 50 whose rough boarded walls and whitewashed beams that ran along the ceiling overhead would suggest a stable rather than a place of worship.'[11] The Salvationists welcomed the newspaper report as proof that they followed the Saviour who was born in a stable.

The report described a march down Germantown Road, 'singing a rousing hymn and keeping step to the air while the leaders beat time with their hands'. When the journalist followed them to the Old Chair Factory he was driven to an orgy of clichés by a scene which 'beggared description'. Moved by the Salvationists' form of sacrament – biscuits broken and pressed from hand to hand in ever diminishing pieces – he was even more impressed by the sight of 'a tall and aged woman with spectacles [who] rose up in her seat and shouted Hallelujah in a voice that . . . made one's hair stand on end'. The climax to the rally was 'a man with a voice like Calliope . . . whose excited exhortation opened the floodgates of eloquence in every part of the room [filled with] men who nearly all claimed to have led a life steeped head over heels and ears in crime and debauchery but had been rescued by the Army and were as white as pure snow'.[12]

The Shirleys had started their Salvationist work in October 1879, advertising themselves as the Salvation Army without obtaining permission from (or even bothering to notify) London headquarters. The new arrivals were so successful that within weeks of opening their first Mission a second corps was formed in 42nd and Market Street – a success that may suggest that the appeal of the Army was more dependent on its evangelistic fervour than William Booth's physical presence.

Amos Shirley, who had paid the rent on the Old Chair Factory out of his own wages, was told to concentrate on silk-making or lose his job. He chose evangelism and became a full-time missionary. The Shirleys, elated by their success and impressed by their own sacrifice, wrote to the Booths describing their achievement in their own words and substantiating their claims with a copy of the *Philadelphia News Report*. Their message ended with the insistence that a visit from William Booth was necessary to consolidate the American victory. No doubt influenced by that knowledge, George Railton had added a comment at the bottom of the letter before he passed it on to his General: 'We must go. This news has come upon us like a voice from Heaven and leaves us no choice.' William Booth was not so sure. He had been doubtful about the advantages of supporting Brother Jermy's earlier initiative, and the failure of that first enterprise had done nothing to encourage his appetite for foreign adventures.

His explanation of the need for caution was convincing enough: 'We are anxious to avoid this for a little longer, seeing how much needs to be done for all the millions who remain in utter darkness even in this land of light.'[13] No doubt he was influenced by his wife's long-standing impatience with foreign missionary societies. But he changed his mind for the most worldly of reasons. Once again he was warned that if he refused to adopt the American Mission, it would go its own way as a separate, and perhaps rival, organisation. And having backed a failure, it would be madness to ignore what looked like being a success. Railton wrote to Catherine predicting that 'the affair in Philadelphia will go with such a sweep that unless we get hold of it, lead it and go at full speed at once, I doubt if we should ever be able to get the reins at all . . . I do not see why they should not let me go.'[14] Railton was doing more than supporting the idea of an American Mission. He was suggesting that he should lead it.

Railton's note revealed his shrewd assessment of William Booth's reaction to the notion that he might encourage the emergence of a rival. His understanding of the General's psychology had been acquired during seven years in which he lived with the Booths, virtually as a member of the family, and enjoyed Catherine's maternal affection. He knew that he could influence Mrs Booth and that she could change her husband's mind. But he also felt, after the intimacy of the 1870s, that the 1880s were a time to move on. Colleagues detected 'an element of disenchantment'. He was thirty-one years old and unmarried, and conscious that young Bramwell Booth – whom he had taught and encouraged like a younger brother – was about to be promoted over his head and become the Army's second-in-command.

It was, however, more than anxiety about his own position that produced Railton's disenchantment. He was a Salvationist and all that interested him was salvation – a blessing which he thought most likely to be achieved by prayer and examination of the gospels. He was growing increasingly disenchanted with the Army's preoccupation with secular matters. Although he had embraced uniforms with the passion of a convert, he remained concerned about the Army's use of music. In the tradition of his Methodist origins he drew a sharp distinction between singing (whatever the words which were used to spread God's message), and bands, which were an artificial barrier between the human voice and the Lord. However, his real objection was to social work. As the Army grew in size and increased its scope, he was torn between pleasure in its achievement and fear that it would forget its true purpose.

Whatever the reasons for Railton's wish to lead the Army in America, the arguments which he used to advance his cause convinced his General that he could not afford a rival in the English-speaking world. And William Booth had no doubt that, with George Railton in charge, the loyalty of the Philadelphians would be guaranteed. The American expeditionary force paraded at the Whitechapel headquarters on 12 January 1880 and received two standards from the hands of Catherine Booth – one from the established Philadelphia Battalion and the other for the unit which William Booth (who was determined to put his stamp on the enterprise) was insistent should be formed in New York. The party consisted of eight in all – Railton, six Hallelujah Lasses and a woman of mature years to chaperone and supervise the young girls. They sailed on the SS *Australia* on 14 February – exactly a fortnight after the *Philadelphia News Report*'s story had been reprinted in *The War Cry*. Those who carry on God's work have no time to waste.

On the morning that the great adventure began, Railton and Booth travelled together by bus to Whitechapel, where they were to meet the guard of honour which waited to escort the expeditionary force to Fenchurch Street Station. As they waited at the bus stop – unembarrassed by the curiosity which their imitation military uniforms aroused – the General gave his subordinate a piece of advice about the movement in America. 'Never forget that it is not what you do yourself as much as what you get others to do that will be the making of the Army.' Thirty years later, Railton recalled, 'It might have been a humbling remark had I aspired to being a great orator. I took it rather as an expression of fear that America might turn my head and create some such tendency.'[15] William Booth always chose to diminish, and sometimes to demote, overmighty subjects. But on that occasion, Railton was oversensitive. Booth was simply setting out his well-known theory of recruitment – the need to make active saints as well as redeem sinners and then use the recently sanctified to redeem others. Railton, however, took it as a reproof, and cheerfully accepted it as he went on his way.

William Booth was temperamentally incapable of moderation. If the
Army and its ideas were to invade America it ought to set out to conquer the whole world. So after Catherine Booth had performed the
ceremony of the flags, William Booth made a speech which made
clear – indeed specified – his territorial ambition. Sweden, Germany,
Russia and, by no means least, 'the lands of the blessed negroes' were
all ripe for salvation. Railton was presented with a cheque to cover the
expedition's early expenses and the proceedings ended with a series of
legal formalities which he believed gave the newest branch of his
organisation status and substance. A solicitor, Thomas Whittington,
read out a declaration which began, in the manner of a Royal Warrant,
with greetings to persons unspecified. It then defined Railton's duties,
obligations and continued subservient relationship with his General.
Railton received William Booth's 'commission' to act as his satrap in
America. The second part of the document was the new Commissioner's official acceptance of his duties. 'I, the said George Scott
Railton, do hereby accept the appointment by the said General of
myself as Commissioner to act in the name of the said William Booth.'
In case the chain of command was not absolutely beyond doubt, it
continued:

> And I hereby agree that I will continue to be, and to act
> altogether and at all times under the command of the said
> William Booth. I further agree that all directions that I shall give
> to any official or officers or any person or persons whomsoever
> over whom I shall exercise any control in pursuance of the
> function delegated to me as such Commissioner aforesaid shall
> be subject to the absolute direction, countermanding and veto
> of the same William Booth.[16]

Railton should have felt flattered by the wholehearted way in which his
chief had accepted his advice. William Booth had no intention of risking America going its own way.

As soon as Railton and his seven ladies landed in New York, they
unfurled their flags and knelt in prayer in Battery Park. Thus fortified,
they set out to conquer the New World. The task proved more difficult
than they had been led to expect. But the evangelists got off to a good,
if slightly embarrassing, start when an impresario called Henry Hall –

having heard that they sang 'Swanee River' and 'My Old Kentucky Home', but not realising that they used words of their own invention – booked them to play at one of his music halls. The congregation, which thought it was an audience, was restless throughout and no one approached the penitent form. The occasion was saved from absolute disaster by Jimmy Kemp, a drunk who had been sent by the local magistrate to spend the day amongst the evangelists as a punishment. Kemp swore never to drink again and became an active Salvationist.

One concert does not make a campaign, and morale was severely damaged by the discovery that Edward Cooper, Mayor of New York, would not allow the Army to preach in Union Square – a privilege afforded only to licensed clergymen.* Railton, having failed to persuade City Hall that he was as good as any clerk in holy orders, wrote to Mayor Cooper in the language of a plenipotentiary from a sovereign power: 'To his Honour, the Mayor, and to the Corporation of the City of New York, G. Railton, by the Grace of God and by the appointment of William Booth, General of The Salvation Army, Commissioner for the various States and countries of North America, sends greetings . . .'[17]

The letter went on to explain that acting 'under the authority granted by the said General' he was commanding operations against 'those who are at present in rebellion against God' and that it was essential to his battle plan that sinners who 'habitually avoid entering a place of worship, should be followed through public thoroughfares'. He therefore respectfully requested and required that the right to preach in Union Square should be granted. He reinforced his request with the warning that, unless his requirements were met, he might be forced to move his headquarters to Philadelphia. The Mayor accepted the risk with unsurprising equanimity and reaffirmed the ban. Railton's *lèse-majesté* attracted brief attention in some newspapers but they described him as a comic rather than a heroic figure. Indeed, hardbitten New York papers were universally less sympathetic than the *Philadelphia News*. Some regarded the Salvationists as dangerous fanatics. Others derided their strange accents and the northern England Hallelujah

---

*The Salvation Army was not granted the status of licensed clergymen in New York until 1917.

Lasses' fine disregard for aspirates. Worst of all, some papers chose to ignore them completely.

Railton did not move to Philadelphia for the very good reason that he did not think himself needed there. A telegram from the City of Brotherly Love announced that the Army's strength in Pennsylvania had risen to 16 officers, 40 cadets and 412 soldiers. Had General Booth received such news he would have gone to Pennsylvania to take the salute at a celebration parade. But instead of joining the Shirleys, Railton set out on a one-man pilgrimage to St Louis, where again he was forbidden to preach on the main thoroughfares, perhaps because of his boast that Salvationists were 'the only white people to whose company, to whose platforms and to whose operations, coloured people had the same welcome as others'.[18] Drawing a line down the centre of the ice which had frozen the Mississippi, he claimed to have marked the city boundary and preached (mostly on skates) from just outside St Louis' jurisdiction. His campaign had mixed success. He kept down costs by sleeping on his office floor, denying himself dinner and wearing such battered clothes that shopkeepers took pity on him and made him gifts from their stock. There were the usual spectacular successes. A salon-keeper was recruited to the colours and the women officers were supported by a group of wealthy ladies.

Just as it seemed that the American Salvation Army was beginning to prosper, William Booth called Railton home. The call was resisted. Railton begged to be reassured that he could 'dismiss all calculations of return', since, as he wrote, 'the spiritual tide is rising every hour. It is only a question of time. It is the chance of a generation . . . The West and by it the States will be in our power in 1881 . . .' His plea concluded with a reaffirmation of his loyalty which was written in such obsequious language that, had it been composed by another man, it might have been taken as intentionally offensive: 'Of course, as I have said before, no conceivable circumstances could be of importance as compared with your health and, rather than risk a breakdown, I can come gladly, however terrible the consequences it may produce in this Army.'[19] Railton was asserting that the welfare of the missionary was, in the long run, more important than the short-term health of the Mission. That view was only sustainable if it was assumed that the whole enterprise depended on one man. That was Railton's view. But while he was right to assume that his recall was not the result of impatience with his results, he was wrong to think that one of the General's sudden illnesses required him at home. The Salvation Army was, in William Booth's view, facing a new threat, and he needed Railton to help him overcome it. The only concession that William Booth could afford to offer was the agreement that Railton's American work could be carried on by his colleagues. The cable that concluded the discussion simply read: 'Come alone.' Railton packed his few personal belongings and left for London on the first ship that would carry him.

Even while he was still in St Louis, Railton's assistance had been recruited to help draft the Salvation Army's Annual Report for 1881. Its contents set out the reason why William Booth wanted his most devoted officer by his side: 'The Army has had to endure opposition such as it never before encountered. The persecutions that have been so joyously endured are themselves taken as the righteousness of our cause.' William Booth really believed that the occasional rough house and periodic attack were good both for morale and recruitment. But although he tried to see the benefits of persecution, the assaults of 1880 were so serious that he began to worry about the safety of his officers and, in consequence, the survival of some provincial stations. The Mission's Annual Report expressed his anxiety:

It was in 1880 that a sister was first wounded in the West End
of London whilst singing in your hall. It was in 1880 that a
little sister was all but trampled to death in the Cathedral City
of Carlisle and that a Bishop first joined his voice to the voice of
the rabble which would do away with you. It was in 1880 that,
in Portsmouth and in Chatham and in Sheerness 'the people
and their rulers' are as never before against you.

And it was in 1880 that there came into existence the strange alliance which menaced the Salvation Army for the rest of the century. 'Professors of religion and haters of religion,' Booth told his followers, 'combined to drive you away.'[20] A coalition of intellectually fastidious bishops and frightened brewers was coming together. The whole establishment, seeing the uniforms and the banners, feared that the church militant might take on a political or military form and that William Booth, having taught the working classes to pray, would encourage them to fight. They were joined in antagonism by the people who simply thought William Booth ridiculous. All together, it was a formidable combination of opponents. Railton was called home to help combat the unholy alliance of church and hooligan.

By 1880 the publicans' wrath had been increased by a new Salvation Army custom. All meetings began with a call to repentance but ended with a plea for total abstinence. On the day that Railton had left England for America, a detachment of Salvationists, under the command of Captain W. F. Day, had been attacked in Carlisle by a drunken gang of youths who had been given free beer as an inducement to break up the meeting. The local police accused Captain Day and his soldiers of having provoked the riot, and Dr Harvey Goodwin, the Bishop of Carlisle, preached a sermon condemning not the assailants but their victims. He took as his text Chapter XIV of the First Epistle to the Corinthians, Verse 34, which bade women 'keep silence in the churches', and Verse 35, which described God as 'not the author of confusion but peace'.

William Booth's charitable reaction was that the bishop had been misled by newspaper reports, but he still believed that an immediate reply was necessary. He was suffering from an ulcerated mouth, so he proposed that 'Mrs Booth answers the sermon next week . . . Not to scold him but to defend and explain.'[21] Although Catherine did not need much encouragement to return to the argument in which she had first engaged in defence of Phoebe Palmer and female teaching, she chose not to deal with the attacks on women preachers but with the assault on the whole Salvation Army. It was not her habit to take half measures. So she hired a theatre in Carlisle and addressed her audience at such length that, when her speech was published, it had to be spread over three editions of *The War Cry*. 'All I can say in respect of the Bishop is that I feel quite certain that, if his lordship is an enlightened man and if he had himself attended those meetings on which he based his remarks, he would have come to very different conclusions.'[22]

Then, for the first time, she argued the pragmatic case for reaching out to the working classes and bringing them to Christianity. It was to become an increasingly familiar justification of her evangelism amongst the poor. 'I have been to sixty-two towns in eleven months. In these towns I have seen hundreds of thousands gathered in our halls . . .

Hundreds of these very men I should be afraid to meet at night . . . As I have said to a gentleman in a high place in London, "My dear sir, the day is coming when these masses will require to be dealt with. Will it not be better to face them with the gospel than with the sword?"'[23] Catherine Booth was advancing her own version of the 'Culture of Contentment' more than a hundred years before J. K. Galbraith gave his stern warning against prosperous complacency.

Continuing in her conciliatory tone, Catherine conceded that some of the Salvation Army's evangelistic methods were unusual. But she explained that the bands and the banners, the combinations of secular music with religious words, the marches and the street meetings and the display of unlikely converts as an example to others were essential to any mission which hopes to reach the masses. 'The Army's achievements were built on the great fundamental principle of adaptation. That is making the means suit the end'[24] – but only in respect of the ways in which men and women could be persuaded to read and accept the truth of the gospels. 'God forbid I should ever teach any adaptation of the Gospel. I teach no adaptation of the Gospel . . . but I contend that we may serve it up on any sort of dish that will induce the people to partake of it.' The great aim of women's ministry was barely mentioned. That had been Bishop Goodwin's text. But he had attacked the Salvation Army in general. Catherine Booth responded because defending it in the same terms was far more important than propagating any single idea.

Unfortunately for the Booths, the doctrine of adaptation was against the instincts of a complacent and essentially conservative country. Their adaptations were dismissed as obtrusive eccentricities by a nation which did not want – either metaphorically or literally – to be woken up to the reality of God's love by a brass band playing in the street on a Sunday morning. The police, on the side of the 'respectable' majority, began to invoke local statutes which prohibited the playing of musical instruments in public places and moved the prayer meetings on from the street corners under the pretext that they were blocking the Queen's highway and causing a breach of the peace.

At Leamington, an officer was convicted of obstruction on the evidence of a policeman and two publicans. He refused to pay his fine and was imprisoned in Warwick Gaol until well-wishers paid it for him. At

Pendle, a woman volunteer was acquitted of causing a nuisance when one publican laid the complaint that she had stood too close to his house. Next day, she was convicted when a police sergeant charged her with the same offence. At Folkestone, a Dover Street shopkeeper had his premises wrecked when it was discovered that he worshipped with the Army. In the Rhondda Valley a Hallelujah Lass was imprisoned for blocking the footpath. Four Salvationists were arrested for singing 'Will You Go?' in the Lincolnshire town of Boston. In London's East End the assaults were severe and continuous. In the early weeks of 1881, William Booth wrote to the Commissioner of Police for London. As always when he dealt with authority, his demands were prefaced with a concession. No instruments would be used at open-air meetings. But he demanded protection for his muted evangelists. There was a brief improvement. Then, 'on account of the changed attitude of the police, matters got worse again . . . The gangs of roughs . . . are now again allowed to congregate. For the last two evenings, there have been the most disgraceful scenes. Windows have been broken and the meetings upset.'[25]

The suggestion that the Salvation Army was breaking the law by using brass bands to accompany its own hymn-singing was made in a letter from the Metropolitan Police Commissioner to John Morley,* the editor of the *Pall Mall Gazette*, who had repeatedly complained that the Metropolitan Police, far from protecting the Army's lawful assemblies, often encouraged the mobs to drive it from the streets. William Booth, neither too proud nor too righteous to accept help from an atheistic radical, had asked Morley to mobilise public opinion behind his cause. The support of the *Pall Mall Gazette* became crucial when the Mayor of Stamford – acting in his capacity as chairman of the local justices – wrote to Sir William Harcourt, the Home Secretary, for guidance about how to protect his town from a Salvationist invasion. The Mayor's question was purely hypothetical, as William Booth made clear in his

---

*Morley subsequently became a Liberal MP and Secretary of State, first for India and then for Ireland. He wrote the classic nineteenth-century life of Gladstone – on whose behalf he interviewed Charles Stewart Parnell. His mistaken conclusion that the charge of adultery against the Irish leader was false was conveyed with the coded message, 'The horse won't run.'

own letter to Sir William. The Salvationists feared a plot to drive them from the streets.

> I observe with some surprise that you have written to the Mayor of Stamford in reply to some communication from him with reference to The Salvation Army in that town. I beg to inform you that no one connected with The Army has ever yet been sent to Stamford. The Salvation Army is not in Stamford. But this incident affords me a sufficient opportunity to point out to you the real cause of disturbances that are complained of. There is no town in this country where any considerable number of ratepayers would approve of any interference with our processions were it not for the violence used against us and the consequent breach of public peace. And from whom comes that violence? Very rarely indeed from any but roughs and cornermen who would not dare to touch us were there not conveyed to them first of all an assurance that they may do what they like with impunity. There has never been a breach of the peace where the authorities have made it plainly understood that assaults on us will be treated as assaults on other people.[26]

Booth was right to be apprehensive. The day after he wrote his letter, *The Times* published Sir William Harcourt's reply to the Mayor of Stamford. It read like a general instruction to magistrates that, when a Salvation Army procession seemed likely to be attacked, it should be prohibited. It admitted, with what read like regret, that 'such processions, not being illegal in themselves, cannot in the absence of other circumstances be legally prevented. But where they provoke antagonism and lead to riotous collisions, and where the peace of the town to be endangered if they are allowed to continue, the magistrates should, by every means in their power, endeavour to prevent them.'[27] There followed a description of the procedures which magistrates should adopt when they anticipated trouble and chose to prohibit the gathering – sworn information laid before the Chief Constable showing grounds for concern, notices announcing that the procession or meeting must not take place, meetings with the leaders of the proposed event to warn them of the consequences of ignoring the magistrates' instructions. 'If, however, in spite of every effort, the attempt to form a procession is persevered in, force may be used to prevent it, and care should be taken to ensure that sufficient force for that purpose is at hand.' The Home Secretary's advice had put the Salvation Army at the mercy of any group of hooligans – motivated by bigotry and encouraged by brewers – who found pleasure in raising a riot. All they had to do was threaten violence and, either as the result of persuasion or coercion, the Salvation Army's lawful assemblies would be prohibited.

The following day, William Booth wrote to the Prime Minister, William Ewart Gladstone. The letter showed signs of real distress. 'Unless something is done immediately to neutralise the effect of the Home Secretary's letter to Stamford (which is already the war cry of roughs everywhere) there will be riot and bloodshed all over the land.' To make matters worse, attacking the Salvation Army was becoming fashionable with the sort of lout who enjoys tyrannising those who do not fight back. All over Britain groups of thugs were proclaiming their rough manhood by knocking Hallelujah Lasses from their soap boxes and hitting male preachers whom they knew would not hit back. To his astonishment, the General received support which was undoubtedly more unexpected and probably more welcome than the endorsement his plea had received from John Morley's *Pall Mall Gazette*. *The Times* published one of its thunderous leaders. Voltaire would have been proud to read it.

The editorial was careful to make plain that the paper had little sympathy for the Salvation Army itself. 'The worship they conduct under cover is not quite of the sober and monotonous character which finds most favour with the English . . . A very large part of our own population, on one ground or another, believed themselves saved already and therefore under no need to go out of their way for a new call' – but *The Times* went on to argue the virtues of tolerance. Although a majority of the population was instinctively 'against the Salvation Army, most of these people are ready to leave it alone . . . But there remain the irresponsible roughs.' Then came the demand for the defence of freedom. 'It is evident that if the roughs are to be allowed to do what they like, the streets can no longer be called the Queen's highway or the land her realm.' Liberty, *The Times* reminded its readers, is indivisible. If Salvation Army marches were to be banned, it would be 'quite impossible to see where such a prohibition might go or where it will stop short . . . The fellows who throw stones and bad language at the Salvation Army are just as likely to take offence at anything else that reminds them unpleasantly of a better life and higher aspirations.' The complaint that 'some of the people whose delicate tastes the Home Secretary is anxious to consult, occasionally claim and are allowed not only the ordinary use of the public thoroughfares but its exclusive possession' led on to what was almost an endorsement of the Salvation Army's aims: 'We must beware how we quarrel with the rude remedies and uncouth methods employed by those who honestly believe there is great work to be done.'[28]

The establishment's newspaper had been guarded in its defence of the Salvation Army's freedom and explicitly critical of its evangelistic methods. But it had supported the right to campaign in the streets and, because of the attention it had given to the issue, stories of the Army were being read at all Britain's best breakfast tables. And William Booth – despite *The Times*'s habit of diminishing his rank with inverted commas – had become a national figure. The harassment continued, but the authorities, magistrates if not police, began to do their duty.

When the Mayor of Basingstoke – himself a brewer – announced that the justices could not provide protection against the brewers' hired roughs, Sir William Harcourt, the same Home Secretary who had advised the Mayor of Stamford to prohibit Salvation Army marches, issued a formal reprimand and the local Salvationists, who had suffered days of persecution, were given protection. At Weston-super-Mare an officer, who was convicted of breaching the peace by organising a procession through the town and sentenced to three months' imprisonment had his conviction quashed on appeal to the Queen's Bench. Costs were awarded against the magistrates who had convicted him. Suddenly the judgement of Mr Justice Field achieved a national significance:

> . . . the defendants belonged to a body of persons whose
> object seemed lawful and laudable and, at all events was not
> unlawful – that is the object of reclaiming a class of people,
> who were not disposed to go to places of worship, by getting
> them together to attend their religious services . . . They were
> not guilty of any offence in passing through the street and why

should others interfere with them? . . . What right have others to resort to force to prevent persons doing what is lawful?[29]

The questions were all rhetorical. But they did more than provide protection from assault. They demonstrated that the Salvation Army was becoming part of the nation's fabric.

14

Mobbing the Apostles

William Booth's life was a continual paradox. So it was not out of keeping with the way in which fate treated him that, just as he was trying to combat the organised violence of his opponents, he should at last be recognised as a major force in British evangelism by his Methodist peers. He was invited to address the 1880 Wesleyan Conference – 'a wonderful chapter in our history', according to Catherine, who rejoiced that he was so 'kindly received and listened to'. Before 'several of the lay nabobs congratulated him most enthusiastically', she would have 'thought it much more probable for him to have addressed the House of Lords than these seven hundred ministers'.[1]

The President ended a chilly introduction with the warning that only a limited time had been put aside for his address. General Booth responded by saying that at Salvation Army conferences anyone who spoke for too long was cut short with a burst of hymn-singing, and he was prepared to endure the same fate if he overstayed his welcome. The good will that his pretence at humility created was immediately put under strain. He first described the Salvation Army as 'the continuation of the work of Mr Wesley', claiming, 'We have gone on, only a great deal further, on the lines he travelled.' It was not a tactful boast to make to the Conference which Wesley set up as his spiritual heir. He then made the reproach-by-implication which explained the necessity for his special brand of evangelism: 'I was told that ninety-five per cent of [the people in] our large towns and cities never crossed the threshold of any place of worship and I thought, cannot something be done about it?'[2] The description of Britain's godlessness could only be interpreted as an oblique criticism of the ministers who had allowed their neglected flocks to stray. The churches and chapels which predated his own conversion were not, in his opinion, up to the job.

According to *The War Cry* there was punctuating applause every time that William Booth repeated (six times in all) his debt to John Wesley, and the Conference must have been reassured by the reassertion of the old idea of Booth as a recruiting sergeant for other denominations. 'We do not fish in other people's water,' he told them, 'or try to set up a rival sect.' Of course he could not resist setting out both the statistics of his success and the methods by which it had been brought about. 'We are moral scavengers, preaching in the very sewers. We want all we can get but we want the lowest of the low.' The account of his speech was interrupted – in the style of House of Commons reports – with the interjection '[Laughter]' at his self-deprecating jokes. Humour was a very unusual feature of a William Booth address or sermon. If the Wesleyans did enjoy the occasion as much as the report suggested it was probably because he began with the concession that he had debts to repay. 'I am,' he said, 'a child of Methodism.' Gratitude did not come easily to William Booth.

He had reason to be grateful for publicity, if nothing else. *The Times* became, temporarily at least, fascinated by the Salvation Army. It was amused by 'General' Booth's military affectations, strong in its defence of his evangelists' right to march the streets, and entirely opposed to the view of redemption which guided his efforts. The characteristics of the Army to which the paper took greatest exception were also the attributes of the founder – the qualities which made him simultaneously an irresistible leader and an always intolerant (as well as occasionally intolerable) human being. The Salvation Army had been built in William Booth's image and acquired his vices as well as virtues.

For the especial outburst of wrath which the Salvation Army stimulates, the cause must be found in the pretensions of the

Army to a superior piety for itself and to its discovery of the
conspicuous reverse in the rest of the world. General and
colonels and corporals in this fortunate body have won their
own spurs and are only intent on leading an unregenerated
world captive. Men do not mind being denounced by sinners in
the company of their accusers. They object to being treated as
the spiritual booty of the boots and spurs of a number of
enthusiasts who have already made their own prospects
comfortable.

William Booth was, in *The Times*'s view, behaving like the Pharisee
and thanking God he was not like other men. But he had also committed other sins, some of them greater than glorying in his moral
superiority. And they had infected his army which, in consequence,
was 'not altogether a pleasant phenomenon'. Having conceded its success, *The Times* set out the vices which made its growth a dubious
benefit. 'It is overbearing, conceited and unreal.' The final condemnation concerned the Salvation Army's intellectual standing. 'Its solitary
weapon for enticing recruits and subduing enemies is spiritual intoxi-
cation. No fruitful ideas lie under its war cries.'[3]

The Times was wrong to accuse William Booth and his army of
having no fruitful ideas. Some of Railton's spiritual innovations
attracted immense and immediate support amongst potential converts.
But the attraction was always their theological extremism and the rejection of more orthodox doctrine. Whether or not they fished in other
people's ponds, the Salvation Army certainly muddied the waters. In
1881, George Railton proposed in a memorandum to his General that
the Salvation Army abandon the Eucharist – a direct challenge to traditional theology and a strange suggestion to be made to a
fundamentalist church which repeatedly claimed to believe, and accept
as holy guidance, every word in the Bible. The Salvation Army, and the
Christian Mission before it, had always had problems with Holy
Communion. The objection to the most sacred of all sacraments was
not the fear of Popish rituals but Catherine Booth's passionate objection
to the use of alcohol for any purpose. When the temperance dilemma
was solved by the substitution of coloured water for wine – thus revers-
ing the process which enlivened the Marriage Feast at Cana – another
problem arose. Although only intoxicated by the hope of salvation, the

communicants often created scenes which were 'sometimes so tumultuous, even so hilarious, that William Booth was shocked and
offended'.[4] Railton had a more fundamental point to make.

He insisted that belief in the possibility of acquiring a 'state of grace'
undermined the whole idea of the Eucharist. Before conversion communion was pointless. After conversion it was superfluous. The
administration of the Eucharist by priests and clergy implied that
common men could not communicate directly with God. The memorandum ended with an argument which appealed, as no doubt it was
intended to appeal, to William Booth's prejudices – which were more
concerned with theatre than with theology. If services ended with the
congregation taking the blood and body of Christ at the altar rail, it
would not be possible to build up to the climax of repentant sinners
approaching the penitent form. Railton's proposed amendment to doctrine was approved.

The decision was not a calculated insult to the Anglican and Roman
Catholic churches. Booth simply did not care whether they were
insulted or not. Of course, most priests and prelates were outraged. But
Dr E. W. Benson – Bishop of Truro and subsequently Archbishop of
Canterbury – wrote to the General in terms which were simultaneously
conciliatory and patronising. 'I am able to understand how the call you
have to make to the dechristianised and degraded may be conducted
by you without the express teaching on these institutions [the sacra-
ments], and rejoice that you so firmly hold that it is no business of your
own system to administer them.' He went on to express his pleasure
that the Salvation Army, unlike other modern heresies (a body of belief
to which he referred by implication), did not propose to 'adopt imita-
tions of the Sacramental system'. He was, however, anxious to be
reassured that 'Church people' who followed the Army's banner should
'not be debarred by compulsory arrangements from partaking of
Communion with their brethren'.[5]

In fact, Bishop Benson was suggesting that Salvationists should be
allowed to receive communion from Church of England clergymen –
and no doubt, if the circumstance arose, from Catholic priests as well.
The Bishop had misjudged his man. For he was, in effect, proposing
that officers of the Salvation Army should accept a second-class status
within the forces of the Lord – yielding to other denominations power
over the Army's own soldiers. That would have involved the sacrifice of

William Booth's authority and dignity – two of his most precious possessions.

The Bishop suggested that the whole question should be examined at a meeting attended by Dr Wescott, Regius Professor of Divinity at the University of Cambridge, who would put the entire subject in its scriptural context. The Archangel Gabriel would not have been able to persuade William Booth to change his mind. What would now be called the Army's 'official position' was based on the central premise of the Salvation Army's doctrine: 'Conversion was the *unum necessitum* and after conversion there was nothing but a life of selfless devotion.'[6] That was certainly Booth's view. But he also had a lively appreciation of the respect owed both to the Church which propagated that view and to its head and founders. Whatever he had said or implied to the Wesleyan Conference, the time when he hoped to do no more than pass on his redeemed sinners to the traditional churches had passed. They had proved incapable of preventing the new recruits from 'backsliding'. They had missed their chance, and *amour propre* – combined with the novel pleasure of leading a church of his own – made him unwilling to give them a second chance. There could be no question of an admission that ministers of other churches possessed a relationship with God that Salvation Army officers lacked. After the correspondence with Bishop Benson and Dr Westcott, the Church of England accepted that William Booth would have no truck with the Eucharist. In consequence, the more theologically minded members of the established Church began to regard the Salvation Army as their natural enemy.

Although the Church of England's anxiety about communion focused attention on William Booth's growing pretensions, it was not, during the early 1880s, only Anglicans who felt threatened by the Salvation Army's increasing power and influence. The Reverend Thomas Rippon, a Wesleyan minister from Warrington, wrote to *The Times* to say that he, like many friends, had received copies of a circular 'begging for aid towards the cost of a new training institution for the Salvation Army'. Despite his 'personal esteem for and very pleasant remembrances of' Mr Booth, he thought it necessary to draw attention to some of the 'fatal flaws' which ought to deter God-fearing Englishmen from 'lending to the enrichment of such a body'. His criticisms, though set out in florid language, were based on the solid evidence of the Salvation Army's 'Orders and Regulations'.

During the early years of the Salvation Army, William Booth had personally interviewed every candidate for full-time employment. But as numbers increased, it became necessary to institute a 'recruitment procedure' to screen potential officers. It began with each officer signing an agreement that he could not 'expect a guaranteed salary . . . or expect to continue his employment should he at any time cease to live up to his promises or show himself to be inefficient in his work'.[7] 'Soldiers', not so much 'other ranks' as volunteers, were required to sign the 'Articles of War', which formed so simple and clear an expression of the Army's 'teachings and system that the most illiterate recruit could at once take in their practical effect'.[8]

The 'Articles of War' were only a beginning. The 'Orders and Regulations' followed. No one could complain that recruits were left in doubt about their duties. The Regulations for Field Officers covered 626 pages, Staff Officers 357 pages, Territorial Commissioners and Secretaries, 176 pages. The Regulations for Soldiers were compressed into a mere 164 pages. As the Army expanded its work, Regulations were also promulgated for Social Officers, Local Officers and Band and Singing Brigades. Each volume provided valuable evidence for those of the Army's critics who wanted to represent it as a tyranny.

It is an 'absolute and permanent monarchy', wrote Mr Rippon, quoting the paragraphs which – echoing the Trust Deed – gave 'the General for the time being . . . absolute control over the Army and all it possesses and decreed that 'each General is to appoint his successor so that there shall always be one person having power and authority'. His contention that the only other religious figure to lay claim to such authority was the Captain General of the Jesuits may have been a little far-fetched. But his quotation from that part of the regulation which warned against fraternisation with other churches was convincing evidence of his view that the Salvation Army wanted to destroy, in order that it could usurp, the other Christian communions. 'Be on your guard against letting any of them know your purposes' the regulations warned.[9] The letter concluded with an echo from the General's travelling past. William Booth's itinerant habits, his emotional style and his determination to make quick conversion all marked him out as a British version of the Revivalist preachers who had come over from America twenty years earlier. By their nature, such preachers were unattached. They did not try to create a firm permanent organisation of their own. Mr Rippon insisted that William Booth should remain true to his chosen calling.

William Booth – rarely able to resist the temptation to triumphalism – began his reply by rejoicing that Mr Rippon's view was so uncharacteristic of the God-fearing public in general that the Salvation Army had been able to 'acquire the Oxford Street [ice] rink, an equally large building in Camberwell and various properties all over the country'.[10] He refuted absolutely the charge that he was antagonistic to other churches and claimed the support of 'several occupants of the Episcopal bench, the president and several ex-Presidents of the Wesleyan Conference and many of the most influential ministers and laymen of all denominations'.[11] The counter-attack was reinforced by a *Times* leader, stimulated by the Rippon letter. It described William Booth as 'perhaps the truer exponent of John Wesley's principles' in late-nineteenth-century Britain, though it was not clear if the comparison was meant as a compliment to Booth or a criticism of Wesley.[12] For the editorial went on to scoff at both the Army's military pretensions and Mr Rippon's fear of despotism.

On 19 March 1882 the opening of the Regent Circus Meeting Room – the converted ice-rink of which General Booth had written so proudly – marked an advance into new territory. At last he had a fashionable address – 271 Oxford Street. And at the inauguration, 'a majority of those in the audience appeared to be well-to-do people attracted by sympathy with the object of this movement for getting hold of the lowest and most brutalised classes rather than from any intention of taking part in the service'.[13] It was not in William Booth's nature to tell his wealthy visitors that they were sinners too. That was, perhaps, just as well. They were the sort of people whose patronage enabled him to pay £20 a week in Regent Circus rent and as much again in working expenses. T. A. Denny – always hovering in the background and occasionally willing to step forward – had financed the first month's operation. But the headquarters staff, looking out on the audience in the hall, must have felt that if they could attract such sympathisers, their future (and that of the Regent Circus Meeting Room) was assured.

The Salvation Army made the most of each little victory. In May 1882 the Lord Chancellor – head of the English judiciary and second in line of precedence after the Royal Family itself – wrote to express 'regret that a movement which he believes to be sincere and well intended should be met with violence and disorder'.[14] The letter was signed by a private secretary and sent in reply to complaints about assaults on the Army in Crediton, and it also observed that it was 'the duty of religious persons to avoid the prosecution of their objects in a way which may give any unnecessary occasion for disorderly proceedings'. But the Salvation Army trumpeted the Lord Chancellor's sympathy and support without adding wearisome details about who wrote the letter and its minor reservations. On 24 June General Booth – who was becoming a regular feature in the correspondence columns – wrote to *The Times* that the Primate of All England had become one of the Salvation Army's patrons: 'His Grace the Archbishop of Canterbury has been good enough to head the subscription list for the purchase of The Eagle Tavern, the Grecian Theatre and adjoining premises.'[15] The Archbishop's contribution was little more than symbolic. For he donated £5 towards a lease which cost £16,750. But William Booth did his best to exploit the unexpected help by suggesting that it gave a lead 'with all who sympathise with our objects . . . without pledging themselves to our modes of operation'. It was a rare public acknowledgement that his methods were controversial.

The Archbishop had not intended to give General Booth such encouragement. Indeed, in the letter which accompanied the token donation, Randall Davidson (the Primate's chaplain) had been careful to distance His Grace from the Salvation Army's general work. Clearly believing that Canterbury's good intentions had been unscrupulously traduced, Randall Davidson wrote his own letter to *The Times*. His rebuke was magisterially understated, simply suggesting that 'some misapprehension appears to have been caused by the publication of one sentence' from the Archbishop's letter and asking for the publication of his full reply.[16] Unfortunately the complete text revealed that William Booth had asked, and been denied, evangelical as well as financial support. The 'nominal' £5 had been accompanied by a clear, though courteously worded, rejection of the suggestion that the Church of England and William Booth's Army might work side by side. 'The question of the co-operation of the clergy of the Church of England in the actual work of your association is one of extreme difficulty.'

Co-operation was not what William Booth wanted, though he would have preferred his overtures to be rejected privately (or better still, quietly forgotten) rather than being publicised in the correspondence columns of *The Times*. The implication that the Archbishop of Canterbury supported his work – with encouragement as well as a £5 note – was made in the hope of persuading other influential Anglicans to follow where (on the General's own disingenuous interpretation of events) the Archbishop had led. Booth never even considered the possibility that he had been less than honest. For he was doing no more than fulfilling his God-given destiny to ensure the prosperity of the Salvation Army.

In the summer of 1882 it seemed, at least to him, that God's will was being done in full measure. *The War Cry* had become so popular that it was published twice a week and *The Little Soldier*, a magazine for Army children, was flourishing. The Commander-in-Chief of the British Army – the Duke of Cambridge, son of Queen Victoria herself – told the Officer Commanding Colchester District that he must allow his men to attend indoor Salvation Army meetings, though the prohibition on marching and public demonstrations must stand. Cardinal Manning wrote a sympathetic assessment of the Army in the *Contemporary Review*. It concluded with a compliment so sublimely judged that it might have been divinely inspired: 'In a wilderness where there is no shepherd, any voice crying a fragment of the truth, prepares the way for Him who is the perfect truth.' And, as if to provide a physical symbol of his Army's success, General Booth bought The Eagle Tavern and Grecian Theatre, decrepit and disreputable premises next door to each other in London's City Road. Within two months of receiving the Archbishop's £5, the Salvation Army had raised £9,000 of the £16,000 needed to purchase the lease. *The Times*, which, one way or another, had played its part in bringing William Booth to public notice, made a judicial summing-up of the first six months of 1882: 'The fortunes of the Salvation Army are in the ascendant.'[17]

The Grecian Theatre was, in terms of property values, nothing like the most significant of Booth's acquisitions. As well as the Regent Circus ice-rink, the Army owned a new headquarters building in Queen Victoria Street and a training college in Hackney. The old training home at Clapham had been rebuilt as Congress Hall and International Headquarters – for the Army, benefiting from its American experience, had now sent expeditionary forces to France,

Switzerland, Sweden, India and Canada. Best of all, at least in terms of wise investment, the old London Orphanage Asylum building, once valued at £6,000, was bought for £1,500 – complete (in the basement) with 'steam engine, boiler, ovens and other apparatus which will enable us to provide refreshments of All Day and All Night meetings to any extent'.[18] As each new property was bought, the Salvation Army rushed unthinkingly towards the edge of bankruptcy, teetered on the brink and was dragged back at the last minute by a spectacular show of faith and generosity. T. A. Denny gave £1,000 towards the rebuilding of the Clapham Congress Hall. But on the day of the official opening General Booth still owed the builders £8,000. More than £4,500 was contributed at the first giant service, much of it from families for whom it was a sacrifice to put even a penny in the plate, and the whole debt was cleared within twelve days. Each new building added something to the folklore. But The Eagle Tavern and Grecian Theatre have a special place in Salvation Army history.

Railton suggested buying The Eagle. After visiting Charles Hadden Spurgeon's mighty Baptist Chapel in the Elephant & Castle, he became obsessed with the idea of the Army acquiring a building of equal size – and Railton's obsessions were not easily brushed aside. William Booth believed that his fits of sudden enthusiasm were essential to the Salvation Army's success, and might well have accepted his idea without the bombardment of letters which Railton fired off day after day. But Railton bombarded him nevertheless. 'If I could set to and build up a concern in some central spot, say near The Eagle, I cannot see why, in the course of years, we cannot build up a really big concern.'[19] That certainly appealed to William Booth. Then the central spot for which he hoped became available not near, but at The Eagle itself – a coincidence which suggests that Railton knew more than he revealed in his first note. However, the availability of the actual site was represented to William Booth as a surprise. 'There is a superbly central spot – The Eagle – within a splendid artisan neighbourhood i.e., black heathens.'[20] Then the prospect improved still further. 'I find that the Grecian Theatre – next door to The Eagle and one of the most notorious in London – which I had coveted for eventual headquarters on Sundays – instead of holding 800, has been rebuilt and professes to hold 5,000.'[21] Booth agreed to buy both buildings.

Raising the money was in itself an historic event. Encouraged by the sympathetic response of the Archbishop of Canterbury, Catherine wrote the first of her many letters to Queen Victoria. Sir Henry Ponsonby, a private secretary, replied. Her Majesty had learned 'with great satisfaction that you have, with other members of your society, been successful in your efforts to win many thousands to the ways of temperance, virtue and religion'.[22] But she did not contribute even £5. However, the royal letter proved to be worth thousands. It was used by William Booth as evidence that the highest in the land were in sympathy with his aims and supported his work.

The private secretary's letter was printed verbatim on the front page of *The War Cry* – the lesson of edited extracts having been learned at the hands of the Archbishop of Canterbury.[23] And it was read to a mass meeting at Alexandra Palace, where the crowd – variously estimated at twenty and thirty thousand – cheered every sentence, including the Queen's refusal to contribute to The Eagle fund. Unfortunately, the drinking classes were less impressed. They determined to frustrate the Army's plans for the regeneration of the City Road and the transformation of one of London's most famous places of entertainment. Three years before George Railton moved in, it had been there that G. W. Hunt had boasted to the world, 'We don't want to fight but by jingo if we do . . .', and twenty years later, when the Salvation Army eventually gave up the lease, it was on the same stage that Marie Lloyd sang, 'My old man said follow the van . . .' But in 1881 it was best known for W. R. Mandale's ditty:

> Up and down the City Road
> In and out The Eagle
> That's the way the money goes
> Pop goes the weasel . . .

'Pop' and 'weasel' were colloquialisms for pawn and watch. They therefore illustrated one of the evils of society which William Booth was dedicated to destroying – the willingness, indeed the determination, to pawn family possessions and property in order to gratify the lust for alcohol. The theatre next door specialised in the cheerful vulgarity that characterised so much of the Victorian music hall – in William Booth's view, a dangerous alliance of 'the Liquor Lion and the Lust Bear'. And the neighbouring 'gardens, with their rustic arbours were, at night, the scene of the most flagrant immorality and thither flocked some of the very worst characters in the town'.[24] The Eagle and its adjacent property offered the Salvation Army the chance to buy out sin and simultaneously buy into new opportunities to promote virtue. Unfortunately, only the sub-lease was for sale. But William Booth bought it without considering – or at least considering enough – what restrictions the primary lease holder might place upon its use.

The Salvation Army took possession of the property in the manner of invading forces occupying enemy territory – and in a way calculated to cause offence to the locals. A thousand Salvationists, led by a brass band and under the command of George Railton, marched down the City Road at six o'clock in the morning. The show of force was regarded as provocative and, in retaliation, The Eagle was immediately besieged by local hooligans. Later in the day, the assailants were reinforced by paid thugs and the violence escalated to the point at which Army officers began to fear for their lives and safety. The police were sent for and, mindful of the Home Secretary's changed attitude, protected both buildings and their occupants. They would not, however, make any arrests. The brewers decided to find out if the law would serve their purpose better than common assault.

A man, claiming to be a local resident and using the name Ebbetts, applied to the Chancery Court for an injunction restraining William Booth from using the Grecian Theatre or Eagle Tavern as a Salvation Meeting House or 'doing anything with them as would endanger the withdrawal or the refusal of the licence granted to certain of those buildings for the sale of beer or spirituous liquors'. Ebbetts based his application on the terms of the bequest by which Thomas Rouse had left the land and property to the parish of St Botolph. A covenant required The Eagle to be used 'as an inn, tavern or public house' and prohibited the licensee from behaving in a way which might cause the licence to be 'revoked, withdrawn or not renewed'. Booth and his advisers hit on the ingenious solution of turning The Eagle into a temperance hotel. Ebbetts rejected the compromise.

Ebbetts's injunction was not granted. Mr Justice Kay could not see how the use of The Eagle for prayer meetings could prejudice its future use as licensed premises. So William and Catherine Booth became the proprietors of a seventy-bedroom hotel and the immediate recipients of a second injunction demanding they sold beer. Mr Justice Fitzjames Stephens found against the Army. It was not possible, he ruled, to sell soft drinks under the provision of an alcohol licence. If The Eagle was to continue as a hotel, it must sell beer, wine or spirits. The ruling went to appeal. While the superior court deliberated, William and Catherine Booth technically were publicans. It was 1884 before the final judgement was made. Then, the Master of the Rolls and two Lords of Appeal unanimously ruled for General Booth – publican but not sinner. The token sale of alcohol ended and The Eagle remained in the ownership of the Salvation Army.

But every new success was matched – indeed became the occasion of – a new form of offence to the wider world outside the bonds of blood and the boundaries of fire. George Railton, waiting for the Appeal Court to give its verdict, sank to his knees and, imitating the way in which some Christians signify they are subjects of the Lord, gave not the sign of the cross but 'The Sign of S'. The obeisance was noticed and reported. Catholics cried sacrilege, Protestants detected Roman influence.

The House of Lords' support was a legal triumph for William Booth. But throughout England opposition to the Salvation Army was growing fast. The Skeleton Armies – founded in Exeter and Weston-super-Mare for the specific purpose of breaking up Salvation Army meetings – began to set up branches throughout the south of England. Although the Armies had no formal structure or high command, the groups which came together in the market towns to give each other comfort and encouragement had four common features – the backing of the breweries, the sympathy of the magistrates, the conservative attitude of the local population and the relatively small size of the towns in which the 'skeletons' operated.[25]

Without the brewers the Skeleton Armies would have been nothing. In one of his many angry memoranda to the Home Secretary, William Booth wrote:

> In nearly every town where there has been any opposition we
> have been able to trace it more or less to the direct instigation
> and often the open leadership of either Brewers or Publicans or
> their EMPLOYEES. The plan adopted is by treating or
> otherwise inciting gangs of roughs.[26]

The Skeleton Army in Honiton produced a professionally printed, if crudely written newspaper. It described the group's original purpose as 'to crush fanaticism and to uphold the dignity and the purity of the borough', a statement of aims not dissimilar from the objectives which were being proclaimed by the Ku Klux Klan in America. But it did not explain why attacks on the Salvation Army were essential to the achievement of that end. The rest of the paper was devoted to abuse of the Salvation Army's local sympathisers and heavy jokes in which the Skeletons' rough-house tactics are described in military jargon. 'The men were then put through some slight exercises, including throwing turnips, artistic decoration with red ochre, and turf planting.'[27] In other parts of England attacks on the Salvation Army were more spontaneous. But they were no less violent.

On 4 April 1882 the Mayor and Corporation of Sheffield met 'to consider what should be done in view of the announcement that the Salvation Army intended to hold a monster demonstration on Easter Monday'.[28] The Chief Constable showed an unusually 'large number of magistrates' an Army poster which proclaimed, 'Heavy fighting is expected and great victories are certain . . . The fighting to continue until four o'clock unless all the rebels surrender before that hour.' The justices were frightened by the knowledge that 'on Easter Monday a great handicap is held there and there is an immense attendance of betting and sporting men from all parts of the Kingdom . . . the rough element is usually predominate'. It was agreed that unless the Queen's Peace could be guaranteed, the Chief Constable should prohibit both march and meeting. The Mayor and Chief Constable were, in the words of the Weston-super-Mare petition, placing the liberty of the people in the hands of a handful of disturbers. Their excuse was that they had attempted the libertarian option three months earlier and the result had been a riot.

The Army's Annual Council of War had assembled in Sheffield. On 15 January the *Sheffield Daily Telegraph*, with a fine regard for its circulation area, reported that delegates had travelled from 'London, Barnsely, Mexborough, Rotherham and Whittington Moor . . .'[29] There were marches on the Sunday, a 'Hosanna meeting . . . at which many of the reclaimed gave their testimonies and a procession led supporters to a mass rally at the Albert Hall – an event for which six thousand tickets had been circulated. The procession through the town was fol-

lowed by a crowd but no interference with the army was attempted.'
Normally the Army's own publicity shared some of the blame for the
antagonism which greeted the great rallies. For it was often couched in
figurative language which the Salvationists' enemies took as a literal
challenge to a passage of arms. The usual posters were on display in
Sheffield: 'Large placards, containing sensational announcements of
what was intended to be done were posted over the town and created
some interest and excitement amongst a certain class.' But the excitement and interest did not turn into violence on the Saturday or
Sunday. There was the occasional hiss, the subdued boo and the suppressed giggle as the parades passed by. But the riot did not start until
Monday.

The day began with a Holiness Meeting 'for Christians only'. Then 'at
half past one o'clock, according to prior arrangements, the soldiers
mustered at the barracks at Thomas Street in readiness for the tri-
umphal march which was to be taken part in by mounted officers and
brass band, female trumpeters and General commanding'.[30] What followed was reported by both the *Sheffield and Rotherham Independent*
and the *Sheffield Daily Telegraph* in language which was almost totally
sympathetic to the Army. For in South Yorkshire – somewhere between
the fearful justices and the violent mobs – there beat the heart of a nonconformist England, men and women of some respectability and little
sophistication who were not offended by vulgar hymns and would
have been scandalised if their local papers had been critical of a man
who claimed to follow in John Wesley's footsteps.

As the procession was assembled – with Catherine and William
Booth in an open carriage – the most conspicuous figure was
Lieutenant Emmerson Davidson, a champion Northumberland
wrestler. 'This man carried the banner at the Stephenson Centenary
Festival in Newcastle . . . and at that time was presented with a scarlet
uniform and dark coloured helmet in which apparel he took part in the
festival.'[31] Cadman commanded the procession, but Davidson – six feet
four and mounted on a white horse – rode at its head. He became a
particular target for a crowd which increased as the column
approached the city centre. 'The yelling of the roughs brought into that
locality all the idlers who may be seen on any Monday morning loiter-
ing about the streets with their hands in their pockets and ready for
anything except work . . . Out of the midst of the yelling mob there was

suddenly thrown a short thick stick . . . it struck Davidson a terrible blow on the back of the head.'[32]

For the rest of the procession Davidson – slipping in and out of consciousness – was held on his horse by men who ran beside it. It had become a matter of honour not to change route, slow pace or admit even a single victory to the enemy. Police and Salvationists combined to prevent the mob from attacking the Booths' carriage. Diversions were attempted but failed to deflect the roughs from concentrating their stones and abuse on the front of the procession, where General and Mrs Booth were sheltered by other Salvationists. 'There was a great deal of fierce wrestling and it seemed certain that the banners would be wrestled from their grasp; but as on the battlefield it is a terrible disgrace to lose the colours and personal safety is forgotten . . . So the soldiers stuck valiantly to the flags.'[33] As they approached the Albert Hall and anxious questions were asked about casualties, Cadman – his nose broken and bleeding – assured the sympathisers that officers of the Army would be 'all right, dead or alive'. General Booth rose in his carriage and urged his followers to make sure that the waiting journalists saw the extent of their injuries.

William Booth was more affected by the events of the evening than he seemed. For at the rally he gave only a 'short address' – an unprecedented concession. To the evident relief of the *Sheffield Daily Telegraph* it offered his forgiveness to those who had assaulted him, with the sad admission that 'all the great towns treated the Army in much the same fashion'.[34] That year, mobs attacked the Salvation Army in riots from Bath to Arbroath and from Guildford to Forfar. William Booth claimed that 669 Salvationists (251 of them women) were injured and 56 Army buildings damaged. The Booths always believed that the mobs were put up to it by the devil acting through the brewers. And perhaps sometimes the ring-leaders were. But there was also a more spontaneous antagonism which, in the northern towns, was expressed by the poor rather than by the middle classes. The Booths had not set their Army outside the society they strove to help. But they had elevated their soldiers morally above it. The combination of social equality and moral superiority worked wonderfully with potential recruits who were inclined towards salvation. But for wholly unrepentant sinners, there was an irresistible desire to drag down men and women who, although no richer or better educated than themselves, sought to dispense uplifting advice. So the riots happened. And it is easy to understand why the town magistrates of Sheffield, who had never read John Stuart Mill, determined that, having had one riot in January, they were not going to have another in April. John Bright (to whom Catherine Booth had written with the complaint that Sheffield was not protecting the rights of free passage as the Home Secretary wished) replied sympathetically but not helpfully: 'The Army's good work will not suffer materially from the ill-treatment you are meeting with. The people who mob you would have mobbed the Apostles.'[35] For once the great Birmingham radical understated his case. The attacks did the Army material good by turning vulgar cranks into heroic martyrs. While that reputation was preserved, the Salvationists were invincible. And William Booth used his unsurpassed talent for publicity to polish both the halo and the image. But it is easy to understand why the Sheffield magistrates did not want to give him a second opportunity for glorious martyrdom.

At about the time when the Yorkshire Justices were considering how to avoid a spring riot, the Church of England was paying General Booth the compliment of considering what its relations with the Salvation Army should be. The debate at the Canterbury Diocesan Conference was as thorough as it was fierce. First, the Reverend R. W. Hoare, Vicar of St Michael's, Croydon, gave an outline of the Army's origins and history. He concluded that its attitude towards the Church was 'at least neutral if not friendly'.[36] He accepted that its view on Holy Communion made a close and permanent relationship difficult to imagine, but he endorsed the view of evangelism which was the justification for the Salvation Army's existence: 'The Church must recognise the fact that vast multitudes of English people are outside religious influences and she must use new measures as well as old to bring them to her fold.'

The Reverend W. E. M. Nunn wondered if there 'was any hope of inducing the new religious body to abandon its more objectionable practices?' He judged, in answer to his own question, that 'the main barrier to compromise was the indisputable fact that the Army was far too much intoxicated with its own success to lay aside its extravagances'. By far the most important speech came from Dr Randall Davidson – Dean of Windsor, Chaplain to the Archbishop of Canterbury and destined himself to become Primate of England.

Davidson, whose attitude towards the Salvation Army was to become crucial to its development, gave the Diocese a long analysis of the Salvation Army's success which remains the classic statement of its strength. He prefaced his speech with the unpalatable truth that whether 'the conference likes it or not,' the Salvation Army was a huge fact which must be faced. His conclusion that it was likely to be a temporary phenomenon was not consistent with his analysis:

> As regards its present strength, he would attribute it first to the extraordinary rapid success which the Army had already met with: secondly to the employment of all its converts (from very first) in the Army's work and the consequent multiplications of countless centres of influence: thirdly to the 'Ritualism' of banners, titles and uniforms: fourthly to the recognition of the value of personal testimony born by speakers on a level with their audience: fifthly by the use of language 'understandable' by people and lastly to the personal ability, administrative power and devout earnestness of its leaders.

The Diocesan Conference ended inconclusively. But it was just one of the many points of pressure on the Church of England to consider its relationship with the new and apparently irresistible force. As a result, the Lower House of Convocation petitioned the Upper House to issue a general instruction on the Church's attitude towards the new religious phenomenon. The Upper House appointed a committee which included two future Archbishops of Canterbury, E. W. Benson, Bishop of Truro, and Randall Davidson himself. The committee must have realised from the start that co-operation was not possible. For the Salvation Army and the Church of England to work in formal union, one of those two proud institutions would have to abandon its most dearly held beliefs. The basic tenets of the Army's faith – sanctity and Holiness – were theologically unacceptable to the established Church. So was the idea of the female ministry. The governance of the Army could not have been grafted on to the episcopal structure of the Church of England. And there would have been personality problems. William Booth would certainly not have accepted a status which did not put him on an equal footing with the Archbishop of Canterbury – with Bramwell at York and Railton in Winchester.

The Salvation Army was prepared 'to give the question of co-operation impartial and disinterested consideration . . . The General was willing for the two organisations to run side by side like two rivers with bridges thrown over and which the members could mutually pass. Nor did he mind the Corps marching at stated intervals to church.'[37] The *lèse-majesté* of an approach which suggested that the established Church should negotiate as an equal partner with a Methodist mutation which was still not twenty years old was justified by the fact that the Salvation Army was expanding at a time when the Anglican Communion was in decline.

The 'two sides' – as represented by Randall Davidson and William Booth – met and talked. Dr Davidson was 'urbane and considerate throughout the negotiations and although he was the rigid, not to say narrow, ecclesiastic, he showed a real ability in fastening on the essentials when in conference with the Founder'.[38] The discussions foundered on the question of William Booth's authority – both over the Army and the doctrine on which it was built. Davidson tried to appeal to William Booth's vanity: 'I am sorry for the Christian teacher, be he cleric, or layman, who has listened to such addresses as those given by "General" Booth, Mrs Booth and by five or six of those "staff officers" and has not asked for help that he may speak his message with the like straightforward ability and earnest zeal.' But he also wrote of 'errors in doctrine and practice' which would certainly have made partnership impossible. Anglican prejudices and William Booth's character prevented progress to the stage at which theological differences were considered.

The Salvation Army itself conceded that 'some adherents of the Army of this period of its existence . . . probably did commit grievous offences against modesty and good taste'[39] – liturgical errors which *The Times* described as 'the consequences of associating sacred mysteries with ludicrous stage properties and forms'. Canon Gridleson of Bristol told his Diocesan Council that Sunday School scholars in the diocese were given copies of *The War Cry* which printed the words of a hymn which ended 'For he's a jolly good saviour'. When General Booth wrote to *The Times* claiming that *The War Cry* had never published such a hymn and that Gridleson refused to support his allegations with evidence the Canon replied that, if he was wrong in particular, he was right in general.[40] Mr Henry Scott came to Gridleson's support with the news that 'the last number of *The War Cry* published an adaptation of "I Wish I Was With Nancy in the Strand", which had, as its refrain, "Oh don't I love my Jesus. I do. I do."' There was also a Salvation Army version of 'Champagne Charlie' and other 'ditties' with words which so offended Mr Scott that he wrote, 'I will not sully my pen or your columns' with further quotations.[41] The Bishop of Durham summed up the whole complaint: 'Awe and reverence are the soul of religious life. He, therefore, who degrades the chief object of religion by profane associations strikes, however unintentionally, at the root of religion.'[42]

Harold Begbie, producing the 'official' version of events after the General was dead, wrote that 'what direction the diplomacy of William Booth could have taken but for the constant influence of Bramwell Booth and George Railton, it is impossible to say. It is fair to assume however that, without this strong and enthusiastic influence the Salvation Army would have been more anxious for a better understanding with the church, more patient and understanding in these fumbled negotiations.' That view of events would have been more credible had it not depended on the notion that William Booth hated controversy and loved to compromise. The idea that Catherine longed for an accommodation is even less plausible, despite the insistence that 'although she was by nature and habit a controversialist and from her youth upwards had been hotly opposed to what is called Clericalism [she] nevertheless felt that some understanding with the recognised forces of religion would have been valuable.'[43]

Randall Davidson, having been the spokesman of Anglican obduracy, is not an altogether reliable witness. But his interpretation of the Booths' behaviour – and, indeed, their character – is more convincing. The General was not 'anything like so original or interesting a person as Catherine Booth . . . I felt strongly during the months of our negotiations that Booth was determined to keep control and an autocratic control, but I could not possibly bring myself to support so dangerous a policy . . . So we had to let go.'[44] Theological disagreements, as well as problems of precedence and organisation, blocked the path to unity. When Archbishop Benson – to whom Randall Davidson reported – wrote a tribute to the 'thoughtful though summary' discussions of 1882, he had no doubt that the key question was Holy Communion. General Booth 'did not hold the partaking of that Ordinance to be essential to salvation and believed that no thoughtful Christian would shut [Salvationists] out of the Pale of Salvation or close the Gates of Heaven . . . because they have not been regular partakers of that Ordinance'. The Archbishop, while at first appearing to agree, went on to argue the importance of the Eucharist. The hope of union – or indeed partnership – was always a chimera. The crucial question is why William Booth pursued or pretended to pursue the idea. The most likely explanation is a tribute to the tactical sense, if not the innocent integrity, of the General and his advisers. The Salvation Army had much to gain from being seen to negotiate on something like equal terms with the Church of England, but nothing to gain from the negotiations succeeding and the Salvation Army being absorbed into, or overshadowed by, the established Church. The Church of England acknowledged the strength of William Booth's support in the country and the attraction of a 'military' organisation by creating a rival unit, the Church Army.

Within days of the negotiations breaking down, the priests who had always hated the Salvation Army renewed their attacks. Dr Magee, the Bishop of Peterborough, used his visitation to Leicester to denounce 'sensational preaching . . . The desire to fill churches by all means, though laudable in itself, might have the very unfortunate result of lowering the teaching and position of the Church . . . [He] did not believe that slang, irreverence and profanity verging on blasphemy were necessary to win the hearts of the people.' He did not suggest an alternative which might fill the increasingly empty churches of his diocese.

The Salvation Army continued to attract great congregations by creating and exploiting opportunities to publicise its work which not only Dr Magee regarded as outrageous. When, on 12 October 1882, William Bramwell Booth married Florence Eleanor Soper, a Plymouth doctor's daughter who had joined the Salvation Army against her father's will and worked for it in France, the service was turned into an Army rally, conducted in Clapham Congress Hall according to the 'Articles of Marriage' which all soldiers were required to accept before the General would agree to preside at their wedding. The articles included the promises 'never to allow our marriage to lessen in any way our devotion to God and the Army' and 'to regard and arrange our home as a Salvation Army officer's (or soldier's) home'.

Six thousand Salvationists assembled at nine o'clock in the

morning – two hours before the arrival of the bride and groom. They sang with such brio that when Bramwell and Florence eventually entered the hall, the bandmaster had to blow his whistle in order to restore order and draw attention to the presence of the young couple. The tumultuous greeting with which they were eventually received included an obvious home-made banner which proclaimed 'Behold the Bridegroom Cometh'. Critics complained that the slogan suggested that Bramwell Booth was regarded in the Army as Jesus Christ. Presumably William Booth was God the Father.

William Booth addressed the assembly, briefly, on the topic of Christian marriage and, at great length, on the subject of press allegations that he was misappropriating Salvation Army funds. He also described in detail his ideas about the succession after he was 'promoted to Glory', as the Salvation Army came to describe death. There was, he insisted, no question of creating a dynasty. But it was only sensible to consider the 'possibilities and probabilities' of Bramwell inheriting the command. The Army would, he knew, rally round its new leader. From then on, dynastic ambitions or not, it was taken for granted that Bramwell was heir apparent.

Catherine followed with a more appropriate speech. 'I cannot say that I am gaining a daughter today, for this dear one is already my own spiritual child.' She was drowned in thunderous applause, as was George Railton when he made an impassioned attack on William Booth's detractors. The strange wedding ceremony was made all the more peculiar by William's decision to charge a shilling for admission. The money contributed towards the purchase price of The Eagle Tavern and Grecian Theatre.

Bramwell's wedding provided a perfect example of William Booth's view of his relationship with the Army which he had created. He was its father and it was his family, and he genuinely believed that his blood relatives (and their husbands and wives when they acquired them) ought to be accepted as specially blessed members. He took it for granted that he should exercise a parent's discipline over the officers under his command – as concerned in their private lives as he was about the way in which they discharged their public duties. In a letter to Cadman principally concerned with staffing arrangements at Heckmondwike, William Booth suddenly veered off into an injunction concerning the amorous activities of an officer called Dent. 'If it is true that he has given up this girl at Beverley for another and has no better excuse for it, it is abominable and I do not feel disposed to cancel his resignation.' His rigid views on sexual morality did not protect him from accusations of condoning the promiscuity of his followers.

When the Upper House of the Canterbury Convocation met on 10 April 1883, Dr John Mackerness, Bishop of Oxford, supported by Dr James, Bishop of Hereford, accused the Salvationists of actually promoting sexual licence. He was echoing the view, first expressed by the Reverend E. Bickersteth, who had claimed that All Night Prayer Meetings always involved 'the grossest immoralities'.[45] That allegation had been categorically denied by William Booth, but it was soon regarded as confirmation of a rumour, rife in south London, that the Hackney Union Infirmary accommodated several young women whose pregnancies were the result of participation in Holiness Meetings. The Bishop of Oxford's claim was even more specific. Soldiers in York practised what they called 'Crawling for Jesus' – two hours each Sunday evening in a darkened room during which the celebrants, on hands and knees, fondled everyone they could touch. The Bishop of Hereford supported the proposal made by Dr Mackerness that an enquiry be set up to determine if the Salvation Army was a force for good or evil. William Booth wrote to both bishops, and to the Archbishop of Canterbury, the day after the proposal was made. Never has indignation been so righteous: 'It seems to me very hard that the outrageous statements constantly made in regard to us should be credited without our having an opportunity to reply to them. There is no doubt that such an accusation made in such a quarter will be used in such a way in the Press as to greatly increase the ill-usage of our poor people on the streets.' And so it was. The Skeleton Armies attacked the Salvationists in the name of sexual morality, indiscriminately assaulting both the men whom they claimed perpetuated the outrages, and the women whose virtue they claimed to cherish.

William Booth himself held an inquiry into the conduct of his officers in the dioceses of Oxford and Hereford. The investigation located one rumour – a woman Salvationist who had been admitted to a workhouse labour ward. Workhouse masters in Oxford and Hereford all denied knowledge of such a pauper. Told of the outcome of the enquiry, the Bishop of Oxford invited representatives of the Salvation Army to visit him. He was in a mood to recant and apologise. Railton and two officers of the Southern Division travelled to Reading for a meeting in St Giles vicarage, but unfortunately the Bishop had failed to enter the date in his diary and at the appointed time of the confrontation, he was consecrating a new church in a neighbouring parish. After the meeting was rearranged Railton drafted a statement which Dr Mackerness agreed to be published. The retraction was very near to handsome: 'He assured us that he had never had any intention of making accusations against the Army still less of exciting public hostility towards it, and that his words used in the midst of a discussion in Convocation must have been ill chosen to create such an impression.'

The controversy did nothing to harm the Salvation Army – at least in terms of membership. In barely two years, General Booth had become a national figure, written about in the national newspapers and even caricatured by August Cramer and his pierrots on the Yarmouth seafront. In 1882 there were 440 Salvation Army corps, staffed by 1,019 officers. In 1883, there were 634 corps and 1,541 officers. By 1884 the numbers had grown to 910 corps and 2,332 officers. William Booth could afford to laugh with the seaside audience at the antics of Colonel Ebenezer Smirky and Captain Mrs Cantwell. The joke was on the established Church, not him.

15

As Quick as Fire

The creation of the Salvation Army had been the result of explosions of not quite spontaneous evangelical fervour. Each sudden expression of piety, though not in the English tradition of reticent Methodism, was certainly nothing like as flamboyant or extreme as the American revivalism which inspired some of its founding members. Its critics in Britain took for granted that it would not travel. The first American experiment, led by Brother Jermy, had failed and the second was not the instant and nationwide success for which its local pioneers had hoped. The rhetoric with which William Booth had sent the American expeditionary force to colonise the New World did not represent his considered view. There was more work in Britain than he could hope to complete in a lifetime. He found no attraction in setting up missions which he could not control. If Brighton and Leicester defected, how could he hope to retain authority over stations in those countries – Sweden, France, Belgium – which he had been moved to mention in a fit of international enthusiasm? So when John Gore, the 'Happy Milkman' of Adelaide, a recently emigrated Bradford butcher called Saunders, and a Mr Whitbourne, late of Plymouth, wrote to say that they had formed themselves into an Australian corps, he was desperately reluctant to respond to their cries for help – despite the dramatic language in which it was composed. 'We need you as quick as fire and steam can bring you. There is no mistake about it, you must come immediately.'[1] The best he could bring himself to offer was Commissioner and Mrs Sutherland to act as his representatives and plenipotentiaries. They discovered that 'the same material which when forced into the unhealthy atmosphere and hopeless squalor of slumdom, and had given birth to the most exaggerated specimens of vice, had blossomed in those brighter and roomier climes.'[2] Even though it was a version of economic determinism more Marxist than Christian, the conclusion was irresistible to an evangelist who believed that God offered all humanity moral redemption. William Booth began to see himself as part of a plan which was worldwide as well as universal. If Australia enjoyed the climate of virtue, he could hardly turn his back on it. And if he could reach as far as the antipodes, he could grasp opportunities nearer home.

A year earlier two Frenchmen, neither actual or even potential Salvationists themselves, had suggested that the Army expand into continental Europe. An unrelated offer of two buildings in the Midi followed. The owner and potential donor suggested that they could become the Army's French headquarters and central meeting hall. William Booth rebuffed the approaches. He did, however, send out one of his officers, Colonel Colville, to reconnoitre the territory, and Colville's report forced him to recognise the potential of planting the flag overseas. For months he had been 'thinking and praying earnestly for a direction from the Lord'. Then a third approach from a Frenchman who 'entreated [the Booths] to do something in his country' convinced him that God was calling him across the Channel.[3] Within weeks he was explaining that the duty to advance into France was being thrust upon him. 'From all parts of France we have received letters – of warning, of advice, of entreaty to come. Of entreaty to stop away. Of impartial enquiry, "What are you going to do?" and so on ad lib.'[4] The honest answer to the question would have been 'expand across the world', for that had become his instinct. His public reaction was more cautious. He simply announced that invitations had also been received from Sweden, Switzerland and China, and added, 'If any of you who read these lines can hand us information respecting these countries, send it along.' All doubts about his international destiny had vanished.

William Booth married his dynastic and territorial ambitions by sending his 22-year-old daughter, Kate, to take command in France. America had been forced upon him. So, in a different way, had Australia. France was his own decision, and he was determined that it should be carried out in the way he chose. So Kate – ever faithful, reliable and an active evangelist since she was a child – was appointed his emissary and consul. She studied French throughout the spring and early summer of 1880. As the year came to an end, she was adjudged ready. She appointed an assistant, Florence Soper – who was to become her sister-in-law – and prepared to set sail.

The Salvation Army never missed an opportunity for a good rally. So the departure of Miss Booth for France was marked by a mighty gathering in St James's Hall, Regent Street, on 4 February 1881. Everyone present was given a letter written by, or at least written on behalf of, Miss Booth herself:

Friends tell me that expenses connected with our effort will be very heavy and this gives me some anxiety. I cannot bear to think of taking money sent for the dear English work. So I feel I ought to ask, in faith, for another thousand pounds today. Will you help me? I have willingly given the Lord myself for France and am leaving home and friends to do what I can to bring the people to Jesus. Will you share the burden with me and send me today what you can?[5]

Mr Denny and his brothers were on the platform, and they immediately contributed £100 each. Sir Arthur Blackwood – a retired Guards officer who had supported the Booths since the days of the Christian Mission – made a speech which was as accurate as it was patronising: 'Of course, there are many things about the Salvation Army that shock those whom we may call refined . . . we must remember that the work which they are carrying out is not designed to meet the needs of these people . . . I heard Happy George at Coventry . . . He got up to speak and the first thing he did was take his coat off.'[6]

William Booth took the opportunity to describe the Army's growth and progress – ten times as many services as three years earlier and the circulation of *The War Cry* risen by 100,000 in a year. When Mrs Booth rose to speak she seemed unusually agitated: 'The papers I read on the state of society in Paris make me shudder and I see all the dangers to which our darling may be exposed. But oh, the joy and honour of giving her to be the saviour of those sin-stricken masses.'[7] It was not a statement which was calculated to endear the Salvation Army to the French, but it seemed that Mrs Booth had other things than an *entente cordiale* on her mind. The tone of her speech was acutely apologetic – a unique example of doubt in a woman who usually triumphed because of her certainty.

> Some friends may think that it does not cost us what it would cost them to give up our children fully to such work. They do not know us. I do not think that any mother in this hall could have realised more keenly than I have done the difficulties and dangers connected with the work and perhaps to few would it have involved so great a sacrifice . . . I have no doubt or question that it is the Divine will that I should offer my child to France.[8]

Miss Booth hired rooms at 66 rue d'Angouleme in Belleville. At first she met more ridicule than hatred. But gradually a pattern of hostility similar to that which the Army had met in England began to build up. Abuse escalated into assault. Particular exception was taken to the bands and the banners. The authorities, anxious to avoid civil disturbance, chose to act against the strange foreign sect rather than its native assailants. Once again the Army was forbidden to march – though an unlikely intervention by the Lord Mayor of London, who appealed to the Mayor of Paris, resulted in the bar being lifted in the capital. As always the Booths triumphed in adversity. Kate – true to family tradition – was then struck down by a mysterious illness. Herbert, aged nineteen, was sent out to help his sister and was comforted by his mother with advice which might have been more appropriately given to a man of fifty: 'Keep your mind quiet. Lean back on God and don't worry. It is His affair and if you have done what you could, that is quite enough.'[9] The Booths could be sanctimonious with each other without fearing to cause offence.

Between them, God and Miss Booth had done quite well without Herbert's help. So many recruits were made in the first year that the headquarters were moved to larger premises on the Quai de Valmy, and in March 1882 the first edition of the French *War Cry* was published. It was called *En Avant* after Miss Booth was convinced, with some difficulty, that the Hallelujah Lasses could not tramp the boulevards of Paris shouting, '*Amour!*' A month later, Mrs Booth visited France on her only excursion outside Britain. She found the French extremely irritating and had 'to scrape together patience to answer the old timeworn objections to our measure'.[10] But she left Paris confident that, although the Army's blasphemous critics were worse than anything that had to be faced in England, the French expedition had secured its base. As she left her final meeting, Arthur Clibborn – an English Quaker who had been appointed Colonel and made Miss Booth's chief of staff – was set upon by the mob. His injuries did nothing to reduce his devotion either to the cause or to Miss Booth herself.

By the end of 1882 the Salvation Empire had spread into each of the five continents. At a great demonstration in Exeter Hall, one hundred officers were 'set apart for service here and abroad'. The foreign contingent had been prepared for service in Switzerland, America, New Zealand, the Cape of Good Hope, India and Sweden, where a Miss Hanna Ouchterlony had been agitating for a unit to be formed ever since Bramwell Booth had made a convalescent visit there. William Booth had been particularly dubious about expanding into India – even though he was flattered by the suggestion that he could become a modern Francis Xavier. But, after intense pressure from Frederick Tucker – a Judge in the Indian Civil Service – he agreed that the subcontinent should be the next target.

Judge Frederick St George Lautour Tucker was the first gentleman to be commissioned into the Salvation Army. He was born in Bombay in 1853 and, after leaving Cheltenham College at the unusually late age of twenty, followed his father into the Indian Civil Service. He was, by nature, a scholar and a reluctant administrator who would have preferred to spend his time studying Greek rather than dispensing imperial justice. As soon as he arrived in India, he began to learn Sanskrit, Hindi and Urdu. He was, as befitted his background, brought up an Anglican, but during one leave in England he attended a Moody and Sankey revival meeting and was instantly converted to Methodism. He thus followed the pattern of conversion which was common to almost all of General Booth's staff officers. None of them spent weeks, or even days, agonising about whether they should join the Salvation

Army. It came to them all in a sudden flash of what they took to be divine inspiration. Tucker was typical of his colleagues in one other important particular. By the standards of the materialistic world, he was slightly crazy. He believed that John Wesley preached the virtues of aestheticism and sacrifice. So, fearing that he was particularly 'susceptible to the appeal of beauty, charm and grace' he married Louise May Bode, a woman eighteen years his senior who could not be accused of possessing any of those qualities. She devoted her adult life to persuading soldiers to give up alcohol and was therefore well equipped to join with Tucker in making himself extremely unpopular, first in Amritsar and then in Dharmsala, by attempting to convert the native population to Christianity. His superiors accused him of fomenting riots, to which he replied, with commendable logic, that no riots had occurred and, with absolute truth, that the Indian Civil Service was far more antagonistic to his activities than were the Indians. In fact, the Indian Civil Service believed that, suttee notwithstanding, it was best to allow the complicated legal and religious pattern of the subcontinent to remain undisturbed by any sort of missionary. That was not Judge Tucker's view. His zeal to convert was increased when he read *The War Cry*'s special Christmas 1880 edition. The magazine so impressed him that he took leave at once and returned to England. As soon as he arrived in London, he attended the first Salvation Army meeting that he could find and, at its conclusion, offered his services as a full-time officer. William Booth, who thought himself both unworldly and untouched by human vanity, was deeply impressed by the sacrifice of income and social status that Tucker was prepared to make. When he introduced him to a mass meeting in Exeter Hall in September 1881, he announced, 'Judge Tucker has thrown up a situation in the Indian Civil Service, where he has been in receipt of £800 a year, to serve God in The Salvation Army.'[11] But the General did not accept his services on God's behalf until Tucker had proved himself to be worthy. Nor was he prepared to let the new recruit plan his own field of operations. Tucker was sent to Bristol to serve an apprenticeship where, much to his wife's horror, he resigned from the Indian Civil Service as a token of his absolute sincerity.

The apprenticeship successfully concluded, Frederick Tucker was enrolled as a soldier and made a clerk in the Army's legal department in Queen Victoria Street. He immediately began to agitate about leading an expedition to India. General Booth continued to have serious doubts. No evangelist was more conscious of the need to avoid sins of the flesh. So he was particularly concerned about his officers having to meet 'the Devadasis, the courtesans, the dancing girls and the attendants at the temples [who] are the common properties of the priests and are at the command of all who can pay for them'.[12] Catherine Booth should have wanted, in all consistency, to save them from more exploitation. But she was still sceptical about foreign missionary work. However, neither her doubts nor William Booth's fears could withstand Tucker's constant pleading and persuasion. For the third time, the Salvation Army expanded its overseas activities with open reluctance – and because of the zeal of one or two converts it was not the ideal formula for success. Great international movements are supposed to thrive on the vision of their founders. Initially William Booth's vision was almost entirely limited to the needs of the British poor. It was his good (and possibly heaven-sent) fortune that his formula – taking Christianity to the people, speaking in a language they understood and using one generation of converts to redeem another – had a near universal appeal. Even in India.

The Indian Party – Mr (now Major) and Mrs Tucker, Captain Henry Bullard, Lieutenant Norman and Lieutenant Thompson (a women's officer who had agreed, at three days' notice, to accompany the party as 'chaperone' to Mrs Tucker) – set sail aboard the SS *Ancona* without anything like the triumphant farewell which had been accorded to the French expeditionary force. Bands, banners and hymns on the quayside were only available to members of the immediate family. But the Indian contingent immediately demonstrated its commitment to the Booth ideal by getting itself arrested in Gibraltar for forming an unlawful assembly and failing to disperse when ordered to do so. The detention did not delay their journey. They landed in Bombay on Wednesday 19 September 1882 'with a great demonstration of military pomp'.

A number of local missionaries and their recent converts were waiting on the quayside and 'a triumphant procession of war chariots, consisting of bullock carts, paraded the streets. The young woman [Lieutenant Thompson] beat a tambourine and one of the men [Lieutenant Norman] attempted to blow a trumpet, but in as much as he was warned that this was a contravention of the police regulations and he declined to desist, he was incontinently arrested.'[13]

Tucker decreed, true to Booth's principles, that the officers must identify with the people with whom they worked. So the men dressed in 'yellow coats reaching to the knees, pantaloons, turbans, shawls and English boots'. Thus attired, the procession not surprisingly 'caused much amusement to the natives who took the Salvationists for circus people and possibly viewed their demonstration as a pageant organised by the government in commemoration of the recent victory in Egypt' (General Sir Garnet Wolseley, whose Orders and Regulations William Booth so admired, had just defeated Arabi Pasha at Tel-el-Kebir). The next day the *Indo-European Telegraph* reported, 'The members of the Salvation Army have all been arrested, except one, a riot being imminent.'[14] The 'one' was detached by Tucker before the march and demonstration to carry on the fight if (or perhaps when) the main body was committed to prison. That too was good military practice: 'detachments' were separated from each of the battalions that advanced into no-man's-land on the first day of the Battle of the Somme. Their duty was to survive and reform their regiments.

The circumstances of the Indian contingent's arrest were in the best traditions of the Salvation Army. The Deputy Commissioner of Police ordered the procession to disperse in the name of Her Majesty the Queen of England and Empress of India. In retaliation – or in the belief of his superior authority – Major Tucker ordered the Deputy Commissioner to stand aside in the name of the King of Kings and Lord of Lords. Unfortunately neither of those authorities could quote the Indian Penal Code in their support. The Deputy Commissioner quoted Section 115, which justified the Salvationists' overnight detention and prosecution. So next day they appeared before Mr Justice Dusaboy Framjee, who fined Tucker fifty rupees and the other officers twenty each. Naturally they refused to pay and their property was restrained. A sympathetic police superintendent bought ninety rupees' worth of the officers' effects and returned them to the Salvationists at once.

The Indian Civil Service was genuinely afraid of a native uprising. For the Salvation Army had breached the rules of religious neutrality which the rulers of the Raj thought essential to the maintenance of law and order. Mr Justice Framjee emphasised the point when he passed sentence: 'In England, the people profess one religion and efforts like those of the Salvationists to reclaim the fallen are met with universal sympathy.' The judge's ignorance of life in the Mother Country should not detract from respect for his attitude towards religious tolerance in Bombay. He went on to say, 'When they come to India to convert people from one faith to another, they must avoid noisy and peculiar demonstrations as they were sure to excite angry feelings and passions and to promote counter demonstrations.' So the British government, 'justly esteemed for its strict neutrality towards all classes', could not risk demonstrations which might 'excite the religious feelings of other sects and so bring the people of different creeds into collision'.[15]

The Salvation Army established itself in India – without either help or instruction from London – in exactly the way in which the Christian Mission had established itself in the Old Kent Road. In France, Australia and America Salvationists were building on the same foundations. The first edition of the Indian *War Cry* was published in English on 11 October. Three days later a Gujerati version was available. It sold two thousand copies – more than half the circulation of *The Pioneer*, Bombay's longest-established English paper. Before the end of the month the Indian advance party was augmented by two additional officers. On arrival they immediately took part in a demonstration to mark the joys of extra-evangelism. As a result, the whole officer corps was arrested on 20 October. Major Tucker, a genuine expert in Indian law, defended himself and his officers, quoting from the Proclamation with which Queen Victoria was pronounced Empress of India: 'We do strongly charge and enjoin those who exercise authority under us that they shall abstain from any interference with the religious beliefs and worship of any of our subjects.' The Chief Presiding Magistrate was not impressed. 'The members of the Salvation Army of Bombay are evidently bent upon winning easy martyrdom and cheap notoriety by insisting on active disobedience to police regulations.'[16]

As always, the Salvation Army reacted to persecution by increasing the activities for which it was being persecuted. Sir Lepel Griffin, the Governor of Central Province, issued a general order: 'Should the Salvationists express any intention to visit Indore or any Native State under this agency with any public demonstration or procession (with or without music) the leader is to be informed that I will not tolerate in Central India the degrading burlesque of the religion of the ruling power.'[17] Tucker decided to leave for Indore at once. He had two hours to prepare his departure. Fortunately 'the Lord delayed the train for us'.[18]

Tucker's success in India was built on more than his audacity – necessary as that was for success amongst the Muslims and Hindus. He had taken a conscious decision to model his work on the life of Francis Xavier, the Jesuit who had converted half of Goa to Christianity by disowning the corrupt missionaries whom he found there and by living like and amongst the native Indians. It was the same principle on which William Booth – without being aware of the precedent – had based his work in England. After a few weeks in India, Tucker decided that his troops must become even more like the men and women they sought to convert: 'The dress was changed to make it more in keeping with real Indian costume. Blankets were abandoned for sacking as being both more simple and more economical. The Salvationists not only lived in the native quarters and on native land but learned to eat with their fingers . . . They took Indian names. They wore Indian caste marks on their foreheads – special caste marks of the Salvation Army.'[19] Occasionally during the years which followed, a few English officers went further than the Army thought decent and 'married Indian wives. However, common sense prevailed. There was strong resentment against a step which received no support from Tucker. It was no purpose of the Salvation Army to be parents to a new race of Eurasians.' Not even a band of unworldly evangelists could totally inoculate themselves against the mores of the time.

When the memorandum for volunteers in India was published it was silent on the subject of mixed marriages. Perhaps someone had reminded Tucker that, whatever the view of the Indian Civil Service, the Salvation Army believed all men and women to be equal in the sight of God. It did, however, deal with the importance of boiling water and using 'a thick cotton umbrella on account of the sun'. It also stipulated that 'a knowledge of some native language will be necessary' and instructed 'leave entirely and forever behind you all Englishness and habits, avoid English quarters and do not live in their bungalows – a shady tree is sometimes all that will be available. Cook as they do and wash your clothes in a stream like them . . . Except in rare cases, Officers will be barefoot like all the rest of the people.' But at least the Army remained incorrigibly English in its determination to break the law and get itself arrested.

In February 1883, Salvation Army members paraded on the Bombay Esplanade and were, once again, brought in front of Mr Justice Framjee. Tucker was sentenced to one week's imprisonment and the rest fined two pounds, ten shillings with the option of seven days in jail. Mr Justice Kenball, who heard their appeal, offered a deal. The sentences would be quashed if the defendants agreed to avoid future disobedience. Of course they refused. Tucker found prison (including the wooden board which was his bed) 'really quite comfortable . . . the uniform tunic is really the most cool and comfortable thing possible. The food is very simple but really good and cheap. Altogether I expect to get a lot of ideas before I get out.'[20] A touch of home awaited him on his release. Mrs Tucker had composed a hymn in praise of his sacrifice.

In what was intended as a reverential reference to Chapter XXV of St Matthew's Gospel, the hymn was called 'I Was in Chauki and You Visited Me Not'.* Each verse ended 'So I'll go to Chauki' – a celebration sung to the tune of 'Wait for the Waggon'.[21] Sir Lepel Griffin would certainly – and perhaps with some justification – have called it a 'degrading burlesque of the religion of the ruling power'. On the release of Major Tucker, his sentence completed, the assembled Salvationists sang their new hymn outside the prison. They were immediately arrested.

At about the time of Tucker's second arrest, in the autumn of 1882, Colonel Arthur Clibborn was sent from the French headquarters to investigate the possibility of the Salvation Army extending its activities into Switzerland. Arthur Clibborn was the second gentleman to be commissioned into the Salvation Army. He was a graduate of Lausanne University who had become a director of his father's linen mills in Bersborough, Northern Ireland. At the age of twenty-six, he became a Quaker minister. Because he could speak five languages he was initially recruited by the Army to translate *The War Cry* into French. There was little local interest in the Army in Switzerland and the decision to cross the Alps was taken in France, without any encouragement from London, and for no particular reason. Arthur Clibborn was expected to live off the spiritual land. So he employed the tactics which he had seen used in London and fly-posted the walls of Geneva with notices which

---

Chauki – pronounced 'choki' – was one of the Hindustani words which was incorporated into English slang by soldiers home from the Raj. *Chauki* was prison.

offered the prospect of redemption. A few curious Swiss citizens turned up at the appropriately named Salle de la Réformation on 6 December and at a subsequent meeting at the Casino St-Pierre. According to M. J. Cart, who wrote a history of the religious sects in the Canton of Vaud, 'He was unnerved by the cultivated and intelligent audiences and made an impression of feebleness on all who heard him.'[22]

Kate Booth descended on Switzerland in mid-December. Ten years later, when Arthur Clibborn (advanced to rank of colonel) married her, she and the family always insisted that *La Maréchale* (as she had come to be called) was not sent to Geneva to remedy the failure of the advance party. As soon as its commander became a member of the family, no criticism (even of his past performance) was allowed. During his early years in Geneva, the usual sequence of events was repeated. Local newspapers announced that 'the proceedings of the Salvation Army . . . are attracting considerable attention and provoking serious disturbances and much angry controversy'. But in Geneva, where their meetings were 'interrupted and their processions attacked by organised bands of rioters', the discrimination escalated to new heights. 'M. Heridier, head of the Department of Justice and Police, has peremptorily refused them the protection of the law . . . He declared that he would not move a single gendarme to help people who were so stupid as to give themselves military titles and seek to obtain converts by talking about blood, battles and fire.'[23] The Salvation Army caused the same sort of offence all over the world and met with exactly the same response from government magistrates and police.

As soon as Kate Booth had arrived in Geneva, she had arranged the usual public meeting and, as always, the news that the Salvation Army had moved into town provoked immediate riots. Much worse was to follow. The first rally at the Casino St-Pierre was broken up by rowdy students and by the end of January 1883 there were regular and open assaults in the streets. During the first week in February an edict was promulgated which prohibited all public demonstrations by *L'Armée de Salut* and five days later, a number of Salvationists were told that if they did not leave the Canton at once, they would be expelled on the following day. Amongst them was Maud Charlesworth, personal assistant to Kate Booth in succession to Florence Sopel, who had married Bramwell. How she had become appointed to that task was to become a subject of national controversy.

Kate Booth was not extradited immediately. Indeed, the Justice Department insisted that she remain in the Canton while the Prefect examined her account books. The clear implication was that campaign money had been fraudulently raised – a charge which Kate Booth was not immediately able to refute because, according to her version of events, her secretary had briefly returned to Paris with all the invoices and bills. Keeping accounts was not the sort of activity at which the Booths excelled, and it is at least possible that no financial records existed besides those in young Catherine's head. Whatever the explanation, the absence of books and the failure to produce a balance sheet seemed, to the orderly minded Swiss authorities, sufficient grounds to confirm Miss Charlesworth's expulsion. Then Kate Booth's name was added to the extradition list. The appeal, which Miss Booth conducted herself, was heroic but hardly calculated to endear the Army to the Swiss:

> We could have sung and danced on your stage and we could
> have dressed in a manner very different (and much less modest)
> than that in which you see us dressed. We could have appeared
> before a music hall audience, men and women, young and old
> and of every class and members of the Grand Council. M.
> Heridier himself and others would have come out to see us and
> we would have got money.[24]

Not surprisingly, the appeal was rejected and both Miss Booth and Miss Charlesworth were expelled. So the same cycle – witnessed in America and India as well as Britain – was enacted once more. Demonstration was followed by the refusal to retreat or apologise and culminated in expulsion and imprisonment. *The Times* struggled hard to prove that the Swiss adventure was more proof of the Army's absurdity:

> Englishmen cannot help watching with some curiosity the
> tortures of the Salvation Army in Switzerland and foreign
> countries which, to keep up their own metaphors, they have
> invaded. Such an invasion is, in itself, somewhat of a
> phenomenon. It is not much more than a year ago that the
> doings of the Salvation Army were hardly thought worthy of

serious public comment. Mr Booth can hardly claim to have
converted any appreciable proportion of his countrymen to his
peculiar modes of worship yet he fits out expeditions to
countries where, comparatively speaking, he has not the
slightest chance of achieving any permanent success.[25]

The Times was not, however, prepared to defend a foreign government which was unable or unwilling to defend British citizens against
the mob. The Canton had treated the Misses Booth and Charlesworth
disgracefully. 'Not only have the usual crowds of rioters been allowed
to attack them with impunity, but the Geneva authorities have inter-
dicted their Salvationist meetings and, to crown it all, suddenly
expelled from the canton Miss Booth and another young lady. The reasons assigned for this summary process were flimsy indeed.' The
reasons for *The Times's* sympathy were made clear in the next paragraph. The story of the Swiss persecution had been revealed by Miss
Charlesworth, who was described as 'narrator and heroine' of the
report. She also, according to the correspondent, 'displayed the self-
possession of a veteran in the trying cross-examination . . . There is,
indeed, in her tales a quaintness almost Puritanic when she dwells
upon the cross and unsaved faces of her examiners and the way in
which they lost their temper while she remained unperturbable.'
Unfortunately her father, the Reverend Mr Samuel Charlesworth, was
less concerned with his daughter's serenity than with her safety. She
had, he claimed, been lured first to France and then to Switzerland
under false pretences. Had *The Times* not treated her like a national
celebrity, he might have kept his dispute with William Booth within the
family – in the manner expected of a Christian gentleman. But, as it
turned out, he wrote to the paper to expose what he believed to be the
truth of his daughter's situation. His letter could have been written by
any one of a thousand distraught parents who, down the years, have
seen their children infatuated by religious movements which, to more
conventional thinkers, appear to be dangerous sects:

Being of a very impressionable and somewhat excitable nature,
deeply imbued with strong religious convictions and feelings,
the Salvation Army took a strong hold of her imagination and
she became fascinated with its meetings and work. Eventually

she was so absorbed in the movement that all her other interest
seemed to merge in her conception of the importance of the
religious work carried on by the Army . . . I shrank with
trembling from the responsibility of allowing a child of so
sensitive a nature and impulsive a disposition to be the subject
of the immense excitement called forth by those meetings . . .
But I found with sorrow that my daughter had already been so
wrought upon by the system that no other form of worship
satisfied her spiritual cravings . . . I must add with respect to
my child and to other young persons of whom I have heard, I
fear that the Army's influence has a direct tendency to wean
from home associates and interests under the idea that the work
is paramount in importance to all other pursuits and
obligations and even to the known wishes of parents.[26]

Samuel Charlesworth was right. Having 'sacrificed' their own
beloved daughter to all the risks of saving souls in France, the Booths
were hardly likely to allow the scruples of an over-anxious father to
stand in the way of their making another recruit to the glory campaign.
Having made the classic complaint of obsession, Mr Charlesworth
went on to accuse the Booths in general, and Kate in particular, of
deception. He had always opposed his daughter's entanglement with
the Salvation Army. But Maud had clearly agitated her father beyond
both his endurance and his power to refuse her wishes. So eventually,
he had agreed that she should go to Paris 'to assist Miss Booth in her
work amongst the poor', but he claimed that he had 'expressly stipulated that she was only to be regarded as a young friend and visitor and
that she should not become an officer of the Army or wear the uniform'. He should have known better than to expect such a promise to
be kept. 'Shortly afterwards Miss Booth went to Geneva to open her
station there and took my daughter with her . . . in direct contravention
of both the letter and spirit of my express stipulation.'

General Booth replied the next day, scandalised by the conduct of
those 'who have chosen the very moment when my daughter is exiled
and silenced to heap reproach upon her'. He quoted, verbatim, a letter
from Mr Charlesworth which expressly referred to Maud travelling to
Geneva and staying there 'in order to save fatigue and expense' during
Kate Booth's brief return to England.[27] The argument, and the

correspondence, continued for weeks, gaining additional venom with each new letter. Before it was over, each man had accused the other of lying. But when Kate Booth did return to London in early May to attend the Exeter Hall celebrations of the French campaign's second anniversary, she believed that the dispute had been amicably resolved. 'Mr Charlesworth was satisfied with the explanation and accepted that he had been misinformed. Miss Charlesworth had neither worn the uniform of the Salvation Army nor received any title, though she had described herself as aide-de-camp when she was taken to Geneva with her father's consent.'[28] The father sat in the Exeter Hall gallery, presumably to confirm the reconciliation for he 'did not dissent'.

The reconciliation was probably not genuine and certainly not permanent. In 1885 Charlesworth wrote, for private circulation, a paper entitled 'Sensational Religion as Resorted to in the System Called a Salvation Army'. As well as repeating all the old allegations he added an accusation of something approaching fraud: 'I agreed to pay a stipend of £100 per annum for board and lodging and instruction . . . on parting with Miss Booth, I gave her a cheque for £25 for the first quarter. It will hardly be credited that the cheque so given was forwarded to headquarters to be entered as a donation from me to the funds.'[29] But the real demonstration of disapproval was to come a year later, when Mr Charlesworth refused to attend the wedding of his daughter Maud to Colonel Ballington Booth. Their wedding came three years after her predecessor in France, Florence Soper, had married Bramwell Booth. In February 1887, Miss Catherine Booth – the woman they had both served – married her second-in-command, Arthur Clibborn. He changed his name, and hers, to Booth-Clibborn. In the month of the marriage, Mrs Frederick Tucker died in India. Tucker returned to Britain to attend a conference on the future of the Army in Asia and – to the consternation of some Army officers – became almost immediately engaged to Emma Booth. It was even rumoured that the General had ordered him to propose. The happy couple were married on 10 April 1888 and took the family name of Booth-Tucker. William Booth had founded a dynasty.

Still in her maiden state, Kate Booth returned to Neuchâtel on 15 April 1883. She was immediately warned that if she resumed her programme of public meetings, all the Army's activities would be banned throughout the country. The warning was accepted as the devil's provocation, a test of both courage and sincerity. So all the campaigns were immediately resumed. On 22 May, the Conseil d'État suppressed the Army's activities in the Canton. The edict was confirmed by the Grand Council three weeks later. Kate Booth, in an unusual fit of prudence, decided that nothing was to be gained by being arrested and returned to the Midi, where she continued to organise the Army in France. She remained satisfied with the routine of careful organisation for almost six months. Then she again yielded to reckless temptation – as much an element in the Salvation Army's progress as divine will – and she went back to Neuchâtel.

Kate was, in temperament, a female replica of her father. That was why William Booth loved and admired her so much. Her evangelistic technique was daringly identical to his. She chose to operate at the very margins of the law (and sometimes wilfully broke it) in order to provoke the authorities into brutal action. Then, with police and magistrates in the wrong, she took the part of saint and martyr. And that is exactly how she behaved as soon as she returned to Switzerland. An open-air meeting was organised in the foothills five miles from Neuchâtel lake. Although warned of the police's approach – estimates of the contingent's strength vary from six to sixteen – the meeting went on. Indeed it continued for two hours after the Prefect of Police made himself known to Kate Booth. When he lost patience, or thought it was time to go home, he arrested the Salvationists and charged them with the usual offence of breaking the injunction to keep the peace. The magistrates granted bail in order that she could attend the funeral of Captain Charles Wyssa, the first volunteer from Geneva – a town which she was forbidden to enter.

Kate Booth intended to leave the forbidden Geneva Canton as soon as the funeral service was over. 'Before she could carry out this intention, however, she was . . . taken to the Town Hall and, after an interview with the Inspector of Police, conducted to the frontier.' She thus 'achieved the distinction of being twice arrested in twenty-four hours'.[30] Back in Neuchâtel she surrendered to her bail and spent the next twelve days in prison awaiting trial. Captain Patrick Beguel, a local officer – although neither arrested nor charged – asked if he could occupy an adjoining cell and was allowed to do so.

The Booths had developed a letter-writing strategy which, although it never righted the wrongs of which they complained, clearly gave them heart and boosted the morale of their supporters. Catherine wrote to those in authority, both as an anxious mother (literal or metaphorical, according to circumstances) and as an outraged woman. William wrote to the newspapers on behalf of God, Christianity, religious freedom and common justice. Mrs Booth explained to the Prime Minister, 'Miss Booth's imprisonment would probably help the cause more than anything else. But for the very delicate state of her health, consequent upon the very trying events of the last few months, I would not intrude on your much needed privacy.'[31] Number 10's reply – sent through the principal private secretary – was depressingly formal. Representations could only be made through the Foreign Secretary and suitable approaches 'Mr Gladstone had reason to know, had already been made and with which he himself heartily concurs'.[32] No doubt, several weeks later, Mr Gladstone was impressed to learn that Miss Booth had spent her time in prison writing hymns: 'Best beloved of my soul / I am here alone with Thee / And my prison is a haven / Since thou sharest it with me.'[33]

When the case came to trial, a window blew open during the prosecuting counsel's indictment and his papers were blown about the courtroom by what the defendant regarded as a 'wind from heaven'. Captain Beguel opened the defence by reading Psalm 150: 'Praise Him with the sound of the trumpet, praise Him with the cymbal and dance. Praise Him with stringed instruments and organs.' Unfortunately the court showed no sign of supporting the view that biblical authority transcended the laws of Neuchâtel, so he offered them the usual social justification for the Salvation Army's behaviour. 'We want to see the drunkards, the thieves, the outcasts washed in the precious Blood of Jesus and changed into peaceful loyal citizens. This being our end, it is in the interest of governments to protect us and, in protecting us, protect themselves.' The jury then considered three questions: 'Did the accused take part in a prohibition meeting? Was the meeting dangerous? Did Miss Booth act with culpable intent to break the law?' To the first two questions the jury answered 'Yes'. They could hardly have done anything else. To the third – despite the overwhelming evidence – they answered 'No'. Kate Booth was acquitted.

The persecutions, however, continued. In April the following year, a march of the Salvationists was ambushed on the St Aubyn road and the Neuchâtel headquarters were attacked and wrecked. It was perhaps only to be expected that Switzerland – notorious for wanting its dubious peace to be undisturbed – should have reacted so violently. And Colonel Clibborn reported with philosophical resignation that he was 'getting beaten regularly every night'.[34] But Switzerland was only typical of what was happening all over the world. In Cape Town officers were arrested on trumped-up charges and imprisoned on the strength of evidence which no British court would have accepted. There were beatings – and prosecutions of the victims – in New Zealand and in the American Midwest, and in Brussels the government prohibited the Salvation Army from holding meetings anywhere in Belgium. In every country the frank judgement with which Mrs Booth began her letter to Mr Gladstone held true: 'Imprisonment would probably help the cause more than anything else.' The more the Salvation Army was prosecuted and persecuted, the more it prospered.

Abroad as well as at home officers and men battled on against all discouragement. In Melbourne, the Prison Rescue Brigade – meeting released convicts on the morning of their discharge and helping them to avoid an immediate return to crime – were so successful that they were incorporated into the penal code of the State of Victoria as places of safety to which magistrates could send first offenders as an alternative to gaol. Then the same colonial government made a grant of £1,000 towards an Army Women's Rescue Home. An 'Inebriates Home' was opened in Toronto and in 1885 the Hartford Brigade in Connecticut launched the Salvation Army's social programme in the United States. Eighteen eighty-five was to be an eventful year in the Army's life.

16

In Modern Babylon

All was far from quiet on the home front and it seemed that fate – Satan, as William Booth would have preferred to call the phenomenon – was determined to force the Salvation Army into situations which required either a dereliction of duty or an increase in unpopularity. Such an incident occurred on a cold February morning in 1885. When the appointed officer opened the door of the Army's headquarters in Queen Victoria Street he found a girl sleeping on the step. She had been there for most of the night and her story – though absolutely honest – might have been constructed to appeal to the passions and prejudices of the whole Booth family. The daughter of a country pauper, she had walked to London in search of work and entered what she believed to be service as a maid in a respectable household. The house in which she was employed was in fact a brothel, and the 'madam' assumed that sooner or later the new girl would be persuaded or coerced into becoming a prostitute. When, late at night, the girl had discovered the true nature of her situation, she had locked herself in the kitchen where she had been left in the belief that she would 'come to her senses when she wants breakfast'.[1] The cook's cynicism was confounded. The girl (a good chapel-goer) remembered that, while she was still at home in the country, she had seen a Salvation Army pamphlet in the back of a friend's Bible. It listed, amongst other activities, the rescue of fallen women. Although she had yet to fall, she escaped through the window of the brothel kitchen and asked a policeman directions to Queen Victoria Street.

Catherine Booth had preached redemption for prostitutes ever since her first visit to the Midnight Movement for Fallen Women in Bermondsey twenty years before, and Bramwell – Chief of Staff and quartered in Queen Victoria Street – shared his mother's burning conviction that prostitutes were more often sinned against than sinning. They believed that the devil worked through men to ruin women and that women were the devil's victims. That view was supported by Benjamin Scott, the City of London Chamberlain who had encouraged the Salvation Army's rescue work, and Josephine Butler, an early feminist, whose views on women in society complemented Catherine Booth's belief about women in the church. Catherine and Bramwell Booth had already supported Josephine Butler's campaign to repeal the 1864 Contagious Diseases Act – a law which both illustrated the extent of prostitution in mid-nineteenth-century England and typified the Establishment's attitude towards it.

The Contagious Diseases Act was the dark side of the reforms in health and hygiene which followed the Crimean War – the reaction to one piece of evidence about the British Army's medical condition which Florence Nightingale chose not to discuss with Queen Victoria. In 1864, one out of every three soldiers who appeared on sick parades was suffering from gonorrhoea or syphilis. Probably one-third of the whole British Army was infected to some degree. Venereal disease was not purely a military problem. Hospitals in both London and the provinces reported that 30 per cent of what were classified as 'surgical outpatients' were said to be contaminated by one or other strains of the virus. But it was the state of 'The Bachelor Army' – regulations insisted on no more than 6 per cent of married men in any one unit – which caused both public concern and parliamentary action. The Skey Committee was set up to examine both causes and remedies:

Two hundred women are newly affected every day in London.
They have no other means of obtaining food and shelter than
by communicating the disease thus contracted . . . These
loathsome diseases are six times more prevalent amongst British

than among French and Belgian soldiers – the number each
year being 70 from France against 442 from England in every
1,000 men. Turning to the army medical reports we find that
the frightening prevalence of the disease cannot be explained
away by temporary local causes although in certain regiments
and on certain stations the numbers are higher.[2]

The government's response – the Contagious Diseases Act – represented the view that since prostitution could not be suppressed, it
should be regulated. In consequence much of the Nonconformist
Church opposed the legislation on the grounds that it gave a form of
official recognition to the activity which was 'immoral, contrary to the
law of God, dangerous'. Libertarians objected to the form of control
that the Act authorised – registration, licensing and compulsory medical examination of prostitutes in eighteen garrison or dockyard towns.
Both groups doubted the provision's ability to 'secure the sanitary and
restraining efforts for which they were professionally enacted'.[3] When
the Act was renewed in 1874, the Wesleyans condemned its continuation. The campaign against the affront to liberty and womanhood
was led by James Stansfield (who resigned from the Cabinet to enjoy
the freedom to oppose the government) and Josephine Butler, who
recruited Catherine Booth to her cause.

Catherine Booth was opposed to the Act from the moment that she
understood its provisions – as much because it placed the blame for
prostitution on women as because of its implication that Parliament
accepted, whether or not it condoned, the practice. The more she
learned of its detailed provisions, the more she objected to them. An
'inspecting officer' was required to certify hospitals as appropriate to
the treatment of venereal diseases. And the Act empowered a Justice of
the Peace to order the examination of a suspected prostitute and, where
syphilis or gonorrhoea was diagnosed, order her detention in a certified
hospital for a maximum of three months. It also created a new
offence – punishable by fine – of knowingly keeping a diseased woman
on premises used as a brothel. Catherine Booth supported Josephine
Butler's reform campaign with unequivocal enthusiasm.

So it was natural enough that Bramwell – 'overwhelmed by the
burden of shame and sorrow' which the girl on the Queen Victoria
Street doorstep had made him feel – should ask Mrs Butler's advice

about what might be done 'to stop these abominations'.[4] The Salvation Army had already become involved in 'rescue work' – not 'born out of any doctrinaire theory but out of the involvement of the Salvationist himself in situations of human need'.[5] Salvationists had tried to arrange the escape of child prostitutes for years, generally under the supervision and encouragement of Mrs Elizabeth Cottrill, Converts' Sergeant of the Whitechapel Corps. It had all begun when she took a young woman – lured to London for prostitution – into her own home. Mrs Cottrill regularly found shelter for homeless families. When she took in the vulnerable girl, 'three families of sixteen people lived under the roof . . . but room was found for yet another'.[6] In May 1884 the Salvation Army had rented a house in Hanbury Street to provide a refuge for 'fallen women'. As a sign of the seriousness with which the subject was taken Florence Soper (Mrs Bramwell Booth) was made Superintendent. She stuck to the work for almost thirty years and, when she died, the Salvation Army, worldwide, ran 117 rescue homes. On that cold morning in February 1885 Bramwell Booth had no doubts about how the Salvation Army should deal with the moral and medical crisis. The question which he asked Josephine Butler was how to mount an assault not on prostitutes but on prostitution.

Mrs Butler believed that the horrors of the trade were intentionally obscured by men in high places who either enjoyed the girls' services or benefited from them. She recommended 'stirring up consciences. We have the votes of the people but we need to reach the upper classes and government too if we are to hope for justice and righteousness in public action.' Josephine Butler's target was the brothel-keepers, the pimps, the procurers and the men who used the girls and left them to die in sickness and poverty. Bramwell Booth shared both her anger and her contempt. But his main concern was the rescue of one class of victim – child prostitutes.

Child prostitution was common – indeed accepted – in Victorian London. Girls as young as nine or ten were 'bought' from their parents and sold to brothels all over Britain and continental Europe. But there is no doubt that numerically, if not morally, Bramwell Booth exaggerated the problem. Like his mother, he believed that prostitutes were victims not villains. If, as he convinced himself, many of them were sold into white slavery before the age of consent it was easy to believe that most of them longed for rescue and redemption. That theory – in fact it was no more than a hope – was supported by the parallel conviction that most adult prostitutes were tricked, bullied or blackmailed into a life of sin.

The pattern of cause and effect was not what Catherine and Bramwell Booth believed. The Royal Society's Report of 1877 had concluded that usually there was a one- or two-year gap between sexual initiation and the move into prostitution, and most often the women, far from being seduced by rich and vicious libertines, 'had their first relationship on a non-commercial basis with a man of similar social status'.[7] However, young girls were certainly bought and sold, and the domestic trade was certainly augmented by a thriving import/export business:

> When [Anile] was fourteen years old, the agent of some English
> speculator in human beings . . . proposed that she should leave
> her native country and proceed to England where, he said,
> there was a great demand for female domestic labour. The
> proposition was entertained by the parents and eagerly
> embraced by the girl herself who, soon afterwards (in company
> with several other girls, all deluded in the same manner) were
> leaving the shores of their native country . . . on arrival in
> England their ruin was soon effected and for some years they
> continued to enrich the proprietors of the house in which they
> resided.[8]

Such women did not, as Bramwell Booth imagined, make up a large part of the prostitute population. But there were so many prostitutes in the capital that total numbers of corrupted innocents was horrifyingly large. Howard Vincent, Director of the Criminal Investigation Department of the Metropolitan Police, giving evidence to the House of Lords Select Committee on the State of Law Related to the Protection of Young Girls, told their Lordships, 'I should think that prostitution in England was considerably in excess of the proportion of prostitution in other countries.' And the police 'were absolutely powerless'[9] to prevent the women from openly plying their trade:

> . . . the consequence is that the state of affairs which exists in

the capital is such that from four o'clock, or many say from three o'clock, in the afternoon, it is impossible for any respectable woman to walk from the top of Haymarket to Wellington Street, Strand. From three or four o'clock in the afternoon, Villiers Street and Charing Cross Station and the Strand are crowded with prostitutes who openly solicit in broad daylight. At half past twelve at night, a calculation was made a short time ago that there were 500 prostitutes between Piccadilly Circus and the bottom of Waterloo Place.[10]

The pattern of prostitution had, he said, not changed since the Royal Society's Report was published. Indeed it had barely altered in fifty years. Twenty years before the House of Lords Committee was set up, the London Police Survey had calculated that of the 30,780 women working the streets, 2,037 were under sixteen in the year of the survey. London Hospital treated 2,700 venereal disease patients between the ages of eleven and fourteen. A quarter of all the prostitutes lived and worked in a single police district, Division H. It included Spitalfields, Whitechapel, Ratcliffe and Houndsditch – the Booths' original London parish. Catherine Booth had been right on her arrival to denounce polite West End society 'which winked at such cruel slavery' and allowed 'the participators in such vice to escape with impunity'.

However, Catherine's view that most prostitutes had been lured, seduced or bullied into a life of sin was not borne out by Appendix B of the Select Committee's Report – 'Statistics About Prostitutes Compiled by the Chaplain of One of Her Majesty's Prisons'. Indeed, they confirmed the findings of the 1877 Royal Society Report.[11] Three thousand and seventy-six prostitutes stated the 'immediate cause' of their decision to work the streets – only 164 attributed their unhappy state to 'poverty or lack of work, 11 to the wish to support old or ailing mothers and 35 to the need to feed lazy husbands'. However, 1,260 'went on the streets as a matter of choice'. The appendix was hardly a scientific analysis of the causes and consequences of prostitution. It was, for example, highly unlikely that all the women gave accurate information about 'Age At Which Seduced'. But in that those figures were worth quoting they confirmed that 10 per cent of prostitutes were fifteen years old or younger. And they were poor. Only 44 of the 3,076 respondents could be described as 'better class', while 1,481 had been orphaned and more than half the total described their previous occupation as 'domestic servants'. Less than one in ten 'could read or write fairly', and 1,213 could not read or write at all. No doubt William Booth was horrified about how few of them attended, or ever had attended, a place of worship. Catherine Booth must have found the survey confirmation of her long-held view that prostitution was as much a social as a moral problem.

Acting on Josephine Butler's advice to stir up consciences, Bramwell Booth recruited W. T. Stead to his campaign. Stead, sometime editor of the *Northern Echo*, had known and admired William Booth in the north-east. He had come to London as John Morley's deputy at the *Pall Mall Gazette* and had been promoted when his editor joined Gladstone's Cabinet. Offered the job of Secretary of State for Ireland, Morley had replied that, having kept Stead out of trouble for so long, he anticipated no difficulty in managing that most distressful country. Stead was a campaigning journalist whose enthusiasm often turned into irresponsibility. His exposition of the 'new journalism' should have made Bramwell cautious about recruiting him to the cause. In 1884 alone he had led the campaign to send General Gordon to the Sudan and 'revealed' that the Royal Navy was incapable of meeting a French attack on British merchantmen. Gordon's expedition to Khartoum ended in disaster. There was no French threat to British shipping and, had one existed, the navy could have repulsed it. However, when Bramwell first told him that there were several thousands of child prostitutes operating in the East End of London he was unusually cautious. Less shocked than sceptical, he refused to believe that girls, still not in their teens, were being exported to France. But Benjamin Scott confirmed the stories from his experiences as City Chamberlain and Rebecca Jarrett, a reformed brothel-keeper who had joined the Salvation Army, added evidence of her own – including several Salvation Army women soldiers who had been taken off the streets when they were less than sixteen. Bramwell hit on the idea of exposing the shameful traffic by infiltrating a bawdy house. So he provided a volunteer who placed herself in a brothel as though she were a woman of doubtful virtue. She lived there for ten days, reporting what happened. Bramwell explained, 'We provided her with money so that she could pay the brothel-keeper suitably and, at the same time, express some fastidiousness in regards to callers.'[12]

We must assume that she was sufficiently fastidious (and sufficiently convincing) to pass the ten days without making the ultimate sacrifice for the cause. She was certainly able – despite her detached relationship with the customers – to confirm Bramwell Booth's worst fears that there were many young girls in the trade. Bramwell believed that his duty was clear. He launched a Salvation Army campaign for the age of consent for girls to be raised from thirteen to sixteen. Attempts to change the law had already been made in the House of Lords, which had three times passed at the Second Reading, what it called the Criminal Law Amendment Bill. But no further progress had been made.

Their Lordships' Bill was based on the recommendations of a Select Committee which had reported to Parliament in the strongest language:

> In other countries, female chastity is more or less protected by law up to the age of twenty-one. No such protection is given in Europe to girls above the age of thirteen. The evidence before the Committee proves beyond doubt that juvenile prostitution from an almost incredibly early age is increasing to an appalling extent in England and especially in London. The Committee are unable adequately to express their sense of the magnitude, both in the moral and physical point of view, of this evil thus brought to light and of the necessities of taking vigorous action to cope with it. They will, therefore, at once state the recommendations which they are prepared to make as to all matters to which they have referred.[13]

The recommendations, embodied in the Lords' proposed legislation, were built around the proposition that the age of consent for girls should be raised from thirteen to fifteen. The Bill was rejected by the Commons three times – largely on the argument that young women, who looked older than they were, would exploit its provisions first by seducing, and then blackmailing, rich old men. When Bramwell Booth heard that the Bill had been 'talked out' in an almost empty House on the day before Parliament adjourned for the Whitsuntide recess, he decided that the time had come to march. He launched his Purity Campaign with the enthusiastic support of his mother and the reluctant acquiescence of William Booth. The General had begun to fear that association with the campaign would prejudice respectable opinion against the Army.

The campaign began with a letter from Mrs Booth to Queen Victoria: 'My heart has been filled with distress and apprehension on account of the rejection by the House of Commons of the Protection of Young Girls from the consequences of male profligacy . . . If I could only convey to your Majesty an idea of a tenth part of the suffering entailed on thousands of children of the poor by the present state of the law on the subject, I feel sure that your womanly feelings would be roused with indignation.' The reply came from a Lady-in-Waiting, the Dowager Duchess of Roxborough. Clearly the Court at Windsor did not regard the subject as suitable for response by a male private secretary. 'Her Majesty,' Catherine was assured, 'fully sympathises with Mrs Booth on this painful subject,' but she could not intervene in what was a purely political matter. Mr Gladstone, to whom a letter was sent on the same day, was no more helpful and less sympathetic. Mrs Booth had asked for immediate action. 'I would entreat you to use your great influence in order to raise the age of responsibility for girls to seventeen and, further, that the Bill should confer power to search any premises where there is reasonable grounds to suspect that any girl under age is detained for immoral purposes.' The reply came from H. W. Primrose, private secretary. It was so terse that it may well have been intended as a rebuff. The Prime Minister 'could not at a moment like the present undertake to examine personally the subject you took on . . . The Government, by introducing the Bill, have shown their sense of the importance of the subject.'[14] The preoccupations of the present moment included the Sudan. General Gordon was besieged in Khartoum.

Catherine demonstrated the importance that she attached to the subject by speaking at a series of public meetings. At Exeter Hall she was particularly severe on a House of Commons which was at best indolent and at worst downright immoral:

I read some paragraphs from reports of a debate in the House of Commons which made me doubt my eyesight . . . I did not think we were as low as this – that one Member should suggest that the age of these innocents should be reduced to ten and,

Bramwell Booth. William's eldest son and heir apparent at the beginning of his long years of preparation.

Because, as Chief of Staff, Bramwell served at headquarters rather than in the field, his authority was constantly questioned by front-line troops.

William Booth conducts the marriage service of Bramwell and Florence Soper. They swore to put the Army before all other considerations.

Florence Booth (née Soper) – Superintendent of the 'homes for fallen women'.

Kate Booth. Sent over to France, 'La Maréchale' carried a banner which proclaimed 'Sang et Feu'.

The Salvation Army in India was required to live and dress as much like the 'natives' as possible. Frederick Booth-Tucker (on the right) illustrates the result.

W. T. Stead, the instigator of the plot to expose child prostitution. Each year, on the anniversary of his conviction, he wore the prison uniform which he regarded as a badge of courage.

Catherine Booth's last sermon. 'When we come to face the great eternity and look back on our past, what will be our great regret? That we have done so much? Oh no! That we have done so little.'

The last portrait. Catherine Booth died, as she lived, under the Salvation Army banner.

The train crash at Dean Lake, Missouri, in which Emma Booth-Tucker died. Her brother and sister – who had defected from the Army – were excluded from the New York memorial service.

In 1900, at the age of seventy-one, General Booth set out on the first of his annual motor tours. He had become a travelling evangelist again.

The Salvation Army flag —which the aged General carried up Mount Calvary — was hung above his bed at the moment of his death.

The General and the Anglican establishment. Nothing pleased him more than the approval of the bishops.

*William Booth in old age –
'Anything is better than
stagnation and being left alone.'*

*William Booth's funeral: 35,000
mourners filled Olympia for the
service and 5,000 Salvationists
marched six abreast behind the
coffin. They wore white
armbands to proclaim that death
was a victory.*

Oh My God, pleaded that it was hard for a man. *Hard – for a man* – having a charge like this brought against him not to be able to plead the consent of a child like that. Well may the higher classes take care of their little girls! . . . But what is to become of the little girls of unprotected widows? Of the little girls of the working class of this country? . . . I could not have believed that in this country such a discussion amongst so-called gentlemen could have taken place.[15]

W. T. Stead pledged the support of the *Pall Mall Gazette* and kept his promise with a form of investigative journalism which was a hundred years ahead of its time. The attack on the opponents of the Criminal Law Amendment Bill was only the beginning of his strategic plan. The full horror of child prostitution could, he believed, only be completely exposed by an eyewitness account of how easy it was to buy and sell a girl. His first attempts to counterfeit a life of sin proved hopeless failures. Two children whom he bought from an old procuress for £10 were so frightened by his cross-examination that they ran away – pausing only to accept £5 notes in compensation for experiencing a fate worse than a fate worse than death. A more professional plan was therefore drawn up, with Bramwell Booth's assistance. An outline of the scheme was sent – both for moral support and self protection – to the Archbishop of Canterbury, Cardinal Manning, and William Temple, Bishop of London. The Archbishop was scandalised. Manning and Temple gave guarded support. When the day of reckoning came, the involvement of the three prelates was of no help. The wrath of society was turned on W. T. Stead as the penalty for drawing public attention to aspects of London life which the Establishment thought best ignored.

The plan was to buy a child and export her to France, thus proving that it was regularly and easily done. Rebecca Jarrett, 'who, being an ex-brothel-keeper, understood the business',[16] worked in conspiracy with Madame Louise Maurez, still a procuress, and Sampson Jacques, a pimp. The first step in the plot was to 'buy' Eliza Armstrong, aged thirteen, for £5. Her mother, resident of Charles Street, Marylebone, was given a down-payment of £3 and promised the rest when Eliza's virginity was confirmed. Stead had heard that there was no demand for damaged goods. Madame Maurez certified the child *virgo intacta* (this being one of the abominable essentials of the transaction) and she was then taken to a brothel where Stead was waiting. Such was his boyish enthusiasm for playing the seducer's part – except the final act – that he prepared himself for the evening by drinking a whole bottle of champagne. He was, by taste and conviction, teetotal, but he had heard that champagne was the usual beginning to such evenings and he was determined to omit no detail of the proper preliminaries. As was the usual practice, Eliza was sedated with chloroform in preparation for her ordeal. According to Stead's later testimony 'she smelt the Chloroform bottle and dozed off into gentle slumber from which she unfortunately woke with a start when I entered the room to see if she was really asleep'.[17]

The dazed child was taken at once to one of the London lying-in hospitals where Dr Heywood Smith confirmed that her virginity had survived intact. Bramwell Booth met Stead and the (no doubt bewildered) child at Charing Cross and gave her into the care of Madame Elizabeth Combe, Superintendent of the Salvation Army's Rescue Home in Nîmes. As soon as she was on the package boat, Stead's story was ready for publication. A thirteen-year-old girl had been bought for £5 and shipped out of the country.

The first article was published on 6 July 1885. Three more followed. They included numerous examples of child purchase and prostitution and were embellished by gruesome anecdotes from outraged midwives and drunken brothel-keepers. The abduction of Eliza Armstrong was described in detail – some of it undoubtedly fictitious. In order to conceal her identity, she was given the pseudonym of Lily. The series of articles was entitled 'The Maiden Tribute of Modern Babylon':

> Then came the chance for Lily's mother. The brothel-keeper
> sent for her and offered her a sovereign for her daughter. The
> woman was poor, dissolute and indifferent to everything except
> drink. The father (who was also a drunken man) was told that
> his daughter was going to a domestic situation. The brothel-
> keeper, having thus secured possession of the child, then sold
> her to the procuress . . . for £5 – £3 paid down and the
> remaining £2 after her virginity had been professionally
> certified . . .
>
> From the midwife the innocent girl was taken to a house of

ill-fame . . . where notwithstanding her extreme youth, she was admitted without question. She was taken upstairs, undressed and put to bed, the women who brought her putting her to sleep. The women then withdrew. All was quiet and still. A few moments later the door opened and the purchaser entered. There was a brief silence. And then there was a wild and piteous cry – not a loud shriek but a helpless startled scream like the bleat of a frightened lamb.

The Booths saw the revelations before they were published and Catherine wrote to her daughter in Switzerland. 'The first article is coming out in the *Pall Mall* tomorrow. It will cause a shaking. And time it did . . . I am going to hold some meetings with Mrs Butler on the subject . . .'[18] She went on to admit, 'I have told Bramwell not to send you the *Pall Mall*. You can do nothing away there and you could not possibly read it without feeling harrowed.' Mrs Booth was right to anticipate a sensation – though what followed was not the reaction for which she hoped.

The wave of almost instant outrage which swept through London was directed not against the perpetrators of the practices which Stead exposed but against Stead for revealing them. WH Smith refused to stock or sell the paper and on the day that the third instalment was published the offices of the *Pall Mall Gazette* were besieged by an angry mob. Only intervention by the police prevented the more violent demonstrators from storming the building. George Cavendish Bentinck MP – who had opposed the Criminal Law Amendment Bill in the House of Commons – demanded that Stead be prosecuted for obscenity. But the young George Bernard Shaw – who was one day to write both about the Salvation Army and a waif by the name of Eliza – made Stead an offer: 'I will take as many quires of the paper as I can carry and will sell them (for a penny) in any thoroughfare in London.' The promise to hold down the price was an oblique reference to the *Pall Mall Gazette*'s black market value. Back numbers of the 'Maiden Tribute' issues were being sold for several shillings a copy. Most other papers ignored the story. But Frank Harris, editor of the *London Evening News*, condemned the series as a squalid and sensational attempt to improve circulation.

It was not the hope of greater sales that drove Stead on. 'The deepest passion which moved him was for the victory of a righteous cause. He was a journalist. But he always subordinated his journalism to what he believed to be right.'[19] However, the interests of circulation and morality coincided. In one sensational week, the *Pall Mall Gazette* sold over a million copies[20] – many of the extra copies being bought by those godly citizens who condemned the publication of the squalid truth. William Booth – suddenly enthusiastic – opened the Salvation Army's international centre as a distribution depot, and cadet officers from the training homes hawked copies in the streets like news boys. The time had come, Catherine decided, for another letter to Queen Victoria.

> Your Majesty will be aware that since your last communication to me, some heart-rending disclosures have been made about the painful subject on which I ventured to address you . . . it would be a great encouragement to thousands of those engaged in this struggle if your Majesty would at this juncture graciously send us a word of sympathy and encouragement to be read at our mass meetings in different parts of the kingdom.

A different Lady-in-Waiting, the Dowager Marchioness of Ely, replied, 'The Queen feels very deeply upon the subject . . . but her Majesty has been advised that it would not be desirable for the Queen to express any opinion upon a matter which forms at present the object of measures before Parliament.'[21] More than the Ladies-in-Waiting had changed. Gordon had been murdered by the Mahdi's followers in Khartoum and Gladstone's ministry had fallen. The new Prime Minister, Lord Salisbury, had decided to revive the Criminal Law Amendment Bill. Catherine Booth responded to the Queen's message of constitutional neutrality with a rebuke which almost turned into a threat: 'I suggest that this is not a political question . . . All I wish to be allowed to convey to the people of England is that Your Majesty is fully in abhorrence of the iniquities referred to . . . I am proposing therefore to read the note which Her Majesty has been pleased to send me by your Grace at a meeting of 5,000 on Monday night in London and also at a large meeting in Yorkshire unless you have reason to believe that Her Majesty would have objection to such a course.'

The letter – or at least the unequivocally supportive paragraph – was read out at London meetings in Princes Hall, St James's Hall and Exeter

Hall and in Leeds, Manchester, Sheffield and Newcastle upon Tyne. Bramwell spoke at some of the rallies, as did his wife. So too did W. T. Stead, Samuel Morley and Josephine Butler. *The War Cry* of 18 July contained a 'Special Notice!' and urged its readers to support the 'Protection of Young Girls'. It announced that 'A PETITION to the HOUSE OF COMMONS for the above purpose will lie for signature at the various corps' headquarters throughout the country for the next few days. All officers and soldiers are earnestly desired to sign it and to obtain as large a number of signatures as possible.' By the end of the month, the petition contained 393,000 names.

On the day when the House of Commons considered the final stages of the Bill, the Salvation Army presented its petition to Parliament. The 'document' was a roll of paper two and a half miles long. It would have stretched from St Paul's Cathedral to Westminster Abbey. It called for four reforms – the age of consent for girls to be raised to eighteen, pro-curement for immoral purposes to become a criminal offence, the right to enter and search premises if it was suspected that young persons were being held there for the purpose of prostitution, and a fourth reform which was surely the work of Catherine Booth. Hitherto solic-iting had been a crime which only women could commit. The petition demanded that it be extended to men who propositioned women.[22]

William Booth would have liked to carry his four hundred thousand names to Parliament at the head of a great procession. But, it being a sitting day, bands and banners were not allowed in the precincts. So it was borne on a wagon, drawn by four grey horses and accompanied as far as Whitehall Place by one hundred and fifty cadets from the Clapham Training Home, 'a fifty-piece brass band and three hundred female members of the Army in their well-known uniforms. On arriv-ing there the petition was removed from the van and carried on the shoulders of eight officers into the House of Commons.'[23] Being too big to deposit in the pouch at the back of the Speaker's chair, it was left on the floor in the well of the Chamber.

Richard Cross, the Home Secretary, supported the Bill on behalf of the government. 'There is,' he said, 'no doubt that a measure of this kind is absolutely necessary.' The Attorney General, summing up, was equally enthusiastic. 'Almost everyone who has spoken has agreed that there is a crying evil to be remedied.' The Purity Campaign had achieved one of its objectives. The age of consent was to be raised to sixteen, a year more than the Lords had proposed. The Bill effectively outlawed brothels. But the clause which granted magistrates the right to search suspect premises was struck out, and the new Clause XI was added by an amendment moved by Henry Labouchere, a radical who warned that the 'greatest care should be taken not to confuse morality with crime'. His new clause contradicted that principle. It made 'acts of gross indecency between male persons' a criminal offence, punishable by prison. The addition was accepted without dissent. It remained law until 27 July 1967.

The Bill became law during the second week in August and seven days later 'a thanksgiving meeting of the Salvation Army . . . was held at the Exeter Hall where the chair was taken by Mr Booth . . . For his own part he did not expect very much from the Act,' but it was a step in the right direction and one for which he was prepared to take much of the credit. Certainly the demonstration which the Army organised had piled on the pressure first created by the *Pall Mall Gazette*. But Lord Salisbury, the Prime Minister, had been at least as much influenced by the findings of the Mansion House Group – including Lord Shaftesbury, Cardinal Manning and the Archbishop of Canterbury – as by the clamour in public meetings. Asked to examine the veracity of Stead's claims, it had done more than endorse his diagnosis. It had given support to his prescription. However, the General did not even acknowledge the contribution made by any of the other protesters. 'Had not The Salvation Army moved on the matter and had it not been for some of the revelations of the press, the Bill would never have become law.' The meeting was not in a mood to quibble about where the praise should fall. And it hardly noticed a strange aside with which General Booth's speech ended: 'Referring to the case of Eliza Armstrong, who was said to have been kidnapped by The Salvation Army, he desired to say that she had been rescued from danger and that she was safe and well and that an offer had been made to return her to her mother.'[24]

Few of the people in the hall had heard of Eliza Armstrong or had the slightest idea about who had accused the Salvation Army of abducting her. But once William Booth gave official recognition to the Fleet Street rumours, the secret was out, and although the meeting moved on – either putting aside or not even realising the risk of troubles ahead – it was only a matter of time before the storm broke. Catherine

Booth promised that the Army would soon 'make a raid upon the streets of London and rescue as many fallen women as they could'. She announced that £20,000 had been provided to set up Rescue Houses, under the supervision of Florence Booth. The Salvation Army did not believe in allowing redeemed sinners to slip back into vice.

W. T. Stead believed that the campaign should escalate. Before the end of August he was telling the St James's Hall Conference on the Protection of Girls that a London Vigilance Society should be set up. But before its work could begin, the story of how the scandal was exposed began to turn into a scandal itself. A heckler at the back of St James's Hall cried, 'Armstrong!' The rumours, to which William Booth had referred a week before, had now become common gossip in London – fuelled by the *Pall Mall Gazette's* rivals who were searching for stories of their own. When he heard the name spoken out loud, Stead lost either his temper or his nerve. 'I will tell you about Armstrong,' he shouted. He then described in detail the bogus abduction and the mock rape. The attacks upon him which followed were as predictable as they were unreasonable. Other newspapers wrote as if, by proving that a girl could be bought and sold, he had (in effect) admitted that he could not find an example of it actually happening. The summer campaign had, they claimed, been built on a sordid fake, created by a sensation-mongering journalist. Although, in the St James's Hall speech, Stead had explicitly absolved William Booth from all responsibility, the Salvation Army was accused of being a willing accomplice in the deception. The General, always determined to put his Army first, decided on prudence. When a rally was held in Hyde Park to support the *Pall Mall Gazette* and its embattled editor, the Salvation Army was 'conspicuous by its absence'.[25]

William Booth's fear, if not his behaviour, was justified when he was interviewed about the part that Rebecca Jarrett had played in the Armstrong case. On 1 September the reformed prostitute and brothel-keeper was arrested and charged with abduction. Once more, W. T. Stead insisted that he must take all the blame for what had happened. The police accepted his version of events and arrested him as well – together with Elizabeth Combe, Madame Maurez, Sampson Jacques, Dr Heywood Smith (who had confirmed that Eliza had not been harmed during the charade) and Bramwell Booth. They were all remanded at Bow Street Magistrates' Court and sent for trial at the Old

Bailey. The Salvation Army's many enemies grasped their new chance to denigrate its work. *The Freethinker* was typical:

> However the Armstrong Case terminates, it is bound to do
> Booth a great deal of harm. The public opened its eyes wide at
> his cadging of twenty thousand pounds on the strength of the
> 'revelations' and now it begins to see what a mischievous and
> dangerous organisation the Salvation Army really is, with its
> thousands of ignorant fanatics under the despotic control of an
> unscrupulous, self-seeking chief whose policy seems inspired
> by Simon Peter, Barnum and Fagin. We believe the trial will be
> a dreadful and perhaps a death blow to the Salvation Army.
> Like other pious adventurers, Booth will languish and perish
> from the disease of being found out . . . Could there be better
> illustration of the morality which flourishes in the atmosphere
> of religion?[26]

Old friends as well as traditional enemies turned on Stead. Almost forty years later, George Bernard Shaw told Stead's biographer that 'nobody ever trusted him after the discovery that the case of Eliza Armstrong was a put-up job and that he put it up himself'. Radicals who had come to Stead's defence were embarrassed that their anger had been directed against a simulated outrage – and irritated by their own gullibility. The Establishment regarded the exposure of Stead's stratagem as proof that the morals of the capital were not as low as trouble-makers suggested. They all awaited the anticipated convictions with undisguised pleasure.

The case turned on a single point. The purchase of Eliza Armstrong had been agreed with her mother, but Charles Armstrong – the child's father – had not been consulted and was not a party to the sale. In normal circumstances, the case might well not have been regarded as strong enough to go to court. But when Mrs Armstrong – abused by her neighbours for 'selling' her daughter – claimed that she had believed that Eliza was going into domestic service, the public outcry which followed made a formal prosecution inevitable. The charge was that 'feloniously and by force and fraud [the defendants] had led away and detained one Eliza Armstrong, a child under fourteen, with the intent to deprive her parents of possession'. Conviction on those charges, the lawyers claimed, would automatically lead to prosecution for assault.

Bramwell Booth remained remarkably cheerful – buoyed up by the belief that he had done no wrong. He had no doubts that, morally at least, Stead was Eliza's guardian and that her prospects were better (and her virginity safer) with the Salvation Army in France than with her family in England. His firm intention was to stand by Stead. But in 1885 he was still in thrall to his father. And the General's instructions were specific: 'You shall not say anything that links Bramwell with Stead. Any day some more unwise thing may come out.'[27]

The trial served to demonstrate how naïve and foolish sophisticated and clever men can be. In an apology to readers of the *Pall Mall Gazette*, Stead conceded that he had 'used a faulty instrument' and added that 'in matters so grave and involving questions so delicate, I ought not to have been deceived on a matter in which I pledged my personal responsibility'.[28] He did himself less than justice. His mistake was not self-deception but failure to understand the law – which allowed a man to buy a child if he obtained the consent of *both* her parents. Indeed, in his passion to expose an undoubted scandal, he had not even paused to consider what the law expected of him. He must, however, have understood that he was exposing the raw, emotional nerve of middle England. Once he was found out, its inhabitants were merciless in their retaliation. They wanted to believe that Mrs Armstrong had behaved in what she thought were her daughter's best interests or at least 'that there was no doubt that in time she became distressed by Eliza's absence'.[29] And they were equally anxious to be reassured that the radicals and social revolutionaries always acted from the most venal of motives. The horrors which he had exposed, even if they existed, ought not, they believed, be described in a way which offended decent people. In his summing up, Mr Justice Lopez reproduced most of the English middle classes' prejudices.

The judge employed his fiercest language in denunciation of the way in which Stead had 'deluged for some months our streets and the whole country with an amount of filth which tainted the minds of the children he was so anxious to protect and which had been, and ever would be, a disgrace to journalism'.[30] *The Times*'s editorial made up for his few omissions:

The name of England has been blackened before the whole world: the Continent has grinned with jealous delight . . . Now the microscopic eye of the law courts has been turned full upon one of the most important pieces of evidence and it has been found to be false and baseless. It is natural that in the circumstances all those who value the good name of their country should rejoice. Things are bad enough we know in all great towns and even villages, but there is no need to believe them to be as bad as fanatical sensation manages to make them out to be. It is a matter for rejoicing that a test case has shown that one of the gravest charges against the English perpetrators – the charge of selling their children for infamous purposes – cannot be substantiated.[31]

Mr Justice Lopez had no doubt that Stead had acted – at least in writing the 'Maiden Tribute' articles – from personal pride rather than moral outrage. 'It appears to me that you made statements which, when challenged, you were unable to verify. You then determined to verify the truth of your assertions by an experiment upon a child . . . An irreparable injury has been done to the parents of this child. They have been subject to the unutterable scandal and ignominy of having been charged with having sold their child for violation.' Having made his generally bogus point about the Armstrongs' wrongly damaged reputation, he then moved on to the question of Eliza's distress. 'The child herself has been dragged through the dirt, examined by a woman who has a vile character, subjected to chloroform . . .'[32] At the end of such a summing up, it was hardly surprising that the jury found Stead guilty of both abduction and assault. But they added a rider to their verdict. They urged the government to ensure the efficient and effective operation of 'the Act recently passed for the protection of children'.

Stead was sentenced to three months' imprisonment. Elizabeth Combe was discharged on the judge's ruling that she had no knowledge of how the girl who had passed into her hands had been separated from her parents. Sampson Jacques, the pimp, was convicted of assault and sentenced to one month's imprisonment. Madame Louise Maurez and Rebecca Jarrett – found guilty on both charges – each went to prison for six months, Maurez with hard labour. Bramwell Booth was acquitted on all charges. Judge and jury had accepted that he honestly believed that Mrs Armstrong was happy to leave her daughter in the care of the Salvation Army in France and that a letter, asking for the girl to return home, had never reached him. William Booth interpreted the acceptance of his son's innocence as complete vindication of the Army's role in the whole affair and determined that it should remain free of all blame. It was not his finest hour. Stead, on the other hand, was scrupulous in his insistence that all the blame should be attached to him.

There is no doubt that Stead felt bitter about the way that William Booth had abandoned him – indeed, refused to play any part in the campaign for his remission and release. That was led by Josephine Butler and certainly had some effect. In November, the Home Secretary announced that Stead was to be allowed the privileges of a 'first-class prisoner' and, unlike Oscar Wilde – convicted under Clause XI of the Criminal Law Amendment Act – came out of prison renewed rather than destroyed. His release was celebrated on the following day by a mass rally in the Exeter Hall. The Young Men's Christian Association presented him with a Bible and Mrs Ormiston Chance handed him a purse which contained 27,000 pennies – 'subscribed by the same number of women, high and low'.[33] Stead, who spoke for more than an hour, pledged himself to carry on the work. No senior member of the Salvation Army was present at the meeting to hear the hero of the hour express his gratitude for the support which the Army had given him, 'from the Chief of Staff down to the humblest private'[34] – thanks which clearly excluded the commanding General. But his resentment did not last for long. Five years later at William Booth's request he helped to write – indeed he probably wrote without acknowledgement – the great work on poverty which was published in the General's name. And the year after that he described his faithless friend as 'one of the greatest men of our time'. The modern Salvation Army has embraced Stead as its own. The broad-arrow uniform which he wore during his weeks in prison and on each anniversary of his conviction is now on proud display in the Army's Heritage Centre.

In the events which followed the trial, Catherine Booth played a far more honourable part than her husband. The great letter-writer petitioned the Home Secretary on behalf of the defendants, for whom she felt the greatest sympathy. 'One of the agents, Rebecca Jarrett, was herself the victim of male criminality at the age of fifteen and lived an immoral life for fourteen years.'[35] The admission 'the greater part of which time she kept a brothel' probably did nothing to encourage leniency. No one spoke up for Dr Heywood Smith, who had done no more than certify that Eliza Armstrong had not been harmed. He was, by resolution of the governors of the British Lying-in Hospital, 'removed from the medical staff of that charity'. He resigned his position as Secretary of the British Medical Association and was severely censured by the Royal College of Physicians. The Armstrongs themselves did rather better, becoming the objects of both pity and (rather more surprisingly) admiration.

In a letter to *The Times* Edward W. Thomas (who, according to the evidence given at the trial, had persuaded the Armstrongs to press for Stead's prosecution) insisted that he had done no more than 'investigate the allegation that [she] had sold her daughter and come to the conclusion that she had not done so but had been duped'.[36] A week later, Harry Bodkin Poland QC contributed to the growing quantity of Armstrong correspondence with the news that, 'since the conclusion of this case several persons have said to me, "Are you not going to do something for the Armstrongs after all the trouble and anxiety they have had in this matter?"'[37] He went on to praise Armstrong as a militia man with twenty-one years' service on his record who had been discharged 'in consequence of weak eyes . . . with a certificate of character, "Very good". I offered to supervise a testimonial fund.' Within three weeks *The Times* was able to report that 'a considerable sum has already been raised . . . Eliza Armstrong was, last week, in Princess Louise's Home for the protection and training of young girls. It is intended to give her two and a half years' schooling and then get her into service.' A dowry would be presented to her when she came of age. Money had also been provided to 'furnish the family [with] a new house and also to ensure for the payment of the extra rent for the first twelve months'.[38] Charles Armstrong himself was not forgotten. In the age of self-help, Mr Poland – who had 'absolute discretion to deal with the funding as he thought best' – made the wronged father a presentation. It was 'two sets of sweeping machines, capable of reaching to the tops of the highest chimneys built'.

17

Light Over the Water

The Times – which had played so inglorious a part in the trial of
Stead, Bramwell Booth and Rebecca Jarrett – had at least the grace
to report that 'for the year ending 30th September 1885 . . . so far from
the Army having been injured, owing to the prejudice created against
it by the Armstrong Case, it is stronger than when the year began'.[1] The
report listed the increase in numbers of both officers and corps at
home and repeated with evident resentment that the Army had claimed
much of the credit for the agitation which resulted in the passing of the
Criminal Law Amendment Bill. It also set out the details of the annual
balance sheet:

> The total income from all sources – apart from trading
> receipts – was £76,108-17-4½, which included £30,849-9-8
> towards the building fund; £13,523-12-7½ for the general
> spiritual fund; £11,973-2-8 for the training homes; £3,958-
> 13-3½ for the rescue homes; £3,634-7-2½ for the corps debt
> extinction fund and £2,607-13-1 for the foreign service fund.
> The balance in hand was £169-5-1½.[2]

No doubt General Booth had read the accounts with quiet

satisfaction – notwithstanding the minuscule size of the surplus which separated the Army from the evil of debt. For although the receipts were only £150 more than the previous year's income, even *The Times* had been forced to acknowledge the success of his work. But the grudging congratulations, far from heralding a new era of acceptance, marked the start of a new campaign of innuendo and vilification. *The Times's* report of December 1885 began the constant scrutiny of the Salvation Army's finances which was to haunt the General for the rest of his life.

Rumours had been spread for years. In the public houses, these had been stories of straightforward corruption while, in more elevated circles, William Booth was accused of the incompetence which comes from ignorance of money matters. Back in 1883 William Booth had launched a scheme by which 'friends, while securing, for their use, interest on their money, can give their capital to the Lord and have the pleasure of seeing it, during their lifetime, employed in His service'. The announcement was headed 'Salvation Army Bonds'. Catherine Booth, speaking at Regent Hall, Oxford Street, took the idea a benevolent stage further. Rich persons who invested in the Army might forgo even the gratuity and use it to finance help for poor families – thus absolving themselves of the sin of usury.[3] The response was immediate. 'Accountant', writing in *The Times*, urged potential investors in the Army to consider both the security of their principle and the likelihood of interest. Since William Booth had no income other than donations neither capital nor income could be regarded as secure. 'Friends of the Army should not allow their zeal to outrun their discretion.'[4] The allegation was naïveté not corruption.

The bonds were not in great demand. Then, in a fit of admirable honesty, General Booth confirmed, at least by implication, that anyone who invested in – as distinct from donated to – the Salvation Army would be entrusting their money to an organisation built on unreliable foundations. The Army, he admitted, had expanded more quickly than its income justified. The 'acquisition of barracks, all over the country, had been a crippling expense . . . Desperate efforts had been made to retrieve the deficiency but had fallen short of success. Present income was below expenditure.'[5] The admission was the product of pessimism which persisted through the year. His annual message to his troops – bitterly complaining about afflictions and persecutions – ended the litany of trials and tribulations with 'the ceaseless wearying fight with financial difficulties'.[6] The admission intensified the crisis by reducing confidence amongst potential investors.

So money continued to be a problem. But William Booth, confident that the Lord would provide, normally left such details to his subordinates. Occasionally he had a sudden inspiration about how to solve the financial crisis. It was the General who developed a chance remark about 'self-denial' into a regular source of income. Major John Carlton had told him, 'By going without pudding every day for a year, I calculate that I can save fifty shillings. This I will do and remit [to Army funds] the amount saved as quickly as possible.' According to legend, General Booth replied, 'There's an idea here. Whilst we ought not to ask our people to go without pudding for a whole year, I see no reason why we should not ask them to unite in going without something every day for a week and to give the proceeds to help the work we have in hand.'[7] By the time he set sail for New York on the *Aurora*, the first 'Self-Denial Week' had raised £4,820.

The Self-Denial schemes caused much rejoicing amongst General Booth's enemies, for they seemed to prove more than that the Army was in financial difficulties. An organisation which pays its employees starvation wages and then asks for a week of extra sacrifice seemed doomed to immediate collapse. But the critics underestimated the Army's resilience and its supporters' devotion. A year of frenzied fundraising produced the necessary increase in income. So the critics' tactics changed. The trading department of the Army 'produced a profit of £6,752 and altogether we arrived at the conclusion that £100,000 passed through the hands of the headquarters staff during the year . . . The chief observation to be made upon the application of this revenue is that, with the exception of the portion invested in building, the whole is spent and none husbanded.'[8] William Booth was not the man to worry about accountants' conventions. In September 1886 he left for the United States confident that the Army's financial future was assured. His enemies were even more certain that the income would be misappropriated. As William Booth boarded the *Aurora* on his way to New York, a man on the quayside shouted, 'That's the last we shall see of him.'

The American tour was not a success. What should have been a triumphant entry into his new kingdom had been badly organised. Worse

still it was, at least in Booth's own estimation, inadequately reported in
The War Cry. He was particularly angered by 'a piece of twaddle about
Quebec and two silly pictures' which recorded his brief trip across the
border into Canada. 'Had it not been too late,' he wrote to Bramwell,
who (as Chief of Staff) he held responsible, 'I would have taken the
reporting into my own hands . . . Never was such a big undertaking
supported by such staff.'[9] He returned to England on Christmas Day
1886, no doubt relieved that the American fiasco was over and hope-
ful that both the Army's income and its international expansion would
continue. The auguries were good. Kate was to marry Commissioner
Arthur Clibborn and the wedding day was set for 8 February. An expeditionary force had been prepared to plant the flag in Germany during
the same month. Ballington was given the title of Marshal and sent to
the United States, to consolidate control of the Army's American kingdom.

William Booth must have looked forward to 1887 with a confidence
which he had rarely felt before. The Army's future was secure and the
whole family was to move to new quarters at Hadley Wood in north
London. Yet it was to become a year of continual trauma which led to
absolute tragedy. Both previous years had been marked by illness in the
high command. In 1885, while William was forming his Cavalry Corps
to tour remote villages in caravans and the Life Guards to preach to
sailors and fishermen, George Railton – who to general astonishment
had found time and enthusiasm to marry a Salvation Army non-com-
missioned officer, Sergeant Marianne Perkyn of Torquay, the daughter
of a Nonconformist minister – was struck down by an unknown disease. He was sent to recover in the sunny atmosphere of South Africa.
In the edition of *The War Cry* which joyfully announced 'his health is
improving', the editor and General also reported, 'my eldest daughter
has been ordered from the field by the doctors. My daughter of the
Women's Training Home at Clapton is still in forced retirement and
likely to be so for many weeks to come. My son, Herbert, is ordered
three months' absence. Miss Charlesworth is also invalided and others,
in every direction, are showing signs of exhaustion . . .'[10] Their sick-
nesses dragged on through 1886 but all the invalids showed a loyal
improvement when the General returned from America at the end of
1886. Then, in the New Year, there was a sudden deterioration.
Herbert was again sent to sea. His second restorative voyage took him

all the way to New Zealand. Eva Booth, doing field work at the Great Western Hotel in the Edgware Road slums, was the victim of one of the contagions which were common in the area and was incapacitated for eight months. Consul Frederick Booth-Tucker, who had withstood every Indian epidemic and infection for almost twenty years, was suddenly struck down by an unknown disease. Worse – much worse – was still to come.

Sometime during 1887 Catherine Booth had found a lump in her left breast. For months she ignored it. When she saw her family doctor, he warned her that the lump was probably a carcinoma. It took him until February 1888 to persuade her to have a proper examination. Sir John Paget of Harley Street confirmed the diagnosis. Catherine Booth had cancer. A second opinion from Mr Jonathan Hutchinson came to the same desperate conclusion. Both specialists recommended immediate surgery. Catherine Booth had only one question. What would the prognosis be if, as her instinct prompted, the cancer was allowed to take its natural course? Sir James was reluctant to answer her question, but, when pressed, gave the estimate for which she asked. If nothing was done to remove the growth, Mrs Booth would die within two years – possibly less. She was on her own when the prognosis was made. Either because of the demands of his calling, or as a result of a misplaced sense of propriety, her husband had left her to visit the specialist alone. Alone she decided to let God and nature take their course. Providence, in its mercy, did not grant her an easy death.

In his now lost diaries, William Booth recalls 'after hearing the verdict of the doctors, she drove home alone. That journey can better be imagined than described. She afterwards told me how, as she looked upon various scenes through the cab windows, it seemed as if a sentence of death had been passed on everything.' Catherine knelt on the cab floor and prayed. Her husband had been watching for her return and went out into the road to meet her. She was crying and it took some time for her to tell him the whole story. Then she asked, 'Do you know what was my first thought? That I should not be there to nurse you at your last hour.' Her husband, not surprisingly, 'was stunned . . . and could say little or nothing'. However, he recovered enough to yield to her insistence that he should honour his commitments. He was 'due that night in Holland for some large meeting . . . and she would not hear of [him] remaining at home'. The General returned to London on the following day. There 'then followed conferences and controversies interminable as to the course of the treatment which it might be wisest to pursue. Catherine's objections to an operation finally triumphed.'[11]

Bramwell Booth, at home when the doleful news arrived, wondered 'how could the war go on without her?' He had to struggle hard to complete the two Notting Hill meetings at which he presided, finding particular difficulty in repeating, with the penitents, 'Not my will, but Thine, be done.' But Bramwell was, by nature, an organiser. Next morning, he saw the doctors himself. 'They urged an operation. Dr Hutchinson spoke most strongly, adding that so important was instantaneous action, that he would not be willing to operate unless he could do so within a fortnight.' Bramwell made anxious and careful enquiries about the results of cancer surgery but they hardly 'justified the very strong opinions expressed in their favour'. Mrs Booth herself was absolutely obdurate, though – in the opinion of her son – for reasons which were less theological than self-protective. 'In all her long experience she had never met one case in which the use of the knife had not apparently increased the sufferings of the patient.'[12]

There was no suggestion, at least at the time, that Catherine either hoped for or anticipated divine intervention. Five years earlier, the Salvation Army – or at least some of its members – had dabbled in 'faith healing', without any recorded rebuke from the high command. In February 1885, Major Pearson had restored the hearing of two stone-deaf women from Hanley in the Potteries and gone on to confound his audience of thousands by successfully commanding a crippled woman to abandon her bath chair and walk.[13] Unfortunately, three days later, he could not repeat the miracle, a failure he attributed to the presence of unbelievers in the hall.[14] But Mrs Booth had no time for such nonsense. She expected God and nature to allow her cancer to take its course. And she was perfectly prepared for their joint will to be done.

A couple of days after William Booth returned from Holland the whole family, and one or two close friends, met at Hadley Wood. W. T. Stead – always full of ideas – had heard that Count Mattei, in Italy, had perfected ameliorative globules which might at least reduce the pain. Dr Kidd, a friend of the family who had attended Mrs Mumford in her final illness, agreed to find out where the Mattei globules could be obtained. It was the sort of treatment that appealed to Catherine Booth. But both her husband and son insisted that, even had the idea not been put to her, the whole family would still have been opposed to what they called 'the knife'. For either psychological or physical reasons, her health began to deteriorate at once. Count Mattei's globules proved entirely ineffective and 'electric surgery' – which Dr Kidd had thought might at least promote a brief remission – caused immense pain without impeding the progress of the disease. Catherine told him, 'Well doctor, if you fail with me, I shall not be altogether disappointed if you are able to obtain some information which will help you to relieve similar suffering in others.'

Either to make sure that Catherine was still alive or guarantee that she was fit to attend, Emma's wedding to Commissioner Tucker was brought forward to 10 April 1888, William Booth's fifty-ninth birthday. Tucker was dressed as an Indian beggar in a ragged turban and he approached his bride barefooted. A begging bowl was placed symbolically on the altar. Catherine's address to the assembled Salvationists was frighteningly frank about her condition: 'I have as you know been wounded and worsted in the fight and I have found it hard, sometimes, not be able to answer the bugle call and jump to the front as has been my custom for the last twenty-six years when there has been a need for me.'

For more than a year, the work of the Salvation Army went on around the dying woman's bed. The Booths lived for nothing except the Salvation Army. So the family home at Hadley Wood was like a railway station. 'There was ceaseless coming and going. Something was always happening. Something was always going to happen. On every side there was a rush, a bustle and a commotion. People called, telegrams arrived, messengers came and went . . . Poor Mrs Booth, to whom order and discipline had ever been the essentials of life, looked on in despair at all of this and grieved that to control such a storm was now beyond her power.'[15] That account of the dying woman's home life, provided by an anonymous lady who claimed to be a family confidante, should not be taken as proof that Catherine Booth wanted to abdicate from the business of running the Army. She would not have tolerated a lull in the Army's activities and she wanted to be part of its irresistible advance right up to the end.

In late June 1888, Mrs Booth preached for more than an hour at the

City Temple – returning, at the last, to a Congregationalist chapel. Her old friend T. A. Denny read the texts on which her sermon was based. She was back with St Paul, telling the London congregation as he had told the Corinthians: 'I am all things to all men that I may by all means save some.' Her sermon included what she clearly believed to be her Nunc Dimittis. In her terrible illness there were to be many valedictions, all of them sounding the advance. 'The great want of this day is the truth that cuts, convincing truth, truth that convicts and convinces the sinner and pulls the bandages from his eyes . . . And those of us who have acted upon it so much as to give up the greater portion of our lives to the service of God, when we come to face eternity and look back on the past, what will be our great regret? That we have done so much? Oh no! That we have done so little.'[16]

As she grew more ill she also grew more restless, and was taken for a time to the Oceanville Army Rest Home in Clacton, where she could hear the sound of the sea. But she was no more contented there than she was in Hadley Wood, and returned to London and the distractions of work at headquarters. It did little to ease the pain. William Booth's diary gives a graphic description of his wife's condition with an attention to detail which is, by any standards, unhealthy. After one graphic description of Staff Captain Carr – the nurse assigned to Catherine – dressing a gaping and putrefying wound, he records that his 'darling had a night of agony'.[17] He had begged her to take morphine to subdue the pain but she had refused:

> When I went into her room at 2 a.m. she had not closed her eyes. The breast was in an awful condition. They were endeavouring to staunch a fresh haemorrhage. Everything was saturated with blood . . . The agony expressed itself in her countenance and especially in her eyes, but amidst it all she managed to gasp out, 'Don't be alarmed, this is only physical. *He* has got me. He has got me.'

The condition described in that passage is not in any doubt and we must charitably assume that what might be regarded as a prurient compulsion to describe its hideous consequences was intended as proof of Catherine's courage and faith. But another diary entry, although almost certainly intended to be just as clear, is almost beyond comprehension – or belief. Had Catherine not been desperately ill – indeed, according to her husband, physically disintegrating – the reader would have assumed that William Booth was recording that they had made love. In any circumstances that would be a strange diary entry for a Victorian patriarch to make. Perhaps William Booth was fantasising:

> She was completely worn out and I sent them all out, resolving to have the night alone with her. What passed that night can never be revealed. It will never be half remembered by myself until the day of Eternity dawns. It was a renewal, in all its tenderness and sweetness and a part of its very ecstasy of our first love. It seemed, I believe to us both, in spite of the painful circumstances of the hour, a repetition of some of those blissful hours we spent together in the days of our betrothal.

Hard as it is to imagine what the passage really means, there is no doubt that it is the expression of an overpowering *physical* emotion. For good or ill, William Booth – a man obsessed throughout his life with his spiritual as well as his bodily health – was for the moment only concerned with things of the flesh. Whatever happened that night, William Booth's description of his feelings reveals a deep truth about his character. In love as in religion, William Booth was moved by a passion which allowed no moderation.

As Catherine grew weaker, she occupied more and more of her time in writing letters, particularly to beleaguered evangelists. The Salvation Army was still under continuous attack – from the newspapers in Britain and from the usual roughs in the countries into which it had expanded. Switzerland remained implacably repressive. In October 1888 a young middle-class Scots woman, Charlotte Lillian Stirling, was charged with the offence of proselytising. The crime had been committed in Orbe where Miss Stirling, a Salvation Army Captain, had invited a dozen children to an afternoon meeting. Her claim that she knew nothing of the law which prohibited evangelism was not an adequate defence, though the testimony of the parents – who raised no objection to the meeting – certainly should have been. Notwithstanding the families' evidence, Miss Stirling was sentenced to a hundred days' detention in the Castle of Chillon. Catherine wrote to her, 'One Prisoner to Another'. They read like a commentary on her own condition: 'I would especially warn you against allowing your present depressing circumstances to cast you down or lead you to fear that this event has happened outside the divine programme . . . remember "whom the Lord loveth he chasteneth".'

He was chastening Catherine Booth more and more. The cancer had begun to affect her right arm and she was no longer able to write in her usual way. For some weeks she persisted in an attempt to produce legible letters with her left hand. Then, with great reluctance, she capitulated and allowed her children to write the letters for her. Her message to the Army to mark the 1888 Self-Denial Week was dictated to a secretary who had been hired to help her. The idea of recording the invalid's words appealed to William's sense of history and to his wife's sense of vocation. From then on a shorthand-taker was continually in the bedroom.

The Self-Denial Week letter left no doubt that the Lord's servant was about to depart in peace. 'I am not without hope that our God, in His own time and way, will yet answer the many and fervent prayers which you have put up on my behalf by allowing me to join you once more in the fight.' She must have known that, without a miracle, she would only be able to reinforce their efforts from heaven. But she was a good regimental officer. The troops' morale had to be kept high. And a miracle of sorts occurred. She was still alive when Self Denial Week came round again in 1889 – a triumph of her indomitable will and her decision to accept the pain and forgo the surgery.

William Booth's sixtieth birthday was celebrated on 10 April 1889 by a Monster Banquet in Congress Hall and Catherine was determined to attend. Her husband, who could never resist an opportunity to publicise the Salvation Army, had already allowed the limelights of the London Stereoscopic Company into the dying woman's bedroom in order to take a final family portrait. The company's manager, two technicians and a photographer crowded round the bed. It would be easy to accuse William Booth of a callous disregard for his wife's feelings, but Catherine, no less than her husband, believed that soldiers should remain at their posts to the end. If her death provided a new opportunity to glorify the Army and the God who inspired its work, she expected her husband to grasp it, as he grasped every chance to fulfil his destiny.

Catherine was too ill to be fully on parade at the birthday celebrations, so she sat in a side room while the Army enjoyed a modest dinner of beef and potatoes under a great banner which proclaimed in letters four feet high 'GOD BLESS OUR GENERAL'. When the crockery was cleared away, she walked with assistance on to the platform and made a brief speech. Incredibly for a dying woman – who had little sense of humour even when in full health but revered her husband next to God – she made what was taken for a joke about William's domineering character.

General Booth – perhaps understandably on that occasion, but typically of his style at any event – had spoken chiefly about himself and dealt in detail with the early years of struggle and tribulation. In youth, he said, his evangelism had been inhibited by his meek nature – a quality which he had inherited from his mother. Perhaps he was (wholly uncharacteristically) caricaturing himself. Certainly the assembled soldiers took the irony for granted and laughed. Mrs Booth confirmed her husband's description of his youthful temperament. Meek he certainly once was – 'though you would not think it. No one knows the bolstering up and almost dragging up, I was going to say, that sometimes I had to do for him in those early years.' It was one of her rare admissions, at least in public, that William had human weaknesses. And it was her only recorded reference to the debt which he owed her. She kept that moment of pride for the last words which she spoke in public. She went back to Clacton expecting to die.

But the 'light over the water' which she saw approaching did not arrive for another year. There were regular bedside vigils which ended in surprise remissions, numerous last words which proved to be no more than loving messages and constant visits from friends who believed that they had come to say goodbye. After the Council of Officers met in London in November 1889, eighteen of the longest serving soldiers – led by Elijah Cadman, who had been with the Booths almost from the start – were deputed to make the sad journey to Clacton and pay the Army's final respects. Catherine, to their astonishment, cried uncontrollably for the first half-hour of the visit and the old friends feared they had brought the end nearer. For some time she was unable to speak. But they knelt together in prayer and sang, perhaps a little insensitively, a hymn which entreated 'Send us where we ought to go'. Catherine suddenly recovered some of her old strength and all of her usual composure. She then addressed them in the language of a soldier. 'I feel at this moment that I could put all my children into graves and go into a workhouse to die rather than I could see those first principles of the Salvation Army, for which I have struggled, reduced.'[18] There was not the slightest risk of the first principles being compromised. But it was a brave thing for a dying woman to say.

One afternoon, what was called a 'representative band' presented itself at Catherine's bedside – not to play but to pay the respects of the scores of Salvation Army musicians who had received so much encouragement from 'The Mother of the Army'. The bandmaster who led the delegation – himself a reformed drunk who had learned to play in order to entertain in public houses – felt 'unable to trust himself to speak' and had therefore prepared a letter which he expected Mrs Booth to be too sick to read. It expressed his determination to remain true to the principles of the Salvation Army and, for the rest of his life, only play for the glory of God. To his astonishment the dying woman read his letter with great care and then responded in detail. Her reply was the classic explanation of the philosophy which governed Salvation Army music:

> I rejoice in one or two points expressed in your letter very
> much; in one especially and that is the importance of keeping
> your music spiritual and using it for only one great end. We
> had a great deal of argument regarding the first introduction of
> Bands in the Army and a great many fears. I have always
> considered music as belonging to God. Perhaps one of you have
> heard me say in public that there will not be a note of music in
> Hell, it will all be in Heaven . . . and God ought to have it all
> here. But unfortunately God has not His rights here and the
> Church has strangely lost sight of the value of music as a
> religious agency. I think that God has used the Army to
> resuscitate and awaken that agency. While the Bandsmen of the
> Salvation Army realise it to be as much their service to blow
> instruments as it is to sing, to pray or to speak and when they
> do the one in the same spirit as they would do the other, I am
> persuaded that it will become an ever increasing power
> amongst us.[19]

And on and on she went – not simply setting out the Salvationists' theory of sacred music but also illustrating the Army's invincible ignorance. Gregorian chant was rising up from the Catholic churches which were encouraged in confidence by the restoration of the English hierarchy. Oratorio was about to be reborn and in the Methodist chapels where William Booth's faith was born hymns written by John Wesley's own brother were raising the roof. And Catherine Booth announced, with absolute conviction, that only the Salvation Army could praise God in song. Her views on secular music also illustrated a sad truth about the Booths and their view of the religious obligation. They cut themselves off from many of the temporal joys of life.

On 15 December she was so sure that death was near that the whole family was called into her room and the shorthand-taker was instructed to record her last message to the Army. 'At 1.18 a.m. the waters are rising but so am I. I am not going under but over. Don't be concerned about dying, only about living well and dying will be all right.'[20] She then spoke to each of her children individually and made each one swear eternal fidelity to the Army and to Bramwell who, by then, was accepted as his father's successor. Herbert was told, 'When the trials and the temper approaches you stick to Bramwell.' No doubt, in the moment of emotion, he swore that he would. But it was resentment against the Chief of Staff – and outright refusal to accept his authority – which, in the end, separated both him and Ballington from the Army. Assured that the family and the Army was united, Catherine settled down, apparently happy to die under the Salvation Army flag which hung above her bed.

Once again, she rallied. W. T. Stead wrote in love and sympathy that, 'like Charles II, she was an unconscionable long time dying' but, he added, 'never was a death bed turned into such good account'.[21] To her sort of Methodist, 'a death well died was as important as a life well lived'.[22] And Catherine Booth's death became an inspiration to generation after generation of Salvationists. But she contributed more than a moral example to admire and follow. Her constant messages – most of them thought, at the time, to be her last – were used to recruit new volunteers. In her quieter moments with William, they talked about his renewed obsession with the relationship between vice and poverty and she held him fast to the idea of setting out the Army's plan for fighting evil by feeding the poor. Through the long months of constant pain, she rarely enjoyed the tranquillity which her doctor prescribed. But the dying woman did not want quiet and rest. Her husband, despite his devotion, was pathologically incapable of providing a peaceful end to her months of suffering. The Army always came first. The logic of his position was impeccable. Catherine was on her way to Glory. He would have betrayed all that she stood for had he neglected a single opportunity to persuade one sinner to achieve the state of grace which had already guaranteed his wife a place in heaven.

Although not strong enough to attend the Annual Anniversary Meeting in July 1890 – special that year because it marked the quarter-century of a fighting force – she sent a message to the twenty thousand people in the Crystal Palace and thirty thousand more in the grounds. Inside the hall special arrangements had been made to make sure that not a syllable was missed. Catherine Booth's words had been printed on a huge strip of calico which was wound around two giant rollers. It slowly rotated to reveal her message, sentence by sentence. The congregation read her farewell out loud: 'My place is empty but my heart is with you. You are my joy and crown. Your battles, sufferings and victories have been the chief interest of my life for these twenty-five years. They still are . . . I am dying under the Army flag and it is yours to live and fight under. God is my salvation and refuge in the storm.'

She was still three months away from the final refuge and, although she slipped in and out of consciousness, she used the time well. There was a letter to Polly Ashton, the first woman to command a Division, expressing the hope that her promotion would 'help forward that honourable and useful employment of my own sex in the Master's service, which I have so strongly desired and laboured for'.[23] And in September there was a long and loving message – almost entirely concerned with the future – to Herbert on the eve of his wedding. Back in 1888, Emma's marriage to Booth-Tucker had been brought forward to make sure that Catherine was still well enough to be there. Almost two years later, Herbert wanted to postpone his marriage to Cornelia Ida Ernestine Schoch – a Dutch Salvationist – as a sign of respect to his dying mother. Mrs Booth insisted that he go ahead. The wedding took place on 18 September 1890 in the Congress Hall. Naturally the General presided. Mrs Booth was too weak to attend but her husband fulfilled her wishes. 'Set me a chair and put my portrait on it, so that I can be there in semblance if not in reality.'[24] Three weeks later she was dead.

There was one last message – a letter published in *The War Cry* on Saturday 4 October to promote the third annual Self-Denial Week. 'Now at his call I am going away from you. . . . The War must go on . . . Fight on and God will be with you . . . Victory comes at last. I will meet you in heaven.'[25] By the time that the Hallelujah Lasses arrived with their copies and collecting boxes in the public houses of Britain, Catherine Booth had, in the language of the Army, been 'Promoted to Glory'.

Ironically, in the days before her death, the doctors – who had so often forecast that the end was only days away – predicted that she would survive the three months to Christmas and the New Year. But on 1 October a massive haemorrhage changed the prognosis. All the family that was in England assembled in Clacton for a four-day vigil at the bedside. They sang 'We Are Waiting by the River', knelt in prayer, sang 'Only Waiting for the Angels' and knelt in prayer again. For much of the time Catherine was unconscious. Occasionally she spoke to God or to her family. 'Lord, let the end be easy for Emma's sake . . . Yes, now, Lord! Come now!' There was a storm on the Saturday night which must have heightened the Gothic climax of the occasion but, throughout Sunday, the weather gradually improved. The sun was shining at half-past three on the afternoon when she died.

William Booth was moved by his wife's death to write with an unaccustomed elegance about the importance of her work to the Army and society. Because of his temperament and because he really believed that death had no sting and grave no victory, he was sufficiently composed to prepare it immediately after her death.

> . . . she will live on and on and on in the hearts and lives of thousands of her daughters. Never before, perhaps, save in the case of one, and that the one 'most blessed amongst women', the mother of Our Lord, has there lived a saint who has had the privilege during her lifetime of seeing so many of her own sex encouraged and emboldened by her example, working out her principles and walking in her steps.[26]

The same theme was taken up by the *Manchester Guardian*, which wrote, 'She has probably done more in her own person to establish the right of women to preach the gospel than anyone who has ever lived.'[27] *The Methodist Times* generously described her as 'the greatest Methodist woman of this generation'.[28]

Catherine Booth's body was placed in a plain oak coffin with a glass cover. The Army was to be given the chance to see her for the last time. The brass plate which bore her name and the dates of her birth and death was also engraved with the words 'More than Conqueror'. The coffin was draped with the Salvation Army's flag for Catherine's last journey to London.

George Railton was given charge of the obsequies. He decreed that first the body should be taken to Clapton Congress Hall and lie in state so that Catherine Booth's soldiers could pay homage. The coffin, under a canopy in Salvation Army's colours, was placed on a catafalque at the northern end of the amphitheatre. Next to it was the empty chair which had filled her place at Herbert Booth's wedding. On it was the last portrait taken on her sick bed. More than 50,000 mourners, kept moving by cadets, passed through the hall in five days – 'ministers, lawyers, doctors, actors, postmen, police, railway officers, grooms, working men just come from their various trades and women from every grade of life'.[29]

At daybreak on 13 October the coffin was carried from Clapton to Olympia. The hall, which Barnum's Circus had 'filled' with 12,000 people, accommodated 36,000 for the funeral. And there would have been more had the turnstiles not been locked two hours before the funeral began at six o'clock. George Railton, anticipating the size of the congregation, had prepared service sheets which contained – as well as hymns and prayers – strict instructions: 'Rise . . . Read in Silence . . . Sing.' So, although barely a word which was spoken could be heard beyond the first half-dozen rows of mourners, the whole mighty gathering sang and prayed in unison. To guarantee harmony, signs were hoisted from the pillars giving the same instructions. When the point was reached at which they, and the service sheets, read 'Give Yourself to God', almost the whole congregation rose in a sign of surrender.

The cortège was led into the hall by Captain Carr (who had nursed Mrs Booth to the last) carrying the flag which had flown in the sick room. William Booth walked alone immediately behind the coffin. He was followed first by the family mourners and then by officers carrying the flags of countries in which the Salvation Army flourished, and the banners of the corps which Catherine Booth had helped to found. The streamers on the flagpoles and the bands on the officers' arms were not black crepe but white linen. They mourned their own loss but celebrated Catherine's triumph. *The Times* could not resist giving its own, not entirely unjustified, version of events: 'The sad occasion had been seized on by the authorities of the Army as an opportunity for making a gigantic display of forces, illustrating the cosmopolitan character and explaining by example the spirit of the movement over which they preside.'[30] Catherine would have applauded all those objectives.

The body was then taken to the International Headquarters in Queen Victoria Street where it lay in state until the next morning. Railton, with his unerring sense of the great occasion, marshalled a funeral parade fit for a Field Marshal. The ranks were formed up outside the Salvation Army's 'Home Office' on the Victoria Embankment, a quarter of a mile from the International Headquarters. The funeral procession was limited to 3,000 officers to avoid what Railton feared would be an unseemly crowd pushing and shoving its way along the road to the graveyard, and divided into fifteen sections, each one separated by flags and banners. It moved slowly until it halted outside the International Headquarters. There, Catherine Booth's coffin was placed on an open hearse and William Booth took his place immediately behind in an open landau. He stood and solemnly bowed to the crowd as the procession passed through the City, into Shoreditch and Dalston and on to Abney Park.

Herbert and Bramwell Booth – British Commander and Chief of Staff – rode behind their father, one on a black mare, the other on a russet gelding. The women – Kate, Emma, Eva, Maria and Lucy – were in the second carriage and behind them the third and fourth carriages bore the daughters-in-law, the grandchildren and the servants. The size of the cortège and its accompanying procession would, in itself, have guaranteed a crowd of gawpers. But most of the people who lined the route and the thousand mourners who were waiting in the churchyard were there out of love and respect for Catherine Booth and gratitude for the work done on their behalf by her Army. At the graveside it was again the words of St Paul that spoke for Mrs Booth. But this time he promised resurrection. 'For the trumpet shall sound and the dead shall be raised incorruptible and we shall all be changed.' Booth-Tucker spoke and so did Booth-Clibborn and Kate. Then William

Booth said his last words to his wife. They ended with a promise about his future rather than a reflection on her past. He was not a man to allow his genuine grief to interfere with his self-absorption:

> What then is there left for me to do? Not count the weeks, the
> days and the hours which will bring me again into her sweet
> company . . . My work plainly is to fill up the weeks, the days
> and the hours and cheer my poor heart as I go along with the
> thought that, when I have served my Christ and my generation
> according to the will of God – which I vow this afternoon I
> shall do with the last drop of my blood – then I trust that He
> will bid me to the skies as He bade her.[31]

Then he kissed the coffin and it was lowered into the grave to the sound of Herbert's hymn 'Blessed Lord, in Thee is refuge / Safety for my trembling soul'. First Railton and then Bramwell committed the ashes to ashes and the dust to dust. Railton, having cried, 'God bless the Salvation Army', Bramwell repeated the words of the Covenant of Service: 'We so solemnly promise . . . That we will be true to our cause. And valiant in Thy service saving souls.' It had been an Army life, an Army death and an Army funeral.

According to Harold Begbie, that night William Booth made a strange entry in his now destroyed diary:

> I am very weary in myself. I had stood balancing myself with
> the jerking of the carriage in its stops and starts for four hours.
> I could not see the people craning their necks trying to see me
> without endeavouring to gratify them. Some may find fault
> with me and say that I made an exhibition of myself. That is
> what I have been doing with myself for my Master's sake all my
> life.[32]

That paragraph of self-justification was written on the night of Catherine's funeral, within a few hours of the supposed offence occurring. It was not the hurt and angry response to press criticism stimulated by bigots of the established Church, nor was it a hurt letter, written to *The Times* to refute the allegations of a country vicar who could not believe in the altruism of the Salvation Army. It was a rare example of self-awareness leading to self-criticism. Perhaps it was the day's emotion that opened William Booth's eyes to the hubris which haunted him all his life. Or it may be that, without Catherine, he lacked the confidence which had once made him feel invincible. Certainly, after her death, nothing was the same again in either the Salvation Army or the family which founded it.

18

In Darkest England . . .

In the year before Catherine Booth died, Charles Booth – her unrelated namesake – published the first volume of *The Life and Labour of
the People of London*. William Booth certainly read the results of the
inquiry into the condition of the capital's poor – probably with and
possibly to his dying wife. The scientific description of suffering and
squalor taught the Booths very little that they did not already know.
And the philosophy of its radical utilitarian author (who spent the
fortune he had inherited from his family's steamship company finishing the work) was entirely alien to the Booths' view of life. But the
catalogue of despair and degradation came at exactly the right time to
stimulate the General into doing what he did best – organising action
to mobilise opinion behind somebody else's ideas.

William Booth's conscience had been stirred during the last months
of his wife's illness by the sight of the vagrant paupers who haunted
London's alleyways. Returning to Hadley Wood late at night after
campaigning in the south of England, he woke Bramwell to ask him if
he knew that 'fellows are sleeping out all night under the bridges,
sleeping on the streets?' His son was surprised by the question and
replied, 'Yes, General. Did you not know?' William Booth was not the
man to accept a moral rebuke. So he asked Bramwell in outrage, 'You

knew and didn't do anything?' When the General decided to do something himself, he had a wide range of texts from which to choose his remedy.

In 1844 Engels had examined *The Condition of the Working Class in England* and prepared the way for Marx's revolutionary prescription. Six years later Henry Mayhew published *London's Labouring Poor*, a lecture he had given to the Committee of West End Tailors. In Victorian England, empirical inquiry was almost always coloured by the moral precepts of the researcher. Mayhew pointed out the dangers of public houses being used as primitive labour exchanges. Forty years later, both Charles and William Booth made the same point.

It was during those four decades that poverty became a moral and political issue. Until the rural peasantry was herded into the crowded slums of the Industrial Revolution, the deserving poor was regarded as a contradiction in terms. In the country, paupers were thought to have the opportunity to help themselves out of poverty. In the towns, destitution was often unavoidable. So the distinction between those who could not work and would not work was born at least amongst radical opinion.[1] Thanks to the difficulty of finding adequate recruits to fight in the Crimea (and subsequent colonial wars), government and Parliament were beginning to count the natural cost of a malnourished and disease-ridden working class. Throughout the second half of the nineteenth century only a third of the men who took the 'Queen's shilling' passed the rudimentary medical examination.[2] And in 1867, the poor (or at least poor men) were given the vote and became a political force which had to be placated, if not offered real help.

Philosophers from the fearsome Karl Marx to the aesthetic John Ruskin warned that poverty would produce a revolution. Even William Morris, who wanted Trafalgar Square to be converted into an apple orchard, believed that the 'basis of change must be the antagonism of the classes. Commercialism and competition have sown the wind recklessly and must reap the whirlwind. It has created the proletariat and the proletariat must destroy it.'[3] Charles Booth's survey of the causes of poverty in *The Life and Labour of the People of London* could not have been made at a more propitious moment.

It was not his first attempt to describe the degradation of the capital's slum-dwellers. In 1883, the year of the Royal Commission on Housing,

he had published *The Bitter Cry of Outcast London*, which simply
recorded his experiences as he moved from hovel to hovel:

> Every room in these rotten and reeking tenements houses a
> family, often two. In one cellar a sanitary inspector reports
> finding a father, mother, three children and four pigs. In
> another room a missionary found a man ill with smallpox,
> his wife just recovering from her eighth confinement and the
> children running about half naked and covered with dirt. Here
> are seven people living in an underground kitchen with a little
> dead child lying in the same room. Elsewhere is a poor widow,
> her three children and a child who had been dead thirteen
> days.[4]

Charles Booth's surveys – which went on unremittingly for thirty
years – were far more scientific than anything to which William Booth
aspired, and they were far more concerned with diagnosis than with
remedy. In their way, they were the social equivalent of the biblical
analysis which the General believed stood in the way of practical
Christianity. On the occasions when Charles Booth did offer a remedy,
it was not the one which William Booth would have chosen: 'His solution to the crux of the social problem, the unproductive presence of
those he characterised class B in his survey – "those deemed very
poor . . . of a wretched and casual character" and "at all times more or
less in want" – was to remove them from the society of the deserving
poor.' To prevent them from infecting industrious workers with their
feckless ways, they were to be 'placed in state-created communes
where they and their children (temporarily separated from their parents) shall be educated to become useful members of society'. William
Booth would never have tolerated such a distinction. Charles Booth
'saw the self-interest of the entrepreneur as the stimulus for production,
distribution and management',[5] while William Booth believed that
every possible force for good, both spiritual and material, must origi-
nate in God. Indeed, both he and Catherine said and wrote, time after
time, that the appearance of progress which was not dependent on the
hope of salvation was a chimera.

However, even Charles Booth was incapable of separating the
evidence of his surveys from moral judgements concerning what

brought the observed phenomena about. In his analysis of London households in 1890 he contented himself with the fact that, despite all the talk of family solidarity, only 30 per cent of all households included grandparents. But when he went further afield he could not resist the temptation to moralise. Families in Barking, Essex showed 'a very wonderful and beautiful loyalty to parents in households' – which was clearly lacking in London. In Richmond, Yorkshire, 'filial duty was at a low ebb'.[6] That was William Booth's sort of sociology.

Charles Booth certainly shared the General's belief in the indissoluble link between poverty and depravity. But he was less romantic about the poor. That may have been because he relied for so much of his fieldwork on Anglican clergymen who, unlike the General, were gentlemen. William Booth, reading the London survey, would not have been surprised to learn that, of the 40,000 children whom it found went to school hungry, half were the victims of their parents' neglect. It confirmed his view that moral and physical regeneration must go hand in hand. His plan to save the disadvantaged and the dispossessed addressed both of those imperatives.

He also had the benefit of Catherine's constant advice – passionate about the needs of the poor but far less coherent than her memorialists suggested. The nearest approach she made to setting out a consistent theory of 'The Social Ministry' was published in *Popular Christianity*, a collection of lectures given at the Princes Hall, Piccadilly some time before July 1887. The lecture was called 'Sham Compassion and the Dying Love of Christ'.

It began with the sort of sharp comment which had made Catherine Booth unpopular – 'Benevolence has come somewhat into fashion of late' – but having produced a passage of radical rhetoric, she rejected, one by one, every radical prescription for reducing poverty. Education was ruled out because 'the cleverest of workmen are frequently the greatest drunkards and the most miserable of men'. Slum clearance programmes were dismissed as treating 'the poor like cattle' and developing 'buildings which pay liberal interest'. Even the importance of total abstinence was diminished by the surprising assertion that 'to look across the channel is to see abundant evidence that people may be almost clear of drunkenness without being, for that reason, any nearer to God'. Catherine Booth went through all the alternatives and came to the conclusion that 'if you want to elevate the masses, go and ask HIM

how to do it and if the answer comes, "Take up thy cross and follow
Me", OBEY.'

A year later, speaking at her daughter Emma's wedding, Catherine
Booth was even more sceptical about secular social policy. 'I am always
glad to hear of anybody doing anything good and kind and true and
helpful to humanity, whether it is feeding little boys and girls of the
poor or enlightening the ignorant or building hospitals . . . but that is
not the particular work Jesus Christ has set His people to do'.
Sometimes she thought that the 'spiritual ministry' was a sacrament in
itself. Often she saw the two obligations – sacred and social – as parallel forms of worship. But she had no clear, fixed, consistent theory of
social improvement. Her response to social injustice was always more
instinctive than intellectual. The passion with which she held her principles often provided a better defence against the Army's enemies than
would have been afforded by careful logical refutation – as she demonstrated when, in May 1888, the Reverend William Adamson, Vicar of
St Paul's, Old Ford, accused the Salvation Army of 'sweating' the
employees in its matchbox workshops. To the allegation that General
Booth was undercutting starvation wages, Mr Adamson added that no
Salvationist 'was allowed to do the work unless ordered by the General'
and that 'male and female members who lived in barracks competed
for laundry work and the price of laundry work came down accord-
ingly'. Bramwell Booth, in his father's absence abroad, denied the
accusations absolutely. Not only had the Salvation Army never under-
cut the price of matchboxes, it had never made, or offered to make,
matchboxes at any price. Nor had it ever competed for washing. The
allegations were pure invention, but they were repeated in newspaper
after newspaper. To some traditional churchmen nothing was too bad
to be believed of the Salvation Army, which they had come to regard as
both a threat to the established order and false friends to the poor, since
its particular brand of heresy encouraged ideas above the working-class
station. Fears that the Booths were about to lead a revolution were
increased by what the dying Catherine had to say on the subject, but
at least it disposed – by force of emotion if not strength of evidence –
of the allegation that the Salvation Army 'sweated' its employees:

It is never convenient for Ministers or responsible church
wardens or deacons (of the class under consideration) to ask

how Mr Moneymaker gets the golden sovereigns or crisp notes
which look so well in the collection. He may be the most
cursed sweater who ever waxed fat on that murderous cheap
needlework system which is slowly destroying the bodies and
ruining the souls of thousands of poor women . . . He may keep
scores of employees standing wearily 16 hours per day behind
the counter, across which they dare not speak the truth and on
salaries so small that all hope of marriage and home is denied
to them.[7]

That polemic summarises Catherine Booth's belief in the insoluble
connection between social and spiritual morality. It was a view of true
virtue which her husband shared, even though it was not always at the
front of his mind as it was of hers. Perhaps it was often pushed out of
his thoughts completely by the sacred hope of mass salvation and the
profane ambition to lead a great international movement.

William Booth resented the suggestion that, before Catherine's illness, he had cared little and done less to help the disadvantaged and
dispossessed. The Christian Mission had run soup kitchens in the
1860s and the gradual expansion of his 'social ministry' had included
the creation of 'shelters' for men and 'refuges' for women. Attempts to
market cheap food had begun in Whitechapel. Selling cut-price meat
and vegetables attracted far more antagonism than the rejection of the
Eucharist. The objection was elevated into a matter of principle.

The notion that providing material help would debilitate rather than
rehabilitate the poor was common in Victorian England. It was perfectly represented by the indomitable Reverend J. Llewelyn Davies
who, as part of his continuing campaign against the Salvation Army, set
out the dangers, as he saw them, of helping the poor in the way that
William Booth proposed:

I see with dismay that it is intended to open a 'food depot' in
this locality 'to supply 4,000 meals per day or 1,248,000 per
year' at a charge from a half farthing to a penny. If we knew how
much the meal is worth, we could calculate how many farthings
the Salvation Army is about to give to each applicant . . . I say
deliberately that I can think of nothing which would more
certainly injure the poorest part of our population than this

distribution of pennyworths to all comers . . . to feed the poor
like animals, with penny-a-liners standing by to report how
hungrily they eat, is an insult to their self-respect and cannot but
weaken what self-respect remains in them.[8]

The Salvation Army's social policy grew gradually with the years –
and with it attacks on the Booths' determination to lift up the poor. A
letter to *The Times* was supported by a correspondent who provided a
perfect illustration of why the Salvation Army was feared as well as
hated. M. D. Pearson of St James's Vicarage, Clapton, complained of
military music which 'disturbed the minds of people who do not like
melodrama'. But that was not his chief grievance. 'Those who have
houses to let are unhappy. Domestic servants are at a premium, for the
Army is largely recruited from this class.'[9] In a society obsessed with
class, William Booth – although he did not realise it – was disturbing
the proper order of things.

For reasons more concerned with status than theology, William
Booth resisted and resented the idea that he only cared for the poor.
His statement about the Army's aims was unequivocal: 'A man clothed
in broad cloth who is without God is just as much an object of pity as
a man clothed in rags.' He denied that the Army had ever claimed that
its exclusive purpose was to spread the word in the slums and casual
wards and amongst the drunkards and harlots. He did, however, feel it
his duty to 'go to those of the working classes who were without Christ,
either down in the whirlpool of vice and drunkenness or regularly
passing towards it'. The implication was clear. The Salvation Army
would help anybody. But the first call came from people who, if the
Army did not help them, nobody else would.

Two weeks after Catherine Booth died, William Booth's plan to rescue
the outcasts of society was published. A hundred years ago the printing industry must have worked at far greater speed than it does today,
for the Preface contained a tribute to the woman who had so often
reminded William Booth of the relationship between poverty and evil:

To the one who has been for nearly forty years indissolubly
associated with me in every undertaking I owe much of the
inspiration which has found expression in this book . . . it will

be an ever green and precious memory to me that, amid the ceaseless suffering of a dreadful malady, my dying wife found relief in considering and developing the suggestions which I have set forth.

In Darkest England and the Way Out began with a passage of autobiography – a temptation that William Booth could never resist. 'The misery of the poor Stockingers of my native town . . . kindled in my heart yearnings to help the poor which have continued until this day and which have had a powerful influence on my whole life.'[10] For most of that time, he had been absolutely certain that the social policies 'usually emulated in Christian programmes and normally employed in Christian philanthropy [are] lamentably inadequate'. A new remedy was required and General Booth was ready to supply it. He demonstrated the need for a radical approach by analogy. Henry Morton Stanley, by writing about his journeys across Africa in *Through the Dark Continent*, had caught the public imagination. William Booth proposed to do the same by making constant comparisons between the Congo and Darkest England.

Stanley had described, in the baroque style of a Victorian explorer, 'the inner womb of the tropical forest' through which he 'marched, tore, ploughed and cut his way for one hundred and sixty days. The undergrowth was so dense and stretched so far that the inhabitants believed the forest to be endless.' The literal description of Africa, by which Stanley had fascinated the civilised world, could have been an extended metaphor from one of William Booth's sermons: 'Some fell sobbing under a spear thrust, some wander and stray in the dark mazes of the woods, hopelessly lost, and some wait to be carved at the cannibal feast. And those who remain, compelled to it by fear of greater danger, mechanically march on, a prey to dread and weakness.' Stanley described the 'denizens of the forests' as 'two kinds of pygmies . . . one a very degraded specimen with ferret like eyes, close set nose, more nearly approaching the baboon than was supposed to be possible, but very human . . . The other [was] very handsome with frank, open, innocent features, very prepossessing.' Upon the pygmies 'had descended a devastating visitation in the shape of ivory raiders' who exploited 'the domestic affections of the forest dwellers in order to strip them of all they possess in the world'.[11]

Victorian moralists delighted in metaphor. William Booth found the

comparison between Central Africa and Britain irresistible. The ivory
traders were no worse than the publicans 'who flourish on the weakness of the poor'. The lower order of pygmies corresponded to the East
End of London's 'vicious lazy louts and toiling slaves . . . Mr Stanley's
Zanzibarians lost faith and could only be induced to plod on in the
brooding silence of dull despair.' So it was in the slums and stews of
Darkest England.

Having extended his image to breaking point, William Booth wisely
warned that it would 'become wearisome if it is pressed too far'. But he
ignored his own warning. The predatory slave traders were no different from London's pimps. 'Here beneath our very eyes . . . the same
hideous abuse flourishes unchecked. A young penniless girl, if she is
pretty, is often hunted from pillar to post by her employer, confronted
always with the alternative – Starve or Sin.' The righteous indignation
was balanced by compassion – a clear reflection of Catherine's view that
most prostitutes were victims of male wickedness. Down in the 'bot-
tomless perdition of prostitution, the fallen woman is far nearer the
heart of the One True Saviour than all the men who have forced her
down, and all the Pharisees and scribes who stand silently by while the
fiendish wrongs are perpetuated before their very eyes'.

The Booths' 'progressive' views on prostitution – condemnation of
the men and sympathy for the women – had already placed them in
firm alliance with a radical element within society, and, combined with
their clear identification with the poor, naturally excited the suspicion
that, in their hearts, they were radicals, or (even worse) socialists. The
introduction to *In Darkest England* contained passages which encouraged those fears:

> Nor is it only women who are the victims though their fate is
> the most tragic. Those firms which reduce sweating to a fine art
> and systematically and deliberately defraud the workman of his
> pay, who grind the faces of the poor and who rob the widow
> and the orphans and who, for a pretence, make great
> professions of public spirit and philanthropy, these men are
> these days sent to Parliament to make laws for the people. The
> old Prophets sent them to Hell – but we have changed all that.
> They send their victims to Hell and are rewarded by all the
> wealth that can make their lives comfortable.

Booth wrote *In Darkest England* against a background of both social unrest and growing political concern. In the previous year, the London dockers had struck for a standard wage of sixpence an hour and, after a month of picketing and protest, won. Public opinion – at least the increasingly educated and articulate working classes – was on their side. The dockers – casual labourers who reported for work each day, but worked at best for three, had once been the powerless poor. But, although they remained amongst the worst paid of British workers, by 1889 they were powerful enough to defeat the increasingly prosperous dock owners. Part of their success was due to the energy and ability of their leader, Ben Tillet. But Tom Mann and John Burns guaranteed the dockers' success by bringing out the engineers 'in sympathy'. Victory for organised labour was, in itself, frightening enough for the political establishment. But building on the experience of the dock strike Tillet, Burns and Mann began to organise unskilled workers. The result was the powerful force of New Unionism. And it was created by men who might – had their inclination not been for politics – have marched with the Salvation Army. Tillet was brought up a Methodist. Mann and Burns were campaigners for total abstinence from drink. Their great victory was won on the battlefield of London's East End where William Booth had first taken up arms against the devil. New Unionism and the Salvation Army were for the poor and of the poor.

So when – probably without realising the significance of his choice of language – William Booth used the vocabulary of the class war, there was general consternation amongst the still ruling classes. No one was more horrified – or expressed their horror more belligerently – than Thomas Huxley: scientist, philosopher and so aggressive an enthusiast for the theory of evolution that he was known as 'Darwin's Bulldog'. Huxley wrote – and seemed, despite his intellectual distinction, to believe – that 'the ultimate object of [William Booth's] plots is the establishment of a sort of Methodist Jacobin Club with vigilance committees, under the name of Salvation Army Corps, scattered all over the country'. Huxley – a wise man behaving foolishly – was deceived by the rhetoric. William Booth, who was anti- rather than unintellectual, took no more interest in ideology than in theology. But his language was fearsome. 'The foul and fetid breath of our slums is almost as poisonous as that of the African swamp . . . Every year children are killed off by what is called defects in our sanitary system. They are really starved and poisoned.' But he did not realise the impact his words made on a nation which feared that continental revolution would be replicated in their green and pleasant land. A view of life which he thought had obviously been made in heaven was assumed by his enemies to have been conceived by Karl Marx in the British Museum. The aggressive language in which *In Darkest England* was written was certainly no more violent than that which William Booth used in a routine sermon. And the allegation that he was taking up a political position caused him astonishment as well as offence. He did not need a man-made ethical framework within which to build his social policy. God had made one for him and called him to turn it into the social salvation of the world.

It took some time for him to accept that more worldly men than he would want to give his theory a political name. But when he was convinced of the dangers of brushing their allegations aside, his response could not have been more emphatic. Undated notes in the Salvation Army's archives confirm his suspicion of politics: 'You will know that it is not my habit to speak on political questions . . . I have resolved that neither the Salvation Army nor any of the agencies shall be employed in political warfare on one side or the other.' Politics, he said, was unnecessary if, as the Salvation Army intended, 'men are made truthful, honest and benevolently disposed towards their fellow men' – exactly the argument used by Islamic fundamentalists against the established political parties. He went on to refute the allegation that he was a socialist. It was one of the few genuine lectures, as distinct from sermons by another name, that he ever gave, and it is reasonable to assume, from its theoretical (if essentially jejune) tone that it was written by somebody else. That somebody was almost certainly George Scott Railton.

Socialism, he said, 'implies compulsion . . . To begin with it involves the absolute supremacy of the state with regard to the fundamental liberty of the individuals composing the community . . . This supremacy would involve the complete mastery by the state of the whole population and their activities . . . For instance it would destroy all liberty in the selection of a wife . . . It would deprive the parents of the right to produce children and train them as they preferred or even to claim them as their own.' That was only the beginning of his denunciation. 'Socialism is unnatural . . . It extinguishes all freedom of action and makes a man a slave to the majority of the community. It stops the wheels of human progress and sinks man down to a lower level than the brute creation.' His belief that socialism would blunt the incentive to improvement and progress – whether or not it was justified – was at least consistent with his general view of human progress. The whole thrust of his social programme – and the central idea of *In Darkest England* – was that God had given men and women the power to improve, both spiritually and materially. Society sometimes prevented the light which shone within them from illuminating their whole lives. The Salvation Army had been created to remove the barriers which Satan had erected along the path of divine progress. He did believe that removing those barriers could, or should, produce a more equal society: 'Every servant would cease to be under any obligation to his master while every master would be brought down to the level of his servant and take the place decided for him by the Government, a leading member of which might be a man whom he had previously employed as a servant.'

In his memorial monograph – written with great affection long after William Booth had publicly criticised his character and conduct – W. T. Stead described the General as always being on the side of authority. But his whole life was devoted to making it possible for both masters and servants to improve themselves. He was not a socialist, or anything else with philosophic base, for his mind did not run to philosophy. Asked serious questions on the subject he always replied in gibberish. Towards the end of his life, W. T. Stead asked, without the slightest suggestion of accusation, if he had socialist inclinations. General Booth replied, 'I am a Socialist, a Salvation Socialist, and always have been. A Salvation Socialist differs from a Fabian Socialist because we begin at the other end. I am working in the tunnel at one end of the tunnel on one side of the mountain and your political parties or Governments are working at the other side of the tunnel.' Asked 'wherein does Salvation Socialism differ from Political Socialism?' he replied, equally vacuously, 'Primarily in this, that I deal with individuals first.'[12]

In fact the thought of questioning – even less of changing – the existing order of society had never passed through his mind. Nor had the notion of defending it. The social programme was no more and no less than an extension of his mission to save souls – necessary in itself but justified by reference to the Bible, not to any ideological text. George Railton, who was always dubious about the propriety of 'diversionary tactics' – both the social programme and the commercial operations by which the Army was financed – sought to put the whole initiative into a more religious context by devoting a whole chapter of his Booth biography to an address given by the General to his 'social officers' a year before his death. The speech was clearly written for posterity. It was intended to prove that *In Darkest England* did not mark a sudden change of his mission from saving souls to succouring bodies. Railton complained that 'most erroneously and unfairly, it has been widely assumed that the great work of the General was the establishment in the world of social institutions'. The evidence of the speech – including an appendix which listed 'the various social enterprises we have in hand' – was based on the view of social progress which William Booth took before he wrote *In Darkest England*. Railton wrote that social work was (in 1890, when *In Darkest England* was published) what it had always been – a means to an end. Its purpose was 'the alleviation or the removal of the moral and temporal evils which cause so much of the misery of the submerged classes and which greatly hinder their Salvation'.[13] William Booth's speech (at least as recorded by Railton) could not have been more explicit: 'Our Social operations, as thus defined, are the natural outcome of Salvationism or, I might say, of Christianity as instituted, described, proclaimed, and exemplified in the life, teaching and sacrifice of Jesus Christ.' That did not mean that its only purpose was the removal of inducements to sin. It meant – whether or not Railton's quietest instincts allowed him to accept the fact or not – that the scriptures proclaimed an obligation to help the poor which was right and necessary in itself.

William Booth went on to explain why he had not developed a co-ordinated social programme until 1890. It was not a convincing explanation. 'For many years after the commencement of my public work – during which time I had, as opportunity served, helped the poor in their distress – I was deterred in launching out in any great direction by the fear (so commonly entertained) that by relieving their physical necessities, I should be helping to create, or at least encourage, religious hypocrisy and pretence.' But he had changed his mind. Instead of fearing that men without homes and food would pretend to seek sanctity in order to gain a warm bed and a good meal, he decided,

'If they won't hear in any other way and accompany the food we give them with a message to which they are so determined to turn a deaf ear . . . In the very earliest days of the Army, therefore in order to reach the people who we could not reach by other means, we gave the hungry wretches a meal and then talked to them about God and eternity.' He did himself less than justice. The more he saw of hungry wretches the more he believed that failing to feed them was a sin in itself.

The claims that General Booth made for his plans were in general strangely modest – and did not honestly reflect his judgement on their importance. He claimed that he had 'left to others the formulation of ambitious programmes for reconstruction of the entire social system' and insisted that he was determined to avoid 'collision' with 'socialists of the state and socialists of the municipalities, with individualists or nationalists or any of the various schools of thought in the great field of social economics'. It was an implausible interpretation of a book which claimed (on the map of the world which was its frontispiece), to resolve the problems of crime, drink, shame, destitution, despair and death. In pursuit of a solution to all those catastrophes, William Booth took issue with 'those anti-Christian economists who hold that it is an offence against the doctrine of the survival of the fittest to try to save the weakest from going to the wall'. He was as much against the biological idea of an 'elect' as he was against the doctrine of preordination.

No matter how insistent General Booth's disclaimers, *In Darkest England* was unavoidably regarded as 'political'. Back in 1876, when he wrote *Heathen England*, George Railton had insisted that his natural parish was made up of those comfortable artisans whose 'houses are thoroughly respectable in position, construction and appearance'. But *In Darkest England* was explicitly concerned with 'those who, having no capital or income of their own would, in a month, be dead from street starvation were they exclusively dependent on money earned from their own work and those who, by their utmost exertions, are unable to attain the regulation of food which the law prescribes as indispensable even to the worst criminals in our gaols'. The 'utmost exertions' was a concession to those who believed help should only be available to the deserving poor. But there was no doubt that Booth intended to cast his net far wider than that.

The metaphor which illustrated the desperate condition of savages living in the industrial jungle was matched by a second image which illuminated the obligation to help in the rescue mission. It was borrowed from Thomas Carlyle, whose arguments in favour of the Zarathusian leader – expressed in *Past and Present* – William Booth found particularly attractive. 'There are not many horses in England, able and willing to work, which have not due food and lodgings and go about sleek coated and satisfied in heart . . . the human brain, looking at these horses, refuses to believe in the same possibility for Englishmen.' Booth seized on the comparison and extended it by insisting that every Englishman (no doubt he meant to include Scots, Welsh and the Irish) should be granted the standard of care enjoyed by a London cab horse – 'shelter for the night, food in the stomach and work by which it can earn its corn'. And he drew a striking moral from the way in which London cab horses are treated that allowed no dispute about his wish to help the undeserving poor: 'When, in the streets of London, a cab horse trips and falls and lies, stretched out in the midst of the traffic, there is no question of debating how he came to stumble before we get him on his legs again.' Booth's view was that he usually fell because he was overworked and underfed. But even if the misfortune was the result of self-inflicted wounds, the horse is helped up as quickly as possible – 'if not for its own sake, then merely in order to prevent an obstruction to the traffic'.

The problems of the poor, Booth explained, affected all of society. But in their selfishness, its prosperous members had foolishly believed that they could be insulated from the product of poverty. There had, he conceded, been a Royal Commission on Housing the Poor and a House of Lords Committee on sweated labour. But *In Darkest England* did not regard their recommendations as worth a mention. Charles Booth, on the other hand, was commended for producing the only analysis which 'even attempts to enumerate the destitute'. It was not a very scientific attempt. And it largely concerned Tower Hamlets, Shoreditch, Bethnal Green and Hackney. But William Booth believed that, from those figures, it was possible to make a rough estimation of the total number of paupers who were starving and homeless in all of London. General Booth conceded that it was a crude calculation. The four boroughs contained less than a quarter of London's total population.

The assumption on which *In Darkest England* based its calculations were, in the author's view, intentionally biased towards moderation.

They assumed that deprivation was not as great in any other part of the capital as it was in the boroughs which Charles Booth examined. He therefore doubled rather than trebled his namesake's figures for his estimate of the destitute in the rest of London and calculated that 'the poorest classes numbered 993,000'. He then made a similar calculation for Britain as a whole – assuming that East London had twice the proportion of homeless and starving families as the entire nation. On that estimate, 1,905,500 British citizens lived in extreme poverty. He then added 60,000 to his interim total to represent the numbers of prisoners in British gaols at any one time, and another 78,966 to include in his figure 'the number of indoor paupers and lunatics living in workhouses and institutions'. Assuming that 'at the very least another million individuals [were] dependent on the criminal, lunatic and other depressed classes', the grand total became 3 million 'or, to put it roughly, one tenth of the population' living in deprivation. Joseph Chamberlain had calculated that 'there is a population equal to that of the metropolis – that is between 4 and 5 million – which has remained in a state of abject destitution and misery'. Robert Giffin (a professional statistician who gave his name to the discovery that a fall in the price of potatoes resulted in a reduction in demand, since it released purchasing power for more desirable food) believed the figure to be 1,800,000. William Booth was happy to build his policy on an estimate modestly in between the two.

Booth saw the poor as inhabitants of three circular kingdoms, one within the other, on the pattern of Dante's vision of hell. 'The outer and widest circle is inhabited by the starving and the homeless but honest Poor. The second by those who live by Vice and the third and innocent region at the centre is people who live by Crime. The whole of the circle is sodden with drink.' His analysis of homelessness depended on often emotive descriptions of individual cases provided by Salvation Army officers. 'No. 7. Good natural looking man: one who would suffer and say nothing: clothes shining with age, grease and dirt. I saw him endeavouring to walk. He lifted his feet very slowly and put them down carefully in evident pain . . . "I have a brother-in-law in the Stock Exchange, but he won't own me. Look at my clothes. Is it likely?"' The 'typical cases' were not, as General Booth had once suggested, invariably sodden with drink. Indeed most of them were the deserving poor. 'Work, work! It is always for work that they ask.' The objective (if *ad hominem*) descriptions were held together by what critics could hardly fail to recognise as class-war rhetoric: 'They perish at the very door of the mansions which, maybe, some of them helped to build.' The questions with which the analysis of homelessness ended confirmed the impression of revolutionary zeal. 'As we have a Lord Mayor's Day, when all the well-heeled, furclad City Fathers go in state coaches through the town, why should we not have a Lazarus Day in which the starving, Out-of-works and sweated, half starved "in workers" of London should crawl in their tattered raggedness with their gaunt, hungry faces and emaciated wives and children in a Procession of Despair through the main thoroughfares, past the massive houses and princely palaces of luxurious London.'

The 'Darkest Africa' metaphor persisted – some of it absurdly far-fetched. Slave owners had managed to balance the demand and supply of labour and nineteenth-century Britain ought to be able to do the same. 'Yet at any moment, let a workman lose his present situation and he is compelled to begin anew the dreary round of fruitless calls.' The Salvation Army officers described the fate of an unconscious man whom they had found in St James's Park. He had walked without food from Liverpool, looking for work. When he died two days later, the Coroner's jury returned a verdict of 'death by starvation'. To prove that 'without God we can do nothing in the frightening chaos of human misery', the examples of the hardship and humiliations endured were completed with a note on the futility of earthly remedies. 'RP was a non-unionist. Henry F. is a unionist. His history is much the same.' No doubt the story of their tribulations was accurate, but it is hard to believe that the docker commented on his plight in the way described – 'Oh dear! Oh dear! Whatever shall I do?'

Richard O. – a man so filled with despair that he attempted to kill himself and his whole family – complained that 'our clergyman had never called on us or given us the slightest consolation, though I called on him a month ago'. William Booth, having damaged the established Church's reputation by repeating the story, added that 'it is no doubt unjust to blame the clergy and the comfortable well-to-do' – a very different view of society from that which he seemed to hold when he attacked the families in the 'massive mansions and princely palaces of London'. To help all the destitute, William Booth argued, would 'drag a Rothschild into the gutter'. Money alone would not be enough. Like

Wesley he believed that, for a new world, we first need new men. A change in human nature 'should be the first object of every social reformer whose work will only last if it is built on the solid foundations of a new birth. You must be born again.'

Politics, whether William Booth realised it or not, kept creeping into both his diagnosis and prescription. 'Avarice and Pride, rebaptised as thrift and self-respect, have become the guardian angels of Christian civilisation.' But at least drunkenness and fornication were still regarded as 'undisguised vices'. Even then there were attempts to call these vices by names which protected some of the guilty parties. Prostitution was a sin in point. 'The word is applied to only half the vice and that the most pitiable . . . The social burden of the vice is borne almost entirely by women . . . It is an immense addition to the infamy of this vice in man that its consequences have to be borne almost exclusively by women.'

That was a repetition of Catherine's view of prostitutes and prostitution and was accepted by her husband as much out of loyalty to her memory as conversion to her beliefs. It was complemented by what amounted to an anticipation of the Cycle of Deprivation – a fashionable sociological theory of the 1960s. 'The bastard of a harlot born in a brothel, suckled on gin and familiar from earliest infancy with all the bestialities of debauchery, violated before she was twelve – what chance is there for such a girl in this world?' Much as William Booth enjoyed denouncing vice, it was the sins of the flesh which he enjoyed denouncing most. So he drew attention to 'the terrible fact . . . that there is no industrial career in which, for a short time, a beautiful girl can make so much money with so little trouble as the profession of courtesan'. He estimated that the most successful prostitutes earned £4,000 in a year. To prove that 'fallen women are often as much the innocent victims of crime as if they had been stabbed or maimed', he gave 'case histories' of one hundred applicants for places in the Army's rescue homes. Only two 'took to the life out of poverty'. Fourteen blamed drink. Thirty-three had been seduced. Twenty-seven had been 'encouraged to sin by bad company' and twenty-four had made a 'wilful choice to go on the street'. Twenty-seven were destitute when they threw themselves on the Army's mercy – though the General did not seem to have considered the possibility that their poverty contributed to their conversion. Twenty-five, poorer still, arrived at the rescue home in rags. It had to be admitted, with obvious regret, that forty-eight were decently dressed.

For a man who hated alcohol – and blamed it for most of the world's problems – William Booth was remarkably understanding about what drove working men to drink. 'The tap room in many cases is the working man's only parlour,' and the 'gin palace, although poisonous, is (like so many other evils) a natural outgrowth of our social conditions'. He based his theory of criminal motivation on exactly the same analysis. 'The hereditary criminal is by no means confined to India, although it is only in that country that they have the engaging simplicity to describe themselves frankly in the census returns.' The notion of an annual Indian census of population only confirms that naïveté was part of William Booth's strength. So was his knowledge, based on personal experience, of the way the poor survived. Theft, he wrote, is 'in many cases due to sheer starvation' and church law allowed a starving man to take bread from wherever he could find it. However, the courts did not, and William Booth's apparent contempt for the law seemed to be confirmed by his judgement on the causes of crime: 'Absolute despair drives many into the ranks of the criminal class who would never have fallen into the category of criminal convicts if adequate provision had been made for the rescue of those drifting down.' *In Darkest England* denied the doctrine of original sin and blamed respectable society for the sins of the criminal minority. It was not the way to win friends in either church or state.

The paradox of William Booth's position was that, although he called for 'adequate provision . . . for rescue', he continually insisted that it was not, in itself, a certain remedy. He was able, to his own satisfaction, to demonstrate that society's mistakes could only be rectified by God. The Salvation Army would create the conditions in which men and women, offered the chance to lead decent lives, would find that the Holy Spirit reawakened the power for good within them. But without the acceptance of God's will and the hope of His love, every scheme for social improvement was doomed. Moral regeneration was a practical, as well as spiritual, necessity.

With his usual disregard for intellectual consistency, William Booth quoted, with apparent approval, a 'Liberal statesman' who 'regarded the present generation as lost'. God's redemption (which in that part of *In Darkest England* its author thought not available to adult criminals) was, however, at the disposal of their children. They were most likely to find that grace in the Arcadia which he hoped to build. It was William Booth's own version of William Cobbett's 'backward glance' – the romantic notion that life was happier as well as healthier before the Industrial Revolution drove God's children out of their rural Eden. 'The country is a breeding ground for healthy citizens,' he wrote. 'But unfortunately the country is being depopulated.'

The country offered the prospect of milk, fresh air and exercise under blue skies. Having presented a risibly romantic view of rural life he concluded from his demand for a return to innocence that one of the alternative schemes for improving the prospects of the working classes – the Education Act of 1870 – was a dangerous irrelevance: 'Educated the children are not. They are pressed through "standards" which exact a certain acquaintance with ABC, pothooks and figures but educated they are not in the sense of development of their latent capabilities so as to make them capable for the discharge of their duties of life.' That led him to a reiteration of his antique view of virtue. 'How many mothers of the future know how to bake a loaf and wash their clothes? . . . Home is destroyed when mother follows father into the factory.' In the country, 'darkness ends the day's labour and restores the father to his little ones'. In the town, 'our crowded homes of the poor compel children to witness everything'.

But there was, in General Booth's judgement, a certain way out of the industrial darkness which he had described. The pathway to light would not be charted by any of the existing relief agencies. The Poor Law offered outdoor relief under 'shameful and repulsive' conditions which destroyed a man's self-respect. It was, he complained – in anticipation of twentieth-century objections to the 'means test' – necessary to sell every piece of furniture in order to qualify for help. Refuge in a workhouse required a man 'to barter his liberty for the sake of food, shelter and clothing'. The Casual Wards were organised in a way which discouraged honest employment. A man was required to break half a ton of stone, 'simply to assuage the cravings of hunger'. And anyone seeking a bed on a Monday night was required to remain in the institution until Wednesday – thus extinguishing hope of any real employment that week. *In Darkest England* had no doubt that 'if anything is to be done for these men, it must be done by other agencies than those which prevail in the administration of the Poor Law'.

He was equally certain that the private charities could not achieve the essential objective of stimulating 'a desire to lead an honest life'. Mass emigration was dismissed as worse than a panacea. 'It is simply criminal to take a multitude of untrained men and women and land them, penniless and helpless, on a new continent.' Trade unions had, in theory, many great advantages. But, in the twenty years since 'combination was set free', only 1.5 million men had chosen to come together in industrial solidarity. Unskilled labour was 'untouched' and women were 'almost entirely outside the pale'. Thrift, although a virtue, provided no solution for men with nothing to save and to urge it upon the indigent poor was a cruel joke. Despite his 'intense sympathy with the aspirations which lie behind socialism' he believed that many of its proponents talked 'claptrap' and 'postponed all redress of human sufferings' until some distant goal is achieved. Having dismissed every other solution to the crisis of poverty, William Booth announced – with fine disregard for the ambitious scope of his own ideas – that he left 'the limitless infinity of the future to the Utopians'. He then described his own vision of Utopia – which he really believed was a practical plan by which, with the help of God, Britain could find its way out of the darkness. Despite all its limitations, it was designed to appeal to generous impulses and tender virtues.

19

. . . and the Way Out

True to William Booth's character – and the practical Christianity which was the hallmark of the Salvation Army – *In Darkest England and the Way Out* devoted 76 pages to analysing the nation's slide into modern barbarism and 200 to prescribing a cure for the moral and social degeneration. The first appendix set out 'the position of our forces in October 1890' – 2,874 corps or societies, 896 outposts, 9,416 officers. It also listed 'the social work of the Army', confirming that – with thirty-three rescue homes for 'fallen women' and as many 'slum posts' – his solution, though Utopian, was based on real experience.

William Booth's analysis of the social crisis which corrupted England ended with the concession that the deliverance from darkness would be a 'stupendous undertaking only to be attempted by men who believe in the reformation of human nature in every form'. The prescription began by describing the 'essentials of success'. The first requirement was 'to change the man when it is his character and conduct which constitute the reasons for his failure in the battle of life'. The second was a 'change [in] the circumstances of the individual when they are the cause of the critical condition and beyond his control'. Having almost bridged the gap between free will and economic determinism, he laid down five other principles which were almost as vital to the success of his crusade. 'Any remedy worthy of consideration must be on a scale commensurate with the evil with which it proposes to deal.' It needed to be permanent as well as large and (as the General might have expected his readers to take for granted) capable of practical application. The warning against creating a scheme which harmed the people it was supposed to help could be dismissed as obvious and unnecessary, had it not been included to deflect the assaults of those critics who believed that charity debilitates all who receive it. The final necessity – the need to avoid assisting one class at the expense of the other – was a pious hope that William Booth should have known could never be realised. The more young women the Salvation Army saved, the more the Reverend H. D. Pearson and his friends would have to pay for their domestic servants. The scheme of national regeneration proposed in *In Darkest England* almost certainly failed all of the tests. Its historical importance was the attention it focused on the problem, not the solution which it proposed.

The 'solution' had three elements, each one indispensable to the others. Three self-sustaining communities – part co-operatives and part benevolent autocracies – were to perform different but related tasks in the general work of reformation and redemption. Each community was to be self-governing. But they were all to be sustained by the unquestioning discipline which made the Salvation Army so steady under fire. The 'City Colonies' were moral and social casualty clearing stations – harbours of refuge to provide basic necessities and temporary employment. They would, above all else, give paupers the hope that, one day, they would work themselves out of their destitution. Ideally, the men and women who had found temporary sanctuary in the City Colonies would, once their confidence and characters were improved, 'float' back to regular employment. Those who did not respond so quickly would pass on to 'Farm Colonies' where they would be settled in cottages and taught to cultivate smallholdings.

If the City Colonies were casualty clearing stations, the Farm Colonies were in part transit camps which prepared their more adventurous inhabitants for life in an Overseas Colony. The Salvation Army's overseas commands had reported that in South Africa, Canada and Western Australia there were 'millions of acres of useful land to be obtained almost for the asking'. General Booth proposed to fill them with refugees from the vice and squalor of the English slums. Nobody could claim that *In Darkest England* lacked imagination or that its author lacked ambition.

By their nature, the City Colonies – filled with the roughs and drunkards who were only one step away from the gutter – demanded the most careful organisation, administration and disciplined control. But William Booth believed that despite these exacting requirements, they could be established without much difficulty. He based his optimism on his experience of the Cheap Food Depots. 'Since the commencement of 1888,' he wrote, 'we have supplied over three and a half million meals.' He did not mention the ill-fated People's Market which Bramwell had struggled so hard and so unsuccessfully to keep solvent. So he was able to report a record of complete success. During the previous year, the Salvation Army's four depots had sold 116,400 gallons of soup, 46,980 gallons of tea and 192.5 tons of bread – a tribute to either the care with which the inventories were kept or General Booth's belief that the evidence of exact numbers, no matter how implausible in their precision, would disarm some of the sceptics.

The new Cheap Food Depots, like those which the Army already owned and ran, would not provide charity. There was to be no 'gratuitous distribution of victuals'. In the existing depots, soup was a farthing a basin for children and a halfpenny for adults. *In Darkest England* set out the full price list from tea at a penny a mug to meat and potato pudding at three pence per portion, as if the same tariff could be applied everywhere and for ever. Despite the rejection of charity, *In Darkest England* acknowledged that 'a certain discretionary power is vested in officers in charge of the Depots and they can, in very urgent cases, give relief'. That principle would be maintained. The text was 'silent' on the subject of whether or not individual officers were expected to meet the cost of compassion out of their own pockets. 'But the rule is that the food is to be paid for and the financial results show that working expenses are just about covered.'

The Depots also provided shelter and, unlike workhouses, welcomed men and women with a few coppers in their pockets. That was not the only difference between the hospitality offered by the Poor Law and the Salvation Army.

We hold a rousing Salvation Meeting. The officer in charge of the Depot, assisted by detachments from the Training Homes,

conducts a jovial free and easy social evening. The girls have
their tambourines and for a couple of hours you have as lively a
meeting as you will find in London. There is a prayer, short and
to the point, there are addresses, some delivered by the leaders
of the meetings, but most of them the testimonies of those who
have been saved at previous meetings.

There was no compulsion to take part in the meeting, though –
according to William Booth – most of the 'dossers' chose to do so.
Perhaps that is what allayed his previous fears about men taking advantage of the facilities not because they wished for salvation but simply
because they were interested in 'relieving physical necessities'. He was,
in consequence, not concerned about 'the risk of helping to create or
to encourage religious hypocrisy and pretence'. The new 'Shelters for
the Destitute', like the four which already existed, would be designed
to encourage clean living. The men would sleep in cubicles which
looked like giant packing cases, and were given mattresses, covered
with impervious American cloth, and under a single leather counterpane. All the beds would be hosed down each day. William Booth
could not recall a single disturbance in the two years since his first shelter was opened. He proposed – confident of success – to open one in
every town. .

He also proposed that a workshop and labour yard would be opened
at every night shelter. Again William Booth's confidence came from
experience. A trial had been carried out in Whitechapel during the
spring of 1889. The workshops had originally made benches and mat-
ting for Salvation Army meeting halls. The work was done on the strict
understanding that a day's labour was necessary to finance a day's food
and lodgings. Workers were classified in two groups. The first and
lowest class of labourers earned no more than their keep. The second
group – whose members had proved their sobriety, industry and cheerful disposition – were to be given five shillings a week to buy tools with
which they could ultimately find outside employment.

The Whitechapel 'factory for the out-of-work' was a simple enterprise. The extension of the idea into dozens of workshops, spread first
throughout London and then all over Britain, was inevitably more
complicated. Some of the proposals were bizarrely impractical. William
Booth proposed to establish household Salvage Brigades which

collected unwanted food from prosperous houses. 'Waste from the kitchens of the West End would provide sustenance for all the Out-of-works who are employed in our labour sheds.' Cast-off shoes were to be mended and sold second-hand. Old bottles were to be made into useful household utensils and tins turned into toys. A chain of second-hand book shops was to be set up and old newspapers collected for pulping and reprocessing. *In Darkest England* proposed to provide every one of London's 500,000 houses with a tub or sack in which to deposit its valuable waste – at an estimated cost of £25,000.

The waste collection schemes, indeed the City Colonies in general, were not, however, anything like as Utopian – to Booth a term of abuse – as his plans for the Farm Colonies. The practicality of the scheme can be judged from a single sentence from *In Darkest England*: 'While other people talk of reclaiming Salisbury Plain and cultivating the bleak moorlands of the North, I think of the hundreds of square miles that lie in long ribbons on the sides of our railways.' That is an idea which has come to thousands of travelling schoolboys who, like the General, never paused to consider the ease with which they could be cultivated or the cost of collecting 'fruit enough to supply all the jam that Crosse & Blackwell ever boiled'.

However, the main work was to be done on smallholdings, into which estates of 500–1,000 acres – leased within easy distance of London – would be divided. There is no evidence that either William Booth, or those who assisted him, made any real estimate of cost or feasibility. He asked himself, 'Do you think you can create agricultural pioneers out of the scum of Cockneydom?' and gave himself the unconvincing answer that 20 per cent of the capital's homeless was made up of old soldiers who would readily take to the new discipline. His view of metropolitan women was even more romantic. 'The poor lost girls on the streets of London' would be overjoyed to 'exchange the pavements of Piccadilly for the strawberry beds of Essex and Kent'. Most farm colonists would, he believed, take naturally to the land. Those who lived up to his expectations would be given permanent tenancies – three to five acres and, of course, a cow. The rest would move on to the Overseas Colonies.

Colonies, wrote William Booth – in a fine exhibition of Victorian imperialism – are 'simply pieces of Britain distributed about the world'. That was, as well as an expression of English pride, a defence against the allegation that he was proposing little more than transportation. There were, he asserted, 'multitudes of people, all over the country who would be likely to emigrate could they be assisted in doing so'. The Salvation Army would provide the assistance by both preparing them for their new lives in the City and Farm Colonies, and by paying their passages. A ticket to South Africa cost £8. A special ship, chartered by the Salvation Army, would save £1 or more on each passenger and allow the organisers to 'avoid the consequences of idleness' by organising work during the journey. There would also be ample opportunities for Army officers to preach and pray. William Booth thought of his ships as 'floating temples'.

The Colonies were certainly crucial to the plan to lead England out of darkness. Their creation, at least on the scale that William Booth envisaged, was incapable of realisation. The Overseas Colonies were destined to be stillborn, the Farm Colonies to have a brief and limited life, but at least the first stage of the plan to guarantee that the rescue homes 'for destitute men and fallen women' were set up in every town of any size was put into operation. And, in a modern form, they operate still. Equally important, *In Darkest England and the Way Out* helped to establish, in the minds of social reformers, the cab-horse principle that Thomas Carlyle had laid down – the need to get a man on his feet first and enquire about the reasons for his fall later. And in the concluding chapters (described almost dismissively as 'More Crusades' and 'Assistance in General') idealism and practicality met in a way which made the Salvation Army the leader of progressive opinion.

The examples of 'practical Christianity' were based on officers' case studies and reported in daily newspapers. St Francis of Assisi was cited in support of the Salvation Army's operating methods – the personal association of the Army with the families which it aimed to help. 'Slum sisters' lived amongst, and in barely better conditions than, the men and women they hoped to save from degradation. As a result, they could speak on the subject with the authority which came from real experience.

According to the people who worked in the slums, the necessities included travelling hospitals (no more than 'a little van drawn by a pony'), designed to meet the needs of the ignorant sick who would not visit the great city infirmaries. *In Darkest England* also suggested the creation of a lost persons' bureau to search for the thousands of missing relatives – 18,000 in London alone – who had disappeared into the great abyss of Victorian cities. It proposed crèches to keep the children of the working poor off the streets, a Poor Man's Bank (as once promised by the Christian Mission) and a network of poor men's lawyers. Some ideas were fanciful. They included a 'matrimonial agency' to take the place of 'the chaste and celibate courtship' which William Booth imagined characterised country life in old England, and a scheme (which the General called Whitechapel-by-the-Sea) that was intended to give the poorest families a day or two of fresh air. The account of how the holidaying families would spend their time contained a rare intentional joke as well as an example of the unconscious humour which was more characteristic of his style:

> There would be shops for tradesmen, houses for residents, a
> museum with a panorama and a stuffed whale. Boats would be
> let out at moderate prices and there would be a steamer to carry
> people so many miles out to sea and so many miles back – with
> a possible bout of sickness for which no extra charge would be
> made.[1]

It was, however, the proposals that he made for prison reform which set William Booth apart from other reformers of his time. His views benefited from the experience of his 'best officers' – men and women who had themselves occupied cells, picked hemp and sewn mail bags. 'When a man has been to prison for the best of causes, he tends to look on the question of prison discipline with a more sympathetic eye . . .' Their judgement was that 'at present there seems to be but a little likelihood of any real reform in the interior of our prison'. So the real work had to begin 'where that of our prison authority ceases'. A hundred years on, that view is sill regarded as dangerously radical.

The Salvation Army had already established a home for discharged prisoners in King's Cross. William Booth promised that more were on the way, each one following the early pattern of preparing the discharged convicts for employment first in its own workshops and then in the wider community. Every discharged prisoner should be met immediately on release to prevent the search for food and shelter driving them back to their criminal ways. The Salvation Army was willing to accept responsibility for teaching trades and finding jobs – as long as it could find the money to finance the scheme. Although, according to *In Darkest England*, rehabilitation would ultimately be dependent on enrolment in a Farm or Overseas Colony, William Booth's description of the steps which he proposed should lead to that blessing were admirably practical and progressive even by the standards of the late twentieth century. Welfare organisations – by which he meant the Salvation Army – should be allowed to enter prisons in order to prepare prisoners for discharge. In Australia the Salvation Army had already first been allowed, then encouraged, and finally officially sanctioned, to perform that task. Ten Prison Gate Brigades had been set up in Britain. Officers of the Salvation Army hovered outside the gaols in the early mornings, waiting to offer bread and redemption to the men who emerged. Giving them official status should, William Booth believed, be only the beginning of a new penal policy. Prison, he argued, was more likely to corrupt than to correct. First offenders should be sentenced to perform socially useful work rather than condemned to a custodial idleness. Of course the Salvation Army was available to organise what amounted to the first 'community service' scheme. Working out of the Army rescue homes would protect the 'ticket of leave men' from the humiliation of regularly reporting to police stations.

The Poor Man's Bank was less intended to hold a poor man's savings, which by definition did not exist, than to finance the small items of capital expenditure which poor men needed to get back on their feet. The proposal was land-banks on the German and Russian models and the aim was to replace the pawnbrokers and loan-sharks and so 'extend to the lower middle classes and working population the advantages of a credit system which is the very foundation of our boasted commerce'. A bank with no depositors or deposits was really not a bank at all, and with no regular income it needed a benefactor to finance its operations. The best William Booth could do to encourage confidence that a patron could be found was the assertion that the scheme would cost no more than 'a piece of a racehorse or an Old Master'.

If the hope of creating a viable Poor Man's Bank was in reality remote, the prospect of creating the ideal justice system for which William Booth hoped was so unlikely that even he accepted that it was unattainable: 'Confession of the most open sort: confession on the public platform before all the main former associates in sin has long been one of the most potent weapons by which the Salvation Army has won its victories.' But that was not the way in which universal justice could be achieved. Instead he proposed an almost equally optimistic scheme – 'a plain straightforward talk with a man or woman, for his or her common sense might remove the weight which was crushing sinners into despair'. The advice bureaux would be divided into several departments. Each one would offer specific legal advice – criminal, commercial, domestic.

Part of the problem with all William Booth's schemes was their names. They were always constructed to attract attention rather than to encourage confidence. A bureau, or series of bureaux, which offered practical advice and assistance with everyday problems – the real cost of hire-purchase, the interpretation of money-lenders' agreements and the dangers of doing business with tallymen and 'bills of sale merchants' – would have received nothing but approval from public persons of all persuasions. But William Booth chose to call his scheme 'The Court of Counsel and Appeal', and his pretensions, which so impressed the class he aimed to help, offended and frightened the people whose help he needed to make the scheme work. When he suggested that his advice bureaux should act as 'Courts of Arbitration', he antagonised more than the lawyers who feared that he wanted to trespass on their territory. His enemies began to argue that he was trying to create a state within a state.

They were wrong. *In Darkest England*, like every other aspect of William Booth's social policy, was intended to ameliorate the worst features of the existing order rather than to change it. 'Capital,' he argued, 'is not an evil in itself, it is good' – a reasonable enough assertion and also one which distinguished him from the socialists of various persuasions who were coming together to demand reform. 'The success of commercial enterprises was,' he believed, 'largely a question of management,' and workers should practice self-denial so as to acquire both the discipline that management demands and sufficient capital to set up on their own account. His view of social rescue was all of a piece with his view on religion and life. Discipline was next to godliness: 'It was the discipline of the revolutionary armies, the stern unbending obedience which was enforced on all ranks from highest to lowest which created for Napoleon the admirable military instrument by which he shattered every throne in Europe.' Discipline, not democracy, would characterise the Colonies on the escape route from Darkest England. Decisions would be taken by those qualified to govern – 'not counting noses but admitting no noses into the concern which are not willing to be guided by the directing brain'. The world was to be governed like the Salvation Army.

Only the Salvation Army – by 1890 boasting 10,000 officers and 4,000 permanent locations – could set up and supervise such schemes. But £1 million was needed to give it 'a fair chance of getting into practical operation'. The Poor Law and other forms of charitable relief cost £10 million a year 'without any real abatement of the evil' which they set out to obliterate. Given a fair start and using the money raised from commercial undertakings, the Salvation Army could do better by spending less.

Anticipating that he would be called mad to even contemplate spending such large sums of money, William Booth defended his sanity with an argument which was as ingenious as it was offensive to imperial opinion. When Britons were in danger abroad, no amount of money is too great to pay for their protection. After the King of Ashanti captured a handful of the Queen's subjects (not even British by birth), General Wolseley was sent to liberate them at a cost of £750,000. Freeing the two diplomats who had been imprisoned by King Theodore of Abyssinia had required the British government to spend the astronomical sum of £10 million. The campaign against Arabi Pasha of Egypt had cost £12 million and the unsuccessful attempt to rescue General Gordon in Khartoum had been almost as expensive. Why not, William Booth asked, spend a fraction of the cost of those imperial adventures on rescuing thousands of slum-dwellers?

In Darkest England ended with an appeal: 'I trust that the upper and middle classes are at last being awakened out of their long slumber with regard to those people who have hitherto been regarded as being forever abandoned and hopeless.' By awakened, General Booth meant become willing to donate money to finance the schemes which he had set out. To help in that process he included a donation form in every copy of the book. But he also needed 'men' to implement the proposals which he hoped to supervise, and he was careful to make clear that 'when I say men, I mean women also'. But there was a problem about recruitment which he conceded. Many of the potential recruits who were willing to serve the poor were not willing to serve General Booth under the conditions of Salvation Army discipline. But that was a detriment which had to be accepted rather than obliterated – 'I cannot soften conditions in order to attract men to the columns.' He made no attempt to explain why that should be. Had anyone dared to ask him he could have spoken of the importance of discipline and the virtues of leadership. The answer, in truth, was more simple. The Army was General Booth's creation and its successes and failures could only reflect the strengths and weaknesses of his personality.

The appendices to *In Darkest England* included a sketch of the Army 'by an officer of seventeen years' standing', an account of 'How Begging was Abolished in Bavaria'; a 'Description of the Co-operative Farm at Ralahine in County Clare' (which unfortunately was closed when its benefactor went bankrupt) and quotations from Thomas Carlyle on the 'Social Obligations of Nations', 'inserted at the earnest request of a friend who was struck by the coincidence of ideas similar to those of this volume'. The quotations all came from Carlyle's *Past and Present*, published in 1843 when William Booth was still a Nottingham pawn-broker's apprentice. But they did bear a striking similarity to the proposals that William Booth made forty years later. Carlyle believed that 'the multiform ragged losels,* runaway apprentices, starved weavers and thievish valets' were part of 'a broken population fast tending towards the treadmill' . They could contribute to their own sal-vation if they were subject to the sort of discipline imposed on the Horse Guards. Carlyle 'could conceive of an Emigration Service, a Teaching Service, considerable varieties of United and Separate Services all doing their work like it – which work, much more than fighting, is henceforth the necessity of these new ages we are got into!'

Clearly, William Booth believed that association with Carlyle was an intellectual distinction in itself, though he was anxious to make clear that he had not read *Past and Present* – quoted in his support as an appendix – before coming to his own, entirely independent conclu-sions. It must therefore have been particularly galling to have Professor

---

*'Worthless persons', according to the *Oxford Dictionary*.

William Ashley, an Oxford historian, condemn *In Darkest England* as no more than 'another Morrison's Pill' – a reference to Carlyle's warning that there is no instant cure to the disease of poverty. Professor Ashley was by no means Booth's harshest critic. He could at least 'in part understand the wonderful changes of character which had been witnessed in Salvation Army shelters as a result of the ardent sympathy and brotherly love' displayed by its officers. But that was a commendation of past efforts, not a sign of confidence in plans for the future. 'The analogy of other Salvation Army efforts and similar movements elsewhere and at other times makes it humanely certain that his regenerating current will not long continue to flow, especially when it is spread over a wider field . . . With such a machinery you must either change the vagrant's character or you will further pauperise him . . . In the long run, the latter result is more probable than the former.'

A second radical philosopher and philanthropist joined in the chorus of condemnation. Bernard Bosanquet – author of *The Philosophical Theory of the State* and Secretary of the London Charity Organisations' Society – produced a pamphlet, '*In Darkest England*, on the Wrong Track', which complained, 'You tempt men into begging with your refuges and free meals and when they have become beggars they go to refuges and to casual wards pretty indifferently'.[2] Bosanquet should have been on Booth's side. His great work, which he had already begun in 1890, argued that individuality could only flourish in a society based on co-operation. He also believed that poverty most often resulted from lack of moral will-power. Both of those concepts were entirely consistent with William Booth's own philosophy. But neither Bosanquet nor Ashley believed that the failures of will which produced unemployment and poverty could be remedied by either faith or prayer. And both of them feared – largely because of the Salvation Army's record of compassion – that when his grandiose plans collapsed, William Booth would have set up a vast network of outdoor relief which, instead of encouraging self-help, dispensed charity. Work was, by near universal agreement, the solution to every moral and material problem. Ford Madox Brown's painting of that name – surrounded by its Old Testament rubrics which asserted that without sweat there should be no bread – was the pictorial paradigm of that belief. Charles Booth's *The Bitter Cry of Outcast London*, published in 1888, described the starving match-girls singing 'One more day's work for Jesus', and one of the most popular sermons of the age, printed as a pamphlet and sold in tens of thousands, was entitled 'Blessed be Drudgery'. Even the most enlightened philanthropists were anxious not to give something for nothing. William Booth was equally against charity in the corrupted form of the word. But because he spoke on behalf of the poor, the rich did not believe him.

Bosanquet criticised *In Darkest England* on the strange grounds that 'want of employment, in nine cases out of ten when the plea is used, is not the cause of the distress. It is, as often as not, drink.'[3] The allegation that William Booth was insufficiently aware of the evils of alcohol was difficult to sustain. The complaint made by Lady Jeune – another pillar of the London Charity Organisations' Society – revealed the real reason that *In Darkest England* was so roundly attacked by social reformers who might have been expected to support it. Booth wrote as if he, and he alone, could solve the problem of poverty. Just as he justified his evangelism with the claim that the traditional churches had failed, he insisted that his new social policy was necessary because of the inadequacy of other welfare schemes and the indifference of the philanthropists who supported them. Not for the first time he offended those who should have been his friends:

> The impression left on the reader is that his scheme is the first
> that has ever been put forward seriously to grapple with the
> terrible problem. He seems to know nothing of the Ragged
> School Movement; or of the Church of England Homes for
> waifs and strays; or of the work done by Doctor Barnardo
> which, whether we agree with all his ways of carrying it on,
> is undoubtedly great. As regards every charitable enterprise,
> General Booth is silent. His book, from beginning to end, is a
> tacit indictment of the Church of England and the
> nonconformists.[4]

And so it was. William Booth was reluctant to acknowledge that any solution – other than that which God had confided in him – could bring an end to poverty and deprivation. He was also convinced, and with good reason, that the respectable churches – both Anglican and Nonconformist – would not reach out to offer either spiritual or material comfort to the undeserving poor. The attacks launched against him by the clergy of the established churches confirmed his criticisms. The biblical scholars with Oxford and Cambridge degrees could not believe that a man of his sort – both lacking education and doubting its importance – could produce a comprehensive plan for the alleviation of poverty. Nor could the Fabians, whose lecture series 'The Basis and Prospects of Socialism' had been published under the title *Fabian Essays on Socialism* a few months before. General Booth – in his silly uniform and supported by the brass bands and banners of his bogus regiment – was not the sort of man whom nineteenth-century reformers of left or right could take seriously, unless they thought of him as an ogre.

The most articulate criticisms of *In Darkest England* were set out with unyielding clarity by Thomas Huxley in *The Times*.[5] He rejected 'that form of corybantic* Christianity of which the soldiers of the Salvation Army are the Militant missionaries'. Huxley was obsessed by the belief that General Booth would, by mistake if not intention, make his socialist nightmare come true. Even if he did not actually hope to become the ruler of a red republic, the collapse of his welfare schemes would result in his regiments of disadvantaged and dispossessed taking over the world. Huxley argued his absurd case with great elegance. His criticisms were also conditioned by his opposition to religion in general and Christianity in particular. So, politics aside, he rejected the notion that 'the excitement of religious emotion (largely a process described by the Army as "rousing" and "convivial") is a desirable and trustworthy method of permanently amending the conduct of mankind'. He attacked what Booth regarded as the Salvation Army's strengths – the unquestioning discipline of its officers and their recruitment from the working classes and argued against all that Booth did and stood for with a savagery and an erudition which the General must have found bewildering. His comparison between the Salvation Army and the Franciscans of the thirteenth century was not the sort of exegesis with which the General was equipped to deal. It began with a description of St Francis' view on the creation of new religious movements:

---

*Corybantes were priests of Cybele (Phrygia in Asia Minor) who celebrated their festivals by clashing cymbals and behaving as if they were delirious.

If there was one rule rather than another on which the
founder laid stress, it was that the army of friars should be
absolute mendicants, keeping themselves apart from all worldly
entanglements. Yet even before the death of Francis in 1226 a
strong party, headed by Elias of Cortina the deputy of his own
appointment, began to hanker after those things, and, within
thirty years of that time, the Franciscans had become one
of the most powerful, wealthy and worldly corporations in
Christendom with their fingers in every sink of political and
social corruption . . . Who is to say that the Salvation Army in
the year 1920 shall not be a replica of what the Franciscan
Order had become in the year 1260.[6]

Huxley's real complaint was not the risk of corruption but the
certainty of religious fervour. He regarded Christianity as an alternative
to thought. William Booth was spreading a dangerously unscientific
doctrine. He mounted a frontal assault:

Few social evils are of greater magnitude than uninstructed and
unchastened religious fanaticism, no personal habit more surely
degrades the conscience and the intellect than blind and
unhesitating obedience to unlimited authority. Undoubtedly
harlotry and intemperance are sore evils and starvation hard to
bear, or even to know of, but the prostitution of the mind and
the soddening of the conscience, the dwarfing of manhood are
worse calamities.

As always, the Booths attributed opposition to unworldly motives.
Huxley was accused by Bramwell Booth of resenting (and therefore
retaliating against) the General deriding Darwin's theories. 'The General
had given an address at a time when there had been a great "push" by
the evolutionists. He said, after briefly describing the new development
that it all began in a patch of mud and that after a long time – ages and
ages and ages – out of the mud there came a fishy creature, something
like a shrimp. Then after more ages and ages and ages the shrimp
turned into a monkey which after more ages and ages and ages turned
into an infidel.'[7] Huxley, Bramwell Booth claimed, was offended by his
hero's work being treated with such disrespect, and when *In Darkest*

England was published 'probably said to himself, "Now is my chance to take it out of him."' Bramwell misjudged and underrated his man. However dubious his tactics, Huxley attacked the Salvation Army with genuine conviction. Given the opportunity provided by a friend asking for advice on the wisdom of (financially) supporting the Salvation Army, he denounced General Booth and all his works with a passion which sprang from the honest belief that religion was a force for evil. 'Darwin's Bulldog' had sunk his teeth into Christian fundamentalists who believed that God had created the world in six days. He was credited with coining the word 'agnostic', but he was essentially an atheist who both denied the existence of a supernatural being and had no doubt that the progress of civilisation depended on the universal rejection of what he regarded as superstition. During the Oxford debates on evolution he had said, and meant, that he would rather be descended from an ape than a bishop. Believing the Salvation Army to be a corrupting influence, he returned time after time to the attack. His second assault sought to expose what he regarded as the self-evident weaknesses which were obvious to anyone who read and understood *In Darkest England*.

In the chapter on 'Fallen Women', Booth had described how a young working-class woman had asked the Army to help her obtain redress from the rich man who had seduced her. 'We hunted up the man, followed him to the country, threatened him with public exposure and forced from him payments to his victim of £60 down with an allowance of £1 a week and an insurance policy on his life for £450 in her favour.' Huxley regarded the story – or claimed to regard it – not as the account of a chivalrous rescue but as a confession of blackmail. 'We consider that anybody, for any reason of jealousy or personal spite or paltry hatred might be thus hunted, followed, threatened and financially squeezed or ruined without particle of legal investigation . . . Surely it is not unreasonable to ask how far does the Salvation Army, in its tribune of the people aspect, differ from the Sicilian Mafia.' Huxley judged William Booth's behaviour to be 'as immoral as he hoped it was illegal'.

Huxley began to search for evidence to confirm his worse fears. He found a pamphlet entitled 'An Ex-Captain's Experience in the Salvation Army'. It was written by J. E. Redstone, a disaffected officer who, according to Huxley, wrote in 'simple direct language such as John

Bunyan might have employed'. The main cause of Redstone's complaint was nepotism. The Salvation Army was 'emphatically a family concern . . . it is Booth all over; indeed, like the sun in your eyes, you can see nothing else wherever you turn'. Huxley then added a few words of his own. 'While he and his family of high officials live in comfort, if not luxury, the pledged slaves whose devotion is the foundation of any true success the Army has met with often hardly have enough to sustain life. One good fellow told me that when he had nothing, he just went begging.' To make sure that no misdemeanour would go unnoticed by the general public, Huxley added that Ballington Booth was in the habit of addressing 'married men, apparently older than himself, as "dear boy".'[8]

Battle was really joined when William Booth spoke at a meeting in Regent Street Polytechnic on 'the subject of the scheme of social amelioration and reformation proposed by him in his book entitled *In Darkest England and the Way Out*'. The General mounted a strangely apologetic defence. His scheme, he said, had been particularly condemned because it was carried out by the Army which he led. 'But that was no part of the scheme itself and the Salvation Army did not oppose it being carried into effect by others.' That was as near to a downright lie as he ever came. The whole programme had been designed on the assumption that only the Salvation Army could put it into practice.

The second criticism was that he had made no provision in his plans for children. Well, he had propounded enough schemes for one man and 'the rest could be left for another* . . . His idea was that men and women should be saved as families.'[9] He was slightly more confident about obedience and discipline – two qualities which he regarded as essential to any successful organisation. But the 'best he could say about the Salvation Army's finances was that its accounts were regularly audited by the firm of accountants that examined the books of the Midland Railway Company'. Had Catherine still been alive, William's response would have been quite different. Instead of making a strategic

---

*This is probably the origin of the story that when William Booth met Dr Barnardo, the General had said, 'You look after the children and I will look after the families' – an incident which was reported in none of the near-contemporary biographies.

retreat, he would have charged his enemies head on and driven them from the field. Without his wife to give him confidence, his trumpet sounded an uncertain note. Encouraged by his adversary's obvious uncertainty, Thomas Huxley struck again at what he believed to be the greatest chink in the General's armour. Salvationists, he wrote, were

> poor, uninstructed and not infrequently fanatical enthusiasts, the purity of whose lives and sincerity of whose beliefs and the cheerfulness of whose endurance of privation and rough usage in what they consider a just cause demands sincere respect. All that I have hitherto said and propose further to say is directed against Mr Booth's extremely clever, audacious and hitherto successful attempt to utilise the credit won by all this honest devotion and self-sacrifice for the purpose of his socialistic autocracy.[10]

Huxley wanted the world to believe that his complaint was not against evangelism or even the Salvation Army. It was against 'Boothism'.

The indiscriminate assaults gave great pleasure to the Salvation Army's opponents – from orthodox churchmen to scientific humanists. But they also heartened the officers and men who served under General Booth's command. They were being persecuted for their beliefs. And the more they were persecuted, the more righteous they felt. Huxley was having the same effect as the Skeleton Armies. General Booth grew daily more famous and daily more certain that he was right. *The Times*, clearly conscious of the penalties of overt prejudice, tried to make Huxley sound more reasonable by announcing that it had made a careful assessment of his allegations before coming to the conclusion that he was correct in every particular.

> Lifelong workers in the cause of religion and of the poor have affirmed that in the districts with which they are intimately acquainted the Salvation Army attracts the more excitable of the adherents of existing sects but does not reclaim those who have resisted other reforming agencies . . . There is not a single charitable or religious effort suggested in his book which is not already being put forth by some existing organisation under conditions of perfect publicity, strict accounting and constitutional forms of management. It is impossible to open

Mr Booth's books anywhere without coming upon evidence of an extreme laxity in all financial conceptions which prove him unworthy of blind confidence in any matter where money is concerned.

Bramwell Booth was calm enough about the criticisms to dismiss them as the work of 'poor Huxley and one or two infidels'.[11] But there were other allegations which it was not so easy to brush aside. Frank Smith, 'one of the few men outside Mr Booth's relations or his connections by marriage who have attained high place in the Salvation Army'[12] resigned his commission. Smith had been in command of the Army's Social Reform Wing and had run most of the policies which, according to *In Darkest England*, pointed the way to a national programme for the alleviation of poverty. His denunciation of the General began with the claim that William Booth had not written the book which bore his name. The introduction acknowledged 'valuable literary help from a friend of the poor'. And, after some speculation in the press, William Booth had conceded that 'he had supplied a professional writer with the material' – getting very close to admitting that he had employed a ghostwriter. W. T. Stead, asked to find Booth an assistant, had done the work himself. The Salvation Army then went to the demeaning length of publishing a facsimile of ten lines of manuscript which were undoubtedly written in William Booth's own hand. That, the Army hoped, would bring the controversy over authorship to an end. But Smith, famous in his Salvation days as an emotional and unpredictable man, suggested that William Booth could not even claim honest credit for the ideas. Both the City and Farm Colonies were, Smith said, his invention.

Suddenly *The Times* decided that *In Darkest England* – a couple of months earlier a fraud or farce – was a brilliant blueprint for clearing the slums, but a plan which could only be put into operation under the personal supervision of Commissioner Smith – 'As long as Mr Smith remained in control of the practical part of the business there was room for hope.' Without him, *In Darkest England* was doomed, and certainly did not deserve the financial support for which William Booth asked.

It would have been easy enough for William Booth to brush his critics aside, dismissing their opinions as the prejudices of the traditional churches whose leaders feared that they would be elbowed out of the way by a new movement which spoke for and to humble people in a way that the traditional denominations could barely understand. The men and women he recruited and converted had never heard of either *The Times* or Thomas Huxley. Amongst the class to which he looked for recruits, jokes about the General's fund-raising had been common for years. Bramwell Booth seemed positively proud of his father's reputation. 'Tens of thousands, especially in London, first heard of us through a queer music hall chorus of the eighties: "General Booth sends round the hat / Samson was a strong man / But he wasn't up to that!" The Founder said more about money, probably, than any other leader in the religious world.'[13] No doubt some of the men and women who laughed and applauded – from the royal circle as well as the upper balcony – suspected that some of the donations went to pay the Booths' rent. But the unjustified suspicions did not have an effect on recruitment. As always, the greater the controversies the greater the number of new recruits. Volunteers were rallying to the Salvation Army's standards more quickly than ever before. In the summer of 1889, before the worst of the allegations had even been made, the Army roll in Britain recorded 2,765 full corps and 8,639 officers. By the end of 1890, the year when the most savage criticisms were published, the numbers had increased to 2,828 full corps and 9,921 officers.

Nor did it seem that *The Times* and Thomas Huxley had prevented the wealthy patrons – on whom the Army depended – from supporting the *In Darkest England* scheme. Cardinal Manning, the Bishops of Durham and Manchester and Sir Squire Bancroft, the idol of Drury Lane and the Haymarket Theatre, all subscribed to the appeal. Sir Squire Bancroft even promised to contribute £1,000 when the schemes, were put into place. When *In Darkest England* was published, the General had asked for £100,000. Four months later the accounts showed that total contributions had reached £129,288.12.6d. In fact *The Times* created only one problem for William Booth. It stood between him and his recently acquired ambition to become socially respectable and accepted in polite society.

20

A Question of Probity

The criticism of *In Darkest England* grew in both detail and violence. And the allegations about the General's cavalier treatment of facts and figures which appeared almost daily in the correspondence column of *The Times* were far more damaging than the fusillades of common abuse. 'Statistics' explained that, although General Booth 'puts the criminal classes of Great Britain at about 90,000, the official figures, from which he professes to quote, give the number . . . as 56,669, to which a comparatively small number must be added for Scotland.' The overall conclusion of the letter was that the figure had been 'inflated' something like 50 per cent above the facts.[1] When William Booth – anxious to found his Poor Man's Bank and finance the building of new Rescue Homes – offered 'safe and useful investment with the Army' at 2.5 per cent, 'Veritas' expressed 'a strong interest in the General's character for straightforwardness' and quoted from the notice published in the back of *In Darkest England* which promised 'rates varying from 2.5 to 5 per cent'.[2] The Salvation Army, he implied, changed the figures to suit its convenience. R. H. Hadden produced a detailed analysis of what *In Darkest England* called the 'submerged tenth'. It was based on the 'official return of outdoor paupers in England and Wales', and concluded that the full total was 592,983 –

including 189,604 children 'who received outdoor relief in only the technical sense' and 57,000 'who were insane, the majority of them in lunatic asylums, registered hospitals or licensed houses'.[3] *In Darkest England* had put the figure at 870,000, and implied that they were all ready and willing to work, if work could be made available. The Reverend J. Mahomed offered an explanation for William Booth's romantic optimism about the industrious character of the London poor: 'All the districts of East London where the Salvation Army has its agents are of the better class.'[4] He added, by way of convincing detail,

> there are no barracks, no slum sisters, no outposts in
> Spitalfields, in South Bethnal Green, in St George's in the East
> or in Wapping. In Whitechapel, two slum sisters began work
> around June 1890 at 79 Wentworth Street. In the Headquarters'
> return it is reported that there are fourteen soldiers (men and
> women) working from that centre. I examined the roll . . . and
> found that there were ten soldiers [on it] not one of whom
> resided in Whitechapel.

The Reverend C. H. Bowden, chaplain to Guy's Hospital, claimed that he enjoyed 'unusual opportunities for measuring a religious organisation's hold on the poor'. During his three years at Guy's, 15,000 patients passed through its wards. 'Almost every variety of Christian belief had its representation here, but of the many hundreds of thousands of members of the Salvation Army we have not, in the last three years at any rate, seen half a dozen.'[5] It is reasonable to assume that he was not suggesting that Army members were more healthy than the rest of the population, or that at times of illness and injury they were more reluctant to receive treatment than those from other denominations. He was claiming that William Booth's estimate of membership was at best wrong and at worst fraudulent.

The last page of *In Darkest England*, as well as offering the controversial interest rates to which 'Veritas' drew attention, advertised the Salvation Army Building Association Limited and announced that, during the six months which followed the publication of the 1889 accounts, 'twenty-eight thousand pounds has been received and placed out again by the directors in valuable securities'. So great had been the society's success that the managers had decided, with the government's agreement, that they should accept a further £50,000 of investment from the public – twice the size of the original limit. An evangelical movement which had created its own social organisations might survive claims that it exaggerated its success. A building society incorporated under Act of Parliament could not.

The allegations – direct and by implication – had begun at last to have their effect on potential investors. George Herring (a bookmaker who, having made a fortune on racing, moved into the city and made another by gambling on the creditworthiness of Central European governments) read *In Darkest England* and immediately offered 'to put up £10,000 of the money required to purchase the proposed Land Colony'.[6] Then he read the criticisms of the Army and withdrew the offer. He remained detached from the Salvation Army for ten years before he returned as a regular benefactor but not a member. Herring was influenced, in his change of mind, by the barrage of adverse publicity – and by what he discovered of the Army's management techniques. All the decisions about major investments were taken by General Booth personally, usually after the receipt of handwritten notes from Bramwell. One of them was what passed for a technical appraisal when making the crucial decision about the location of the first Farm Colony. General Booth 'finally decided that Hadleigh in Essex was the right place'[7] after his son – on another scribbled half-page – told him, 'I have just come back from Hadleigh. I have not time to go into particulars but, to sum up, while I think we have paid quite enough for the land, I think it can be made into a very valuable and successful undertaking.'[8] At the time, they had not quite despaired of persuading Herring to invest in an adjacent property. 'Whether or not Herring will buy Thundersley, I think we ought to do.'[9] In fact, the plan did not turn out quite so well as Bramwell had hoped. So another note conveyed the bad (and extremely expensive) news: 'We cannot erect houses there at present. We have neither the men nor the material. We must provide accommodation within the next three months for at least 100 men.'[10] The solution was temporary accommodation – 'shelters to contain 6,000 cubic feet to which would have to be added dining room and washing and latrine facilities'. Bramwell Booth proposed to go ahead 'unless I hear from you to the contrary by telegram'.[11] The extraordinary feature of the Salvation Army's form of personalised management was not that men like Herring chose not to invest in its capital projects, but that any of its business activities survived the casual way in which decisions were taken.

The Salvation Army's enemies (assuming that survival was impossible) began to rejoice at prospects of its death. H. H. Cooper wrote to *The Times* with the totally unjustified claim that the £99,000 which Squire Bancroft had offered to make up to £100,000 had not been collected 'even in smaller sums'. He attributed the failure of the appeal largely to the way in which Thomas Huxley and other critics had 'combined together, not without some success, to tear *In Darkest England* to shreds, to upset and disprove most of its figures and facts and ridicule Messrs Booth's and Stead's social theories and to thoroughly discredit the machinery by which they were to carry it out'.[12] Mr Cooper went on to argue – in absolute opposition to his original argument that no one was contributing to the *In Darkest England* appeal – that contributions to Salvation Army funds had 'seriously injured' the level of contributions made to other churches. Then (reverting to his original argument) he asked if, in the absence of the other ninety-nine matching donations, Squire Bancroft was still going to contribute his £1,000.

In February 1891 the complaints took on a new form. A Mr George Kebbell – whose sudden interest in the Salvation Army's constitution was never adequately explained – wrote to William Booth's solicitors. His contention was that the Trust Deed on which the Salvation Army was founded allowed General Booth to spend all or any of the money in whatever way he chose. The allegation was technically correct. But both sides in the argument chose to dispute slightly different contentions. The Army did not deny that the General had supreme power. But it insisted that 'after the first ten or twelve years of the life of the Movement, he never himself touched the money. All the financial arrangements though, of course, carried on in his name, were attended to by others.' According to Bramwell Booth, his father had lost interest in managing the finances ten years before *In Darkest England* was published. 'By 1878–79 I was already signing all the cheques.'[13] The assertion did not invalidate the claim, amply justified by examination of the Trust Deed, that General Booth could do what he chose with the Army's money – as long as he could argue, in the unlikely event of being challenged in court, that he was acting in the general interests of the organisation which he led. Kebbell's description of the legal position was as accurate as it was offensive.

The confiding public have, in fact, given their money to a man who is at liberty to use it entirely for his own individual purposes and without the smallest control from anyone whatsoever. It is not necessary to discuss what Mr Booth will do with all this wealth. It is enough to show what he can do with it. I know that he could walk into a bank tomorrow and, without consent of anyone in the world, draw out every penny that the too credulous community has confided in him. After that the smallest question of 'trust' might be evaded by a happy pilgrimage to, say, Boulogne, where he could pose as a martyr for the rest of his remarkable and (in one sense) useful career.[14]

The Kebbell allegations were damaging because informed opinion knew that the hypothesis on which they were based was correct. The fund set up to support *In Darkest England* was controlled by a special Trust Deed entered in the Chancery Closed Roll on 30 January 1891. It gave 'the person who is, from time to time, the General of the Salvation Army' the right 'to determine and enforce the laws and to superintend the operation of the scheme'. What was more, it also placed in his hands 'the power to expend, invest or otherwise dispose of or deal for the purposes of the Darkest England scheme (or of any part thereon) all money or other property contributed, collected or received for the purposes thereof'. The deed was also explicit in stipulating that 'all money and property contributed, collected or received for the purposes of the Darkest England scheme . . . shall at all times hereafter be held and applied upon trust for the social and moral improvement of such manner indicated, implied or suggested in the said book'. Clauses of that sort never prevent the principal proponents of such a scheme from receiving 'reasonable remuneration' or 'legitimate expenses'. And, despite suspicions that General Booth was exploiting the scheme in that way, there is no reason to doubt his absolute probity. But although he had no intention of misappropriating a pound, he was absolutely determined to manage every penny. The *In Darkest England* scheme was governed by the rule which governed everything the Salvation Army did. William Booth had supreme, indeed sole, authority.

William Booth – or Bramwell on his behalf – attempted to repudiate each allegation in letters to whichever newspaper repeated the old charge or reported new accusations of malpractice. Occasionally a supporter or sympathiser would write in the General's defence. J. T. Cunningham ('late Fellow of University College Oxford') observed that philanthropists like Mr Booth and economists like Alfred Marshall 'are approaching nearer and nearer to harmony'.[15] That intellectual endorsement of *In Darkest England* concluded with an encomium which, although no doubt welcomed at International Headquarters, must have added to the concern that William Booth's real intention was to overthrow the legitimate government and seize power. Mr Cunningham speculated about the time when society had learned 'from Mr Booth's colonies that the first requisite of true progress in human life is to check and control individual competition and individual liberty with a strong, stern hand' – a prediction which made a letter sent by an anonymous Salvation Army officer insisting that his General had no authoritarian instincts sound particularly unconvincing. Archdeacon F. W. Farrar of Westminster – the author of *Eric, or Little by Little* and one of the few churchmen to rally to the Salvation Army's support – defended the General in the *Daily Graphic*. A more senior figure expressed his sympathy in a way that alienated previous supporters. Cardinal Manning wrote to Ben Tillet (the dockers' leader) revealing both that he supported *In Darkest England*'s prescription and that he had not been able to muster 'the patience to read Professor Huxley's letters'.[16] The publication of his letter raised widespread fears that Rome and the trade union movement were going to combine in support of the Nonconformist who, although he claimed to regard socialism as a godless heresy, was planning to usurp the powers of the state. It was General Booth's misfortune not to appeal to the class of person who wrote letters to *The Times*.

At the centre of the storm, William Booth – still mourning and desperately missing his wife – was struggling to manage his growing international organisation in the personal, and therefore profoundly demanding, way which was the only form of management which he knew. The Army was still expanding fast. Within the space of three months, while the financial controversy was raging round him, the General was able to report that a night shelter was to be established in Paris, a study was made of the German *Arbeiter Colonian* and a mission hall was opened (and closed by the police) in Buenos Aires. At the same time, William Booth and his family were, as always, regularly if only periodically ill.

Success, as well as deep conviction, helped the General to brush aside attacks which he had no doubt were motivated by evil and envy. The Army's expansion was virtue rewarded. God would provide and protect him against his tormentors. Faith saw him through every crisis and encouraged him to embark on continual new adventures. *The War Cry* announced that 'a Salvation fleet of eight splendid steamers, carrying nearly 4,000 passengers, will escort the General to RMS *Scot* on Saturday July 25th 1891'. Soldiers were invited to travel from Waterloo to Southampton and back at a cost of five shillings – paid out of their own pockets. General Booth left behind an ailing and disturbed family.

Emma Booth-Tucker – weakened first by the strain of nursing her dying mother and then by the privation of living, as 'Raheemah', the life of a low-caste Indian – was thought to be on the point of death and ordered to return to England. Lucy Booth, ill with an undiagnosed respiratory disease, was sent out to the subcontinent partly to take her sister's place and partly in order to benefit from the warmer climate. When she returned to London in April 1892, she brought with her Colonel John Lampard, a Salvation Army officer who was previously stationed in Bombay. *The War Cry* announced that Colonel Lampard and Miss Lucy Booth were engaged to be married. On the day that the news was published, Lampard wrote to William Booth – his commanding officer, employer and (it was assumed until then) his future father-in-law – to say that he felt unworthy to become the husband of such a paragon as Lucy. The letter was written in such a bizarre style that there was some doubt about its authenticity. Lampard was an essentially serious man, but he withdrew from his engagement in the language of a poltroon. The charitable interpretation of his strange behaviour was that, having lost his nerve at the thought of becoming William Booth's son-in-law, he chivalrously chose to portray himself as a weak-minded irresponsible whom Lucy was lucky to escape. If Lampard did draft the letter with honourable intentions, his high-minded behaviour was not reciprocated. His letter was published in *The War Cry*.[17]

Colonel Lampard's breach of promise – cause for civil proceedings in Victorian England – was regarded by General Booth as a betrayal of the Army as well as his daughter. Lucy collapsed. And her father thought it his duty to report the cause of her illness and the consequences of the desertion to what he regarded as his extended family. Lucy's condition was, therefore, described in *The War Cry* in distressing detail. 'Colonel Lucy is, we regret to say, very ill. The shock to her system caused by the mysterious and sudden termination of what seemed to her to be the path of true happiness, together with the tossing of spirit inevitable from conduct so unreasonable, has prostrated her. Since Friday she has remained in a state of permanent collapse.'

In the next edition of *The War Cry* General Booth wrote that he had received numerous enquiries about the disciplinary action to be taken against Colonel Lampard. He clearly thought that a stern response was essential and tried to satisfy his soldiers' curiosity – real or counterfeited – with the information that 'five of our most widely known and trusted officers (Commissioners Howard, Carleton, Cadman and Colonels Higgins and Pollard) investigated the facts and reported on them'.[18] The report, if it was ever written, was not published. Instead, the Army issued what amounted to a medical bulletin:

> Since the inquiry took place, an opinion on the subject has
> been formed by the physician who enjoys a leading reputation
> in the treatment of mental disease. He states very explicitly that
> in this particular direction, Colonel Lampard was (in his
> opinion) so far mentally deranged as not to be responsible for
> his action. In view of the grave doubt this raises as to Colonel
> Lampard's moral accountability, the General feels that he can
> only suspend his further judgement on the matter and hope
> that God will make plain his will. We are glad to be able to add
> that Colonel Lucy is gradually recovering her strength . . .

Few people, even at the time, believed the diagnosis to be medically reputable. It is more difficult to decide if William Booth cynically regarded Colonel Lampard's 'madness' as the best way of defending his daughter and the Army or if his admiration for both the woman and the organisation made him honestly believe that only a lunatic would miss the opportunity to become a Booth. Lucy, on the other hand, was at pains to emphasise that she had only benefited from the experience. Thanking the many Salvationists who had written to her to express their sympathy and concern, she seemed far more anxious to offer comfort than to receive it. 'I want to tell you something that proves that your pleadings with the Lord have not been in vain . . . While being tossed on these strangely wild billows, and when almost overwhelmed by mysterious darkness which so suddenly clouded my sky, Jesus has come to me – come as never before.' Jesus told Lucy to return to India, where she took the Indian name of Ruhani and met a Swedish officer, Emmanuel Daniel Hellborg. They were married – in the absence of the General in America – by Bramwell Booth in October 1894. In preparation for the wedding the groom had changed his name by deed poll to Booth-Hellborg.

Although William Booth, managing his Army and guiding a family which had relied on Catherine for so long, was anxious to put the disputes about money behind him, some of his closest friends, as well as his natural enemies, persisted in doing what they regarded as clearing his name. Francis Peek, a wealthy philanthropist, had been so impressed by *In Darkest England* that he donated £500 to the fund to finance the implementation of the scheme. He decided to back his investment with proof of William Booth's integrity. He judged that the best way to demonstrate that his money was being well and properly used was to initiate an investigation into the administration of the scheme.

Peek did not pretend that he was acting in the spirit of objective inquiry. He had already expressed his approval of both the book's analysis and conclusion in the *Contemporary Review* for December 1890. He admitted 'a strong desire to promote the success of General Booth's efforts' but made the usual criticisms of statistical methods and sources. But he admitted that 'the first thought that occurs . . . is the total inadequacy of the amount asked for'. The second was that the size of the problem had been underestimated. The calculations had been made on the basis 'of the hungry Out-of-work who stands before your door . . . not the hungry Out-of-work with wife and family'. But he concluded with the balanced judgement which was so lacking in most of the press comment. Although *In Darkest England* lacked intellectual rigour, 'those parts of General Booth's scheme which are open to unfavourable criticism are not essential to it'. His review ended with the sort of judgement with which publishers – planning a paperback edition or reprint – dream of printing in large letters on the new jacket: 'The book itself is touchingly and powerfully written and the scheme it sets forth is fascinating.' But the general public still needed to be convinced of its merit. Indeed, opinion was moving against it.

Having so firmly made up his own mind about the virtues of *In Darkest England*, Peek was not in a position to conduct the examination himself. So he employed G. Penn Gaskell, a barrister who had been a member of the Charity Organisations' Society's investigation into the homeless poor – a double qualification for the job since it gave him some knowledge of the social crisis which *In Darkest England* addressed and guaranteed that he was not a Booth acolyte. The COS had been continually critical of *In Darkest England*. Indeed, C. S. Loch, the Society's Secretary, had specifically attacked William Booth's supreme authority over the implementation of the scheme and unchecked control of the money which funded it. Most of the charitable organisations affiliated to his association felt about William Booth as the Methodists had felt about him twenty years earlier. Not only was he intruding into their preserve, he was justifying his intrusion by accusing them of failing in their duty.

Penn Gaskell based all his analysis on figures taken from the Salvation Army's 'Review of *The First Year's Work*', so he made no comment on the accuracy of the statistics. He did, however, point to what he regarded as a basic weakness and illustrated it by an examination of the proposal to provide comfortable lodging houses at specially low prices – sometimes subsidised by the men's own work. 'In the common lodging houses,' he wrote, 'fourpence is the ordinary charge for a bed and by establishing their penny and twopenny shelters, the Salvation Army have made the homeless life more easy and to many more attractive. I need hardly dwell on the consequences which are likely to ensue.'[19] William Booth himself would have been perfectly happy to dwell on them. The consequences he anticipated would be an improvement in the character of the men who sought refuge in his shelters. He believed that human nature thrived on encouragement. Men given a decent place to live would want to live decently. And their prospects would be even more dramatically improved by their regular attendance at the nightly prayer meetings. Far from wallowing in the easy luxury of a penny bed, covered in a single cloth counterpane and separated from its neighbour by a two-foot-high partition, they would long for, and work towards, the day when they could play an industrious part in respectable Christian society.

Penn Gaskell did not think that the prayer meetings were doing their work. He judged them to be

> in every way appropriate to the class for whom they are
> intended . . . But excellent though these meetings are, there is
> only a small percentage of the men who show signs of being
> seriously impressed by them . . . As a result of investigations
> on this point, I feel little doubt that the real and permanent
> conversions amongst the men received in the factories (attached
> to many of the shelters) is less than 2 per cent and my
> impression would be that at the farms (the second stage
> of the *Darkest England* project) there is certainly not a
> higher proportion than in the factories.

More damning still, Penn Gaskell concluded: 'In the "Review of *The First Year's Work*" it is remarked, "*The factory is not like an ordinary workshop but an actual 'elevator' designed to lift up all who are willing to be helped: intended as a means of transport not a place of residence.*" This unquestionably is what the factory ought to be, but I cannot agree that for the majority of the men it really is so.'

William Booth took what comfort he could from the report's more positive comments on the selfless devotion of the Salvation Army's officers, the imaginative scope of the *In Darkest England* aspirations and the extent of the work already in place. There were ten shelters in London alone, providing nightly accommodation for 2,000 men and providing 307,000 beds in the first year of their operation. The workshop had employed 14,000 previously unemployable men and 1,567 destitute women. The Salvation Army, on the evidence of a less than laudatory report, was the biggest and most comprehensive welfare organisation in Britain.

In one particular, the report was, however, unequivocally helpful. Penn Gaskell absolved the Salvation Army from another charge of 'sweating labour', this time brought against it by the Firewood Trade's Association – a more credible critic than the Reverend William Adamson. Penn Gaskell reported that, at some of the shelters, 'a man, by chopping a certain amount of wood, can earn a penny' by which to pay for his night's lodgings. 'By chopping double quantity [he] may earn twopence which can be used either to pay for a twopenny bed or

divided between a cheaper night's sleep and a supper.' At the
Westminster shelter, men were allowed to chop enough wood to earn
fourpence. The result was that firewood was produced far more
cheaply than in one of the commercial yards.

The private firewood companies feared that the Salvation Army
would force prices down to a level at which it was impossible for them
to stay in business. Penn Gaskell accepted that costs were so low in the
Rescue Home workshops that other factories could not compete with
their prices. But he judged that the Army could legitimately argue that
the firewood choppers were 'under training' – to return to society if not
to take up a trade – and that their wages were increased in kind, if not
in cash, by the food and accommodation which they received.

However, the building trade's union persisted in the allegation, and
the London Committee of the Associated Society of Carpenters and
Joiners monitored pay rates at the Hanbury Street Works and published what it believed to be the highly damaging results in *Reynold's
News*. The ASC & J had been against *In Darkest England* from the start.
Its objections were essentially ideological. But it backed them up with
irrefutable statistics and even more compelling simple arithmetic. Its
basic complaint was with William Booth: 'Not only did Booth display
no understanding of the root cause of poverty, but his plans for regenerating the hapless victims of our social system were so constructed as
to be agencies for mischief.' They were not warning against the risk of
creating willing paupers. Their concern was that vulnerable men would
be exploited. The ASC & J proved its point by recourse to the *ad
hominem* technique on which the *In Darkest England* prescription had
been based:

> A long period of unemployment had caused this Aldershot
> joiner to pawn his tools for bread and when he was quite
> destitute he tramped to London . . . He was given to
> understand that employment as a joiner at the Hanbury Street
> Works would mean wages which would eventually enable him
> to redeem his tools and start life afresh outside . . . This
> unfortunate joiner was given joinery work to do from 6.30 a.m.
> to 6.00 p.m. each day with 45 minutes for breakfast and one
> hour for dinner. The first week he received board and lodgings
> estimated to cost 9/- and one shilling in cash. The second week

and for each succeeding week during his six weeks' stay with
the 'Army' his compensation for work done was board and
lodging and 2/- cash. There did not appear any prospect of
being able to save enough to redeem his tools.

The union's conclusion was that the Army was paying at most 12/-
a week for work which, if carried out for a private company, would
have attracted wages of £2.7.3d, and, more damagingly, that the central purpose claimed for the scheme by William Booth was not being
achieved. The men were not being prepared for work in the world
beyond the Salvation Army nor helped to redeem their tools from the
pawnbroker's shop. They were simply cheap labour.

In a typical week, the Hanbury Street Works employed sixty-five
carpenters and joiners. 'Some of the most competent men receive cash
grants from 1/- to 3/- a week'; others received only 6d. The Army told
the union that, even with that rate of pay, the Hanbury Street Works
lost £1,500 a year – a deficit made up by private donations. Since the
Army calculated the cost of board and lodging at 9/- a week, the donations alone would pay for the upkeep of the total workforce. The
average payment – in cash and kind – was not therefore 12/- a week,
but 3/- a week, or a little less than a farthing an hour. The trade union
rate was 10½d an hour.

The Associated Society of Carpenters and Joiners made its complaints (and its calculations) public. The TUC passed a critical
resolution and General Booth – saying that he was offended by the allegations – refused to meet its delegation. The Parliamentary Committee
of the TUC did however meet representatives of the Salvation Army
and asked that all Hanbury employees should be paid at trade union
rates and their products sold at normal market prices. The proposal
was politely declined. The TUC modified its position. Its revised proposals included the suggestion that some of the profit made at Hanbury
Street be used to provide tools for each man who left the Works after
a period of successful employment. The Salvation Army, which did not
accept that any profit was being made, was unable to accept the
Congress's request.

It was not the sort of complaint that William Booth was likely to
take seriously. Everybody who worked with, and for, the Salvation
Army was expected to make sacrifices which employees in other

enterprises would not be expected to accept. But despite the General's lofty refusal to discuss the subject and his subordinates' unwillingness (indeed inability) to carry on real negotiations with the union, the question remained. What happened to the money that might have been earned in a commercial concern? Some of it was undoubtedly lost through inefficiency. The rest found its way into the funds which supported William Booth's first love – preaching. Evangelism, on the scale in which it was carried out by the Salvation Army, was expensive.

So the suspicion persisted that William Booth was not to be trusted with money. The accusation that he misappropriated donations to finance a life of luxury could easily be brushed aside. And the more sophisticated claim that donations towards the welfare schemes were sometimes used to finance evangelical expeditions could be ignored – even though there were certainly occasions when the two accounts were confused. The third indictment was, however, certainly plausible and occasionally justified. Donations were often squandered because of the Salvation Army's lack of adequate managerial experience. Yet William Booth relied for funds on people who, in the competitive economy of Victorian England, expected value for money.

In his critique of *In Darkest England* Francis Peek explicitly commended William Booth's plans for improving conditions in the slums as an essential free enterprise solution to poverty and, for that reason if no other, superior to more radical alternatives which required the government to perform tasks best left to private companies. In his 1890 review he had written, 'the state should not build houses for the poor but should compel the owners to keep them in sanitary conditions' – a Benthamite solution which Joseph Chamberlain in Conservative Birmingham would have regarded as timid. In his preface to the Penn Gaskell report, Peek had complained, entirely gratuitously, about the folly of 'rendering it unprofitable for the capitalist to build houses'. William Booth needed to appeal to men who held such opinions and he could not afford to be found guilty of chronic inefficiency. The most damaging judgement made about his stewardship was *The Times's* conclusion that 'it is impossible to open Mr Booth's books anywhere without coming upon evidence of an extreme laxity in all financial concepts which proves him unworthy of blind confidence in any matter where money is concerned'.[20] Francis Peek's enquiry, which had found him honest and well intentioned, had not found him efficient. As the attacks mounted, William Booth – or his advisers – hit on a bold plan of vindication. The Salvation Army, on its own initiative, would set up an independent 'Commission of Inquiry Upon the Darkest England Scheme'.

Perhaps it was the publicity given to *In Darkest England* by *The Times* – almost all of it adverse – which persuaded six men of public distinction to spend so long investigating a scheme which most of their social circle must have thought of as, at best, sentimental and at worst corrupt. But whatever the reason, William Booth was able to recruit a committee of men who might easily have made up a Royal Commission. The chairman was Sir Henry James MP. He was a particularly cunning choice since he had just defended *The Times* (albeit unsuccessfully) against the charge that it had libelled Charles Stewart Parnell. In consequence, he could hardly be accused of bias against the Establishment or its paper. The other members were Walter Long (soon to be elected Member of Parliament and eventually, as reward for standing aside when Andrew Bonar Law was elected leader of the Tory Party, to become a Viscount); Sydney Buxton MP; the Earl of Onslow and Edwin Waterhouse, President of the Institute of Chartered Accountants. Their judgement on the success of the *In Darkest England* scheme would, it was assumed, be accepted by everyone except its most prejudiced opponents. William Booth still took an enormous risk in asking them to pass judgement on his scheme. Because of his character, he did not realise how great that risk was. He had complete faith in his project and had no doubt that men of judgement and integrity would confirm that it was certainly the best, and possibly the only, way to deliver England from darkness. His reckless confidence was exemplified by the terms of reference which he laid down. They were absolutely comprehensive and in no way pointed the committee towards the desired conclusion:

1. Has the money collected by means of the appeal to the public for the *In Darkest England and the Way Out* scheme been devoted to the objects and expended in the manner set out in that appeal and in no other?
2. Have the methods employed in the expenditure of such money been of a business like, economical and prudential

character and have the accounts of such expenditure been
kept in a proper and clear manner?

3. Is the property, both real and potential, and are the
   moneys from the above appeal so vested that they cannot
   be applied to any purpose other than that set out in *In
   Darkest England*, and what safeguards exist to prevent the
   misappropriation of such property either now or after the
   death of Mr Booth?

Committee members were given a memorandum of guidance –
officially based on the reasonable assumption that members could not be
expected to possess an expert knowledge of the Salvation Army's constitution and activities. It also performed the important function of
putting on record the General's personal financial position, a subject
which pride made it impossible for him to include in the terms of reference. The memorandum began with the categorical assertion that
neither General Booth himself nor any of his family had ever received
either salary or expenses from the Social Fund. Indeed, the £7,838
received in *In Darkest England* royalties (a very large sum indeed in
1891) had been contributed towards the implementation of the schemes
it proposed. The rest of the guidance followed the course set out by the
terms of reference. The method of accounting made misappropriation
impossible. All books and balance sheets would be made available to the
committee. No money subscribed to the Social Fund had been used to
cover the expenses of speaking tours, the payment of officers or the erec-
tion and maintenance of barracks. The prudential conduct which the
memorandum described was, William Booth concluded, guaranteed by
the Trust Deed which governed the *In Darkest England* fund.

The determination to be exonerated without the indignity of an
inquiry into his private finances was typical of William Booth's haughty
attitude towards the wicked world he hoped humbly to serve. It was
also the cause of suspicion which surrounded him until he died.
William Booth lived in an age of financial reticence and the idea that he
might be 'accountable' to anyone but God never passed through his
mind. But he encouraged such suspicion by matching the enthusiasm
by which he refuted all allegations of misappropriation with a dogged
reluctance to explain how he financed his comfortable, though never
luxurious, life. Much was made of his decision not to make *The War*

Cry his private property and live off the profits – not so much an act of grace as obvious obligation – and similar publicity was given to his insistence that in prosperous middle age, he repaid (to the Salvation Army) the £500 which, in his impecunious early married years, the Christian Mission had contributed to an endowment fund. But the quite unnecessary mystery still surrounded his income.

The committee held eighteen meetings and took evidence from most of the Booths. Elijah Cadman – Commissioner in charge of the Social Programme – met the inquiry twice. The dedication with which they discharged their duties, as well as the social class from which they came, can be judged by a footnote to the first report of their proceedings. 'The Earl of Onslow, when visiting the Farm Colony, was accompanied and assisted by his land agent, Mr Bowles.'

The report published in the *Contemporary Review* on 19 December 1892 left no doubt about the success which the Salvation Army had enjoyed in establishing and extending its social schemes – long before *In Darkest England* was published. The Army's experience of welfare work had been constantly cited by General Booth, and the committee endorsed that view. Waterhouse confirmed that the Social Fund had £129,288-12-6 to spend – more than £5,000 subscribed before the *In Darkest England* appeal was launched, £108,000 during the year of active collection and the rest thereafter. The committee then described how the money was being spent.

The 'elevators', city workshops which prepared men for social rehabilitation by subjecting them to the discipline of employment, supervised eighteen different activities – carpentry and joinery, firewood chopping, cabinet making, basket making, mat making, carpet weaving, tambourine making, brush making, mattress making, painting, engineering, wheel making, sewing, tin beating, rag and paper sorting, tailoring, shoe making and cardboard-box making. Anxious not to overstate the Army's success, the committee made clear that the tailoring mostly consisted of cutting down and mending second-hand clothes and that the rag and paper sorting (which earned the Army 27/- per ton) had been reduced 'after the restriction of collections for economic reasons'.

With the allegations of sweating in mind, the committee made a careful analysis of the way firewood was costed. One hundred bundles were said to put a man one shilling and twopence-halfpenny in credit.

That was said to pay for breakfast (threepence), dinner (fourpence), tea (threepence) and bed (twopence). Twopence-halfpenny was then left to contribute towards the cost of his Sunday keep. The committee expressed surprise at the size of the Army's firewood enterprise – including the acceptance of a contract from the London School Board for one million bundles in a year. Bramwell Booth 'gave an undertaking never to sell below the price of the commercial trade' – no assurance about wage levels was asked for or offered. Bramwell's promise did not prevent the committee from recommending that 'every care should be taken when disposing of the articles produced at the institutions under the control of the Social Wing, that prices charged should not be lower than those which may fairly be demanded by ordinary tradesmen and women'. The trade unions remained so dissatisfied that the parliamentary agitation which they stimulated lasted for almost twenty years. General Booth's social work was, they wrote, 'looked upon with favour by the wealthy class and the Government which represented it as a useful way of diverting attention from the fundamental cause of social wreckage'. Catherine Booth had said as much – in a rather more elevated way – twenty years earlier. It had no effect. Indeed, put in a slightly different way, William Booth shared their view. Rather the Bible than the sword as a weapon against revolution.[21]

The Farm Colony – 1,629 acres bought at Hadleigh and 67 acres leased nearby – received a positive commendation. Mr Bird, Inspector of the Board of Agriculture, 'did not think that a more desirable, suitable and appropriate property for the purpose could be obtained'. The analysis of the Army's rescue work was at once more analytical and more emotive. A table, purporting to evaluate the work of the Rescue Homes, set out the way in which 3,070 fallen women, who had been persuaded to leave the streets between 1 October 1890 and 30 September 1892, had settled down in their new moral state. Only 640 were said to have responded 'unsatisfactorily'. More than twice as many – 1,364, or 44.5 per cent of the total – had been 'found situations' and 133 (3.5 per cent) had learned trades. Only four had married, but 547 (17.75 per cent) had gone to live with respectable friends. Nine had died, four emigrated and three hundred and eighty-nine had moved to infirmaries, hospitals and other homes. The committee noted with approval that 'in order to guard against the girls from the Rescue Homes being [exploited], on account of their [being] given very much lower wages than could be obtained by girls of good character, Mrs Bramwell Booth requires an assurance that the wage shall not be less than £10–12 per annum in every case'.

Florence Booth had described to the committee the older women who sought refuge in her shelter:

> The majority who come here are utterly destitute, degraded, old and struggling to keep out of the workhouse. They earn pennies by picking up scraps in the street, picking fruit etc. In many cases the inmates pay for one meal and lodgings and leave before the streets of London are swept in the morning with the object of picking up enough rags, paper and other refuse to bring in 2d for the next night's lodging. While doing this they pick tealeaves out of the dustboxes and pick up bread and rotten fruit around the market and actually live on this, asking the shelter only for hot water to turn the tealeaves into tea.

The committee had a clear duty to put such emotive facts aside. And it was careful to make clear in the last paragraph of its report that it had 'simply considered the matters coming within the determination set out at the commencement of the report' and the Conclusions and Suggests dealt with nothing else. That was enough to vindicate completely William Booth and the *In Darkest England* scheme.

With the exception of investment in the building of barracks at Hadleigh, all monies donated to the scheme had been used for the welfare initiatives which it proposed – and the Spiritual Wing of the Army was paying rent for use of the barracks. The management of the fund was 'businesslike, economical and prudent'. The accounts were 'kept in a proper and clear manner' and, although the Trust Deed did not prevent misapplication of funds, using any of the money for any other purposes would subject the General (or his successor) either to civil or criminal proceedings for breach of trust.

Edwin Waterhouse made some minor suggestions for greater efficiency. Some of the jobs in the Farm Colony could be amalgamated. Investment in stock should be held in the name of independent trustees. But the report made no major criticism or fundamental recommendation for change. And it contained a paragraph which, although outside its terms of reference, must have filled William Booth with delight:

> In examining the accounts, the Committee was careful to inquire whether any portion of the travelling expenses of the Salvation Army had been born by the Darkest England Fund and whether Mr Booth or any member of his family have drawn any sum for their personal use therefrom . . . No such expenditure appears to have been incurred . . . He has a small income, partly settled on him by personal friends and partly derived by the sale of his literary works, the amount and nature of which he explained to the Committee and which seemed to be commensurate with the maintenance of his personal establishment.

At the age of sixty-three and with the organisation he founded now established in such diverse countries as Italy, Uruguay and the West Indies – as well as providing a quarter of a million meals a year to the British poor – William Booth must have thought that vindication by the Committee of Inquiry removed the one obstacle that had barred his way to a triumphant old age. But the seeds of the final crisis in his life had already been sown.

21

The Devil Does His Worst

During the agonies of her last few weeks, Catherine had talked more of the future than of the past. About her own resurrection she had no doubts. She lived in the belief that eternal life for sinners who repent was God's promise to the world and she died in the certainty that He would keep His word. However, she was deeply troubled about the family which she was to leave behind. The shorthand writer, who took down all she said, recorded the constant return of her wandering thoughts to the importance of the Booths standing shoulder to shoulder in the fight against evil. 'When trials come and the temper approaches you,' she told Herbert, 'stick to Bramwell.' And time after time she repeated the valediction which was both a promise and a warning: 'Stand fast together and the devil can do his worst.'[1]

Perhaps she knew that she was the force that held the family close. Or she may have recognised the tensions which were building up before her death. William – watching the great movement which he had created expand all over the world – seemed to have lost all enthusiasm for its management. He was, at heart, an itinerant preacher. The success of the Salvation Army offered him the chance of world-wide evangelism. Bramwell (his heir apparent) was, he rightly believed, a first-rate administrator. So while the General retained both the wish

and the inclination to interfere and intervene as he thought appropriate – usually with handwritten notes which confirmed or
countermanded his subordinates' judgement – he left more and more
of the strategy which guided the Army to his oldest son, a man more
admired by his father than by his siblings.

Bramwell had been ill for almost all his life. In 1876 he had broken
down completely and although he insisted that his health and confidence had both recovered, he had become badly deaf. His main
handicap was a disability that every staff officer must avoid. He had
little or no experience of active service. Yet, despite his background as
a non-combatant, he was given increasing authority over his brothers
and sisters who had, since childhood, been in hand-to-hand combat
with the devil. No one could blame Bramwell for his long absence from
the field of battle. Since he had given up his ambition to be a doctor, he
had wanted to be an evangelist rather than an administrator. At sixteen
he had managed the 'Food for the Millions' shops which his father had
set up in East London, and that had set the pattern for his life. When
he was called back into headquarters, he had spent much of his spare
time preaching in the streets. But his brothers and sisters still thought
of him as a civilian, while they were more than simple soldiers. They
were the shock-troops of the Lord.

All the children, out in the field, had been encouraged in that belief
by their father who genuinely believed that to be a Booth was to be one
of the Lord's Anointed. *The War Cry* exalted them each week. And, as
if to prove their inherent superiority, they were all appointed to
demanding commands over the heads of more experienced officers and
before they knew much about the world which they were supposed to
save. Ballington was made his father's Viceroy in the United States in
1887, when he was thirty. Herbert commanded the Salvation Army
throughout Great Britain in 1890 when he was twenty-eight. William's
daughters were given even more prodigious responsibilities. In 1880
Kate, aged twenty-two, had been sent to France and Emma, aged
twenty, had been charged with running the women's training homes.
By the time of their mother's death, they were all battle-hardened.

Ballington had the peculiar distinction of being one of the first
Salvation Army officers to be prosecuted, convicted and imprisoned.
After presiding at a Manchester meeting 'where many of the worst
characters were saved, [he] spent twenty-four hours in Belle Vue Gaol

for upholding the Master's name to the perishing multitudes'. He was 'placed with the common felons, lived for twenty-four hours on a few ounces of bread and a little skilly, scrubbed the cell and slept on a plank'. His account of the ordeal ended with the assurance that he 'never felt more blessed or encouraged'.

It was not only hubris which encouraged William Booth to promote his sons and daughters above all others. By placing each of his children in strategic commands, both at home and abroad, William Booth believed that he had guaranteed his continued worldwide control of the Salvation Army. But that was not his primary motive. He regarded the whole Army as his extended family, and his sons and daughters inherited responsibility for its care as they would have gradually assumed responsibility for the success and welfare of anything else which was precious to him. His assumption that the Booths and the Army were indistinguishable produced a peculiarly personal and paternal style of management. It also guaranteed the series of family desertions which were to haunt his old age.

All the children had been taught the importance of discipline. And disciplined they remained – at least when they were under their father's command. They had been brought up to accept his authority without thought or question and to obey his orders no matter how uncongenial they might be. Bramwell, having learned his trade from an autocrat, assumed that autocracy was essential to leadership. So when his father devolved power to him, he assumed that – despite his deafness, his weak chest, his nervous breakdown and his lack of experience in the field – he had to treat his subordinates in the way in which they had been treated by the founding General. The first signs of open resentment came from Herbert who believed that, as British Commander, he should work *with* rather than *under* Bramwell, the Chief of Staff. William Booth recognised the problem without being able to solve it. His pleas that the brothers should 'work together with unlimited good will' were ignored. Herbert – at least accepting that continued bickering was bad for the Army – asked to be sent to South Africa. Bramwell could see the wisdom of his suggestion but he was not willing to accept it outright. So Herbert was given command in Canada.

It was not only the Booths, with their exaggerated sense both of mission and their own importance, who were beginning to feel dissatisfied. George Scott Railton – the most saintly of men – was on the point of

revolt. Railton had been given command in Germany, where one newspaper summed up all the reasons for the Salvation Army's unpopularity
in a single paragraph:

> The way the Salvation Army people try to convert others is
> really against all manners and customs and if they could only
> keep before themselves the example of Our Lord and Master
> (who did not call his disciples 'saved') they would not go to
> such extravagances. One could only think what a pity if this
> sect should gain ground in our country, for it does not
> represent quiet and sober and serious Christianity, but
> encourages self-righteousness and spiritual pride.[2]

Railton seemed totally unconcerned. When he was denied entry to
Worms – a city which, thanks to Martin Luther, had immense symbolic
significance – he returned the following day assuring his followers
that 'if we happen to get into prison, we shall be all right, for I find
from those who have been there for selling *The War Cry*, it is a very different affair from England'. Bramwell Booth – directing operations
from London – was less happy about the prospect of imprisonment. He
was worried about the risk of what he portentously called a 'diplomatic
incident'. Anxious for the Army to be accepted by the German authorities and fearful that Railton was exacerbating the situation, Bramwell
recalled him – and then agreed that he should return in secret to direct
operations incognito.

He did not direct them very well. William Booth visited Germany in
1891 and spoke to a meeting of seventy-three people – eleven officers,
forty-one members of the public and twenty-one police officers. The
General travelled to what he had believed would be a mass rally by
tramcar. Thanks to his distinction, he was awarded the privilege of
standing alongside the driver while Railton had to sit with the other
passengers. During William Booth's second visit to Germany the travel
arrangements were even more unsatisfactory. He missed his train at
Frankfurt because Railton had thought it a waste of sixpence to buy a
new timetable. So the General passed most of the journey in a crowded
third-class smoking compartment. The complaints came not from the
victim but from the Chief of Staff. Railton was already conscious that
his style of leadership was going out of fashion in the Army and that

new officers were gaining favour at his expense. He was thought to have failed hopelessly in America whereas Frederick Booth-Tucker, the General's son-in-law, had been such a success in South Africa that William Booth had announced, 'I have always felt that the Salvation Army would have to settle the Zulu difficulty.' Bramwell Booth bombarded the German headquarters with instructions, directives, requests for statistics, evidence of improved performance and additional income from Self-Denial – an unreasonable request from officers who were obliged to live on five shillings a week.

Despite disapproval of Railton's performance, William Booth – who remembered Catherine's love for her oldest friend and 'adopted son' – allowed him liberties which were forbidden to other officers. He was allowed publicly to express his distaste for trade and, by implication, the Salvation Army's growing participation in the private economy. 'It remains a painful fact that eighteen hundred years after Jesus Christ's plain declaration on the subject those who profess to Him are just as ready as others to hear about the securities with which to lay up treasures on earth.' Had he left his criticism there, no more would have been heard about it. But that was not George Scott Railton's way.

Railton loathed commercialism but, because of the need to finance the *In Darkest England* scheme, the Salvation Army had grown increasingly commercial. It sold summer underwear, Gladstone bags, visiting card photographs (twelve copies, two positions, 6/6), soap with embossed pictures of the Booth family attached, and shares in the increasingly successful building society, which was then growing at a greater speed than the Prudential. The 1894 Jubilee International Conference – planned to mark the jubilee of William Booth's conversion – was announced in a copy of *The War Cry* which also advertised Salvation Army matches 'made by methods which protected the workers from phosphorous jaw'. The announcement listed the great men who had been invited to attend. Lords Rosebery and Carrington, H. H. Asquith, A. J. Balfour and the Duke of Westminster all declined with thanks. Their courteous, if formal, regrets were described as proof that the Salvation Army was acknowledged in high places.

The public rally, which was always the emotional highlight of the Army's international conferences, was held in the Exeter Hall on 6 July 1894. Railton arrived, not in his Commissioner's uniform, but barefoot and wearing sackcloth. He was not one of the advertised speakers but rallies invariably ended with an invitation to testify. Normally members of the audience proclaimed their continued conversion. But, at the Exeter Hall, George Scott Railton was the first to rise. He held a copy of a handbill which had been produced by Colonel Bremner, the first managing director of the Salvation Army Assurance Society. His 'testimony' was not recorded. But he possessed a verbatim copy of his speech and he gladly distributed it to press and public. 'I was so glad to hear our General, at the Holiness Meeting this morning, lay down the principle of self-sacrifice which he deemed necessary to salvation. Judge then my surprise when I found lying at my feet a dirty piece of paper . . . It invited officers to pay twenty shillings of the Lord's money and offering them thirty-three farthings, a farthing for each year of Christ's life, in return.' Neither the syntax nor the arithmetic stand much examination. But the audience at the rally had no doubt about Railton's meaning. He emphasised his point by tearing up the 'dirty piece of paper', throwing it on the ground and stamping on it.

It was just two years since *The War Cry* had published the 'eminent physician's diagnosis' of Colonel Lampard's state of mental health. The Army's senior officers were quick to act on the precedent. If refusing to marry William Booth's daughter was a sign of madness, insulting the General in public must be conclusive evidence of an even more serious condition. Their round-robin to William Booth may have been an attempt to protect him from greater wrath. 'We all feel the importance of your taking some definite action in the grave matter, but we cannot but think that Commissioner Railton would never have so acted but for the physical and mental strain from which he is evidently suffering. We would suggest that you should order the Commissioner upon a lengthy furlough before coming to any final decision.'[3] But the General wanted, and asked for, an immediate apology. Railton declined with regret and received a sullen reproof. 'Since our interview I have hoped and waited for some definite expression of regret.' The errant Commissioner's invaluable service to the Army was weighed against 'the necessity of maintaining discipline'. The General had come to the conclusion that his senior officers were right. Railton 'was not responsible for the extraordinary conduct referred to'. The remedy was 'a few months' rest'.[4]

Railton replied that he would prove himself 'capable of understanding and obeying orders' and awaited new instructions. Commissioner

Coombs suggested that Railton join him in Australia. But Coombs was thought to have been insufficiently forthright in his condemnation of the original offence and Bramwell Booth feared that, by putting Coombs and Railton together, he would create a hotbed of dissent on the other side of the world. So the miscreant was sent, safely it was thought, to South America. He was then moved on to Spain. There he wrote to Arthur Booth-Clibborn, whom he thought to be his friend, and in what he believed to be confidence. Some of Railton's letters complained mildly against his treatment. Booth-Clibborn sent them on to the Chief of Staff.

Bramwell was not equipped to accommodate even the mildest form of criticism. He was pondering how to deal with Railton when he received an urgent request. Marianne Railton – in Switzerland for the health of her sickly children – longed to return home and her husband had written to Bramwell asking for an English posting. The reply to his request began with the warning that the 'subversive' letters to Booth-Clibborn had been seen at the International Headquarters. It asked for assurances 'not only do you accept [the General's] decisions and the arrangements and regulations he lays down, but you accept them in the sense that he makes them and the interpretations which he puts on them'.[5] George Scott Railton had the grace and humility to accept the old man's autocracy. The Booth children did not – particularly when it was exercised, in fact if not in theory, by Bramwell.

In some ways the Chief of Staff was even more autocratic than his father. Towards the end of 1895, he wrote to Ballington in America instructing him to mortgage all the American property – bought by the hard work and sacrifice of the United States Command – and send the proceeds to the International Headquarters in London. The property then had to be re-registered as being in the ownership of William Booth. That was only the beginning of his show of strength.

In late 1895, with William Booth on tour in India, Bramwell decided that the time had come to impress his authority on the whole international organisation. He insisted that he was doing no more than improving the efficiency of the Army, but whatever his motives, they led to a reorganisation of commands which his brothers and sisters described as 'musical chairs'. Herbert, briefly back in London for a conference, was informed that he had been transferred (without consultation) to the Australian Command. Eva was to abandon her duties in the London training homes and succeed Herbert in Canada with the new rank and title of Field Commissioner. The Booth-Clibborns were moved from France and Switzerland to Holland and Belgium and the Booth-Hellborgs from India to France. Ballington Booth was relieved of the United States Command and recalled to London. The Booth-Tuckers, who had returned to London with the intention of becoming the joint Foreign Secretaries of the Army, were warned of the possibility that they would succeed him.

At first, Ballington accepted the order – bitterly and resentfully, but with the discipline of a front-line officer. His valedictory letter to his troops not only announced that he was proceeding with arrangements to say farewell but added 'the fervent prayer that no officer of any rank, or soldier or recruit in any corps shall allow the tidings to interfere with the progress of his own advance in the organisation that we have fought so long to upbuild and uphold'.[6] As is usual on such occasions, he denied categorically that he was in any way responsible for damaging stories in the local press. He had never said, and did not believe, that London was determined to 'Anglicise' the Army in America. The letter also revealed the bungling insensitivity with which Bramwell had implemented a decision which, in itself, was entirely consistent with the Army's policy. Wesleyans had always believed in the importance of preachers – whatever their seniority – moving from appointment to appointment, rather than sinking into familiar indolence in a permanent post. But that did not mean that normal courtesies should not be observed. Ballington Booth and his wife 'had no knowledge whatever of their successors . . . and [were] not in a position to explain what or how the General may decide in his instructions to them'. No doubt resentment combined with the pleading of his officers to break down Bramwell's discipline. Whatever the cause of his insubordination, after a few days of personal turmoil, Ballington decided to disobey the instruction. He would stay in America.

The initial explanation for Ballington's disobedience was the implausible fear that diplomatic relations between Britain and America would suffer if a new territorial commander – insensitive to the details of the then not-very-special relationship – was appointed in his place. The Venezuelan government (supported by the President of the United States) was again claiming territory which Britain believed to be part of

British Guyana. Ballington feared that his removal (and replacement by a jingoistic Englishman) might well provoke an international incident – a result no less likely than the Salvation Army negotiating a land settlement with the Zulus. In fact, as well as resenting Bramwell's authority, Ballington – alone amongst the children – had begun to react against his father's absolutism. In the six months before Bramwell made his changes, father and son had not exchanged a single letter – an extraordinary state of affairs in a family of obsessive correspondents. Paradoxically, Ballington began to rebel against his father's personal domination of the Army just as the 67-year-old General was either relaxing or losing his grip. Five years earlier, with Catherine still by his side, he would never have allowed either the Army or the family to disintegrate in the way which followed Ballington's defection.

There was no doubt that Ballington was highly popular in New York. A mass rally to demand that he be allowed to stay was planned for Carnegie Hall. The Mayor of New York promised to be on the platform. Twenty years earlier, his predecessor in Gracie Mansion had refused George Railton the right to preach in the streets. Salvation Army officers were still not recognised as registered clergy, but Ballington had made them sufficiently respectable for 'many distinguished men to lend their aid . . . to an occasion of such dignity and importance that the echo of its sentiments may sound across the sea and the weight of adverse opinion presented may induce General Booth to reconsider his orders to the present leaders of the Army's work in America to [say] farewell'.[7]* Six-seater boxes were available at $10.

Major Strong, a local officer, had already sent a cable of complaint to London and was reassured by the Chief of Staff that 'CHANGE IN COMMAND INDICATES NO DISAPPROVAL WHATEVER BUT CONFIDENCE THAT LEADERS IN STATES LIKE MANY OTHERS CHANGING THIS YEAR REMAIN TRUE TO WORLD PURPOSE OF ARMY'. A copy was sent to Ballington, but it did nothing to reconcile him to the decision.

The Carnegie Hall rally was a huge success. Estimates of attendance

---

*It is worth noting that Ballington's valedictory letter and the notice of the Carnegie Rally in his support both contain the same strange grammatical construction. We must assume Ballington wrote both.

varied, but the hall, with a seating capacity of 2,700, was virtually full. The organisers urged Bramwell to think again. The best he felt able to do was plead with Ballington to change his mind. Eva and Herbert were sent to New York to beg their brother to remain true to the Salvation Army and its founder. It was a hopeless task. Major Strong, judging the local mood, telegraphed London again. Feeling was hardening against the Chief of Staff's decision. 'SEVENTEEN HUNDRED AND NINETY-SIX AUXILIARIES THREATEN WITHDRAWAL. WITHDRAW ORDER FOR PRESENT. ONLY WAY TO SAVE FROM CHAOS.'[8] William Booth was in India. To keep him informed, a more doleful telegram was being drafted by Bramwell at International Headquarters: 'EVA AND H. HAVE FAILED – COMMANDER B. ALREADY COMMITTED – WILL VERY SHORTLY BE MADE PUBLIC THE REASONS FOR . . .' The Chief of Staff went on to urge General Booth to decide on the succession: 'IT IS OF THE UTMOST IMPORTANCE – SUCCESSOR BE PUBLICLY ANNOUNCED – EVERY MOMENT IS OF CONSEQUENCE.'[9]

It was despatched to Bombay on 21 January. The reply (dated the following day) was signed 'Salvation' and was in code. It concluded 'magnifying badger havenby'.[10] Whatever its deciphered meaning, it did nothing to solve the problem.

The bitterness increased. Ballington and his wife, Maud, denied 'the opportunity to bid a loving farewell to write through *The War Cry* or to speak (to officers and men) personally', issued a detailed refutation of the statements – mostly emanating from London – which had 'misjudged and still more misrepresented' their position. They were particularly severe on their brother and sister who 'in place of calm and loving persuasion' had employed 'threats and cutting insinuations as to our motives'. According to Ballington's version of events, he and his wife were offered three courses of action – withdraw their resignation letter, leave for England immediately or resign their commissions by ten o'clock on the morning which followed the confrontation. He denied categorically the allegation that he had found sufficient 'financial and influential' support to enable them to form a rival organisation. 'We have told officers and soldiers to stand by the Army.' They did not, however, stand by it themselves. Ballington and Maud formally seceded from the Salvation Army on 9 March 1896 and founded the Volunteers of America, of which Ballington became General and Commander-in-Chief. In an implied rebuke to his father, he announced that, as he was a democrat, he would only serve for five years, after which there would be an election. He was re-elected every five years for the rest of his life.

The Salvation Army's High Command hit back. Its attack on Ballington and defence of Bramwell was based on the surprising proposition that General Booth would not contemplate favouring his family. A large meeting had asked him 'to allow America to be an exception to the rule' that commands should rotate. 'To this, however, the General could not agree and for this faithful adherence to principle and justice . . . when affecting a loved and trusted member of his own family we heartily praise God!'[11]

William Booth liked to give God what practical assistance he could. And his family, in that as in other things, followed his example. So instead of waiting for divine retribution to engulf the apostates of Ballington's new organisation, Eva did all that she could to sabotage its creation. When, shortly after failing to persuade him to change his mind, she heard that he intended to invite his whole command to defect with him, she planned to gate-crash the meeting and speak up for the Salvation Army. She was denied entry to the New York headquarters in 14th Street – according to the *New York Times*, 'a cross between a skyscraping office building and an armoury'[12] which, by its size and shape, confirmed that the Army was in America to stay. Eva ran round to the rear of the building, forced her way through the house which backed on to the hall, climbed the fire escape, pushed open an unlocked window and arrived, uninvited and unannounced, in the hall. At first Ballington refused to allow her to speak, but she insisted and proved that her brother's caution was justified. After her emotional appeal, most of the officers and men decided to remain in the Salvation Army. Ballington left the 14th Street headquarters as soon as his sister finished speaking and never entered them again. But Eva's remedial work was not quite finished. She thought that the case for the Army had to be made in all the places where, in happier days, it had enjoyed untroubled popularity. At one meeting she was hissed by Ballington's supporters. Seizing the Stars and Stripes which was hanging over the platform, she draped it over her shoulders and cried, 'Hiss that if you dare.' The theatrical gesture was not even original. John Greenleaf Whittier had immortalised Barbara Frietchie who, at the height of the American Civil War, had wrapped herself in the Old Glory and told the Confederate soldiers, 'Shoot if you must this old grey head / But spare your country's flag she said.' The gesture evoked brave memories in the American audience. The hissing stopped.

The Booth-Tuckers set sail for America, leaving behind (in the care of a nurse) Tancred, their youngest son. Tancred was seven weeks old and seriously ill. Just as the pilot boat was about to cast off from their liner, a telegram arrived warning them that the little boy had only hours to live. Emma was adjudged too frail to be lowered over the side of the ship. So Frederick Booth-Tucker returned to shore with the pilot. Tancred's condition improved and his father again embarked for New York. He had been three days at sea when news reached him that Tancred was dead. The next morning the Booth-Hellborgs' baby died of dysentery in Bombay. The Booths never flinched from sacrifice – their own or others. No doubt Emma and Lucy, like their mother and grandmother before them, thought of their dead children as happy in heaven rather than deprived of life. And they had both died in the noble cause of strengthening the Army.

In America, Ballington struggled on, leading a poor imitation of the great international movement from which its General's son had seceded. The bitterness which the secession caused, instead of fading with the years, increased in its intensity. On 28 October 1903 Emma Booth-Tucker, Consul and Commander-in-Chief of the United States Forces, was killed in a railway accident on the Topeka and Santa Fe Railway at Dean Lake, Missouri. When Ballington and Herbert Booth – together with their wives – arrived at the memorial meeting in New York, they were refused permission to hold what they described as a 'family gathering . . . around the remains of our departed sister', although they had been given the impression that the local Salvation Army had agreed to arrange 'a room at the Carnegie Building to conduct a family funeral service with none other present than members of the family'.[13] The Chief Secretary of the Army in the United States – a local officer, temporarily in command – sent London a long and convoluted explanation of the incident.* Letters had been sent but not received. Messages had been misunderstood. Ballington and Herbert had not wanted to sit on the platform of the principal memorial

---

*The letter, in the Salvation Army Heritage Centre, has been damaged by fire. The words in brackets are what seem likely to have completed the sentences.

meeting. Certainly a family gathering before the main event had been suggested. But the Chief Secretary had said, 'No! There could be no meeting before the Carnegie [service]. All our arrangements had been made and it would simply [put the] program considerably out.'[14] Like every Booth marriage, christening and funeral, Emma's memorial meeting was not a family affair dedicated to one individual, but organised for the great glory of the Salvation Army.

The American secession was the most dramatic of the rebellions because Ballington, the proudest and the most impetuous of William Booth's children, reacted to Bramwell's instructions with a public show of defiance which his brothers and sisters understood but deplored. Their discipline held, even in the face of the Chief of Staff's provocation. But, although they suffered in silence, their suffering was no less than Ballington's. Kate in particular was heartbroken at being required to leave France. She had served there for most of her adult life. Her seven children spoke English (when they spoke it at all) with a French accent and she had intended that her ninth (already on the way) would be brought up to share her own emotions which she described in the strong assertion, 'I love France. I love its people as much as me.'[15] She could also cite, in support of the argument that she should stay, a remarkable record of achievement. In ten years, she had established 200 stations and commissioned 400 full-time officers. She wrote to her father pleading that she be allowed to stay. The replies over his signature were either terse or evasive and were posted when he was out of the country on speaking tours. Kate was convinced that they were drafted by Bramwell.

Even before she received her orders to leave France, Kate was becoming increasingly impatient with the rigid autocracy of the Salvation Army's organisation. 'I was,' she wrote, 'territorial commander in France and I could not make a corporal or sergeant without permission from London.'[16] Brother Herbert sympathised and encouraged her resentment. 'It is not in the will of man to devise a stricter code of laws than those which relate to a Commissioner's expenditure of funds'.[17] The Army was growing too fast to accommodate the style of personal management on which William Booth insisted and which Bramwell chose to copy. Herbert was inclined to excuse rather than to excoriate his elder brother. He had no doubt where the blame lay for the Chief of Staff's excess of zeal and, in a moment of reckless anguish, asked his father, 'Who taught us so well the autocratic principle? Are we not as familiar with discussions at home concerning leaving your hands untied and your will unfettered as we are with our alphabet?' However, it was not just the pervasive bureaucracy of the international office which was coming between Kate and the Salvation Army.

Her husband, Arthur Booth-Clibborn, was at heart still a Quaker. At least he was still a pacifist and remained (despite being promoted to Colonel) uneasy about ranks and titles. On to those basic beliefs he had grafted a theology which the Society of Friends would have found abominable. He believed in faith healing and justified his view with a biblical quotation: 'The Lord Himself took over our infirmities and bore our sickness.' And he believed that the Second Coming was imminent. That, in itself, should not have disqualified him from holding a commission in the Army. Long ago, in the East End of London, John Eason, William Booth's first recruit, had insisted that the end was nigh. But Booth-Clibborn, because of his manner as much as his beliefs, irritated the High Command.

Kate and Arthur Booth-Clibborn accepted the new posting in the Low Countries. Lucy and Emmanuel Booth-Hellborg took their place in France. Dissatisfaction in the ranks, which broke out as soon as the news of their transfer was announced, escalated into open revolt. Peace was not restored until George Railton – ever willing and always available – took the Booth-Hellborgs' place. However, the arrival of the new commander at the Weesperzijde in Amsterdam was marked by the sort of recognition that William Booth thought appropriate to his senior officers. Queen Wilhelmina sent a message of welcome.

Whatever their doubts and disappointments, the Booth-Clibborns did their best to make a success of their new command. All the proper Salvation Army rules were obeyed. The men's shelter was improved and extended to include a meeting hall and on Christmas Day 1,000 dinners and 500 suppers were served to the Amsterdam poor. Copies of *The War Cry* were sold in the bars and public houses and Kate felt sufficiently confident and contented to mount a three-week campaign in Brussels – where, to her delight, she could speak French. On the first night she had an audience of 800 enthusiasts in the Salle de la Grande Harmonie where, on the eve of the Battle of Waterloo, the sounds of revelry by night had echoed from the Duchess of Richmond's ball. Kate made a dramatic entrance, wearing sackcloth and with ashes on her head. 'I come to you in mourning,' she said. 'I come to you in mourning for your sins, for your selfishness, for your rejection of God. It fills me with sorrow and, unless you forsake it, it will bring upon you the judgement of God.' Everything seemed normal.

But Arthur Booth-Clibborn was not prepared to accept the rigid discipline of the Salvation Army and Kate was supportive of whatever her husband did and believed. Three times they requested permission to visit London for a conference of the China Inland Mission and three times they were refused. They came nevertheless. Arthur then declined to visit a music festival on the grounds that it was designed for pagans not Salvationists. He chose, instead, to visit dockland public houses where he played hymns on an instrument called an autoharp which rested across his knees as he sang. Kate spent the time visiting striking miners.

While Kate was defying her father, William Booth was offending his son. In the New Year of 1899 he visited Australia. During his visit he gave Herbert a copy of the 'New Rules and Regulations' which he warned, gratuitously Herbert thought, must be observed to the letter if penalties and punishments were to be avoided. After the General left, Herbert told him 'The result of your visit was to leave us utterly dispirited and broken hearted.'[18] But the immediate problem was in Europe. Kate – with or without encouragement is not known – read the new regulations to which her brother had taken such exception and announced her intention to ignore them. She and her husband again formally asked for formal permission to evangelise on their own terms – as pacifists, millenarianists and advocates of 'faith healing'.

It was Arthur Booth-Clibborn's enthusiasm for pacifism which caused the immediate embarrassment. England was at war in South Africa, and Bramwell Booth was unequivocally on the side of the Boers – not least because of his view of Cecil Rhodes. 'I have,' he confessed, 'never met anyone, always excepting the old General, who made such an impression on me.'[19] William Booth as always judged the conflict by the way it affected the Salvation Army. 'He grieved over the possible shooting of Salvationists by each other.'[20] Arthur Booth-Clibborn's demand for an end to shooting in general added to his distress. The behaviour of Salvationists during that war was the beginning of one of the Army's greatest glories – support, under fire, for the Armed Forces of the Crown. Ever since the first mugs of tea and sandwiches were distributed to the 20,000 horse and foot who went to Table Bay, British servicemen have expected the Salvation Army to have its mobile canteens up in the front line.

Arthur was distributing tracts to soldiers – Kipling's 'gentlemen in khaki going south' – when he heard that Dr John Dowie, an American faith healer, had arrived in Britain. Dowie, who claimed to be the reincarnation of the prophet Elijah, led a sect called the Zionites. His followers believed that he could perform miracles. After two secret meetings it seemed that Booth-Clibborn agreed with them. Having come to the conclusion that a rival prophet at the head of a competing mission was the harbinger of a 'gigantic truth', Booth-Clibborn could hardly be expected to remain an officer of the Salvation Army. In fact, Bramwell spent six weeks attempting – in more emollient language than usual – to persuade him to change his mind. William Booth had insisted that the Booth-Clibborns be given no quarter. 'Regards Holland,' he wrote to Bramwell, 'let us be straight and plain and firm as a rock. Make them understand that it must be so.'[21] However, Kate occupied a special place in both William and Bramwell Booth's affection. She was *La Maréchale*, the indomitable campaigner who, in the view of her father, embodied both her mother's virtues and his own strengths. Her brother had preached with her on East London street corners when they were both children. And neither father nor son had any doubt that, if Arthur were to be expelled, Kate would immediately resign.

Arthur Booth-Clibborn was unyielding in his commitment to his bizarre beliefs. He resigned from the Salvation Army on 10 January 1902. Immediate attempts were made to 'save' Kate. She reacted with the accusation that her father and brother were trying to break up her marriage: 'How can you demand I turn my back on my husband. I love him with all my heart and all my soul. What is there in the rules of the Salvation Army that takes precedence over the conviction between a man and his wife and demands the renunciation of the vows and faithfulness of marriage?'[22]

Kate – who loved her father and was proud to be like him – had nevertheless not realised that he was 'a General first and a father afterwards' and that he had 'no children outside the Salvation Army'. Eleven years later, with her sister dead in America, she learned that William Booth really thought of deserters from the Army as deserters from the family. Hearing of Emma's death, she sent him a message of love and condolence. His diary recorded the receipt of 'a letter from Mrs Clibborn full of assertions of her great love for myself and Bramwell and sympathy with us in the tragic death and her lamentation over the loss suffered by the death of Emma'. The entry reads as if he did not want to remember that 'Mrs Clibborn' was his daughter. He knew that she believed very little of the nonsense that attracted her husband to Dowie. But he did not realise – indeed he was incapable of realising – that she loved her husband more than she loved the Salvation Army.

On the fifteenth anniversary of their wedding, Arthur and Kate Booth-Clibborn announced the creation of the Friends of Zion Christian Mission. Her defection made Herbert's inevitable. He felt himself exiled in Australia – possessing the name and limited power of a territorial commissioner, not because his father and elder brother had any faith in him but because he was a Booth. As always, the High Command attempted to hide revolt behind the pretence of sickness. The official announcement seemed actually to regret that Commissioner Herbert Booth had resigned his command because of ill health and was to take charge of the 20,000 acre sheep farm on the bank of the River Collie – part of the *In Darkest England* scheme.[23] The hope that fresh air would clear his head as well as his lungs was sustained for six months. In May 1902, he and his wife resigned and set out their reasons in a letter which, for all its self-pity, explained with great cogency the problem which faced a rapidly expanding Army:

> . . . since the Army has now become such an immense concern, involving such mighty interests not alone as regards *property* but more unfortunately as regards *personality* we see no escape from the conclusion that it demands for its future safety, happiness and unity a Government in which its leading spirits throughout the world shall have a voice and a vote in some constituent assembly.

William Booth replied to his son – in sorrow and at great length – four months later. His time had been taken up 'in European tours with their continued travelling and [with] meetings which have occupied . . . the greater part of the summer'. His only family was the Salvation Army.

22

Promoted to Glory

William Booth was as restless in old age as he had been in youth. Catherine's death and the rebellion of his children had made him uncertain about the future direction that the Army should take. But he had no doubts about the path which he should follow. He wanted to be a preacher again, with (like Wesley) the world for his parish. When Emma and Frederick Booth-Tucker arrived in America to replace Ballington and Maude Booth, there was a letter from the General waiting for them. 'It is,' he wrote, 'a curious piece of comfort that anything is better than stagnation and being left alone.'[1] General Booth enjoyed both the battle and the victory. He wanted simultaneously to be admired by the Establishment and excoriated by the brewers. In fact, the Salvation Army still had implacable enemies. But the struggle was not as dramatic as it once had been. In his sixties, William Booth imagined that he wanted to be back on the streets running the gauntlet of angry publicans. In fact he did not have the enthusiasm to engage in the new sort of warfare which his success had made inevitable.

The Charity Organisations' Society was still on his trail. In the spring of 1895, their Whitechapel Committee alleged that the Salvation Army free shelters in their area were insanitary. At the end of July they made an official complaint. Between the 15th and 26th of that month, 'seventeen persons suffering from smallpox were admitted to the Whitechapel infirmary'. All of them had 'recently been inmates of Salvation Army shelters'.[2] When the Vestry of St George the Martyr, Southwark made a similar complaint, a question was asked in Parliament. The Board of Local Government had already inquired into the matter. 'The general result of the inquiry would appear to be that the Salvation Army authorities realised their responsibility in the matter of smallpox and are anxious to do all in their power to prevent the spread of the disease'[3] The Chief of Staff – who had not always been well treated by the House of Commons – was no doubt gratified by the answer. But the condition of Salvation Army shelters had become a matter of public debate. Everyone who was opposed to William Booth and his work, from high churchmen to scientific atheists, took the opportunity to reveal examples of insanitary overcrowding.

The Salvation Army officer responsible for the shelter at Blackfriars was charged with overcrowding and the courts, in their judgement, instructed that no more than 500 vagrants should sleep there on any one night. As a result, 'at least 250 unfortunate and hungry men were turned out on to the streets with little prospect of other shelter than those streets can afford'.[4] A technical, as well as emotional, debate followed. Two doctors who had visited Blackfriars said that they would rather have slept in the street. An engineer who had installed a ventilation shaft argued that, thanks to his device, the shelter was more hygienic than other establishments which allowed greater space between the beds. *The Times* adjudicated in one of its editorials. 'It is simply monstrous that, in such circumstances, Mr Booth should be allowed to breed infectious diseases in shelters which may be philanthropic but are also commercial speculations.'[5] Mr Booth himself was entirely detached from the controversy. He said not a public word from start to finish.

The General wanted to become a preacher again. His new passion was for travel, both in Britain and abroad. For his tours were, in effect, peripatetic evangelism on a grand scale – opportunities to confirm the Salvation Army's position in respectable society and illustrate how far he had travelled since his birth in Sneinton. By holding highly publicised meetings with the great figures of his time – emperors, kings, the political leaders of the new democracies and the potentates of those

Eastern countries which had allowed his soldiers within their borders – he was exalting his Army and its Commander-in-Chief.

On the afternoon of Monday 21 December 1896 he visited William Ewart Gladstone at Hawarden. Gladstone had, he knew, read *In Darkest England*.[6] The meeting gave him such delight that he published a pamphlet which reproduced, as far as the General's memory allowed, 'a talk with Mr Gladstone at his own fireside'. The result was an embarrassing demonstration of the awe in which the General held the powerful and famous. It was also an illustration of his invincible insensitivity. The Grand Old Man's letter with which the pamphlet begins comes very close to being a reproof: 'I thank you for the promise contained in your kind note that you are sending me, besides the books you refer to, a note you have made of the conversations between us . . . Your account will go forth on your own responsibility and will not, I apprehend, require me to take any steps with regard to it.'

Mr Gladstone need not have worried that General Booth would produce a version of their discussion which caused embarrassment. The tone was set by the introduction. 'Mr Herbert Gladstone met me at the entrance to the Castle – kindness itself, as he always is – where we found Mrs Gladstone and Mrs Drew. Our formal introductions over, they made me feel at home in a moment.' There followed a dialogue which showed every sign of Mr Gladstone fulfilling an unwelcome commitment with patience and courtesy:

> I mentioned the fact that I had been allowed to hold two
> successive meetings in the King's gardens, the gates being
> closed to the public for a session, in order that entrance money
> might be taken for the benefit of our work there among the
> poor. 'Indeed,' Mr Gladstone remarked, 'but that was Denmark;
> tell me, what is the attitude of the authorities in Sweden
> towards your labours there?'

Twenty years earlier William and Catherine Booth would have exploited a visit to Hawarden in order to popularise and publicise the work of the Salvation Army. But the pamphlet which followed the 1896 meeting was unmistakably written for the glory of the General rather than his soldiers. The two grand old men were, William Booth wrote, 'in absolute agreement about the relationship between church and state'. No doubt he referred, with dubious justification, to disestablishment. Booth was for complete separation. Gladstone abstained in House of Commons votes on both Scottish and Welsh church independence. Although William Booth did not describe the principles of church government which they held in common, he did record that he was 'unexpectedly gratified' by the similarity of their views on most subjects. Mr Gladstone expressed his disapproval of 'the objection he found running through many religious works to what was described as self-righteousness'. General Booth had no hesitation in supporting that view. The tone of the Gladstone pamphlet was at once obsequious and anxious. General Booth wanted to be on equal terms with the greatest of all English Prime Ministers but was too overcome with the privilege of meeting him to express anything but agreement. However, as an exercise in sycophancy, it does not compare with his account of the audience with Edward VII in June 1904:

> I had come to expect a selfish, sensuous personage, popular
> because of lending himself to the recreations etc. – showy
> functions – a change from the quiet role his Queen Mother had
> played – unwilling to pose as treading in the shoes of Albert the
> Good. And all at once, the embodiment of a simple genial
> English Gentleman was sprung upon me.[7]

Perhaps the General felt particularly warm towards the King because of the way in which he had treated Bramwell at the time of his coronation. The Chief of Staff had been the Army's choice of representative in Westminster Abbey, but the formal invitation stipulated 'Court dress'. Bramwell wrote to the Earl Marshal to ask permission to wear his Salvationist uniform, explaining that 'it was much more than a badge of office or rank. It represents the great principle for which we are contending'.[8] The Earl Marshal was not impressed. Court dress was *de rigueur*. The coronation was postponed while the King's appendix was removed. So Bramwell had time to argue. When the new date was announced, he wrote to the King himself asking for gracious permission to 'attend in the uniform of my rank as a Salvation Army officer'. Lord Knollys, the principal private secretary, telegraphed the King's personal agreement and Bramwell, in full regimentals, took part in a service which reminded him of a Salvation Army meeting. 'There were

banners . . . there were uniforms . . . there were the responses of the
congregation to the prayers . . . there was the reading of moving passages of Scripture . . . there was the note through it all of glory to God
and abounding joy.' He went on to illustrate the presumption which,
above everything else about the Salvation Army, irritated the established Church. 'The possibility occurred to me that the Church of
England had taken some lessons from the Salvation Army while hesi-
tating to acknowledge the source.'

Bramwell's judgement on the coronation liturgy was a rare example
of Booth *lèse-majesté* – at least in the presence of royalty. His father – on
a tour of world capitals – had only to see a crowned head to reach, at
least metaphorically, for his forelock. In Copenhagen the King and
Queen were 'most friendly'. He was 'much impressed by the Queen, a
serious personage. Dressed very neatly without any attempt to do the
grand or queenly.' In Stockholm, the King was ill, but the Queen was
'a very superior woman . . . with a perfectly free and easy manner'.
William Booth was always very grateful for being put at his ease and
always noted the civil questions of the great and good. King Edward
had 'with extended hand and cheery countenance . . . pointed to an
easy chair a few feet away from him'. The General longed to be
accepted.

The visit to Japan, like every other, began with apprehension and
ended in unqualified admiration for, and gratitude towards, his host.
The Emperor was wearing 'royal costume with various stars, representing different orders, glistening on his breast'. However, despite his
decoration, the General found 'nothing showy about his appearance
and . . . The event proved that we had been mistaken in our forebod-
ings . . . His face appeared, during the few moments when I had the
opportunity of observing him, to indicate determination, strength and
kindness.'[9] Presidents impressed him as much as kings and emperors.
The man who had led the ragged boys into the Wesley Chapel and
believed that poverty bred vice had begun to behave as if power, fame
and wealth were, in themselves, virtues.

As early as February 1898 he had, during a tour of America, been
asked to open a session of the Senate by saying the prayer with which the
day's business began. During the afternoon he spent half an hour with
President William McKinley. Five years later he was back in the White
House to meet President Theodore Roosevelt who, to the General's

delight, was accompanied by the Vice-President, the Speaker of the House, the Secretary of State and the Secretaries for War and for the Interior. The endearing naïveté of his account of the meeting does something to mitigate its sycophantic tone. Commissioner McFarland – a local official of the Army in America – 'interposed the remark . . . I am sure the President would be pleased to hear about the Oxford Function . . . the President at once said, "Yes, General, I would like to hear about it very much." Then came another suggestion from McFarland. "The facts concerning the General's recent visit to Japan would, no doubt, be of equal interest."' Commissioner McFarland was clearly destined to go far in the Salvation Army.

The Oxford function to which McFarland referred was the ceremony at which General Booth had been made an honorary Doctor of Civil Laws. Combined with the Freedom of the City of London, recognition by the University of Oxford ought to have convinced him that he had at last joined the Establishment – an ambition which he had once justified as part of the strategy to secure support for, and investment in, the social programme which he proposed.

Although he walked with kings – without entirely retaining the common touch – he was still deeply involved in organising at least the more grandiose parts of the *Darkest England* scheme. It was not so easy to inspire interest in the more ambitious parts of the project. Nobody took wholly seriously his plans to establish Overseas Colonies. Cecil Rhodes seemed briefly excited by the idea – particularly the notion that they would turn out to be extensions of England established in Africa. When he visited the Farm Colony at Hadleigh during 1898 he encouraged the idea that Rhodesia would be the natural site of William Booth's most ambitious project. But the Overseas Colony scheme needed capital and that Rhodes was unable or unwilling to provide. Perhaps Rhodes's confidence in the entire project was undermined when he became the victim – William Booth would have thought of it as beneficiary – of one of the General's most disturbing habits. It was the General's practice, apparently on a sudden impulse, to demand that whoever he was with should kneel with him and pray. It was an eccentricity which he gratified in public as well as in private. Margot Asquith 'after a mere half-hour's acquaintance prayed with General Booth . . . in a railway carriage they happened to be sharing'.[10] But Margot Asquith often prayed on what more reticent souls would have described as inappropriate occasions. She even persuaded her husband, during his years as Home Secretary, to join her on his knees in prayer. Cecil Rhodes, on the other hand, was not a naturally pious man. Indeed, on the railway journey back from Hadleigh he told the General, in response to some searching cross-examination, that 'it's not quite so well with my soul as I could wish'.

The journey from Essex to London was made in the company of Lord Loch, sometime Governor of the Cape and High Commissioner for South Africa, and Bramwell Booth, who made a note of every detail the same night. He recorded a discussion between his father and Rhodes on the relationship between material and spiritual welfare. Rhodes recalled that during the Commission of Inquiry which had followed the Jameson Raid, the General had prayed for him. Lord Loch complained, 'He has never prayed for me.' William Booth was notably deficient in humour and incapable of comprehending a joke, however slight, about anything even remotely spiritual. So, assuming that Lord Loch had made a genuine complaint, he announced, 'I will pray for you now' and sank to his knees. According to Bramwell, who was there in the carriage, Cecil Rhodes did not join him on the compartment floor 'because it was physically difficult for him to do so'.[11] Harold Begbie – in whose 'official' biography William Booth always wears a halo – had him down with the General, side by side in humble supplication between the seats.[12]

If William Booth prayed for the success of his Overseas Colonies, his prayers were not answered. The Charter Company, which effectively governed Rhodesia, could not finance the planned settlement. So, during the summer of 1908, he began to lobby politicians for help. Lord Rosebery – briefly Gladstone's successor as Liberal Prime Minister – told him the Rhodes Trust, which he controlled, was virtually insolvent. Then, after a brief discussion about the dangers of socialism, his lordship left for Goodwood races with the depressing admission that, much as he supported the General's idea, he had no influence with the current Liberal leadership. Next day, William Booth saw David Lloyd George, the Chancellor of the Exchequer, in the House of Commons and, to his obvious delight, passed Winston Churchill, the President of the Board of Trade – 'piercing eyes and glowing countenance' – on the stairs. He asked Lloyd George for £100,000 'on condition that the South Africa Company will furnish

£150,000'.[13] Lloyd George cross-examined him on the details of the scheme and then took him along the corridor to see the Prime Minister. Mr Asquith arranged for him to see Lord Crewe, the Colonial Secretary. There is no suggestion in his diaries that William Booth feared that he was being passed from hand to hand. On the day that he visited the Colonial Office, he also met A. J. Balfour, the Leader of the Opposition, who, as always seemed to be the case in such interviews, first offered his visitor a choice of chairs and then proved himself to be as admirable as every other famous personage who entertained the General. 'His feature, while retaining every expected element of strength, appeared to indicate a nature as tender as a woman's.'[14] It was a view of the ex-Prime Minister which was not shared by those Fenians who, in the response to the way in which he put down the Irish Rebellion, called him 'Bloody Balfour'. William Booth was at least honest with himself about the faint hope of retaining the friendship of politicians of every stripe. A Licensing Bill was making its weary way through Parliament and, because of obstruction by Tory peers, was preparing the way for the constitutional crisis which ended in limiting the Lords' power of delay. Since it restricted opening hours, William Booth felt a moral duty to support it. But he deeply regretted that, after forty years of conscious neutrality, he had to take political sides.

Yet, paradoxically, William Booth suffered in old age from a disease which is usually associated with politicians – an inability, in a *tête-à-tête*, to show the strength of feeling which he was able to express to a mass audience. So he believed, because he wanted to believe, that everybody he met was gracious, complimentary and kind. No doubt they were in private conversation. But none of them could find the money to finance an Overseas Colony of such a size that, as William Booth had once believed, it would change the world.

By then, William Booth's enthusiasm for the whole *In Darkest England* scheme had changed in character. He began to have doubts about his own motives and feared that he was supporting social reform for social reform's own sake – not as a necessary prelude to the redemption and salvation of the wicked poor. In old age, he wanted to be an evangelist again, saving souls and pointing the way to heaven. He was, by temperament and experience, no more an administrator than he was a theologian. Yet he was the head of a mighty international organisation. And the *Darkest England* scheme seemed more and more to demand management, which was not his forte, rather than missionary zeal, which was. He was God's salesman, not His chief executive. And it was to that role which he more and more reverted during the last ten years of his life.

By 1908 he was sending Salvation Army medical missionaries to work with lepers in Java. So he travelled great distances, often – because of recurring ill health – in considerable distress, to spread the word of the Lord. In a single year he visited France, Germany, Holland, Denmark, Norway, Sweden, Switzerland, Italy, the United States and Canada. Overseas he made carefully planned celebrity appearances at meticulously staged events. In Britain he became an itinerant evangelist again. Much to his credit, his revivalism was organised in a way which, although immensely demanding on him, was wholly appropriate to the new century.

The idea had come to him in 1900.[15] He described, in language uninhibited by false modesty, how one day in Banbury he first thought of modernising the organisation of his campaigns. 'A crowd of my own people and friends came to the station to give me a send-off. Such was the affection shown and so manifest was the pleasure derived from my visit that I said to myself, "Why should I not impart the satisfaction to those comrades and friends who have never had the satisfaction of seeing my face or hearing my voice?" and then the idea occurred to me that the automobile would not only be the readiest means of transit but the only plan by which I could reach the small towns and outlying hamlets.'[16] The penalty of a motor tour for a man in his mid-seventies was that the cavalcade could move so easily from town to town – stopping at villages on the way to meet small groups of supporters – that there was barely a moment for rest and recuperation. That was its attraction to General Booth. His appetite for evangelism was insatiable. In the days before motor transport was available, he had always complained bitterly about the wasted time while waiting for railway connections.

On 9 August 1904 he set out on the first of what was to become his annual motor tour – an evangelical version of Gladstone's Midlothian Campaign – spread along the length of the country rather than over a single constituency. At the age of seventy-five – and in poor health since his teens – he travelled 1,224 miles in twenty-nine days from Land's End to Dundee, and addressed 164 meetings. Seventy-four of them were indoor rallies at which he spoke, on average, for seventy minutes. In the spring of the following year, he first went to the Holy Land – where he climbed Mount Calvary carrying a Salvation Army flag – and then sailed on to Australia. Thus prepared, he set out on the second of his motor tours. It was both more spectacular and more extensive than the first. He travelled in a distinctive car – white with red wheels – and covered the whole country by pressing on from Dundee to John o'Groats. In all, he covered 2,250 miles and spoke in 121 towns. The third motor tour was less ambitious. He visited only 98 towns and travelled barely 1,700 miles. The fourth covered almost exactly the same distance, but lasted three days longer. The fifth motor tour began in June 1908 as far north as Dundee and ended as far south as Crystal Palace. But the General still completed 1,000 miles and addressed 140 meetings in 78 towns. A year later, the sixth motor tour was planned to take him across, rather than up and down, England and into Wales. It was not completed.

William Booth had always been blessed with extraordinary energy and resilience. But at the end of his life he was driven on by more than duty to his vocation. The old man was lonely. It was a strange state of affairs for an octogenarian who, after Emma's death, still had seven surviving children and thirty-eight grandchildren. But too many of those he loved had been driven away, or forced by his unyielding autocracy to turn their backs on the family and the Army which was its extension. The officers who had been with him since the days of the Christian Mission were dying, one by one. They had been less friends than subordinates but at least he had felt at home with them – able to express his true feelings and his honest fears. By the end, only one was left – Commissioner John Lawley, who became guardian, companion and nurse but never confidant. Railton and Bramwell remained – both of them too loving and loyal to be alienated by his determination to dominate them. Even in exile, Railton was William Booth's man. But he was far away in Canada. So it was to Bramwell that he confided his secret doubts. They often revealed the worst, which was the most sanctimonious, aspect of his character.

One letter began, 'I have been much exercised during the night with thoughts about our interview with WTS [Stead]. After seeing him, I am always more or less tormented with the feeling that I have not dealt faithfully with him.' Stead had stood by and supported General Booth through every vicissitude, even though at the height of the 'Maiden Tribute' crisis the General had ordered Bramwell to leave the campaigner against child prostitution to sink or swim alone. Yet William Booth's concern was not that he had treated an old friend badly but that he had failed to bring him to the penitent form and salvation. 'Why don't we say to him, as we would say to a servant girl, if she came to the PF, "Come out from amongst them?"' He then went on to list Stead's failures. 'He had the *Pall Mall Gazette* . . . he threw it away. He had the love of the Salvation Army . . . he threw it away. He had the esteem of nearly every generous Christian . . . he threw it away with his Julia Fantastic notions.'[17] Julia was the American spiritualist who had convinced Stead that she could put him in touch with his dead son. Stead's reaction to Julia's promise of reunion was uncharacteristically gullible, but William Booth's reaction to his weakness was typically unyielding – it was the hard edge of his belief that made him an irresistible leader. But it was not a quality that surrounded him with friends in old age.

Nor did he go out of his way to endear himself to those who befriended him. The well-to-do supporters in whose houses he stayed during his motor tours were all warned, a week in advance, of his requirements – 'In making the toast, the bread should be cut tolerably thin and gradually toasted until it is dry and hard but not too crisp.' When the arrangements failed to please – or when the accommodation was inadequate – he simply took over the house and reorganised it according to his own taste. 'He demanded his dinner at once and simply wolfed it, putting his knife in the salt and in his mouth. He next retired upstairs but didn't like the bedroom I had prepared as it was at the front of the house. So he took possession of the rose room . . . During the afternoon the fire must have annoyed the General in some way because he put it out by throwing water over the fire and the hearth . . . Nearly all our doors had to be padded with dusters to prevent them banging and orders were sent down to "shut the dog up".'[18] But he was as indomitable in his faith and work as he was intolerable in his private conduct.

In August 1908 he made one last desperate effort to revive the Overseas Colonies with a visit to South Africa. His efforts were hampered by deteriorating sight and a pain behind his left eye. As soon as he was back in London he went to see a noted eye specialist, Dr Bell-

Taylor, and told him he believed that he had a cataract. The problem was worse than he had imagined. 'Dr Taylor says that I have a cataract in both eyes, one of which is ready for an operation, but recommends that I wait for the other to ripen so that both can be operated on at the same time.'[19] The operation took place ten days before Christmas in Guy's Hospital. William Booth described the procedure in the loving detail that characterised all his diary entries – evidence of both an endearing simplicity and a less attractive self-obsession. 'The actual work on the eye did not last for more than two minutes. Both eyes were then bandaged up with sticking plaster to prevent any movement whatsoever.'[20] He was consoled by a message of good will from Queen Alexandria.

A house had been built for him at Hadley Wood where Adjutant Helen Treen joined his staff as housekeeper and assistant to Commissioner John Lawley. He paid the Salvation Army rent, as did Bramwell, who lived in The Homestead half a mile away. Bramwell and his family joined William for lunch on Christmas Day. The old man did not pretend that he enjoyed such gatherings. And he ate his usual toast, steamed vegetables and rice pudding. But, as he explained, Catherine would have expected him to make a seasonable gesture towards his eldest son.

The work went on. The 1909 motor tour paused at Hereford where the General had been invited to lodge with the Bishop. He dined on hot milk and roast apple and retired to bed in apparently good health and spirits. When he woke next morning, he could barely see. But he drove on to Pontypool where his host, a doctor, warned him that his condition was potentially serious and urged him to return to London. William Booth ignored his advice and left for Newport. There, the pain was so bad that another doctor was summoned. He confirmed the Pontypool diagnosis. The scar had given way in his left eye and the iris was damaged. The motor tour was abandoned and the General returned to London for an immediate operation. He again described the surgery and the ghastly complications which followed with an almost prurient attention to detail. He had recorded the facts of Catherine's terminal illness with the same unrestrained interest in decay and decomposition. Perhaps he thought that flesh was inherently unclean. It was certainly frail. William Booth was left blind in the left eye.

It did not make him rest. Indeed for a month or two he worked harder than ever – preaching in England and travelling abroad to give his blessings to the divisions of his Army in foreign lands. In early 1910 he visited Holland, Germany and Sweden. Then he moved on to America. He was in Zurich when Edward VII died. When he returned to Britain, he visited the Home Office to discuss extending the Salvation Army's work inside prisons and with discharged prisoners. Not surprisingly, the remaining eye began to deteriorate. At the end of 1911, he gave a lecture in Rome on the Salvation Army's principles and purposes and he addressed the Army's International Social Council at such length that his address was published as a book. The eye deteriorated still further.

William Booth – half blind and eighty-three – was still travelling in early 1912. He visited Holland in February and March and was apparently coming to terms with his disability, despite several heavy falls. But by April he could barely see at all and his doctors recommended yet more surgery. An operating theatre was put together in Hadley Wood. When the doctors had finished, they insisted that Bramwell break the bad news. He found it impossible to set out the terrible fact in simple English. 'You mean,' his father asked him, 'that I am blind?' Even then Bramwell could not bring himself to say the words. 'Well General,' he answered, 'I fear that we must contemplate that.'

Blind old men can often live on for years. But William Booth, his work over, sank gently into oblivion. Sometimes he talked about doing more work with discharged prisoners, extending the Army's work to China and setting up a special unit to deal with homeless children. But despite the moments of lucid enthusiasm, it was clear that he was fading away. On Sunday 17 August he lost consciousness just before a great thunderstorm – equal to that which marked Catherine's death – broke over Hadley Wood. He hung on to life, drifting in and out of consciousness, for almost two months. The Salvation Army flag which he had carried up Mount Calvary was hung above his bed. He died under its shadow at thirteen minutes past ten on Tuesday 20 October 1912.

The Army's High Command asked for him to be buried in Westminster Abbey. Mercifully, and no doubt for the wrong reasons, the Dean refused. So he was buried as was appropriate, and as he would have wished, next to Catherine and with his officers in Abney Park. He was given a soldier's funeral with his cap (his badge of rank) and his Bible (his sword) on the coffin. A window had been cut into its lid. Through it General Booth could see the picture of his dead wife which hung above him. It was, in its way, an essentially pagan gesture. For William and Catherine were, according to the canons of their faith, already united in heaven. But its purpose was theatrical not theological. William Booth had taught the Salvation Army always to put on a good show.

Sixty-five thousand mourners passed by the coffin, a congregation of 35,000 filled Olympia for the memorial service and 5,000 Salvationists marched six abreast behind the cortège. The King and Queen sent a wreath to the churchyard. So did a dozen other heads of state. That night, in the East End of London where General Booth's first and best work had been done, a rumour swept through the public houses. Queen Alexandria, they whispered, had walked incognito in widow's weeds and veil, behind the coffin. It was not true and that, in a way, was its importance. William Booth had become part of English folklore.

Epilogue

William Booth died in the certainty of resurrection and eternal life and – being a man of simple faith – the belief that he and Catherine would be reunited to live together in heaven very much as they had lived together on earth. During the last weeks he was often unconscious and sometimes delirious. So he was denied the chance to send a final message to his Army or attempt a death-bed reconciliation with his estranged and alienated children. Had he, in full command of his senses, known that the end was near, he would certainly have wanted to say farewell to his soldiers, telling them that, if they continued to advance against the enemy, the forces of evil would not prevail. He would not have attempted to reunite his divided family. Kate, Ballington and Herbert had disobeyed their General and ignored the commandment to honour their father. For them, there could be no forgiveness. William Booth possessed the attributes, as well as the appearance, of an Old Testament prophet. Those characteristics made him a great man but an unsympathetic human being.

No doubt, in his more lucid moments, the dying General believed – as a good Christian – that, although sanctified on earth by the Holy Spirit, he was unworthy to meet his maker. But he could have had few doubts that he would be welcomed at the gates of paradise as God's

Soldier who had fought the good fight ever since the early battles in the back-streets of Nottingham. More often than not, he beat the devil. The enemy, which he regularly routed for almost fifty years, was a strange alliance of godless Mammon and complacent Christianity. Hatred of the brewers and publicans was matched by contempt for those churches (self-satisfied Methodists no less than sanctimonious Anglicans) who thought that they should wait for sinners to offer themselves for redemption rather than take God's message into the slums of the Industrial Revolution. Active Christianity was not his invention. He had little capacity for original thought. But he possessed a genius for putting other people's principles into practice.

General Booth followed his calling with absolute confidence and conviction. The Church of England denounced him. The Wesleyans ostracised him. The Establishment derided him. The brewers and the publicans assaulted him. But he never flinched from his vocation. His physical courage was immense and his moral courage even greater. General Booth's whole life was a triumph for certainty.

He was not an easy man to serve, but he inspired unquestioning loyalty in men of great talent and strong opinion. William Booth was both arrogant and autocratic in his relations with everyone except his wife. And he was at his most dictatorial and inhuman when he feared that personal failings and foibles imperilled his Army's good name. In all his relations – with the single exception of his marriage – he lacked warmth, sympathy and understanding. Born leaders often do.

Men of destiny also find it hard to separate their own success from the success of their cause. William Booth believed that God had called him to redeem the world. He therefore regarded anyone who stood in his way as defying the divine will. Every new authority that he acquired and new power which he assumed was justified, at least in his own mind, by the prospect it provided of saving more souls.

The work was easiest in the slums. Although William Booth instinctively accepted that Christians have a duty to the disadvantaged and the dispossessed, he was no class warrior. Unlike Catherine, he never used his sermons to denounce the callous rich. But he did understand that the poor were the victims of exploitation and he treated them without social condescension. Other churches refused to descend to the level which attracted industrial labourers and their families. Booth was happy to lead an organisation which he believed could match the

public houses and the music halls for colour and life. He had no time
and no capacity for the classical scholarship of the Church of England
or the theological speculation which won Methodist ministers their
doctorates. The Salvation Army always claimed to embrace every section of society, yet most of its officers were working men and women
and its most successful recruiting sergeants were repentant sinners
who renounced their working-class vices – drunkenness, petty theft
and wife-beating. The principles on which the Army operated – service and sacrifice, duty and discipline – were made especially attractive
in Bow and Bethnal Green by the addition of bands, banners and uniform.

Because he understood the people whom he hoped to serve, William
Booth was the most successful evangelist in Victorian England. Half a
dozen new churches were founded during the nineteenth-century doctrinal disputes which tore Wesleyan Methodism apart. Only the
Salvation Army survived, separate and independent. And it became a
worldwide movement. Before William Booth died there were 'Blood
and Fire' battalions in Confucian Korea and Catholic Colombia. In
Korea the Salvation Army was run by Koreans and in Colombia by
Colombians, not foreign missionaries. The same philosophy was
applied to its work in the East End of London, the factory towns of
northern England and the mining villages of Wales. The Salvation
Army was always home-grown – of the people, for the people and by
the people.

The creation of the Army – measured by numbers alone – was, in
itself, a triumph. William Booth's success was made even more extraordinary by his unpropitious beginnings. Sceptics who doubt the extent
of his personal triumph have only to consider how they would have
reacted, back in mid-Victorian Nottingham, to the prophecy that the
pawnbroker's apprentice would found a church which swept through
the world and, at the approach of the twenty-first century, be the one
voluntary organisation which the federal government of the United
States regularly made responsible for disaster relief. But the continued
existence and expansion of the Salvation Army was only the beginning
of William Booth's historic achievement. The ideas on which it was
built were at least as important as its size and scope. They played a crucial part in changing the social climate in Victorian Britain. William
Booth – believing in the Christian duty to help both the deserving and

undeserving poor – stirred the conscience of a whole generation and contributed mightily to the great vision of social justice which, paradoxically, sprang from those hard times. No one did more to convince society that we are all members one of another.

That conviction came gradually to William Booth, encouraged by his wife who discovered poverty in Middlesbrough and thereafter spent much of her life denouncing causes and demanding remedies. William worked in more practical ways to defeat the devil who made men wicked by first making them cold and hungry. In the beginning he did little more than provide cheer in dismal lives by distributing Christmas puddings. Then came the night shelters, which offered men cheap lodging and the girls' 'rescues' which took women off the streets. Gradually the aspirations increased. The itinerant paupers were offered work and officers of the Army waited outside prison gates to convince time-served convicts that the future offered them something better than crime, conviction and gaol.

William Booth was always over-optimistic about the enthusiasm with which prostitutes would exchange prosperous degradation for honourable penury. But thousands of men chose hard labour in Salvation Army workshops rather than remain idle. And they accepted, with moderately good grace, the obligation to sing a hymn and say a prayer at the end of the working day.

In a rare moment of intellectual inspiration – stimulated by his dying wife's passion for social justice – William Booth set out his great plan for building the New Jerusalem. Perhaps he stole some of the ideas. He certainly did very little of the actual writing. But that is of no consequence. *In Darkest England and the Way Out* was his in spirit. Without him, it would never have been written. It was certainly over-ambitious to the point of Utopianism – ironically one of its terms of abuse. The Farm Colonies which would have taken families out of the fetid cities and given them a new life in the fresh air of rural England were not a success, and only a couple of Army ships set sail for Africa with pioneers to build Overseas Colonies. But his more practical proposals prospered. Working men still find shelter in the Salvation Army's hostels and unmarried mothers are still helped to meet the challenge of single parenthood in Salvation Army homes – modern, if not totally contemporary versions of William Booth's century-old plans to create a green and pleasant land.

The greatest achievement was both ideological and intellectual –
two characteristics which William Booth certainly despised and probably feared. Fabians, Marxists, Christian Socialists and half a dozen
other groups of social reformers had long argued that poverty bred sin
and crime and that the self-interest of the well-to-do obliged them to
support better housing, education and health-care for the working
classes. But their views – although increasingly popular with the radical intelligentsia – were not held with any great enthusiasm by the
industrious working classes who thought that paupers had only themselves to blame. William Booth spread the idea of constructive
compassion, as he spread the idea of redemption, in places where the
good news had not been previously heard.

Catherine encouraged the idea of a Ministry to the Poor. But William
Booth would have embraced it – perhaps later and with less passion –
without her influence. The beliefs which they eventually shared about
women's place in society would never have entered his head had his
wife not held them with absolute conviction and advanced them with
unrestrained passion. Perhaps the General – although he certainly
shared his wife's view of a woman's right to preach – never quite
endorsed her views on church governance. But he agreed that women
in the Salvation Army should have authority over men. It was in direct
conflict with his other, essentially patriarchal, views on the family. But
because he loved Catherine, he at least adopted her advanced view of
women's religious rights. When, during their early months in London,
Catherine became the senior member of the evangelical partnership –
better known, more in demand and, in consequence, the principal
breadwinner in the family – he showed not the slightest resentment.
His attitude was almost unique in middle-class Victorian England.
And, because he treated Catherine as something approaching an equal,
the Salvation Army was the first organisation to prove that working
women possessed the talent to lead.

It was Catherine Booth who convinced her husband that prostitution was a male, not an exclusively female, vice, since most prostitutes
had taken to the streets because of male brutality and exploitation. It
was a view of vice to which he was already susceptible since it matched
his beliefs about why drunkards turned to drink and thieves to theft.
Indeed, *In Darkest England* displayed a naïve sentimentality about the
causes of, and remedies for, prostitution – a social problem he hoped

to solve by turning fallen women into domestic servants. But he lived at a time when excuses for sin were in short supply. Catherine and William Booth held views on prostitution which are still regarded as dangerously progressive in some parts of society. And they promoted them in the name of Jesus in the slums from which the prostitutes came and the public houses where they carried on their business.

The Salvation Army which William Booth founded – although sometimes derided as an essentially nineteenth-century organisation – can take pride in having helped ease Britain out of its nineteenth-century attitude to sin and poverty. It can also boast a million little miracles – wounded soldiers in the front line given tea and two-inch-thick sandwiches; drunks sleeping under bridges persuaded to dry out, wash up and look for work; girls escaping from tyrannical parents convinced that it is better to live under friendly supervision than in the unprotected custody of pimps. It is not necessary to believe in instant sanctification – or in sanctification in any form – to admire and applaud their work of social redemption.

Innumerable incidents illustrate the extent of that achievement. Sometime in the early 1880s, Bramwell Booth – visiting the East End poor – rashly agreed to a dying widow's request that he should look after her infant son. The baby – Harry Andrews – was adopted by Emma Booth who, when she married Leonard Booth-Tucker, took the child to India. Harry took a precocious interest in medicine and was sent home to England and enrolled in the University of London medical school. After he qualified, he studied surgery in Chicago before returning to India, where he first became Superintendent of the Army's Punjab hospital and then, on the outbreak of the First World War, volunteered for military service. Captain Harry Andrews was awarded the posthumous Victoria Cross for 'devotedly attending the wounded under heavy fire' and showing 'the utmost disregard for danger'. He was a true Salvationist. Neither General nor Catherine Booth ever flinched under fire. Both died victorious.

Note on References and Sources

During their long engagement (which began in 1852) and through-out their marriage, William and Catherine Booth were often separated. Whenever they were apart, they wrote to each other almost every day – often starting the letter in the morning, continuing it in the afternoon and finishing it in time to catch the evening post. Catherine wrote to her mother at least three times a week and, after her mother's death in 1869, sent a weekly letter to Sarah Billups, the wife of the Cardiff building contractor who befriended the Booths when they were on tour in Wales.

Most of the letters written between 1852 and 1865 were kept by the family. Commissioner Catherine Bramwell Booth – granddaughter of William and Catherine – gave them to the British Library. Letters writ-ten after 1880 – many of them handwritten notes to subordinate officers of the Salvation Army – are now in the Salvation Army's International Heritage Centre.

The letters written between 1865 and 1880 are missing. So is the journal which William Booth kept in his youth and from time to time in middle age. It is assumed that both letters and the journal were lost when the Salvation Army headquarters were part-destroyed by fire during the London Blitz.

Two official biographies – *The Life of Catherine Booth* by Frederick Booth-Tucker (1892) and *The Life of William Booth* by Harold Begbie (1926) – quote many of the missing letters at length. Indeed, some chapters of both books contain little else. The quotations from earlier letters in both Booth-Tucker and Begbie are accurate. It is reasonable to assume therefore that the same can be said for quotations from letters between 1865 and 1880. Often the authors neither identify precise dates nor the places where the letters were written. The references to these letters therefore relate to the books in which they are quoted. The Salvation Army printed many editions of both Begbie and Booth-Tucker – each one slightly different from its predecessor and none of them clearly identified. Some of the quotations change (though not materially) from edition to edition. References refer to the original (two-volume) complete edition of both books.

All other references relate to the original source.

References

Abbreviations

Begbie	Harold Begbie, *The Life of William Booth* (London: Macmillan, 1926)
BL	British Library
Booth	William Booth, *In Darkest England and the Way Out* (London: Salvation Army, 1890)
Booth-Tucker	F. de L. Booth-Tucker, *The Life of Catherine Booth* (London: Salvation Army, 1892)
CMM	*Christian Mission Magazine*
ELE	*East London Evangelist*
Ervine	St John Ervine, *God's Soldier: General William Booth* (London: Heinemann, 1934)
NCM	*New Connexion Magazine*
SAA	Salvation Army Archives (International Heritage Centre)
TWC	*The War Cry*
WT	*Wesleyan Times*

1: God's Apprentice

1. TWC, 19 October 1901.
2. TWC, 10 April 1909.
3. Edward Hind, *The Nottingham Enclosures*.
4. *All the World Magazine*, August 1893.
5. Ibid.
6. *Social Gazette*, 11 November 1905.
7. Begbie, Vol. 1, Ch. II, p. 25.
8. Ibid.
9. *All the World Magazine*, August 1893.
10. Ibid.
11. Ibid.
12. *Social Gazette*, 11 November 1905.
13. Ibid.
14. Begbie, Vol. 1, Ch. III, p. 38.
15. Ibid.
16. Ibid., Ch. II, p. 28.
17. *Social Gazette*, 11 November 1905.
18. Begbie, Vol. 1, Ch. III, p. 52.
19. *Nottingham Citizen*, 14 April 1834.
20. TWC, 19 October 1901.
21. Ibid.
22. Ibid., 10 April 1909.
23. John Kent, *Holding the Fort* (London: Epworth, 1978), p. 316.
24. Begbie, Vol. 1, Ch. III, p. 46.
25. George Scott Railton, *General Booth* (London: Hodder & Stoughton, 1912), Vol. 1, Ch. II, p. 11.
26. TWC, 10 April 1909.
27. See William Chadwick, *The Victorian Church* (London: A & C Black, 1966).
28. Kent, *Holding the Fort*, p. 80.
29. See Richard Carwardine, *Transatlantic Revivalism: Popular Evangelism in Britain and America, 1790–1865* (Westport, CT: Greenwood Press, 1978).
30. See Kent, *Holding the Fort*.
31. Ibid., p. 81.
32. Begbie, Vol. 1, Ch. II, p. 34.
33. *The Young Soldier* (Christmas Number), 25 December 1889.
34. TWC, 10 April 1909.
35. W. T. Stead, *General Booth* (London: Isbister, 1891), Ch. II.
36. Begbie, Vol. 1, Ch. V, p. 81.
37. TWC, 2 August 1919.
38. TWC, 19 October 1901.
39. *Nottingham Weekly Gazette*, 4 November 1939.
40. TWC, 19 October 1901.
41. Begbie, Vol. 1, Ch. IV, p. 70.
42. Ervine, Vol. 1, Book I, Ch. VII, p. 40.
43. Begbie, Vol. 1, Ch. III, p. 51.
44. Ibid., Ch. VI, p. 88.
45. Booth-Tucker, Vol. 1, Ch. VIII, p. 52.
46. Begbie, Vol. 1, Ch. VI, p. 93.

2: Forward With the Crowd

1. See Dunn, *Shetland and Orkney Journal, 1822–1825*, collated and introduced by Harold R. Bowes, 1976.
2. Ibid.
3. SAA, 'Booth the London Pawnbroker'.
4. Begbie, Vol. 1, Ch. VII, p. 101.
5. SAA, original letter.
6. Ibid.
7. SAA, 'Booth the London Pawnbroker'.
8. Begbie, Vol. 1, Ch. VIII, p. 105.
9. SAA, original letter (to John Savage, I).

10. SAA, original letter (to John Savage, II).
11. SAA, original letter.
12. Begbie, Vol. 1, Ch. X, p. 116.
13. Stead, *General Booth*.
14. Ibid.
15. Booth-Tucker, Vol. 1, Ch. VIII, p. 56.
16. Railton, *General Booth*, p. 30.
17. TWC, 8 October 1910.
18. Begbie, Vol. 1, Ch. XI, p. 131.
19. Booth-Tucker, Vol. 1, Ch. II, p. 12.
20. Ibid.
21. Booth-Tucker, Vol. 1, Ch. IV, p. 25.
22. Ibid., Ch. V, p. 33.
23. Ibid., p. 31.
24. BL, AM 64801, Brighton, 12 May 1847.
25. Ibid., May–June 1847.
26. Ibid., 1847 letters.
27. Booth-Tucker, Vol. 1, Ch. IX, p. 65.
28. Ibid., p. 66.
29. BL, AM 67999, 6 June 1852.
30. Ibid., 9 June 1852.
31. Ibid.
32. Ibid.
33. Begbie, Vol. 1, Ch. XI, pp. 139–40.
34. Ibid., p. 140.
35. Booth-Tucker, Vol. 1, Ch. X, p. 72.
36. Ibid., p. 71.
37. SAA, 'Home Mission Society Minutes', December 1852.

3: A Star in the East

1. BL, AM 64799.
2. Booth-Tucker, Vol. 1, Ch. X, p. 75.
3. Ibid.
4. Begbie, Vol. 1, Ch. XI, p. 136.
5. BL, AM 64799.
6. Ibid., 5 December 1852.
7. Ibid.
8. Ibid., 14 December 1852.
9. Ibid., 12 December 1852.
10. BL, AM 64801, 6 January 1854.
11. Ibid., 9 October 1854.
12. Ibid., 8 January 1854.
13. BL, AM 64802, 6 February 1855.
14. BL, AM 64801, 13 September 1854.
15. Ibid., 15 September 1854.
16. BL, AM 64799, 5 December 1852.
17. BL, AM 64806.
18. BL, AM 64801, 10 January 1854.
19. Begbie, Vol. 1, Ch. XIV, p. 201.
20. Booth-Tucker, Vol. 1, Ch. XIV, p. 105.
21. Begbie, Vol. 1, Ch. XIII, p. 193.
22. Booth-Tucker, Vol. 1, Ch. XV, p. 107.
23. Ibid., pp. 108–9.
24. BL, AM 64801, January 1854.
25. Begbie, Vol. 1, Ch. XV, p. 225.
26. NCM, 1854.
27. Booth-Tucker, Vol. 1, Ch. XVI, p. 114.
28. Ibid., Ch. XVIII, p. 127.
29. Begbie, Vol. 1, Ch. XV, p. 230.
30. BL, AM 64801, 13 January 1855.
31. BL, AM 64802, 29 January 1855.
32. Begbie, Vol. 1, Ch. XV, p. 270.
33. Ibid., p. 272.
34. Ibid., pp. 258–9.
35. Booth-Tucker, Vol. 1, Ch. XII, p. 88.
36. *All the World Magazine*, 10 October 1910.
37. Ibid.
38. See Bramwell Booth, *Catherine Booth*.

4: *Abundant Labours*

1. Booth-Tucker, Vol. 1, Ch. XIX, p. 137.
2. BL, AM 64803, Leeds, 8 December 1855.
3. BL, AM 64802, 9 October 1855.
4. Ibid., Chatsworth, October 1855.
5. BL, AM 64802, 9 October 1855.
6. Ibid.
7. Booth-Tucker, Vol. 1, Ch. XX, p. 144.
8. BL, AM 64803, Leeds, 8 December 1855.
9. Ibid.
10. BL, AM 64802, Sheffield, October 1855.
11. Ibid.
12. BL, AM 64801, 6 January 1855.
13. Ibid.
14. BL, AM 64802, 13 February 1855.
15. Ibid.
16. Ibid., 12 February 1855.
17. Ibid., October 1855.
18. BL, AM 64803, Leeds, 8 December 1855.
19. Booth-Tucker, Vol. 1, Ch. XXI, p. 151.
20. Begbie, Vol. 1, Ch. XVII, p. 293.
21. BL, AM 64802, Chatsworth, October 1855.
22. Booth-Tucker, Vol. 1, Ch. XXI, p. 148.
23. BL, AM 64803, 21 November 1855.
24. Begbie, Vol. 1, Ch. XV, p. 225.
25. Ibid., Ch. XVI, p. 284.
26. Ibid., Ch. XVIII, p. 302.
27. Ibid., p. 306.
28. BL, AM 64803, 12 November 1855.
29. Ibid.
30. Begbie, Vol. 1, Ch. XVI, p. 227.
31. BL, AM 64803, Dewsbury, 5 November 1855.
32. Ibid., 2 November 1855.
33. Ibid., 21 November 1855.
34. Ibid.
35. Ibid., 5 November 1855.
36. Ibid.
37. Begbie, Vol. 1, Ch. XVIII, p. 298.
38. Booth-Tucker, Vol. 1, Ch. XXIV, p. 171.
39. J. Sigson, *Memoir of W. Bramwell Booth* (London, 1934), p. 405.
40. Booth-Tucker, Vol. 1, Ch. XXV, pp. 182–3.
41. *Chester Chronicle*, 14 February 1857.
42. Booth-Tucker, Vol. 1, Ch. XXVI, p. 192.
43. Ibid., Ch. XXVII, p. 195.
44. Ervine, Vol. 1, Book I, Ch. IV, p. 211.
45. Booth-Tucker, Vol. 1, Ch. XXVII, p. 200.
46. Ibid., p. 202.
47. Ibid., p. 204.
48. Minutes of 61st Annual Conference of the Methodist New Connexion.

5: *A Fool for God*

1. Booth-Tucker, Vol. 1, Ch. XXX, p. 219.
2. Ibid., p. 220.
3. Begbie, Vol. 1, Ch. XVIII, p. 309.
4. SAA, Ordination in Gateshead.
5. Ervine, Vol. 1, Book II, Ch. V, p. 214.
6. George John Stevenson, *Methodist Worthies: Characteristic Sketches of Methodist Preachers of the Several Denominations, With Historical Sketch of Each Connexion* (London: T & C Jack, 1855), pp. 623–7.
7. Ibid.
8. *Gateshead Observer*, July 1858.

9. BL, AM 64804, June 1858.
10. Booth-Tucker, Vol. 1, Ch. XXXI, p. 230.
11. Ibid., Ch. XXXII, p. 232.
12. Ibid., Ch. XXXIII, p. 241.
13. Kent, *Holding the Fort*, p. 318.
14. Ibid., p. 90.
15. Ibid., p. 317.
16. Ibid.
17. Phoebe Palmer, *The Way of Holiness* (London, 1856), p. 19.
18. BL, AM 64805, 16 September 1859.
19. Booth-Tucker, Vol. 1, Ch. XXXIII, p. 243.
20. BL, AM 64805, 25 December 1859.
21. Catherine Booth, *Female Teaching*, pp. 14–15.
22. BL, AM 64806, 19 March 1861.
23. Ibid.
24. Booth-Tucker, Vol. 1, Ch. XXXIV, p. 250.
25. Ibid., p. 251.
26. BL, AM 64804, 23 December 1857.
27. Ibid.
28. W. T. Stead, *Mrs Booth of the Salvation Army* (London: J. Nisbet, 1900), p. 42.
29. 'Our Army Mother's First Sermon', *All the World Magazine*, 1891.
30. BL, AM 64805.
31. Ibid.

6: Not Called but Chosen

1. Booth-Tucker, Vol. 1, Ch. XXXVII, p. 273.
2. WT, 17 June 1861.
3. NCM, May 1861.
4. Booth-Tucker, Vol. 1, Ch. XXXVIII, p. 283.
5. Ibid., Ch. XXXIX, p. 285.
6. Ibid.
7. Ibid., p. 287.
8. NCM, June 1861.
9. Ibid.
10. Ibid.
11. Ibid.
12. WT, 17 June 1861.
13. Ervine, Vol. 1, Book II, Ch. XIV, p. 243.
14. Ibid.
15. BL, AM 64805, June 1861.
16. Ibid.
17. Ibid.
18. Ibid.
19. Ibid.
20. Booth-Tucker, Vol. 1, Ch. XLI, p. 301.
21. Kent, *Holding the Fort*, p. 328.
22. Booth-Tucker, Vol. 1, Ch. XLI, p. 303.
23. BL, AM 64805, Nottingham, July 1861.
24. Booth-Tucker, Vol. 1, Ch. XXXVIII, p. 284.
25. Ibid., Ch. XLII, p. 312.
26. *The Revival*, Vol. 5, No. 110, 31 August 1861.
27. Ibid.
28. Ibid., No. 112, 14 September 1861.
29. Ibid., No. 114, 28 September 1861.
30. Ibid., No. 118, 26 October 1861.
31. Booth-Tucker, Vol. 1, Ch. XLII, p. 313.
32. Ibid.
33. Ibid., p. 314.
34. Booth-Tucker, Vol. 1, Ch. XLIV, p. 328.
35. *The Revival*, Vol. 5, No. 123, 30 November 1861.
36. Ibid., Vol. 6, No. 152, 19 June 1862.
37. BL, AM 64806, 12 January 1862.
38. Ibid., 2 December 1862.

39. Ibid., January 1862.
40. WT, 31 March 1862.

7: *God's Gypsies*

1. BL, AM 64806, Penzance, 10 August 1862.
2. Booth-Tucker, Vol. 1, Ch. XLIX, p. 367.
3. Ibid., p. 369.
4. BL, AM 64806, 6 August 1862.
5. Ibid., 26 November 1862.
6. Ibid., Cardiff, 16 February 1863.
7. Booth-Tucker, Vol. 1, Ch. XLVIII, p. 360.
8. George Scott Railton, *Twenty-One Years Salvation Army* (Introduction).
9. Ibid.
10. BL, AM 64806, 18 February 1863.
11. Ibid., 23 February 1863.
12. WT, 6 April 1863.
13. BL, AM 64806, Cardiff, 12 February 1863.
14. Ibid.
15. BL, AM 64806, June 1863.
16. Booth-Tucker, Vol. 1, Ch. XLIX, p. 371.
17. Railton, *Twenty-One Years Salvation Army* (Introduction).
18. Booth-Tucker, Vol. 1, Ch. XLIX, p. 368.
19. BL, AM 64806, Walsall, June 1863.
20. Ibid., Cardiff, 11 April 1863.
21. Ibid.
22. Ibid., Walsall, June 1863.
23. Ibid., Birmingham, 24 November 1863.
24. Ibid., 29 February 1864.
25. Ibid., Leeds, March 1864.
26. Ibid., Nottingham, 28 March 1864.
27. Ibid., Leeds, July 1864.

28. Ervine, Vol. 1, Book II, Ch. XXIV, p. 268.
29. Ibid., p. 269.
30. Booth-Tucker, Vol. 1, Ch. LI, p. 383.
31. WT, 13 March 1865.
32. Ibid., 3 April 1865.
33. Booth-Tucker, Vol. 1, Ch. LII, p. 393.
34. WT, 27 March 1865.
35. Booth-Tucker, Vol. 1, Ch. LI, p. 387.
36. Ibid.
37. Railton, *Twenty-One Years Salvation Army* (Introduction).
38. Ibid.
39. Catherine Booth, Lecture V, 'Sham Compassion and the Dying Love of Christ', *Popular Christianity* (1889), p. 134.
40. Ibid., p. 135.

8: **When Men Shall Revile You**

1. Railton, *Twenty-One Years Salvation Army* (Introduction).
2. ELE, Vol. 1, October 1868.
3. WT, 4 September 1865.
4. ELE, Vol. 1, October 1868.
5. Ibid.
6. WT, n.d.
7. WT, 4 September 1865.
8. Ibid., 25 September 1865.
9. Ibid.
10. TWC, 10 April 1909.
11. Catherine Booth, Lecture V, 'Sham Compassion and the Dying Love of Christ', *Popular Christianity* (1889), p. 133.
12. Railton, *General Booth*, p. 56.
13. ELE, November 1868.
14. Ibid., 1 December 1868.
15. Ibid.
16. Ibid., 1 January 1869.

17. ELE, 1 December 1868.
18. Ibid., March 1869.
19. Ibid.
20. Ibid., April 1869.
21. Ibid., May 1869.
22. Ibid., 1 January 1869.
23. SAA, letter, 20 April 1869.
24. ELE, 1 June 1869.
25. Ibid., 1 September 1869.
26. Ibid.

9: Suffer Little Children

1. Ervine, Vol. 1, Book II, Ch. XXIV, p. 269.
2. BL, AM 64806, Walsall, July 1863.
3. Ervine, Vol. 1, Book II, Ch. XXIV, p. 271.
4. Begbie, Vol. 1, Ch. XXI.
5. BL, AM 64806, Birmingham, 24 January 1863.
6. Ibid.
7. Ibid., 12 October 1863.
8. Begbie, Vol. 1, Ch. XXI.
9. Ibid.
10. Ibid., Ch. XXIII, p. 378.
11. Ibid., Ch. XXI.
12. Ibid., p. 357.
13. Ibid., p. 345.
14. Booth-Tucker, Vol. 2, Ch. LXVI, p. 39.
15. Ibid., Ch. LXXVI, p. 147.
16. Ibid., Vol. 1, Ch. LIX, p. 456.
17. Ibid., Vol. 2, Ch. LXIX, p. 85.

10: Singing All the Time

1. CMM, 1 January 1870.
2. Ibid., 1 October 1870.
3. Ibid., 1 March 1870.
4. Ibid., 1 May 1870.
5. Ervine, Vol. 1, Book III, Ch. XII, p. 312.
6. CMM, 1 April 1870.

7. Ibid., 1 October 1870.
8. Ervine, Vol. 1, Book III, Ch. XV, p. 322.
9. Booth-Tucker, Vol. 2, Ch. LXII, p. 22.
10. SAA, Chancery 1875, Part 64.
11. ELE, 1 December 1870.
12. Walker, *Pulling the Devil's Kingdom Down* (Ph.D. thesis quoted in Roger Green, *Catherine Booth*).
13. CMM, June 1871.
14. Ibid., January 1871.
15. Ervine, Vol. 1, Book III, Ch. XVII, p. 331.
16. Ibid., pp. 331–2.
17. Booth-Tucker, Vol. 2, Ch. LXIII, p. 27.
18. Ibid., p. 28.
19. Eileen Douglas and Mildred Duff, *Commissioner Railton* (London: Salvationist Publishing, 1921), p. 5.
20. Ibid., p. 9.
21. Ibid., p. 21.
22. ELE, 20 September 1872.
23. Ervine, Vol. 1, Book III, Ch. XVII, p. 333.
24. See Bernard Watson, *Soldier Saint* (London: Hodder & Stoughton, 1970).
25. See Bramwell Booth, *Echoes and Memories* (London: Hodder & Stoughton, 1925).

11: Well Instructed Saints

1. CMM, January 1873.
2. Ibid., September 1873.
3. Ibid., January 1874.
4. Ibid., July 1874.
5. Ibid., May 1874.
6. Ibid., Summer 1872.
7. Ibid., 20 September 1872.
8. Ibid.
9. Humphrey Wallis, *The Happy*

Warrior (London: Salvationist Publishing, 1928), p. 7.

10. Ervine, Vol. 1, Book III, Ch. XXIII, p. 348.
11. Ibid., Ch. XXV, p. 356.
12. CMM, 1873–74.
13. Ervine, Vol. 1, Book III, Ch. XXVII, p. 362.
14. Closed Roll (Chancery 1875), Part 6A, p. 173.
15. CMM, July 1875.
16. Booth-Tucker, Vol. 2, Ch. LXXIII, p. 116.
17. Ibid.
18. Walker, *Pulling the Devil's Kingdom Down* (Ph.D. thesis quoted in Roger Green, *Catherine Booth*).
19. CMM, July 1876.
20. Bramwell Booth, *Echoes and Memories*, p. 169.
21. CMM, July 1876.
22. Ibid.
23. Ibid.
24. Ibid.
25. Ervine, Vol. 1, Book III, Ch. XXVIII, p. 366.
26. Ibid.
27. Begbie, Vol. 1, Ch. XXIV, pp. 395–6.
28. Ibid., p. 398.
29. Ervine, Vol. 1, Book III, Ch. XXIX, p. 369.
30. Ibid., p. 370.
31. Ibid., p. 371.
32. Ibid.
33. George Scott Railton, *Heathen England* (London: S. W. Partridge, 1877), pp. 143–4.

12: Into Battle

1. Douglas and Duff, *Commissioner Railton*, p. 57.
2. Booth-Tucker, Vol. 2, Ch. LXXV, p. 133.
3. Railton, *General Booth*, p. 73.
4. Ibid.
5. Booth-Tucker, Vol. 2, Ch. LXXV, p. 134.
6. Henry D. Rack, *Reasonable Enthusiast* (London: Epworth, 1989), p. 42.
7. Walker, *Commissioner Cadman*, p. 58.
8. Bramwell Booth, *These Fifty Years* (London: Cassell, 1929), p. 82.
9. Ibid., p. 33.
10. Ibid.
11. Watson, *Soldier Saint*, p. 28.
12. Ervine, Vol. 1, Book III, Ch. XXXIX, p. 398.
13. CMM, January 1878.
14. *Whitby Gazette*, 5 January 1878.
15. Ibid., 5 January 1878.
16. CMM, June 1877.
17. Ervine, Vol. 1, Book III, Ch. XL, p. 404.
18. Bramwell Booth, *Echoes and Memories*, p. 53.
19. CMM, February 1878.
20. Ibid., December 1878.
21. Ibid.
22. Begbie, Vol. 1, Ch. XXV, p. 349.
23. Ibid., p. 439.
24. Booth-Tucker, Vol. 2, Ch. LXXV, p. 139.
25. Roger Green, *Catherine Booth* (Grand Rapids, MI: Baker, 1996), p. 203.
26. Begbie, Vol. 1, Ch. XXVII, p. 440.
27. Douglas and Duff, *Commissioner Railton*, p. 64.
28. Ibid., p. 65.
29. Booth-Tucker, Vol. 2, Ch. LXXV, p. 143.
30. Ibid.

13: *The Voice of the Rabble*

1. Douglas and Duff, *Commissioner Railton*, p. 193.
2. Booth-Tucker, Vol. 2, Ch. LXXXIV, p. 227.
3. Ibid., p. 215.
4. Ibid., p. 216.
5. Ibid.
6. Ibid.
7. *Northern Echo*, May 1879.
8. Booth-Tucker, Vol. 2, Ch. LXXXV, p. 225.
9. Ibid., p. 226.
10. Begbie, Vol. 1, Ch. XXIX, p. 478.
11. Booth-Tucker, Vol. 2, Ch. LXXXIII, p. 208.
12. *Philadelphia News* (reprinted in TWC, 31 August 1880).
13. TWC, 7 February 1880.
14. Douglas and Duff, *Commissioner Railton*, p. 68.
15. Ibid.
16. Ervine, Vol. 1, Book IV, Ch. XVIII, p. 488.
17. Watson, *Soldier Saint*, p. 58.
18. Ibid.
19. Ibid.
20. Railton Papers.
21. Begbie, Vol. 1, Ch. XXIX, p. 479.
22. TWC, 9 October 1880.
23. Booth-Tucker, Vol. 2, Ch. LXXXVI, p. 233.
24. TWC, 16 October 1880.
25. Begbie, Vol. 1, Ch. XXIX, p. 480.
26. Ibid., p. 481.
27. *The Times*, 11 October 1881.
28. Ibid., 13 October 1881.
29. Booth-Tucker, Vol. 2, Ch. LXXXVII, p. 244.

14: *Mobbing the Apostles*

1. Robert Sandall, *The History of the Salvation Army* (London: Thomas Nelson, 1947), Vol. 2, p. 141.
2. Railton, *General Booth*, p. 76.
3. *The Times*, 26 January 1882.
4. Begbie, Vol. 1, Ch. XXVIII, p. 461.
5. Ervine, Vol. 1, Book IV, Ch. X, p. 470.
6. TWC, 3 February 1881.
7. Railton, *General Booth*, p. 79.
8. Ibid.
9. *The Times*, 14 April 1882.
10. Ibid., 18 April 1882.
11. Ibid.
12. Ibid.
13. Ibid., 20 March 1882.
14. Ibid., 5 May 1882.
15. Ibid., 24 June 1882.
16. Ibid., 28 June 1882.
17. Ibid., 26 June 1882.
18. TWC, 24 November 1881.
19. Watson, *Soldier Saint*, p. 34.
20. Ibid.
21. Ibid., p. 35.
22. TWC, 13 July 1882.
23. Ibid.
24. Begbie, Vol. 2, Ch. I, p. 10.
25. Dr G. H. Horridge, *The Salvation Army in England* (Ph.D. thesis).
26. Ibid.
27. Ibid.
28. *The Times*, 5 April 1882.
29. *Sheffield Telegraph*, 17 January 1882.
30. Ibid.
31. *Sheffield and Rotherham Independent*, 17 January 1882.
32. Ibid.
33. Ibid.
34. *Sheffield Telegraph*, 17 January 1882.
35. Booth-Tucker, Vol. 2, Ch. XCI, p. 278.
36. *The Times*, 29 June 1882.
37. Booth-Tucker, Vol. 2, Ch. XCV, p. 316.
38. Bramwell Booth, *Echoes and*

Memories, pp. 60–1.
39. Ibid.
40. *The Times*, 7 November 1882.
41. Ibid.
42. Ibid., 20 December 1882.
43. Begbie, Vol. 2, Ch. III, p. 32.
44. Ervine, Vol. 1, Book IV, Ch. LV, p. 608.
45. TWC, 3 August 1882.

15: As Quick as Fire

1. Booth-Tucker, Vol. 2, Ch. LXXIII, p. 210.
2. Ibid., p. 211.
3. TWC, 3 February 1881.
4. Ibid.
5. Ibid., 17 February 1881.
6. Booth-Tucker, Vol. 2, Ch. LXXXVIII, p. 249.
7. Green, *Catherine Booth*, p. 320.
8. Ervine, Vol. 1, Book IV, Ch. XXXII, p. 529.
9. Green, *Catherine Booth*, p. 221.
10. Ibid., p. 222.
11. Ervine, Vol. 1, Book IV, Ch. XXXIX, p. 539.
12. Ibid., p. 543.
13. *The Times*, 25 September 1882.
14. Ibid., 26 September 1882.
15. Ibid., 2 October 1882.
16. Ibid., 30 October 1882.
17. Ervine, Vol. 1, Book IV, Ch. XLVI, p. 561.
18. Ibid.
19. Ibid., p. 570.
20. TWC, 11 April 1883.
21. Ervine, Vol. 1, Book IV, Ch. XLVII, p. 567.
22. See M. J. Cart, *Histoire de la liberté des cultures dans le canton de Vaud, 1798–1889* (Lausanne, 1890).
23. *The Times*, 1 February 1883.
24. Ervine, Vol. 1, Book IV, Ch. LIII, p. 592.
25. *The Times*, 20 February 1883.
26. Ibid., 21 February 1883.
27. Ibid., 22 February 1883.
28. TWC, 28 March 1883.
29. Ervine, Vol. 1, Book IV, Ch. LII, p. 586.
30. *The Times*, 12 September 1883.
31. Booth-Tucker, Vol. 1, Ch. XCVI, p. 323.
32. Ibid.
33. Ibid., p. 325.
34. TWC, 23 April 1884.

16: In Modern Babylon

1. Bramwell Booth, *Echoes and Memories*, p. 119.
2. *Saturday Review*, 12 September 1863.
3. *Methodist Archives*, 1871.
4. Booth-Tucker, Vol. 2, Ch. XCIX, p. 344.
5. Green, *Catherine Booth*, p. 248.
6. *William Booth in London* (London: Salvation Army, 1886), p. 31.
7. See Judith Walkowitz, *Prostitution and Victorian Society* (Cambridge: CUP, 1980).
8. See Hemying Bracebridge, *Prostitution in London*, Vol. 4 of H. Mayhew, *London Labour and the London Poor* (1861).
9. House of Lords Report from Committees, 1881, Vol. 9, p. 74.
10. Ibid.
11. Ibid.
12. Bramwell Booth, *Echoes and Memories*, p. 123.
13. SAA, House of Lords Select Committee, 'The Armstrong Case and The Salvation Army'.
14. Booth-Tucker, Vol. 2, Ch. XCIX, p. 350.
15. Green, *Catherine Booth*, p. 254.

16. Bramwell Booth, *Echoes and Memories*, p. 126.
17. Ervine, Vol. 2, Book V, Ch. IX, p. 646.
18. Booth-Tucker, Vol. 2, Ch. XCIX, p. 351.
19. Bramwell Booth, *Echoes and Memories*, p. 142.
20. See Jones, *Saint or Sensationalist*, quoted in Green, *Catherine Booth*.
21. Booth-Tucker, Vol. 2, Ch. XCIX, p. 353.
22. TWC, 25 July 1885.
23. *The Times*, 31 July 1885.
24. Ibid., 18 August 1885.
25. Raymond Schults, *Crusader in Babylon* (Lincoln, NE: University of Nebraska Press, 1972), p. 179.
26. SAA, G. W. Foote, *The Free Thinker*, 13 September 1885.
27. Begbie, Vol. 2, Ch. IV, p. 48.
28. *The Times*, 11 November 1885.
29. Booth-Tucker, Vol. 2, Ch. XCIX.
30. *The Times*, 11 November 1885.
31. Ibid.
32. Ibid.
33. Ibid., 19 January 1886.
34. Begbie, Vol. 2, Ch. IV, p. 42.
35. Booth-Tucker, Vol. 2, Ch. C, p. 360.
36. *The Times*, 9 November 1885.
37. Ibid., 13 November 1885.
38. Ibid., 7 December 1885.

17: Light Over the Water

1. *The Times*, 21 December 1885.
2. Ibid.
3. Ibid., 1 March 1883.
4. Ibid., 7 March 1883.
5. Ibid., 13 July 1883.
6. Ibid.
7. Ervine, Vol. 2, Book V, Ch. XV, p. 659.
8. *The Times*, 29 November 1887.
9. Begbie, Vol. 2, Ch. VI, p. 72.
10. TWC, 8 July 1885.
11. Booth-Tucker, Vol. 2, Ch. CV, p. 412.
12. Ibid., p. 414.
13. *The Times*, 17 February 1885.
14. Ibid., 20 February 1885.
15. Ervine, Vol. 2, Book V, Ch. XVIII, p. 673.
16. Ibid., p. 672.
17. Begbie, Vol. 2, Ch. IX, pp. 104–5.
18. Booth-Tucker, Vol. 2, Ch. CVIII, p. 444.
19. Ibid., Ch. CX, p. 461.
20. Ibid., p. 456.
21. Stead, *Mrs Booth of the Salvation Army*, p. 209.
22. Rack, *Reasonable Enthusiast*, p. 429.
23. Green, *Catherine Booth*, letter cited in possession of Mrs L. T. and Colonel Roy Oldford, Salvation Army, USA.
24. Ervine, Vol. 2, Book V, Ch. XXIV, p. 685.
25. Booth-Tucker, Vol. 2, Ch. CXI, p. 463.
26. Ibid., p. 469.
27. *Manchester Guardian*, 18 October 1890.
28. *Methodist Times*, 9 October 1890.
29. Booth-Tucker, Vol. 2, Ch. CXII, p. 475.
30. *The Times*, 14 October 1890.
31. Booth-Tucker, Vol. 2, Ch. CXIII, pp. 488–9.
32. Begbie, Vol. 2, Ch. IX, p. 112.

18: In Darkest England . . .

1. Gertrude Himmelfarb, *England in the Early Industrial Age* (London: Faber & Faber, 1984).
2. Ibid.
3. Asa Briggs, *William Morris*:

Selected Writings
(Harmondsworth: Penguin,
1962), p. 150.

4. Charles Booth, *The Bitter Cry of
Outcast London* (London, 1888),
p. 5.
5. A. Kershen, *Henry Mayhew and
Charles Booth: Men of Their Time*,
p. 105.
6. Ibid.
7. Catherine Booth, Lecture V,
'Sham Compassion and the Dying
Love of Christ', *Popular
Christianity* (1889), p. 136.
8. *The Times*, 5 January 1889.
9. Ibid., 7 January 1889.
10. Booth, Preface, p. 1.
11. Ibid., pp. 10–11.
12. TWC, 18 April 1908.
13. Railton, *General Booth*, p. 187.

19: . . . and the Way Out

1. Booth, p. 239.
2. See Bernard Bosanquet, '*In
Darkest England*, on the Wrong
Track' (London: Swan
Sonnenschein, 1891).
3. Ibid.
4. Lady Jeune, *Lesser Questions*
(London: Salvation Army, 1894),
p. 257.
5. *The Times*, 1 December 1890.
6. Ibid.
7. Bramwell Booth, *These Fifty Years*,
p. 204.
8. *The Times*, 11 December 1890.
9. Ibid., 17 December 1890.
10. Ibid., 20 December 1890.
11. Bramwell Booth, *These Fifty Years*,
p. 205.
12. *The Times*, 26 December 1890.
13. See Bramwell Booth, *Echoes and
Memories*.

20: A Question of Probity

1. *The Times*, 26 December 1890.
2. Ibid.
3. Ibid., 2 January 1891.
4. Ibid., 11 March 1891.
5. Ibid., 13 March 1891.
6. Bramwell Booth, *Echoes and
Memories*, p. 111.
7. Ibid.
8. SAA, letter from Bramwell Booth
to William Booth, 14 April 1891.
9. Ibid.
10. Ibid., 5 May 1891.
11. Ibid.
12. *The Times*, 22 January 1891.
13. Bramwell Booth, *Echoes and
Memories*, p. 109.
14. *The Times*, 19 February 1891.
15. Ibid., 24 February 1891.
16. Ervine, Vol. 2, Book V, Ch. XXXV,
p. 725.
17. TWC, 21 May 1892.
18. Ibid., 28 May 1892.
19. *Contemporary Review*, December
1892.
20. *The Times*, 14 April 1892.
21. Booth-Tucker, Vol. 2, Ch.
LXXXVI, p. 236.

21: The Devil Does His
Worst

1. Ervine, Vol. 2, Book V, Ch. XXIII,
p. 684.
2. Watson, *Soldier Saint*, p. 102.
3. *All the World Magazine*, October
1893.
4. Watson, *Soldier Saint*, p. 130.
5. Ibid., p. 141.
6. SAA, letter, undated.
7. SAA, letter, 23 January 1896.
8. SAA, cable from Major Strong to
Bramwell Booth, 30 January
1896.

9. SAA, cable from Bramwell Booth to William Booth, 21 February 1896.
10. SAA, cable from 'Salvation', 22 February 1896.
11. *All the World Magazine*, April 1896.
12. Diane Winston, *Red-Hot and Righteous* (Cambridge, MA: Harvard UP, 1999), p. 57.
13. SAA, letter from Ballington Booth to William Booth, undated.
14. SAA, letter from unknown author to William Booth, 2 November 1903.
15. Carolyn Scott, *The Heavenly Witch* (London: Hamish Hamilton, 1981), p. 177.
16. Ibid., p. 178.
17. Ibid., p. 179.
18. Ibid., p. 183.
19. Bramwell Booth, *Echoes and Memories*, p. 147.
20. Begbie, Vol. 2, Ch. XIX, p. 239.
21. Scott, *The Heavenly Witch*, p. 189.
22. Ibid., p. 194.
23. TWC, 8 June 1901.

22: *Promoted to Glory*

1. Scott, *The Heavenly Witch*, p. 185.
2. *The Times*, 29 July 1895.
3. Ibid., 23 August 1895.
4. Ibid., 23 November 1895.
5. Ibid., 10 December 1895.
6. Begbie, Vol. 2, Ch. XVII, p. 213.
7. Ibid., Ch. XXIV, p. 325.
8. Bramwell Booth, *Echoes and Memories*, p. 215.
9. Begbie, Vol. 2, Ch. XXVII, p. 387.
10. Daphne Margot Bennett, *A Life of the Countess of Oxford and Asquith* (London: Victor Gollancz, 1984).
11. Bramwell Booth, *Echoes and Memories*, p. 150.
12. Begbie, Vol. 2, Ch. XVIII, p. 227.
13. Ibid., Ch. XXVIII, p. 401.
14. Ibid., p. 404.
15. Railton, *General Booth*, p. 201.
16. Ibid.
17. Begbie, Vol. 2, Ch. XX, pp. 255–6.
18. Ervine, Vol. 2, Book VI, Ch. XVII, p. 800.
19. Ibid., Ch. XV, p. 793.
20. Begbie, Vol. 2, Ch. XXVIII, p. 412.

Index